THE SOUTHERN FAULT LINE

THE SOUTHERN FAULT LINE

HOW RACE, CLASS, AND REGION SHAPED ONE FAMILY'S HISTORY

BRYAN D. JONES

OXFORD
UNIVERSITY PRESS

OXFORD
UNIVERSITY PRESS

Oxford University Press is a department of the University of Oxford.
It furthers the University's objective of excellence in research, scholarship,
and education by publishing worldwide. Oxford is a registered trade mark of
Oxford University Press in the UK and in certain other countries.

Published in the United States of America by Oxford University Press
198 Madison Avenue, New York, NY 10016, United States of America.

Library of Congress Cataloging-in-Publication Data
Names: Jones, Bryan D., author.
Title: The Southern fault line / Bryan Jones, JJ "Jake" Pickle Regents'
Chair of Congressional Studies, University of Texas at Austin.
Description: New York, NY : Oxford University Press, [2025] |
Includes index. |
Identifiers: LCCN 2024039684 (print) | LCCN 2024039685 (ebook) |
ISBN 9780197770429 (hardback) | ISBN 9780197770443 (epub) |
ISBN 9780197770450
Subjects: LCSH: White people—Alabama–Biography. | Jones, Bryan D.—Family. |
Dean family | Carr family. | Davidson family. | Jones family. |
African Americans—Segregation—Southern States |
Blount County (Ala.)—Race relations. | Sumter County—Race relations. |
Civil rights—Southern States. | Southern States—Social conditions. |
Southern States—Politics and government—1865–1950.
Classification: LCC F326.J656 2025 (print) | LCC F326 (ebook) |
DDC 976.1/06—dc23/eng/20241031
LC record available at https://lccn.loc.gov/2024039684
LC ebook record available at https://lccn.loc.gov/2024039685

DOI: 10.1093/oso/9780197770429.001.0001

Printed by Sheridan Books, Inc., United States of America

To My Family, Inherited and Acquired:

To those who were there then; to those who are here now; and to those who are to come.

AND

To Donald S. Strong (1912–1995), who taught me more than I learned.

Contents

Foreword

I knew how to succeed in the courses Professor Donald Strong offered in political parties and Southern politics at the University of Alabama. Strong kept a steady barrage of questions coming, and he always knew the names of all the students by the first day. The secret to success was simple: read the assigned material before each class.

One day in class, seemingly out of nowhere, came "Mr. Jones?" I half-grasped the question in my dreamland, so I blurted out what I immediately knew was way off-base. Strong commented in his classic acerbic style, "Mr. Jones I had become convinced you were a genius, but you have now disabused me of that notion." Ouch. There was another key to success: pay attention in class.

As an undergraduate at the University of Alabama I was introduced to the methods of political geography, a system of county-by-county mapping of political trends, comparing those trends to similar trends in different regions. The approach reached its pinnacle in V.O. Key's magisterial *Southern Politics*, based on research conducted at the University of Alabama's Bureau of Public Administration in the late 1940s. The reflected glory of that achievement was still glowing in the Political Science Department in the mid-1960s, when I studied there—with one of the contributors to the research, Donald Strong.

The research from that program led to the inference that the one-party system in the South led to oligarchical rule that perpetuated white supremacy and poverty. The answer from Key and his allies was that vigorous two-party competition would foster class-based divisions and move the region away from the politics of race division that characterized oligarchic rule.

I was so taken with both the substance and the methods of the approach that I knew this was what I wanted to do for my life's work. I had become enamored with the idea of becoming a professor, partly because of the influence of Strong. I got accepted into graduate school at the University of Texas and headed west.

My first graduate student paper was a V.O. Key–style analysis of Lurleen Wallace's smashing victory in her run for Alabama governor in 1966 as a stand-in for her husband George. The professor teaching the course was, unbeknownst to me, a student of V.O. Key.

In the summer of 1967, I attended the Inter-University Consortium for Political Research (ICPR) at the University of Michigan. ICPR was the major vehicle for a set of ideas that were changing the very underpinnings of political science, especially the study of voting behavior. There four scholars, Angus Campbell, Phil Converse, Warren Miller, and Don Stokes, were unifying systematic polling of mass publics with a theory of voting choice, soon to be labeled "the Michigan Model."

The Michigan scholars saw citizens as captives of simple cognitive dynamics. Most people had emotional connections to churches, groups, and political parties, but these connections were not really rooted in cognition. Some voters made decisions based on issues or ideology, but that group was vanishingly small. Other voters lacked even the capacity to link emotionally to a party; they simply followed the crowd. But most identified with a party, and generally did not change that identification. While the notion of partisan identification was not new, the Michigan scholars gave it a firm psychological basis. They laid out the full theory and empirical foundation in *The American Voter*, published in 1960.

The Michigan Four, as they came to be known, obtained National Science Foundation grants to support their studies, which they conducted at each presidential election, producing an invaluable time series of data that is a critical resource to this day.

The Michigan scholars did not stop there. The organizational genius of the operation, Warren Miller, worked to set up a network of universities that would support the development of a more robust foundation for quantitative political science. In 1963 the Michigan group began a summer program for students from member colleges and universities for the propagation of quantitative political science. Fundamental to the program, which was (and still is) first rate, was the assumption of cognitively limited voters.

The whole enterprise was brilliant. It had a core set of ideas based on sound psychological studies. It had a network of supporting universities across the country and soon the world. It had a mechanism for transmitting these ideas to other scholars.

Unfortunately the approach also carried with it an attack on the political geography method I was wedded to at the time. The problem, claimed the Michigan scholars, was the "ecological fallacy," the notion that inferring individual behavior from aggregate data on geographical units was a fallacy. True. But the political geography approach examined the regional aspects of voting over time and did not generalize to individuals. Nevertheless, I knew an academic steamroller when I saw one. I could not pursue political geography in political science.

V.O. Key's final book, *The Responsible Electorate*, took aim at this steamroller. Key famously characterized his work as showing that "voters are not fools." Certainly their rationality was bounded, but not absent. I was horrified when the Michigan scholars teaching in the summer program denigrated the book. I knew that I could not in good faith pursue a political behavior career either.

In my career, I thought and taught about political institutions, how they operate, and how they produce public policies. I studied how the cognitive and emotional facets of decision-makers influenced the institutions they inhabited. I especially focused on the politics of attention because attention is a key measure of how people, political parties, and policymaking organizations prioritize the problems they face.

My work with Frank Baumgartner led to the notion of applying punctuated equilibria to politics. We saw punctuations in large part as due to the limits of human abilities to foresee and attend to the correct path of action. The resistance of institutional "gridlock" and the grasp of ideology and belief systems allowed decision-makers to ignore problems over long periods of time before a problem got so severe that it presented a crisis. Then the political system had to play "catch up" to address the problem.[1] The result was a large policy change.

If such punctuations influence political elites and policymaking institutions, then they must affect the general public as well. The Michigan model had no explanations for such changes. Maybe a return to political geography and historical analysis and the insights of V.O. Key was warranted.

I Return to My Alabama Roots

The U.S. Supreme Court's decision in *Shelby County v. Holder*, announced in 2013, was a wake-up call. The Court's conservative majority struck down as unconstitutional the most important mechanism for protecting the right to vote for minorities enacted in the Voting Rights Act of 1965. The long title of the Voting Rights Act is "An Act to enforce the fifteenth amendment of the Constitution of the United States, and for other purposes."

The Fifteenth Amendment, one of three amendments passed after the Civil War, guaranteed that "The right of citizens of the United States to vote shall not be denied or abridged by the United States or by any State on account of race, color, or previous condition of servitude." Further, it gave Congress the responsibility of enforcing the amendment. And Congress did so, passing a series of Enforcement Acts to implement the amendment. In response the Southern states enacted restrictive electoral policies that did not explicitly mention Blacks but were correlated with being Black. Unfortunately, the Supreme Court upheld these efforts, undermining the Enforcement Acts. Black citizens throughout the South lost the right to vote, and much more.

The Voting Rights Act of 1965 reasserted Congress's role in enforcing the Fifteenth Amendment. Its provisions were to run for a limited number of years, but the act was broadened and extended several times because Congress judged that the issue of voter suppression continued to be a problem. In 2006, with hard work by both political parties and the G.W. Bush administration, Congress produced an in-depth report showing how the problem continued to exist and extended the act for 25 years. Surely this was Congress at its best.

Yet there we were in 2013: a Court usurping Congress's enforcement powers based on the erroneous argument that voting suppression was no more likely in the South than in the rest of the nation. The Court and conservatives more generally were in the act of destroying the consensus that all Americans have the right to vote. A major punctuation in the American equilibrium of the second half of the 20th century was occurring.

I hoped that the nation would reject the thrust of the Court to undermine voting rights, or that at least the remaining enforcement mechanisms would be sufficient to keep voting suppression attempts at bay. Was not there a national consensus on the right to vote? After all, had not even the conservative President George W. Bush gathered civil rights and Congressional leaders together as he signed the reauthorization in 2006? Alas, that proved not to be true; Southern states enacted and implemented a barrage of voter suppression laws and ordinances as soon as the decision was announced.

I began to think back to the days of Jim Crow that I naively thought the nation had moved beyond. Instead, Republicans adopted a more racially conservative stance to attract the white Southern voters who abandoned the Democratic Party as Democrats moved toward a more inclusive stance on race. Many of us had noted the trend, and it has been documented both by scholars and by participants in the increasingly white supremacist stance of the

Republican Party.[2] But we had ignored or downplayed the trend, just as my models of attention predicted. It is hard to realize you have been a case study in your own models.

Realizing I was a member of the last cohort of Southerners to have observed directly the horrors of the Jim Crow oppression even if I had not experienced that horror, I dropped my cherished introductory course in public policy to develop and teach a new course, "The Politics of Voter Suppression."

As I developed and taught my new course, I came to appreciate more deeply the sordid record of the United States on defending the right to vote. This realization led me to a more ambitious project. I wondered if I could tell the story of the long fight—and continued failure—for Southern democracy through the stories of my own quintessential Southern ancestors, ending with my own observations as de jure Jim Crow died an agonizing death.

This insight led me back to where I started as an undergraduate—Southern political development through the lenses of political geography. V.O. Key wrote of the deep division between the lower and upper South. The plantation and slave-dependent lower South developed a different economy, culture, and politics from the upper South, rooted in the small-time tenant and yeoman (landowning) farmers of the Appalachian Mountains. Key saw oligarchy in the former and democracy in the latter. He thought that vigorous two-party competition would bring about a more democratic system, fostering an alliance between Blacks and uplanders based on class rather than the racial divisions promoted by the one-party white supremacist system that existed.

My ancestors were divided along the lines of these two Souths—and lived different lives as a consequence. The South Alabamians lived in an oligarchic and hierarchical world, a caste system where a majority of people were Black and unfree. Some of my South Alabama ancestors benefited from this arrangement as slaveholders; others inhabited a less productive agricultural region and were yeoman and tenant farmers. My nonslaveholding North Alabama ancestors lived the harsh lives of mountaineers—lives in which vigorous democracy could occasionally break out in rebellion against the slaveholding oligarchs.

The Decline and Fall of the American Apartheid

I grew up in the American apartheid. For Black Alabamians that meant separate housing, churches, schools, political offices held only by whites, police repression and brutality, limited economic mobility. They could not use public facilities or most private ones without being separated into restricted areas. For whites, it provided better schools, nonrestrictive entrance to public facilities, voting rights, more economic opportunities, safety, and a sense of entitlement.

I had a front-row seat to the demise of legal apartheid in the 1960s. I was a freshman at the University of Alabama when Governor George Wallace "stood in the schoolhouse door" to block the University from being integrated. I edited the yearbook that for the first time in history included Black students, and worked to make sure they were represented in the *Corolla*'s pages. I was mostly a bystander, but it was a turbulent period in which it was hard not to take sides. Donald Collins, a young Methodist minister in the South Alabama Conference during the time, captured the essence of the time well when he wrote, "To live through [the 1950s and 1960s] in Alabama was to live through a vortex of crisis, conflict, and confrontation on an almost daily basis. . . . Everyone was impacted. Not only those who chose to be directly or indirectly involved in the happenings of those days, but also those who had no interest to become entangled in the crisis of those years."[3]

Southern politics is an ongoing morality play in which moral choices are clearer and more consequential than in the rest of the nation. I was lucky to be able to work through these moral choices during a period when they were most vivid. That journey involved dealing with the Lost Cause myths that saturated the white culture of southern Alabama, where I grew up. As former Congressman Carl Elliott wrote in his autobiography 30 years after I was grappling with these choices, "The Confederacy thing still hovers over the South like a fog that refuses to lift."[4] It also required seeing through the veil of nonsensical justifications for segregation offered by white participants. Finally, it required the recognition of the moral repugnance of the white supremacist system that most white Southerners at the time unquestioningly accepted.

As I tried to put together these end-of-an-era memories, I increasingly felt that I was starting the story at its end. How could I comprehend Jim Crow segregation that seemed so normal in the 1950s and 1960s without understanding how it developed and the roles my family played in that system? I set out to understand those roles, focusing on the dual South that they inhabited. This book is the result of those efforts.

This is mostly an Alabama story. Its themes, however, characterize much of the South, especially those states that are divided between fertile lowlands and harsh hills and mountains. And the general dynamics—the struggle over who governs between oligarchy and democracy—are general ones for all social systems at all times.

Acknowledgments

I owe many for supporting me in this endeavor. First is a posthumous bow to my undergraduate professor, Donald Strong, whose courses in Parties and Interest Groups and Southern Politics introduced me to the work of V.O. Key and political geography. I appreciate the support of two of my friends and colleagues, Paul Pierson and Chris Wlezien, who urged me to continue when my will faltered as the project stretched out over the years. Paul graciously reviewed the manuscript for Oxford University Press, as did Rob Mickey, offering great insights into what I was trying to accomplish. Chuck Myers, my former editor at the University of Chicago Press, warned me not proceed without a firmer theme than I had at first. Clarence Stone, Frank Baumgartner, Bat Sparrow, Wilbur Rich, Carter Wilson, Michael Shepherd, Elizabeth Sanders, Brooke Shannon, and E.J. Fagan read all or parts of the manuscript, making it much better. Clarence not only read the manuscript but also engaged with me in a long-running discussion of our similar Southern backgrounds, helping me think more clearly about the project. Maggie Corwin did the cartographic work.

My wife, Diane, agreed to read and react to the full manuscript, and became a superb editor of content, theme, and style, often telling me all sorts of things I didn't want to hear; she was almost always right. I'm not sure how she tolerated me throughout the task, but I am so grateful she did. David McBride of Oxford University Press took a strong interest in the project, carried it forward, and edited the book for theme and style.

I found few letters or documents to guide my genealogical work; as in many families, mostly these were lost or discarded. Two sources made this project far more feasible. One is Mildred Davis Davidson's superb *Frederick Davidson: Revolutionary Soldier and His Descendants*, 1987. The other was my Grandfather Thomas G. Jones's partial autobiography, "Records and Recollections of Thomas G. Jones." Modern tools made available by Ancestry.com, newspapers.com, the U.S. Census, and the archiving on the internet of so many documents, especially newspapers, made the ancestor research possible.

CHAPTER I

Southern Democracy or Southern Oligarchy?

Alabama is always swinging between the politics of class and the politics of race.

—Wayne Flynt[1]

As the American farm crisis climbed to its peak in the 1880s, John Dean served as the tax assessor of Blount County, located in the mountains of North Alabama. Most of the county's inhabitants were white yeoman and tenant farmers, scratching out hardscrabble livings on small farms backing up against the beautiful mountains. There they grew corn and raised pigs but produced no cotton, the major cash crop in the South. There were few big farms and no plantations in Blount; the land would not sustain large-scale agricultural operations.

Dean, my great-grandfather, traversed the county to assess land, around and over Sand Mountain, setting up shop at 33 different locations accessible to the farmers—hamlets like Foster's Chapel, Harmony, and Summit. In traversing his circuit, year after year, Dean became increasingly disturbed by the deteriorating conditions on the farms. Crop prices were low, and cartels monopolized the railroad and fertilizer markets. The "hard money" policies of both national political parties caused currency deflation, resulting in special hardships for the agricultural economy.

Throughout the South, Midwest, and Great Plains, the railroads were strong symbols of the rich man and his corporations taking advantage of the poor man. The railroads received land grants and low assessments from the Blount County Court but provided scant benefits to the farmers Dean interacted with every day.

In 1885, Dean could bear it no more. He refused to accept the claimed valuation presented to him by the Louisville and National Railroad, the most politically powerful railroad in the state. Instead he raised the valuation, and hence the company's taxes, by a large amount. Seeing where the agrarian political winds were blowing, the Blount County Court upheld Dean.

Dean became a regional leader in the Populist movement that challenged the white Southern "Bourbon" power structure composed of planters on the great estates in the Black Belt and their allies among the industrialists and bankers in Birmingham. Enemies of the conservative oligarchs called them "Bourbons" because they aimed to restore the old antebellum order in a way reminiscent of the French attempts at restoration of the Bourbon dynasty.

Today "Populism" is used to indicate racism, jingoism, and conservative economic policies, but it certainly was not that in the late 1800s. Dean and his like-minded colleagues constructed an alliance with Blacks that was economically liberal and moderate on race.[2] The alliance was more than a marriage of convenience; the mountaineers that Dean represented "disliked slavery but also resented the control of government by and for the benefit of the people who lived in the big houses of the lowlands."[3]

Through a campaign of white supremacy, intimidation of Black voters, and massive electoral cheating, the conservative Regular (Bourbon) Democrats defeated the threatening Populist interracial alliance, and terminated it for good by building segregation into the new constitutions which the Regulars wrote at the turn of the century.

When the Populist revolt collapsed, Dean saw no future in Alabama, and headed for Texas.

.   .   .

In 1865, James Powell Carr returned to his plantation in Sumter County, Alabama, after his surrender in North Carolina at the end of the Civil War. Sumter was the mirror opposite of Blount. It lay astride the Black Belt, a region of deep rich soils, and was one of the highest slaveholding counties in the United States in 1860. Carr, my second great-grandfather, had no intention of participating in the war; as a plantation owner he was exempt. Then the Confederacy changed its draft laws, requiring a planter to hold more than 20 slaves for the exemption, and Carr, a small-time slaveholder, received a bounty and signed up with a partisan ranger cavalry company.

Returning home, he faced slaves who were ill-prepared for independence, according to family lore, and Carr set up a sharecropping system. The system ensured that the traditional hierarchical system of white supremacy and deference to authority remained in place.

The white planter reconstruction of a racial hierarchy ran headlong into Blacks determined to exercise their rights as citizens. Blacks outnumbered whites more than three to one in Sumter, and the quasi-slave system based on sharecropping and tenant farming did not stop some labor mobility. Reconstruction was empowering Blacks both economically and politically. Sumter Blacks were not interested in perpetuating the Old South system of hierarchy and caste deference. They wanted democracy.

Sumter whites resorted to intimidation. In 1868, a gang of whites attacked a group of Republican candidates on a wagon tour of the region in the village of Gaston, near Carr's farm. Massive vote cheating took place in the Gaston Beat (precinct), and indeed all over the county. Carr almost certainly participated in this fraud, as he was an election administrator during the period. As a minor Black Belt oligarch, he sided with the Regular Democrats during the Populist Revolt.

Two Minds on Democracy

The South has always been of two minds on the desirability of democracy. Throughout U.S. history some white Southerners were vigorous proponents of the American democratic project. Others thought that participation in governing was more of a privilege granted only to those who proved themselves worthy through education and wealth. Blacks, treated as chattel property under slavery, were at first omitted from the discussion, but when emancipated they joined the prodemocracy side of the debate.

My ancestors were representative of these two mindsets. Dean supported democracy and worked to integrate Republicans, including Black Republicans, Populists, and disaffected Democrats, into a reform coalition capable of challenging the oligarchic Southern power structure. Carr was part of the oligarchy, supporting vote suppression, white supremacy, and hierarchic social and political arrangements.

For much of Southern history, the division was geographic—basically upland small farmers inhabiting the Appalachian regions supporting the democratic project and the lowland planters and slaveholders opposing it. It reflected a politics of class—poor uplanders versus well-off planters.

The debate was not so much over petty regional squabbles, but rather whether the uplanders fell in line with their "betters" when crises came. After the Civil War the plantation owners, joined later by bankers and industrialists, carried the banner of white supremacy that, the plutocrats claimed, unified all whites against Yankee and Black rule. That was the one-mind Solid South based on white supremacy.

The uplanders, though, were capable of revolting against the elites, and did not always fall into line. They were sometimes less motivated by white supremacy and more by class interests, and not infrequently defied the plutocrats, most notably in the Populist rebellion of the 1890s. They did so by forging alliances with Blacks. This was the South of two minds.

Around 1900, Southern states passed constitutions that suppressed Black votes and instituted legal segregation between the races. This action ended the possibility of interracial democracy, but did not destroy the class-based antagonisms between the lowland aristocrats and poor white uplanders. Sadly, the white backlash to the civil rights movement's successes in the 1950s and 1960s undermined the politics of class. Today the Southern uplands, once the home of more liberal politics and a more benign approach to race, is the most Republican region of the country in a period in which Republicans increasingly looked to racial and cultural resentment for support.

In this book, I use historical narratives from my Southern family to explore this political division, where it came from, and what happened to it. Because my lineage incorporates both uplanders like John Dean and blackland planters such as James Powell Carr, I am able to use their stories to map out more fully this division, trace it through history, and explore its impacts on the politics and history of the South. I carry the narrative of the dual Souths up through the 1960s, when I observed directly the last throes of Jim Crow and the final attempts to revive an interracial coalition of North Alabama whites and Blacks. The attempt failed, overwhelmed by the intense politics of racial demagoguery as the civil rights movement reached its apogee.

The dual Souths, one anchored in a commitment to democracy, the other steeped in hierarchy and oligarchy, cannot be separated from racial relations. The side of the Southern mind committed to oligarchy was desperate to prohibit Blacks from participating in politics, as that participation threatened white supremacy and hierarchical deference. The democratic side supported Black participation, but not necessarily enthusiastically. Often the democratic alliance occurred out of a sense of pragmatism that could be disrupted by the cries of "Black rule" from the oligarchs.

As a consequence, the narratives I develop are often based in issues of race. Interracial democracy is possible even when the groups are wary of each other, even distrustful, but cannot be achieved without pragmatic leadership.

There is clear evidence of two white mindsets—ways of thinking about social, political, and economic systems—for the period from 1800 to 1965.

The system dissolved in the stresses of the 1950s and 1960s. Alabama Governor George Wallace represented the concluding chapter of the collapse of the sectional system dividing uplanders, augmented by urban labor, from the Black Belt plantation society, bolstered by industrialists, bankers, and the urban rich. These divisions were replaced later with coalitions more based in the national pattern of urban and rural divisions, but that is a story left for others to tell.

Family Lineages Embedded in History

We may think of a family lineage as a long series of family developments and specific events taking place across several linked lifetimes. This conception gives us the opportunity to understand the two Souths across time through the eyes of the participants, to the extent that we can reconstruct them. Within a person's life, the outcomes we observe, such as wealth, status, or achievements, are affected by the person's biological, social, economic, and political inheritances; his or her decisions through life; and the advantages or disadvantages that are conferred on the individual because of class, race, and gender.

The characteristics of the time and place in which the person lives and the historical events that occur that disrupt that time frame also matter. These historical events can occur at the societal level, such as war, economic boom or bust, or other large-scale events. Or the events could be localized disasters or fortuitous circumstances, such as floods or droughts, or living in a city with a localized economic boom.

Here I trace four lines of my ancestors through Southern history. All four lines, which trace back from my grandparents, have been in the country for a long time—since before the Revolutionary War—allowing for the examination of long historical timelines. My objective is to intertwine individual lives with the historical period in which they lived.

Each line represents different migratory patterns and even different genetic traces. The Carrs were slaveholders and lowland southerners, moving from the Cape Fear region of North Carolina to Black Belt Alabama. The Joneses started as minor slaveholders in South Carolina but gave up slavery early and hewed frontier lives out of the pine barrens of North Florida and South Alabama. The Davidsons and the Deans were nonslaveholding uplanders, always moving west along the Appalachian Mountains into North Alabama.

I weave the stories of these people and the history of the American South together, showing how history molded their life opportunities and how they, and people like them, affected the trace of history.

Using these reconstructed lineages, I explore two central themes. The first is the pervasiveness of race in ordering the lives of white Southerners. White supremacy was the legal organizing principle of the Southern social structure from early settlement to the 1960s (and the informal structure beyond). For most of that period for whites this system was akin to the foundation and structural beams of a house: it was the critical structure, but it remained mostly unseen and blithely assumed.

The second is whether there existed two white Southern mindsets, one based in democratic ideals, the other in oligarchic rule. Did white Southerners think similarly on major issues, stemming from the slave system? Or were there two mindsets, one derived from the plantation economies of the fertile Black Belt soils, the other from the rugged nonslaveholding Appalachian Mountain regions? If there were two distinct mindsets, could they be forced into one through the rhetoric of racism and the disproportionate power of the plantation oligarchs?

Eras

The effect of history on our lives today is unmistakable. Some years ago, Paul Pierson urged political scientists to explore "the insights to be gained by shifting from a 'snapshot' to a moving picture of important social processes."[4] Journalist Kyle Whitmire put it this way, "History is the backstory for everything that happens today—without it we can no more understand the present than keep up after walking into a movie that's halfway over."[5] William Faulkner returned again and again to the heavy hand of history that particularly plagued the South: "It's all now, you see. Yesterday won't be over until tomorrow and tomorrow began ten thousand years ago."[6]

Granted, but how does that work? History does not unfold smoothly and uniformly; it proceeds in fits and starts. Political scientists use the term "critical junctures" to denote those major events that affect the course of history.[7] In between these critical junctures plenty of history goes on, but it unfolds under a set of "rules of the game" that hold steady. During the Jim Crow period Black activists and their allies pushed against the oppressive status quo, while the white political elites of the day resisted, but for the most part segregation remained in place. During the 1960s the rules of the game changed as de jure segregation collapsed, even if de facto segregation continued in many arenas.

We may point to four major critical junctures that disrupted the trace of Southern history: Indian removal and the opening of the frontier; the Civil War and Reconstruction; the Populist Revolt of the 1890s; and the civil rights movement of the 1950s and 1960s (Figure 1.1). These dramatic punctuations were not just disruptive of the trace of history. They resulted in reordering the social structure and opened the possibilities to change the trajectory of history.

The Indian (Native American) removal led to vast new opportunities for both slaveholding and nonslaveholding whites but devastated Native Peoples' rights and opportunities. The Civil War and Reconstruction opened the possibility of a cross-racial society that instead fell into the white supremacist Redemption Period. The failed Populist Revolt explicitly envisioned a class-based Black and white coalition but was derailed by rampant corruption and racism, ushering in Jim Crow. The civil rights movement opened the modern period of struggles toward multiracial democracy or its failure (either path is possible as I write this).

In between the catastrophic disruptions were periods of relative quiet that resulted in little or no change in the existing social structure. These form general eras between the disruptions. Each of these eras endured turbulence, such as economic cycles including radical changes in the price of cotton and challenges to chattel slavery from Northern abolitionists. This within-era turbulence did not upset the socioeconomic status quo.

The periods during which social stability is occasionally dented but not seriously challenged are what historians would term historical eras—relatively calm seas divided by social tsunamis. These eras are the Colonial Period, the Antebellum Period, Redemption, and the Jim Crow era.

Following the historical traces of family lineages affords a particularly effective way of shifting from a snapshot to a moving picture. Examining family lineages comparatively, as I do here, offers the opportunity to compare moving pictures through the same set of eras.

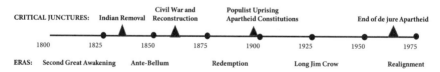

Figure 1.1 Timeline of Eras Punctuated by Critical Junctures
Source: Author's chart.

The Matthew Effect

A final important concept that we all grasp intuitively is the Matthew effect, which is the notion of cumulative advantage. This effect takes its name from a biblical reference to the Gospel according to St. Matthew. "For unto everyone that hath shall be given, and he shall have abundance: but from him that hath not shall be taken away even that which he hath" (Matthew 13:12).

The stability of the social structure benefits some people, allowing them to accumulate wealth, and works against others, prohibiting them from successful accumulation. While we think of this maxim as applying to wealth, it can apply to many other areas of life. The sociologist Robert Merton used the concept to explain the tendency of scholars who had lots of citations to their published work to gain more citations.[8]

The Matthew effect describes inequality among individuals. It can also apply to family lineages which, through gifts or inheritances, can lead to between-family inequality. In the case of slavery, masters could pass on slaves to their offspring, but of course slaves could pass on nothing to theirs, increasing inequality between races through history. The Matthew effect can apply to physical capital or wealth, but it can also apply to human capital, with different access to education or other human skills that can lead to higher levels of wealth or skills in the future.

The Matthew effect may or may not survive a major disruption. Many Black Belt slaveholders, such as the Carrs of Sumter County, were still relatively well-off after the Civil War even after much of their wealth had been wiped out. This was partly a result of the formal and informal rules established after the war concerning sharecropping and land tenancy, and partly because of the human capital built up during the antebellum period. My great-grandfather Robert Bryan Carr was able to attend formal medical school, the sole great-grandfather of my ancestors who attended college.

I cannot tell the full story of Black Southerners, those most negatively affected by oppressive slavery and the following decades of white supremacy. They challenged the system from the moral high ground but suffered not only immediate economic, political, and physical harm, but also historical legacies that continue today.

Oppressive societies take a toll on the oppressors as well. I hope I can illuminate the damage a corrupt stable social system such as the long period of Jim Crow can impose on the presumed white supremacist victors as well. The mindless moral depravity that occurs in racially unequal societies corrupts whites as well as the social structure more generally. A downward spiral in morals occurs in oppressive societies as they come under pressure, causing the defenders of the system to invent more and more falsehoods to justify the oppression, generally resulting in social or economic sanctions against the challengers and often resulting in violence.

Stories Intertwined in History

Narratives are stories that represent something broader. They are often stories that people tell themselves to justify their status. Political science, economics, sociology, anthropology, and history have all experienced upswings in the study of narratives.[9] For these disciplines, the subject matter is the primary concern; the characters in the story are secondary.

The narrative method is used in two ways. Scholars study the narratives that people tell themselves to show how these stories affect behavior. These stories can be mostly true or mostly false. For example, Southerners have constructed the myth that the Civil War was fought not to defend slavery, but for the high moral cause of states' rights, and that narrative has been passed on across generations in the face of contradictory evidence.

A second way that the narrative method is used is by reconstructing the lives of people as they lived history. Historians pursue what is called microhistory to offset the "great man" and "determinism of history" approaches that once characterized the field. They link narrative histories of real people to study the underpinnings of history. Historians of slavery have used individual stories to bring home the horrors of the practice, generally combined with analyses of available data.[10]

One part of that approach is the study of family history. Historian Kendra Field notes that the study of family history has developed into a scholarly subfield and uses this approach to reconstruct her family's history after Emancipation.[11] The family narrative approach is especially important in prying open the myths that survive more sweeping historical accounts. Edward Ball, whose slaveholding family kept intricate records, traced his genealogy from the slaveholders to the modern former slaves held by these owners.[12] Ball is a pioneer in slashing through the myths of the plantation society, illustrating with records and stories the cruelty of the system.

There is nothing new about people being interested in ancestry. The newly developed tools for tracing where Americans today "came from" make that much more possible. But there are pitfalls. Too many students of their family's past stop at who their ancestors were, and perhaps what they did. Less often do they pause to understand the sweep of history their ancestors lived through, except to locate their forbears in time and place.

I've tried mightily to keep the history, political science, and sociology at the forefront. However it is easy to fall into the trap of becoming mesmerized by the stories, and many of the stories I tell here are strong, as would be the case of most Americans' ancestors.

A second trap for the ancestor hunter is the tendency to whitewash the ancestor and his or her role in the brutal history that is the American South.[13] I have tried to avoid that by comparing my slaveholding ancestors with the non-slaveholding ones. It is certainly easier to write about ancestors who intervened to stop a lynching or save a Black man from the gallows than it is to describe a one who aided in the removal of the Cherokees in Georgia or conspired to steal Black votes after Reconstruction (and yes these were real events).

Structure of the Manuscript

I have structured the manuscript to develop the "two minds" theme, stressing geographical differences and exploring family lines simultaneously. This chapter and the next explain the thesis through the lenses of an initial comparison between two Alabama counties where my ancestors lived—the mountain county of Blount and the Black Belt county of Sumter.

Then I divide the manuscript into sections, each following a major theme developing the tensions and hostilities, on the one hand, and solidarity on the other, between the two Souths. I show how race and class interplay to produce the dynamics of the divided white South over time.

Part 1 develops the story of the slaveholding Carrs in Sumter County, Alabama, and the lasting legacy of slavery. Although they were minor slave-holders compared with the vast plantations nearby, they nevertheless accumulated substantial wealth from slavery and passed down both wealth and human capital across generations.

Part 2 explores the nonslaveholding Davidsons and Deans, who moved into North Georgia and Alabama thanks to Indian removal. In the rebellious mountains where they settled, both families assumed leadership roles in the 1890s Populist agrarian revolt against the Black Belt planters. Disgusted when the corrupt conservative Democrats defeated Populism, both families moved into the Republican Party.

Part 3 shows how the Joneses, religious frontiersmen, traversed the pine barrens and sandy soils of the Wiregrass of South Georgia, Panhandle Florida, and Southeast Alabama. They were the archetypical "common white men," craftsmen and poor farmers living a life similar to the mountain yeoman farmers. The county they hailed from was solidly Populist, but the Joneses were politically apathetic, and when they took political positions they generally sided with the officers turned conservative Democrats who led them in the Civil War.

With Part 4, I shift toward the central story of a more unified white South during the Jim Crow period. Black disenfranchisement made Black–white class-based political allegiances impossible. The South became solidly one-party and put in place mechanisms that would ensure economic stagnation and racial injustice. Objections to this system were more individual acts of resistance, mostly by Blacks but by some whites as well. Great Uncle Julius saved a Black man who killed a justice of the peace from being lynched. J.O. Sentell played a lead role in the writing of the Alabama segregationist constitution of 1901. His son, J.O. Sentell Jr., my uncle by marriage—Uncle J.O. to me—helped to convict the Klan murderers of Viola Liuzzo, a civil rights activist participating in the Selma-to-Montgomery march in 1965.

Part 5 focuses on the collapse of the efforts of Southern moderates to bring about step-by-step change in the segregated social structure and describes the long period of Jim Crow. Black participation in the Second World War opened a new era. Uncle Mac was a D-Day veteran who worked for race-moderate political candidates and as a lawyer represented Black defendants. As Jim Crow collapsed in the 1950s, the pressures on Southern moderates to conform to massive resistance to desegregation were severe. I examine the responses of three moderate Southern editors in their editorials, including my father, a small-town South Alabama newspaper editor and publisher, and two other Southern editors.

Part 6 concludes the manuscript with the observations of a white boy insulated from the horrors of segregation in its heyday in a small South Alabama town, and my realization of the senselessness of the system. Then I recount legal segregation's agonizing end as I observed it as a student at the University of Alabama in the 1960s. When legal segregation ended, so did the "two Souths" under the weight of the racist demagoguery of George Wallace. A new "two Souths" has replaced the old one, a politics of rural Blacks and urban Black and white progressives.

CHAPTER 2

Two Souths or One?

Blount and Sumter

In 1889 the *Sumter County Sun* published a furious front-page editorial directed at alleged miscreants in the North Alabama mountain counties. The commentary centered on North Alabama's increasing calls for reform of the corrupt Black Belt voting system during the agrarian reform era of the late 19th century. The editorial dripped with the haughty status distinctions of the day—the slaveless planters could still look with contempt on the hillbillies of the backwoods.

"These two sections of the greatest State in the South never could get along well together," wrote the *Sun*'s editorialist. "Before the war all the prosperity and wealth of the State centered in the cotton belt, and the long, lank mountaineers of Blount, Jefferson, and other northern counties picked up a precarious living by raising apples, making hard cider, and jug ware for the planters of the blackbelt." In 1860, the population of Sumter County was 75% slave, while Blount was only 6% slave, the second lowest in the state.

The editorial went on to complain about the weak support for the Civil War in the mountains, noting "When the war broke out they laughed at the idea of facing the foe; they said it was a 'rich man's war and a poor man's fight.'" The editorial then moved to the agrarian calls for electoral reform, calling the uplanders "these Republicans, in Democratic garb, clamoring for fair elections and a just representation."[1]

My mountain ancestors, the Davidsons, were potters in Blount County; my Black Belt ancestors, the Carrs, were planters in Sumter County (Figure 2.1). I cannot shake the image of my potter ancestors making jug ware for my planter ancestors.

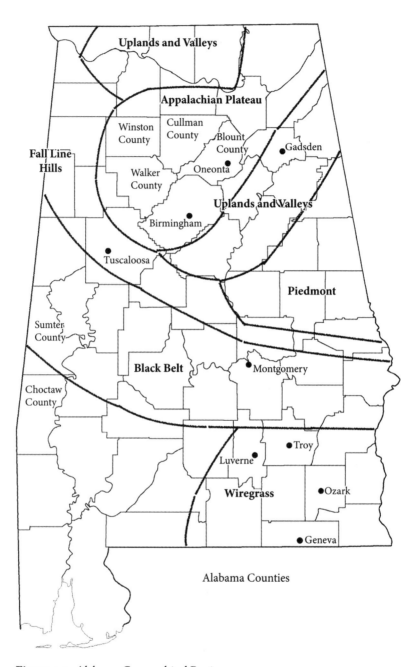

Figure 2.1 Alabama Geographical Regions

Source: Author. Modified from Physiographic Regions and County base maps, Department of Geography, University of Alabama.

Migration Patterns and Sectionalism

The Blount-Sumter divide stems from a South that was historically cleaved into two parts. They developed separate political identities, cultures, and economies. Historical geographer Colin Woodard mapped U.S. cultural differences across the United States, distinguishing Greater Appalachia from the Deep South.[2] His dividing line sliced the Deep South states of Georgia and Alabama cleanly into two parts, highlighting the differences between the plantation economy and the nonslaveholding upland regions. Similar divides characterize the Upper South states of Tennessee, North Carolina, and Virginia.

Southern sectionalism was defined by economic opportunities offered by geographic variations, but it was also affected by the migration patterns followed by European immigrants who brought cultural and political differences along with them. These differences even follow genetic variations. Using a technique called network analysis on DNA collected from 770,000 individuals, a group of geneticists analyzed the genetic structure of postcolonial North America.[3] These clusters connect genetics with migratory patterns of European immigrants. These westward migratory patterns followed Indian removal, often through a series of land cessions after massive intrusions of white settlers and at times violent conflict between the natives and the immigrants.

The geneticists detected two primary white Southern migratory patterns, Upland South and Lower South, very closely matching Woodard's cultural classifications. The Upper South cluster, which included my relatives the Davidsons and the Deans, stretched down from northern Virginia along the east side of the Appalachians into western North Carolina, eastern Tennessee, northern Georgia and Alabama, and over to Arkansas and central Texas. These regions are primarily white to this day.

The Lower South genetic cluster stretches from the eastern parts of Virginia and North Carolina to most of South Carolina, southern Georgia, Alabama, and Mississippi. The Sumter County Carrs fit this pattern. A distinct subgroup of the Lower South is located in the sandy pine barrens (often called the Wiregrass region) of Georgia, Alabama, and Florida. My paternal lineage Joneses followed this path.

Black patterns closely trace the Lower South cluster, but of course Blacks did not migrate. Their masters took them to new plantations in the Black Belt regions of these states. In a second wave of Black settlement, "drovers"

marched slaves from the slave-overproducing regions of the older South—
Virginia and North Carolina—to sell in the new frontier regions of Alabama
and Mississippi.

When we trace the historical family settlement patterns, we are also tracing family genetic distributions. Culture is not determined by genetics but can
emerge out of similar people following similar paths of migration. New places
were settled by westward streams of migration, and the streams of migration
brought people with different orientations and outlooks from their points of
origin. As political scientist V.O. Key Jr. noted, "The westward travelers carried
their partisan loyalties with them and the paths they followed can even today be
traced on the maps of party voting."[4] A white uplander in Alabama had more
in common both culturally and politically with an uplander in North Carolina
than a white slaveholder in the Alabama Black Belt.

The Fall Line

A wide swath of deep black prairie soil crosses central Alabama east to west. It is
narrower in the east, wider on the west, and centers on the state capital, Montgomery. The Alabama Black Belt is part of larger pattern of rich soils running
from Virginia to the Mississippi River in Mississippi and Louisiana, between
the coastal plains and the Piedmont.

The political fault line of Alabama is just north of the Black Belt, generally
along the Fall Line, dividing the Piedmont and Appalachian regions from the
coastal plains. North of the fall line, the topography is rugged and generally
unsuited to plantation farming. The great exception is the Tennessee River Valley, where the river bottom provided rich soil and a gentle terrain, and hence
was more suitable to the plantation economy.

The fall line divided Alabama politics and culture, and Southern politics
more broadly. It divided the region over the key issues of slavery, secession,
Reconstruction, and partisanship. Political scientist Walter Dean Burnham
wrote of this divide:

> Ever since the organization of modern political parties in the 1830's, the most
> enduring political cleavage within Alabama has been a sectional antagonism
> between the poor whites of the North Alabama hills and the wealthier whites
> of the plantation counties in the South. This struggle recurs again and again
> throughout the state's history: in the contest of the 1830's and 1840's between
> the "homespun" Jacksonian Democrats of the North and the "broadcloth"
> Whigs of the Black Belt; between unionists and secessionists in 1850 and 1861;

between Populists and Bourbons in the 1890's; and even within the Democratic gubernatorial primary of 1946.[5]

From the period of settlement to the 1960s, much of the political dialogue involved Black Belt politicians appealing to the racial sentiments of North Alabamians. In a famous editorial in 1874, just before Alabama was "redeemed" from Reconstruction, the *Montgomery Advertiser*, the voice of the Bourbon Democrats in the Black Belt, pleaded, "South Alabama raises her manacled hands in mute appeal to the mountain counties. The chains on the wrists of her sons and the midnight shrieks of her women sound continually in their ears. She lifts up her eyes, being in torment, and begs piteously for release from bondage. Is there a white man in North Alabama so lost to all the finer feelings of human nature as to slight her appeal?"[6]

North Alabama whites could be incited to action on the race issue and were mobilized on the question of "redemption" from Reconstruction, but often were much more concerned with economic well-being. In North Alabama, it was respectable to be a unionist before the Civil War and a white Republican after the War.

One Mind

The political cleavage between white uplanders and white lowlanders was certainly enduring, but was it durable? During the mid-20th century, historians and political scientists engaged in a spirited debate on this issue. On the one hand, journalist W.J. Cash argued that one mindset prevailed. On the other, political scientist V.O. Key Jr. and historian C. Vann Woodward maintained that there were two distinct Souths, with cultures different enough from each other to generate distinct politics that opened the possibility of an interracial democratic order after the Civil War and again in the 1890s. With the "one mind" of Cash, an interracial democracy would always have been unattainable.

Cash argued that the Blount-Sumter difference was superficial—that there was a more fundamental underlying unity to the white Southern identity. "If there can be said that there are many Souths, the fact remains that there is also one South. That is to say . . . there is a fairly definite mental pattern, associated with a fairly definite social pattern—a complex of established relationships and habits of thought, sentiments, prejudices, standards and values, and association of ideas" common to most [white] Southerners.[7]

Scholars and journalists promoting the single solid South conception depicted a white population whose historical experiences were similar. They shared the view of a frontier economy where ambitious whites accumulated wealth at first slowly and then rapidly, following the Matthew principle. The less ambitious "crackers" were less successful because they were less industrious.

This led, in the one-South conception, to a hierarchical system of deference to those destined to rule—the successful planters in antebellum days; the officers of the Confederacy in the post–Civil War period; and the cotton mill owners and new industrialists, bankers, and utility company executives in the emerging "New South."

Deference alone was not enough. To keep the lower classes in place, the lowland oligarchs employed a propaganda of white racism along with a culture of violence. Ralph Bunche, first Black president of the American Political Science Association and Nobel Prize–winning diplomat, described the Southern class system this way:

> There have always been severe class distinctions in the South. Negroes and "poor whites" have consistently occupied the two bottom rungs on the Southern social and economic ladders, and the white landholders, bankers, and industrialists—the Southern "Bourbons"—have always perched at the top. . . . Between these upper and lower white classes in the South there has been a traditional and deep-seated hostility. Only the clever manipulation of the threat of black dominance has kept the underprivileged white masses and the privileged upper classes of the South from coming to a parting of the ways.[8]

Cash argues that the oligarchs manipulated the racism of the bottom white rungs by acting as the instigators of most racial violence that the "common whites" carried out. He blamed the "master classes" for stirring up the racist masses in lynchings. He saw the hand of the Southern oligarch behind the repeated rise of the Ku Klux Klan and other white terror groups. Although common whites made up the foot soldiers of Klan terror, "the people who held it together and coordinated it and directed it were very near to being coextensive with the established leadership of the South . . . they usually maintained liaison with it through their underlings and the politicians."[9] Similarly, Cash saw the Southern race-baiting demagogues as allies of economic oligarchs who almost always preached economic betterment of the lower classes but practiced economic conservatism.

A second voice in the single-mind thesis was the distinguished historian W.E.B. Du Bois. Writing half a decade before Cash, Du Bois saw one Southern white mindset, but argued that it was built on deliberately constructed institutions designed to implement a caste system of white supremacy and "a determined psychology of caste" to support the white supremacist institutions.[10] The psychology dictated Black inferiority; a parallel sociology and history justified the structure. While Cash saw a single white mind born of distant history, Du Bois saw that single mind as emerging from more recent manipulation of political and economic institutions.

Cash saw oppression as a side effect of the deference to hierarchy that, he argued, affected both poor whites and Blacks. Du Bois depicted a South upside down from Cash—he saw a race-based hierarchy designed to subjugate Blacks because of racism. In both approaches, one white supremacist mindset prevailed. It encompassed all whites–rich and poor; yeoman farmer and planter; industrialist and mill worker. In both models, Southern oligarchs used the system to manipulate common whites into acting against their class interests.

Slavery and Deference

> There was a land of Cavaliers and Cotton Fields called the Old South . . .
> Here in this pretty world Gallantry took its last bow . . .
> Here was the last ever to be seen of Knights and their ladies Fair, of Master and Slave . . .
> Look for it only in books, for it is no more than a dream remembered.
> A Civilization gone with the wind . . .

Such was the gauzy prologue to the 1939 movie *Gone with the Wind*. It captured well the antebellum myths that upper-class planters repeated to themselves to downplay the brutality of the Old South.

The antebellum myths of the Old South carried over to the Lost Cause justification for the Civil War—that it was fought for a good cause, states' rights. The Old South romanticism justified slavery and the destruction of the Union. The "moonlight and magnolias" view of the South made popular the notion that plantation society generated magnanimous slave owners with compliant and generally contented slaves. Today that version lives in plantation tours, and plantations are even used as sites for weddings.[11]

The single-mind thesis did not ignore Southern class and sectional differences but gave the uplander a place low in the oligarchic hierarchy. The uplander was not romanticized, but denigrated as an ignorant hillbilly, seen as far more racist than the benevolent planter of the Black Belt. They supposedly lived isolated lives in the mountains, hardly connected to civilized Southern society, making moonshine and bootlegging alcohol—along with some jug ware for the better classes. It was easy to depict them as ignorant bigots, not traveling far from their small farms and isolated villages, alienated from the better classes, and faring unfavorably in comparison to the slaveholding gentry of the Black Belt. This classic hillbilly caricature is alive and well even today.[12]

The "Unknown South"

For the most part this picture is backward. In 1949, V.O. Key noted, "It is the whites of the black belts who have the deepest and most immediate concern about the maintenance of white supremacy."[13] Both historical and systematic social science research support Key's observation. A team of political science researchers recently showed convincingly that whites in Southern counties with high proportions of slaves in 1860 are more racially conservative today than counties with low slaveholding proportions in 1860. This effect is independent of how many Blacks live in those counties today, along with other variables such as economic well-being. The history of the county matters, not just the conditions of today. The research team called this phenomenon "behavioral path dependency," a technical description for Faulkner's observation that "yesterday won't be over until tomorrow."[14]

Many Alabamians back in the 1960s thought that the Black Belt harbored the worst forms of racism. I recall a discussion between my mother and my outspoken aunt Mary Elizabeth, who had complained that an aunt by marriage treated her Black maid harshly. I was surprised that Mother agreed; usually she demurred from my aunt's gossip. But this time she nodded, and Mary Elizabeth, or Woo as we knew her, said quite definitively, "Well, she IS from Demopolis." Demopolis is in Marengo County (78.3% slave in 1860) in the Black Belt. Mother nodded.

Even though the earlier presence of slavery and today's percentage of Black residents are both related to higher levels of racism among whites, that is not the whole story. The handful of North Alabama counties in the Tennessee Valley with high percentages of slaves in 1860 voted against secession in 1861. In those counties there is now among whites a weaker identification with the

Confederacy than among South Alabama whites. Or, as one Huntsville commentator on the Southern sectional division remarked that "Y'all, in North Alabama, we don't have that much 'Confederate heritage' to preserve."[15] One of my cousins from South Alabama put it this way: "We saw anything north of Birmingham as Yankee territory."

One other issue not addressed in the behavioral path dependency research is how attitudes from the 1860s are carried forward to today. The passing down of narratives and myths is one likely mechanism, and the examination of family lineages can be one way to study this. I explore some of these aspects in later chapters.

The white oligarchic status hierarchy built on top of a racial caste system requires deference from the lower orders. That is, the lower orders need to believe the upper class came by their status and power legitimately, so its power to rule is not questioned.

The proponents of the two-minds side of the debate were not persuaded by the "falling in line behind the oligarchs" argument. Historian C. Vann Woodward claimed that in the Reconstruction Period both Black and white citizens were in the process of developing cultural norms adjusting to the new, integrated South.[16] Although there was plenty of racism among whites, the norms of behavior were changing, moving toward a more open South.

Political scientist V.O. Key was less concerned about evolving norms and more about political power. He wrote of a South that was artificially unified because of the disproportionate political control exerted by the Black Belt regions of southern states. The problem for oligarchic control was the regional concentration of lower-class whites who were extraordinarily hostile to the governing Bourbons. "Outside the black belts southern political behavior often takes on a tone distinctly at odds with the planter-financier stereotypes. . . . [This area] in several states consists largely of the highlands which have been marked by an almost unbroken strain of political rebelliousness."[17] He called these regions "the unknown political south." These regions constituted enclaves of democracy capable of making alliances with Black voters and causing serious problems for Bourbon rule.[18]

Key saw the Populist rebellion of the 1890s as a critical moment in Southern politics, one that could have yielded a different more democratic South by empowering the uplanders in their challenges to the Bourbon oligarchs. The time was ripe. Among the common folk deference to the "governing classes" was far weaker than before the War. That was especially true among the upland nonslaveholding craftsmen, farmers, and laborers. There was great resentment against the slaveholders who had led the South on a fool's crusade to protect and extend slavery. This resentment grew during the agricultural hard times of the 1880s, blossoming into the Populist Revolt in the 1890s. Nationally the Populists targeted the railroad and banking monopolists and the hard money policies they demanded. In the South, Populists allied with Black Republicans in a struggle against planters and industrial oligarchs. This alliance generated a "vigorous upsurge of the lower-class whites and what may have happily developed into a process of more extensive democratization of that region."[19] Instead, Bourbon political leaders achieved victory through a massive white supremacist propaganda campaign aided by violence, economic intimidation, and election cheating.

Unlike Key, Cash dismissed Populism as an epiphenomenon, claiming "the common white of the South did in overwhelming tide abandon his advance upon class consciousness and relapse into his ancient focus."[20] As we shall see in Part 2 of this book, I find little of the hierarchical deference required for a return to the single mind among my uplander ancestors. They led a democratically exuberant challenge to the Bourbons, and when that was crushed, rather than crawling back to Bourbon rule they left the Democratic Party or left the state.

The work of Woodward and Key implies that a one-minded Southern history was not inevitable, but that it could have turned out differently. Keri Leigh Merritt's research into the lives of poor whites supports the Key-Woodward thesis. She shows that in antebellum years whites were deeply divided on the issue of slavery, and the division was class-based.[21] Poor whites were despised by plantation elites, and law and custom operated against them. She argues that a cross-race politics would have been possible even before the Civil War.

The Southern Politics of Class and Race

Most historians and political scientists today reject Cash's single-mind concept. The second civil rights revolution would seem to have undermined the old Southern hierarchy. Yet that rejection may well be premature. Many modern students of race politics, following Du Bois, have taken the fixed, hierarchical social structure argument more seriously. In her National Book Award–winning book *Caste*, Isabel Wilkerson writes of a fixed caste system that generates status distinctions and a panoply of social rewards based on an immutable trait.[22] Hannah-Jones et al.'s *1619 Project* analyzes the unrecognized contributions made by Blacks to American economic success, and shows how a single mind similar to that put forth by DuBois holds the racial hierarchy in place.[23]

In his Pulitzer Prize–winning book, Jefferson Cowie accepts the single-white-mind thesis, writing of a Southern white supremacy that allocated one's social standing and political claims according to race. In that system "freedom" includes the freedom to oppress others (especially Blacks). He shows how Southern-style freedom led to white resistance to federal interventions. He does so by dissecting the politics of a single Alabama Black Belt county from its settlement to the George Wallace years.[24] Had he picked a North Alabama county, however, Cowie may have found a different and more complex storyline.

The prominence of the single-mind approach emerges out of a focus on the politics of status while minimizing the politics of class. There exist two kinds of politics in any social system, side by side, intertwined like DNA's double helix. They are a politics of class, centered on wealth, and a politics of status, based on race, ethnicity, and gender. This tension constantly shows up in the geography of the South, and the two struggled for ascendency more times than we often imagine. A solid South based in white supremacy was repeatedly challenged by class-based and geographically-based coalitions, as Bunche noted.

The major issue of class politics revolves around wealth accumulation versus wealth redistribution. Should government promote the accumulation of wealth for future investment in developing the region economically? Or should government redistribute wealth to the poor to better their lives in the present? One perspective allows the wealthy to become a governing class that should be trusted to make the system better over time. The wealthy demand low taxes and cheap labor, claiming that such policies lead to economic prosperity. The other perspective sees the wealthy as untrustworthy and sees wealth as a collective asset to be redistributed for the betterment of the general population. In this case arguments center on increased wages, pensions, education, and roads.

Status politics always centers on the politics of ranking the worth of identities. In the South, that has invariably involved the caste system based on race, but it also involved how whites are ranked as well. Wealthy planters and businessmen scorned poor upland farmers, and saw the landless poor as less worthy.

In the politics of class, people ask, "What do I have? Why can't I live bet-ter? and Why do other people have more?" In the politics of status, people ask, "How am I viewed? How do I view myself compared to others? What is my reputation? How are people like me viewed?"

Class politics is about worth; status politics is about self-worth. Class politics is about countable assets; status politics is about identity and reputation.

Both generate inequalities, but class is measurable and status consists of all sorts of incommensurate elements. It is easy to calculate what I am worth by adding up my economic assets. It is not so easy to calculate whether I am *worth* something. In the United States, race is used as a critical allocator of status, held in place by notions of white supremacy. Critically, are groups I belong to or just identify with worth something? If they are, then I am. If they are not, then I may not be.

Both class and status politics lead to one overwhelming consideration: I cannot be worth something if someone else is not worth less. Political scientist Ted Robert Gurr saw this struggle over worth as *relative depri-vation*; absolute well-being matters less than deprivation relative to other groups.[25]

Wealth grants status, but status need not be wealth-based. As historian Harvey Jackson has written about the early settlers of Mobile, "like the first settlements throughout America, a certain status is granted the founders and passed on to their descendants, whether they deserve it or not."[26] Yet such sta-tus is not granted to the descendants of Black slaves, who arrived in Mobile soon after the first whites, even after they were freed. Nor to the displaced Native Americans who first inhabited the area. Race has been an integral part of status politics, and it continues to be.

Because so much of Southern life historically revolved around race, the ten-sion between class and status mostly plays out as a politics of race. For many disadvantaged whites, being white is the basis for their identities. For all South-ern whites, to some extent or other, being Southern means (or at least used to mean) having a shared historical experience—especially the Civil War.

After the Civil War, if the uplanders identified as "poor men," then they could ally with Blacks, and sectional and class interests would dominate Southern politics. If they identified as "white men," then race would domi-nate Southern politics, and the South would be solid and white supremacist. When uplanders identified as white, the South presented a solid front against outside influences on "our Southern way of life," "our customs and traditions," and other such similar phrases. By identifying as such, uplanders effectively handed power to the Black Belt conservatives and their big business allies. White supremacy always led to rule by economic elites.

Even though white supremacy has been the "strong force" in Southern politics, it has been regularly challenged, generally at the critical junctures in Southern history. Whites demanded the lands of natives during the Removal of the 1830s. Unionists and secessionists clashed before the Civil War. In the 1890s Bourbons and Populists exemplified the struggle between oligarchy and democracy. In the 1950s and 1960s a strategy of court action, legislative maneuvering, and direct democratic action by Blacks resulted in the dismantling of the most egregious legal underpinnings of white supremacy by federal intervention. Overcoming the strong force of white supremacy is very difficult, but not impossible.

The two mindsets in the white American South rely on different cultural understandings and political coalitions. One tends toward hierarchy and oligarchical rule and relies on white racial resentment for enforcement. The other mindset is based in the American democratic ideal and relies on cross-race coalitions based on shared class interests. In Southern history they have existed side by side, in different geographic regions. In the past, the difference was between Appalachia and the lowlands. Today it divides rural from urban regions.

Blount and Sumter

I started this chapter with a vignette of Alabama's Blount and Sumter Counties, locales where branches of my ancestral tree rooted. I did so because the contrast is so stark and so illustrative of the difference between Margaret Mitchell's romanticized South and V.O. Key's unknown South. In coming chapters, I carry through stories of the Davidsons, the Carrs, the Joneses, and the Deans and how they dealt both with the tidal waves of the critical moments as well as the calmer eras of Southern history.

In this literary journey, I discovered continual surprises and moments of great decency, on the one hand, and poor moral choices on the other. But mostly I found that the eras between the massive disruptive events were simply the backdrop of life, just there, structuring almost all aspects of behavior but generally ignored. Jim Crow was just there. Only when great social tsunamis are building do the injustices become obvious.

None of my family members today lives in either Sumter or Blount counties and have not for a long time. Nevertheless I think of Sumter County as a metaphor for white status and white identity politics. Until recently few whites attended public schools with Blacks. Sumter is solidly Democratic, because it is solidly Black and the Voting Rights Act freed Blacks from the bars that kept them from participation. The few whites there are Republicans, and Southern Republicanism has in recent decades undergirded white identity politics.

Blount, once a bellwether of whether status and identity politics, on the one hand, or class on the other, would be central to Alabama politics, is today strongly Republican. The Republicanism there today is far from the unionist Republicanism of the 1890s. There is little doubt, though, that status and identity dominate, and southern Appalachia today is both overwhelmingly white and solidly Republican.

PART 1

Slaves, Owners, and the Black Belt

Of the four family lines we are following, one enslaved people. The Carrs were slaveholders from at least the time of the Revolutionary War, and perhaps before. They never left the slaveholding world once they entered it until Emancipation forced them to do so. They practiced slavery in both North Carolina and Alabama. While the Carrs were not major players in the slaveholding South, they nevertheless were closer in wealth and attitudes to the richer slaveholders of Alabama than to the yeoman farmers and simple craftsmen who constituted the Davidson, Dean, and Jones lines.

The Carrs of Duplin County, North Carolina, serve as exemplars of the Matthew effect, or accumulated advantage—those that have get more. In the antebellum South that Matthew effect worked not only by rich planters buying more land and slaves and passing them down to their sons and daughters but also by the tendency of slaveholding families to intermarry.

The story of the Carr family is one of wealth-building throughout the antebellum period, but they experienced harder times after the Civil War. Still, many advantages survived. Planters carried with them relative wealth through the war and Reconstruction. The failure of the federal government to engage in substantial redistribution of wealth after the war left the Southern hierarchy in place. The planter class carried forward wealth in the form of human capital such as education and other skills that foster upward mobility even in a stagnant society as the South was.

In finance, we know the Matthew effect as the principle of compound interest. If you reinvest the interest on a bank account back into account, the base grows exponentially. This effect leads to increasing inequality in a seemingly open system because of a feedback process in which those that have assets can leverage them into more assets, while those lacking assets will fall further behind.

Although the Matthew effect alone explains increases in the inequality of wealth across time in the plantation South, the effect was augmented by the white planter elite taking control of state governments after the Civil War. The restored planter elite used governmental power to continue many elements of the system of racial hierarchy carried over from slavery.

The Carrs were relatively minor players in the plantation society of West Alabama, with land on the edge of the Black Belt. They were well-off but by no means in the league of the great planters of Sumter County. Yet as slaveholders they identified with the planter class. They took part in the rebuilding of the Southern hierarchy and were involved in the massive Black Belt vote suppression of emancipated slaves in the post–Civil War period.

My grandmother of Carr lineage played a part in the transmission of the old plantation and Lost Cause myths and was active in the Daughters of the Confederacy, an organization whose adopted mission was to keep the memory of the Confederacy alive. The sons and daughters of the lost antebellum plantation waxed nostalgic for the earlier period, and those myths, their falsity, and their resiliency form an essential part of the Carr story.

I cannot claim the Carr story is typical, but it is illustrative of the mindset of Southern planter society and how its values were passed down through the years. To help keep characters and their actions in context, I've provided a lineage chart for the main characters, from Joseph the immigrant to my grandmother, Laura (Carr) Jones (Figure P1.1). Main characters are in all capitals.

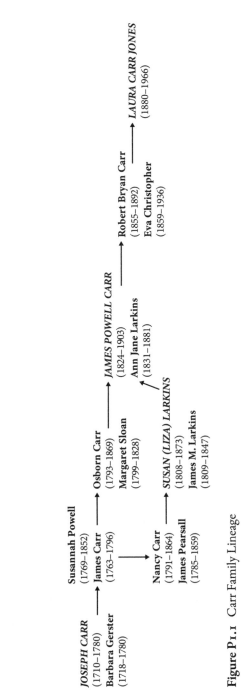

Figure P1.1 Carr Family Lineage
Source: Author.

JOSEPH CARR
(1710–1780)
Barbara Gerster
(1718–1780)

Susannah Powell
(1769–1852)
James Carr
(1763–1796)

Osborn Carr
(1793–1869)
Margaret Sloan
(1799–1828)

Nancy Carr
(1791–1864)
James Pearsall
(1785–1859)

SUSAN (LIZA) LARKINS
(1808–1873)
James M. Larkins
(1809–1847)

JAMES POWELL CARR
Ann Jane Larkins
(1831–1881)
(1824–1903)

Robert Bryan Carr
(1855–1892)
Eva Christopher
(1859–1936)

LAURA CARR JONES
(1880–1966)

CHAPTER 3

The Lasting Legacy of Slave Ownership

On Christmas day, every year in the late 1950s and early 1960s we would open our family presents, and then get bathed and dressed to drive from our home in Troy, Alabama, to the small bungalow of my grandparents Thomas and Laura Jones, in Montgomery, 50 miles to the north. It was the annual gathering of the Jones clan for a wonderful Christmas dinner organized by my grandmother, a talented Southern cook. In attendance were my father's brother, James Bryan, whom we called Casey; his sisters, Jane and Virginia; and spouses and cousins (Figure 3.1).

At some point in these gatherings, and at other times during our trips to Montgomery, my grandmother would beckon me over to her and have me sit down next to her. She would lean over to talk directly in my ear. These were wandering conversations, but they boiled down to a theme: her pride in her Carr family's history.

As a preteen, I was unsure how to react to these interchanges. They made me extremely uncomfortable. She discussed her landowning heritage and lavished high praise on the fine people in the West Alabama Black Belt country where she grew up. I got the firm impression that my grandmother felt that she had married beneath her class. She made clear that she felt downwardly mobile in the status system, given what she thought of as her superior background in comparison to my grandfather, a tenant farmer and logger before going into the ministry.

Years later I got some verification of my childhood impressions. Two of my cousins interviewed my aging Aunt Jane about her recollections. She commented that her mother, our grandmother, "looked down on the Joneses because they did not own slaves." The key to status, apparently even a century

Figure 3.1 Jones Family Reunion: Laura Carr Jones and Thomas G. Jones and
Their Grandchildren, Late 1950s (I'm on the far left.)
Source: Author's collection.

after slaves were freed, was prior ownership. The wealth of the South, after all,
was in antebellum times concentrated in land and slaves. A key indicator of
one's wealth, and hence status, was the number of slaves one held.

Joseph Carr Comes to America

In 1736, the British Crown granted to Henry McCulloh, a wealthy Lon-
don merchant, almost 72,000 acres of land in eastern North Carolina, under
the condition that he settle the land with Protestant immigrants. McCulloh encouraged Scots-Irish Presbyterians to settle there, but the area was
also attractive to Swiss and German Protestants. Many Scots-Irish were
ready to emigrate because of the hard times in Ulster due to English
tariffs.[1]

A decade later, my fifth great grandfather Joseph Carr, or Kerr, a Presbyterian born in Londonderry in 1710, received a grant of 100 acres from
McCulloh "on a branch of Maxwell's Swamp, on the west side of the Cape Fear

River" (now in Duplin County).[2] Joseph likely came from a family of lowland Scots who moved to Ulster from Scotland in the 17th century. The Carr clan was a borderlands tribe that spent time feuding among themselves or with the Highland Scots. Many of the clan later moved to Ulster because of incentives from the English King James I.

Joseph was a man of at least modest means; the grant of 100 acres indicates that Carr traveled from Ireland at his own expense. A smaller grant of land would have indicated that the ship's captain took a cut to pay for the passage.

It is unclear whether Joseph acquired slaves during his lifetime, but that is a distinct possibility. Early white settlers with even modest means could begin to assemble wealth through the accumulation of land and slaves. Much of the land in Southeastern North Carolina was rich and fertile, with ample rainfall and a nearby harbor at Wilmington. Wilmington's port made it relatively easy to transport slaves from the Caribbean via Charleston. By the Civil War, over 46% of the population in Duplin County was slave.

In 1750, Joseph married Barbara Gerster Beverett, a widow from a family of Swiss immigrants. Her first husband, a sea captain, had been lost at sea.[3]

Joseph's building of his rudimentary plantation was not a simple and smooth process. The Revolutionary War was on the horizon. After the end of the French and Indian War in 1763, tensions built between Great Britain and its American colonies over taxes imposed on the colonies. North Carolina was far from the center of the antitax fervor in Massachusetts, and for the most part farmers like Joseph were able to conduct business as usual.

The colonial discontent continued, and in 1775 the colonies declared independence from Great Britain. The Revolutionary War divided loyalists from revolutionaries, and the intensity of the rivalries was particularly severe in the South. A major reason was slavery; it was not completely clear to slaveholders which side might best protect the practice. On the one hand, the British had brought chattel slavery to America, and participated vigorously in the slave trade, bringing slaves from Africa to America and the Caribbean. In addition, Great Britain was a major market for New World commodities. On the other hand, after the outbreak of war, the British promised freedom to slaves if they left the American plantations, hoping to damage the American economy.

There were risks for slaveholders in joining the Patriot cause as well. The Patriot ideology, based so thoroughly in Enlightenment thinking, ran the obvious risk of getting out of hand (from the slaveholder's point of view) and being applied universally to Blacks as well as whites. Indeed, Jefferson's first draft of the Declaration of Independence singled out the slave trade as one of King George's sins.

There were other cleavages, and probably the most important was the notion of the oppressed colonials as subjects and the clear attraction of the ideal of the rights of man (at least the white man). But slavery cannot be ignored as a factor in dividing the Southern colonists, even if the "proper" choice may have been unclear.[4]

Duplin County generated both Loyalist and Continental militias, and Joseph Carr and his family sided with the Continentals. The British had block-aded the port of Wilmington, which interfered with commerce in the area, but mostly North Carolina was unaffected by the conflict happening to the north and in nearby South Carolina.

In May of 1780 British armies captured Charleston, gaining control of most of South Carolina. To counter British successes, General George Washington sent Nathaniel Greene to command the Continentals in the South. Greene lured British General Charles Lord Cornwallis away from Charleston, with Greene steadily retreating into North Carolina. After winning a pyrrhic victory at Guilford's Courthouse, Cornwallis moved his army to Wilmington. Unable to trap Greene, Cornwallis decided to invade Virginia to cut off supplies to the Carolina Continentals. He met no serious resistance as he marched north to his destiny at Yorktown.

Major James Craig, left in charge at Wilmington, raided the local coun-tryside, which stimulated the building of local Continental militias. In May of 1781 Joseph's youngest son and my fourth great grandfather, James, was drafted into the Duplin County Militia of the North Carolina Continental Army. The extent of Loyalist support in Duplin led to difficulties in recruit-ment, and most draftees failed to appear. James Carr was one of only 24 of 70 men in the draft call who reported for duty.[5]

The Duplin Militia marched south with other North Carolinians to rein-force General Greene, and participated in the critical Battle of Eutaw Spring, northwest of Charleston, in early September. Greene's army lost the field but held such a strong strategic position following the battle that he forced the British back into Charleston. Eutaw Springs effectively ended British activity in the South Carolina countryside.

James Carr was grievously wounded at the battle, was discharged, and returned home. Major John Armstrong wrote a note requesting that friends in America come to the aid of James due to the loss of the use of his left arm.[6]

Chattel Slavery and the Carrs

Joseph Carr died in 1780, before James was drafted. Joseph's will, written in 1773, divided his lands on Maxwell Swamp between his three sons. His will does not explicitly mention slaves. He refers to his "plantation" and his "houses," suggesting a substantial agricultural operation.

His son James reported holding six slaves in the first U.S. Census, taken in 1790. Perhaps James inherited slaves, or perhaps he acquired them after his father died. In any case, by 1790, the Carrs were slaveholders.

James died in 1796, at the age of 33, probably due to his wounds at Eutaw Springs. He left a widow, Susannah, and four small children. His death was probably sudden, as he seems to have died intestate. The estate was still tied up in court four years after his death as his debts were paid and beneficiaries determined. Court papers provided a property list: 12 Negroes, 3 heads of horses, 21 or 22 heads of cattle, 25 heads of sheep, 21 2-year-old hogs . . . the list goes down to 3 weeding hoes, 2 grubbing hoes, a stone pot. Even with modern research on the horrors of slavery, it is still jarring to see people—enslaved unwillingly by James Carr—listed as chattel property along with pigs and grubbing hoes.

The Carrs may have been lesser slaveholders, but through the acquisition of land and slaves they benefited from the Matthew effect, rapidly acquiring wealth and the status that came with it. They intermarried with other slaveholding families. As one observer noted, "(W)hen it came to marriage the young people whose parents were better educated and were wealthier and owned many slaves seldom married into families that had less."[7]

The wealth generated through slavery was enormous. "The 'human capital' consisting of Black men and women held as chattel in the states of the South was more valuable than all the industrial and transportation capital ('other domestic capital') of the country in the first half of the nineteenth century." Picketty and Zucman estimate that the market value of slaves was between one and two years of the country's total national income.[8]

The price of a slave in 1810 is estimated to have been just under $300 in current dollars. Translating this into today's prices is tricky, because mercifully there is no longer a slave trade. But Williamson and Cain offer some illuminating comparisons. During the antebellum period, annual per capita income was roughly $110, so a slave was worth almost three times the average yearly income of a citizen of the period. They estimate that the value of a slave in today's prices to be around $40,000, depending on the age and gender of the slave.[9]

James's wife, Susannah, found herself widowed at 27 with 4 small children. In 1797 Susannah married James Dickson, a well-off planter in his late 40s. Dickson reported holding 19 slaves in the 1810 Census. He died 2 years later, leaving Susannah a widow again at 43, holding a substantial amount of wealth inherited from her two husbands. She did not remarry.

The short lifespans of Americans at the time and the resulting multiple marriages had two consequences for life in the slaveholding regions of postcolonial America. One was the role of women as heads of plantation households, perhaps more common than is generally realized. The second was the acceleration of wealth-building among slaveholding families, benefiting Susannah's firstborn son, Osborn, and those like him.

James and Susannah's son and my third great grandfather Osborn lived and died in Duplin County. Born in 1793, Osborn accumulated wealth by acquiring slaves and land, some perhaps as gifts from his mother. By 1850, when he was 57, he owned 19 slaves and was a wealthy and successful man by North Carolina slaveholding standards. Osborn died in 1869. He lived long enough to accumulate substantial wealth through the ownership of other humans and lost much of it because of the emancipation of his enslaved property.

Three generations of Carrs—Joseph, James, and Osborn—had lived in Duplin County since Joseph's arrival. The Carrs were settled and successful North Carolinians. Joseph's land grant in 1748 had led to the sizable plantation of Osborn. In 1850, Osborn reported the value of his real estate to be $2,500. Comparisons can be misleading, but in buying power (assessed by the Consumer Price Index), his land today would be worth over $300,000.

Osborn's oldest son and my second great grandfather, James Powell Carr, started his productive life following along the Carr slaveholding path. In 1850 James Powell lived in Duplin County and held real estate worth $1,000, which would be quite a start in life for a 26-year-old. It is possible, even likely, that this was a gift from Osborn. James Powell worked his land with the help of three slaves—a 65-year-old man and two boys, one 13, the other 12. He probably hired slaves from other owners to aid in planting and harvesting, or in other duties.

Abruptly James Powell Cerr's life changed. He left North Carolina in 1852 for Sumter County, Alabama, in the Black Belt, to marry Ann Jane

Larkin, a distant cousin. James Powell Carr's grandfather was Ann Jane's great-grandfather—James Carr, the Revolutionary War veteran. By the 1860 Census, James Powell Carr and Ann Jane Carr were prosperous planters, with real estate estimated to be worth $2,560 and a personal estate of $14,336. The latter figure would include their slaveholdings.

Wealth inequality was substantially worse in the South than the North during the antebellum period and increased throughout the period. The inequality was present in the slave system itself; it occurred in the distinction between slaveholders and yeoman and tenant farmers; and it happened even within the slaveholding class.[10] The accumulation of family wealth by the Matthew effect does not tell the whole story of inequality because it omits a set of associated behaviors that also lead to inequality. These include intermarriage of wealthy families and investment in human capital as the wealthy educated their children and taught them the keys to wealth accumulation.

Governments can contribute to inequality, and did so in the antebellum South. In a classic feedback loop, unequal societies generally lead to oligarchic rule; oligarchic rule leads to unequal societies. Social capital, a form of capital in which people cooperate with one another to achieve collective goals, adds to wealth accumulation as the aspiring offspring of the well-off build social connections with politically and economically important individuals. These connections foster wealth-building. Oligarchic governments institute policies to protect wealth and stifle democratic movements, facilitating inequality between the connected few and the less fortunate.

A final mechanism for increasing inequality was the consolidation of plantations into a smaller number of very large plots. The volatility of the price of cotton gave rich planters the opportunity to buy out the smaller less viable plantations during economic downturns. Throughout the antebellum period class differences increased and became more rigid.

Native American Removal in Sumter

Native removal was the first of the four post-independence critical junctures discussed in Chapter 1. Like all so-called critical junctures, Forced removal did not occur in a single instance; instead, it spanned several years characterized by turbulence and an unclear and unsettled set of social rules for citizen

behavior. At the end of a critical juncture, rules stabilize and political, economic, and social life proceeds under the new set of rules. Many historians see
the Indian Removal Act of 1830 as a marker of just such a change.[11]

As the native tribes were removed, the land became available, and the seemingly endless frontier beckoned white settlers. Such was the case for the Larkins
and the Carrs, who were unified by the marriage of James Powell Carr and Ann
Jane Larkin in 1852.

Choctaw removal offered the Larkins opportunity. Susan Elizabeth Pearsall
(who went by her middle name, Elizabeth, or Liza), the mother of Ann Jane
Larkin, was the daughter of well-off North Carolina planter James Pearsall. In
1829, Liza married James M. Larkin, also a planter's son, in North Carolina.
Liza's father, James, owned 24 slaves in 1830.

In 1837, Liza, James, and their four children moved to Sumter County on
land purchased for them by Liza's father, who also gave Liza and James five
slaves and $1,200 in cash.[12] Liza's dowry, plus James Larkin's holdings, includ-
ing his four slaves, allowed the couple to establish a plantation near Ward in the
southern part of Sumter County.

Liza and James settled on land made available to white settlers after the
Treaty of Dancing Rabbit Creek, signed in September of 1831. The treaty was
the first signed under President Jackson's Indian Removal Act of 1830, but it
was not the first Choctaw cession; rather it was the last. Whereas earlier treaties
were cessions that left the Choctaw free to move to other lands in Mississippi
and Alabama, the Treaty of Dancing Rabbit Creek removed all the Choctaws
in Alabama and Mississippi to Oklahoma, and thus initiated the first "trail of
tears."

Early Southern history (indeed, American history) is a story of forced Native
land cessions, and the removal of the Native populations to Oklahoma (then
designated as Indian Territory). The Choctaw ceded several territories to the
United States before the final removal in 1832–1833 from Mississippi and
Alabama. The story of the Cherokee Trail of Tears is best known, but the
Choctaw removal came earlier.

The Choctaw left peacefully, but the first group of Choctaw who were
removed suffered terribly along the trail, causing one chief to call the journey
"a trail of tears and death."[13] The tribe members took their Black slaves with
them; sadly the "civilized" tribe had adopted the practice of chattel slavery from
white settlers. Later the Choctaw allied with the Confederacy in the Civil War,
in part to protect its slave ownership.

Religion Embraces Slavery

James Larkin owned 4 slaves which he brought from North Carolina, and with Liza he owned 5 more: Swan, Hannah, Stewart, Jerry, and Adaluhe. By 1840, the Larkins acquired 2 more, for a total of 11 slaves.

Larkin died suddenly in 1847 of meningitis at the age of 38, leaving Liza a widow at age 36 with 7 children but with substantial assets in land and slaves. Liza, known as "Lady Liza" by her slaves, managed the plantation with her son as overseer (the 1860 census lists him as a "clerk") until the Civil War.

James was both a Methodist minister and slaveowner; he was converted to Methodism in 1832 in North Carolina and "felt the calling" immediately, according to his obituary in the *Southern Christian Advocate*. Frederick Douglass was scornful of slavery dressed up in religious piety, and held the religious slave master in particular contempt. "For of all slaveholders with whom I have ever met, religious slaveholders are the worst. I have ever found them the meanest and basest, the most cruel and cowardly, of all others." Elsewhere the former slave continued, "the bitter cries of the heartbroken slave are drowned in the religious shout of his pious master."[14]

Methodism had once stood as an antislavery beacon, but by Larkin's time it had made its peace with the practice, even promoting a religious defense of slavery.[15] As Methodism settled down from its radical peak, it incorporated slavery into its doctrines by finding supportive biblical passages and knitting them together into an interpretation that justified the horror. Douglass was observing the result of the moral certainty of the religiously committed.

The *Advocate* continued Larkin's obituary, "His character as a minister of the gospel was without spot or blemish,—a firm, zealous, and devoted champion of the cross—a devotion that never prevented him from owning slaves, buying and selling them, and accepting them as gifts"—although the *Advocate* characterized him as "an indulgent master." I suppose that was the Christian way to manage slaves, and perhaps indicates just a slight hint of discomfort at the terrible bargain Methodism had made with slavery.

James Larkin was not the only ancestor in my Grandmother Jones's line who embraced religion and slavery. R.G. Christopher, Grandmother Jones's great-grandfather through her maternal line, left detailed recollections of the captivating enthrall of religion during the Second Great Awakening.

Christopher was born to poor parents in the Piedmont region of Virginia.[16] He writes, "we had no schooling and as such in great ignorance as to the Bible."

Members of his family, "as far back as we have any account" were Episcopalians, or the "High Church," implying an impersonal, haughty, and remote church.

By the first decade of the 19th century, Methodists and Baptists were traversing the country with their exhorters and camp meetings, but R.G. was not swayed. "I had objections to shouting or any kind of noise about religion . . . the Methodists I disliked and particularly their shouting."

R.G. nevertheless began to attend Methodist camp meetings, where the exhorters brought the crowd to a state of collective emotional frenzy with people coming forward and openly expressing their religious conversions, but R.G. remained a skeptic. Then suddenly at a camp meeting while listening to a minister "of the suffering of Christ to redeem the world, my soul was filled with something I had never felt before; tears flowed freely." Soon "I was praising the Lord aloud, shouting. . . . I felt that I loved everybody, my soul was filled with love, I felt it in my whole system."

Joining the Methodist Church, R.G. was licensed to exhort. He then became a local preacher, and began riding various circuits in South Carolina and Georgia. Along the way he apprenticed to study medicine, married in 1822, and moved to Black Belt Sumter County in 1823.

R.G. got busy in the plantation business in Sumter County. He and his wife acquired 11 slaves by 1830. In 1834, R.G. served as the first minister of the Methodist Church in Livingston, the county seat, and oversaw the building of a new sanctuary, complete with slave gallery in this slave-rich region.[17] Apparently R.G. allowed his slaves to attend church, which was not the practice of the Larkins.

In his autobiography, R.G. focused solely on his religious conversion and later participation in the Methodist Church. Yet he probably moved to the Alabama Black Belt to profit from the rich soil and the availability of slaves being herded south from Virginia into Alabama and Mississippi. Was he aware that the founder of Methodism in England, John Wesley, thought slavery evil, and described in detail the horrors of the slave trade? Did he learn that the Church in 1785 prohibited ministers from owning slaves and denied church membership to any who owned slaves? Or that in 1800 the Methodist General Conference called slavery "the great national evil of the United States"?[18] R.G. writes nothing of this in his autobiography; religion and slavery were handmaidens in his worldview. The Church had made its peace with slavery, and R.G. had made himself well-off in the slave business.

One element of religion caused slaveholders some discomfort. Methodist philosophy stressed that adherents should read the Bible to save one's soul. This led to a dilemma for the churches, which once decried slavery but had come to support it. Should slaves be educated so they could read the Bible? Church-men sometimes made the argument that Blacks could not be saved if they were illiterate, as they could not read the Bible. Slaveholders were wary of abolition-ists who produced all sorts of pamphlets arguing against chattel slavery, which could fall into the hands of literate slaves. The version of the Bible provided to literate slaves omitted large parts of the King James Version, including the Moses story of escape from bondage.[19]

Caste and Class in the Black Belt

In 1860, more than three-quarters of Sumter County's population was slave, and Sumter was the epitome of plantation society. Sumter, as in the rest of the Alabama Black Belt, was sharply divided between the free and well-off whites and unfree Blacks, with a sliver of a middle class made up of merchants and a few professionals. For all practical purposes the division was stark: either you were white, owned land and slaves, and were well-off, or you were Black and slave.

In the Black Belt regions of the South almost all farming occurred on plan-tations, not on freehold farms. The small-time yeoman farmer so common in North Alabama and the Wiregrass was virtually absent in plantation society. In 1860, Sumter County accounted for more than 18,000 slaves, the 18th highest in the United States. The average slaveholder in Sumter held 20 slaves, but this average masks vast differences in the number of enslaved Blacks held by slave-holders. Fifty percent of the slaves in the county were held by 122 slaveholders, each of whom held at least 40 slaves. The other 50% were held by 767 owners. Planter Jerrit Brown alone held 540 of those slaves.[20]

In 1860, Liza Larkin reported to Census takers that her plantation was worth $2,400 while she valued her personal property at $13,380; she held 16 slaves. Her total worth was similar to that of her daughter Ann and son-in-law James Powell Carr, whose plantation was close by. Her 24-year-old son, S.R., a planter listed in her household, owned land worth $960 and personal property of $2,000, likely a gift from his mother. He held two slaves, and his brother Willie, the plantation's overseer, held four slaves. Willie did not report his wealth to the enumerator (or it was included with his mother's wealth). So the plantation harbored some 22 slaves, considerably more than the Carrs' 13.

The number of slaves on a plantation correlated highly with the quality of the soil for raising cotton. Generally the plantations in southern region of the county where the Larkins and Carrs farmed, had poorer soil than further north and the landholdings were more modest. In 1860, James Powell Carr's farm was 320 acres, while the Larkin spread was 480 acres.

Southern antebellum society was both a caste and a class system.[21] Slavery divided Black from white, imposing a caste order and an extreme one at that. Class divided slaveholders from nonslaveholders, the latter divided between yeoman farmers and nonlandholding free whites. Most of the small farmers, landholders or tenants, tilled the less productive lands. Even where freeholders settled on productive farmland, larger plantation owners bought them out as larger slaveholders invested in more slaves, which required more land. The Panic of 1837 devastated many marginal farmers, and the influx of slaves during the 1840s from older slave states to the newer states of Alabama and Mississippi further damaged the economic prospects of small farmers and white laborers.[22]

The thick rich clay soils of the Black Belt region made subsistence farming difficult. A local Sumter County historian noted that "The black, waxy soil was too heavy for the average farmer of that day to till with the equipment he brought with him from sandy areas, so he sold out to his neighbor who had slaves to work the soil. In that way, the whole area fell into the hands of a few landlords."[23] The same logic applied to owners with small numbers of slaves, who often sold out to the more efficient larger plantations. This led to the increasing concentration of wealth in the hands of fewer and fewer landowners in Sumter County and other productive regions.

The comments by the local historian also belie the common slur that Blacks are lazier than whites. As Kerri Leigh Merritt and Edward Ball separately argue, the prevailing notion among Southern elites was that Black slaves worked harder than free whites, and the explanations were both genetic and economic. Blacks were thought to have a greater capacity for work and a generally better work ethic. Planters opined that the more imported Blacks were exposed to the corrosive influence of American culture, the weaker as workers they became.[24] Ball notes that landowners complained that they had more trouble with indentured servants than Black slaves, buttressing the notion that poor whites were simply poorer workers. Hence the local Sumter historian, writing in the 1950s, simply assumes that white yeoman farmers could not compete with slave labor.

As the Civil War approached, Sumter and the Southern Black Belts generally lacked a middle class as well as a white working class. Yeoman and even tenant farmers had disappeared, and most craftsmen were slaves leased out by the largest landholders. Even ministers were climbing the status ladder through the acquisition of slaves, as were James Larkin and R.G. Christopher. The economic system had bifurcated into increasingly wealthy slaveholders and the slaves themselves. The concentration of wealth among a very few planters, along with the lack of a middle class, signals oligarchic rule.

Within the slaveholding class, wealth differences were large, and status was allocated accordingly. The large slaveholders were the cream of slaveholding society. They provided the models of plantation societies often romanticized in literature. Smaller slaveholders such as the Carrs and Larkins were held in less regard, but they were considered part of the upper class.

Ank Bishop

My grandmother Laura Carr Jones romanticized Black Belt plantation society, even though she was born 15 years after the Confederate surrender freed the slaves. Slaveholding was a family tradition on both her paternal and maternal sides. Lady Liza Larkin was her great-grandmother and her paternal grandfather, James Powell Carr, owned 12 slaves in 1860. Her mother, Eva Christopher, was from a slaveholding family as well.

The reality of slave life was starkly different from the "Old South" view Laura Carr Jones held. Direct pictures of life on Lady Liza's plantation can be roughly reconstructed thanks to reliable slave narratives from Sumter County and census records.

The slave narratives were sponsored by the Works Progress Administration, a New Deal Agency created to employ destitute workers on public works projects. Among its programs was the Federal Writers' Project to provide jobs for writers, editors, and researchers. In 1937, the project organized an initiative to record and archive narratives of former slaves, who were reaching old age at the time. Field workers in former slave states interviewed around 2,000 former slaves.[25]

These interviews are treated cautiously by historians due to the age of the respondents and the biases of the interviewers, most of whom were white. These issues led to a lack of candor on the part of the respondents. One former Sumter County slave told an interviewer who was obviously prompting him, "slaves in Sumter County mus' hab a mighty good time, had plenty of ebery t'ing an' nothin' to worry 'bout."[26] Today historians of slavery have found these narratives highly useful, if treated with care.

Most of the slave narratives collected from Sumter County former slaves were especially reliable. One of the Federal Writers' Project's best interviewers was Ruby Pickens Tartt, who was open to hearing the horrors of slavery in a manner that most interviewers were not.

Fortuitously, one of the slave narratives came from Ank Bishop, who told Tartt, "Us belonged to Lady Liza Larkin at Ward."[27] Ank said he was born in 1849, and that his mother "was brought out from South Car'lina in a speculator drove, an' Lady Liza bought her at de auction at Coke's Chapel" (Figure 3.2).[28] A speculator drove was a group of slaves purchased by a speculator in one of the established slave states and brought to a newly settled region. Another former slave whose parents were brought to Sumter County in a speculator drove told Ruby Tartt that "they was driv' down to Alabamy lak cattle."[29]

Cotton prices were down in the 1840s, and East Coast planters sold the excess slave labor supply in Alabama and other developing regions. Planters expected slaves to breed—one slave narrative refers to a particularly fecund slave as a "breeder woman." Another respondent noted how little pleasure there was for slaves on the plantation and that the work was all-consuming. "Dey want you to have plenty of chillum, though."[30] Slave children were profit centers, and planters built them into their business plans.

The auction took place at a local church—Coke's Chapel—making the mixture of religion and slavery complete in Sumter. Ank's mother and her siblings were taken from her mother and father, and "never did see 'em no more in dis life." Ank continued, "She was bidded off an' Lady Liza got her, jes' her one from all her family."

Ank related to Tartt that his mother was bought to serve as "Lady Liza's house gal" but she often cooked, cleaned, and did the milking as well. On Lady Liza's plantation all slaves, women and men, worked as field hands except for

Figure 3.2 Ank Bishop, Age 88, Slave on the Plantation of "Lady Liza" Larkin
Source: Library of Congress, WPA Slave Narrative Project: Container A917, vol. 1, Federal
Writer's Project, US Works Project Administration, published between 1936 and 1938
[https://www.loc.gov/resource/mesnp.010035/?r=-0.225,0.092,1.82,1.007,0.]

house servants. Women with small children came back from the field twice a
day to nurse their children, then returned to the fields. One slave, Ellie Larkin,
called Mammy Larkin, tended all the children. None of the slaves received even

a rudimentary education, and none were allowed to attend church, although some owners did allow it. Forbidding church attendance or any form of religious education on the Larkin plantation is ironic, given the religious calling of Reverend James Larkin. According to Tartt, slave education was uncommon, although the largest slaveholder in the county, Jeremiah Brown, educated his slaves.

Tartt's narratives make it clear that beatings and intimidation were common. Many slaves blamed overseers rather than masters, but the extent of the beatings were so common and so severe that clearly they were part of plantation routine. Plantations differed in the severity and pervasiveness of punishment, but the whip was the common instrument. And, not surprisingly, the punishment was often counterproductive. One slave told Tartt of a particularly cruel overseer who regularly whipped slaves. "I been whooped till I tell lies on myself to make 'em quit. Say dey whoop till I'd tell the troof, so I had ter lie 'bout my se'f keep 'em from killin' me."[31]

Occasionally severe punishment yielded even more dire unintended consequences. One former slave tells of a woman so severely beaten that she turned on the overseer and killed him. Nor did punishment seem to deter runaways—clearly they were not uncommon in Sumter County. Runaways were so common that planters relied on gangs of men—slaves called them "patterrollers"—to chase runaways and recapture them. The patterrollers used what the slaves termed "nigger dogs" to track them, often viciously attacking the slaves when they were found.

According to Ank Bishop, slaves on the Larkin plantation were treated relatively well, which he attributes to Lisa Larkin's son, Willie, acting as overseer. Using family members as overseers was a common practice on smaller plantations. Then Ank qualified his observation by noting that Willie was quite capable of using the whip, or, as Ank put it, he "thrashed 'em out." When a slave, Caesar Townsy, ran away, "dey sent for Dick Peters to bring his nigger dogs. Dem dogs were trained to ketch a nigger the same as rabbit dogs is trained to ketch a rabbit . . . but them nigger dogs didn't' never ketch ol' man Caesar." Rather than stay on the roads for a quick escape, as Larkin and Peters assumed, Caesar stayed in the area until "well after S'urrender and de War done ceaseted."[32]

Caesar probably felt as did another slave, Rich Parker, who ran away from a particularly abusive planter and also stayed in the area. As another of Tartt's sources told the story, he hadn't heard of the end of the war, and emerged complaining: "He say 'Why didn't somebody come tell me "twas S'rrender?' Den he start—singin,

> Slav'y chain, slav'y chain.
> Thank God a' mighty I'm free at las',
> Free at las', Free at las'.
> Thank God a' mighty I'm free at las'."[33]

CHAPTER 4

Plantation Politics

On March 31, 1863, James Powell Carr enlisted in the newly formed Boyle's Regiment of the 56th Alabama Calvary, known as the Partisan Rangers, for a period of three years or the duration of the war. He received a bounty of $50 for signing up. Why did James Powell Carr sign up so late in the war? He had received the slaveholder exemption until the draft law changed in 1863, requiring a planter to hold at least 20 slaves to receive it. His 13 slaves made him ineligible for the exemption and caused him to enlist.

Carr's service in the 56th Alabama Calvary began in North Mississippi, and then moved to Georgia in 1864. He took part in the Atlanta Campaign, and was part of the failed attempt by General John Bell Hood to invade Union-controlled Tennessee. The Alabama 56th harassed Sherman as he marched through Georgia and South Carolina, and surrendered near Greensboro, North Carolina, on April 25, 1865.[1]

Carr's regiment was part of a larger phenonmen known as "partisan rangers." These were independently organized military units not subject to the traditional standards of warfare; they were in essence guerrillas. Confederate guerrilla units organized first in Virginia, but soon the rest of the South demanded some of the action. In the summer of 1861, an Alabamian wrote to the Confederate secretary of war that some "men of undoubted respectability" wanted to serve the Confederacy by "organizing companies to fight without restraint, under no orders, and would convert captured property to their own private use." This was a request for the well-off partisan rangers to harass the Union supply chains, to keep what they captured, and to maraud and plunder the civilian population behind enemy lines. The Secretary rejected the idea, stating that such units would have to be subject to normal military organization and rules.[2]

In the spring of 1862, the Confederacy passed the Partisan Ranger Act to encourage recruitment of guerrilla units, but to subject them to regular military control. The act failed in its second aim, and General Robert E. Lee among other regular army leaders pressured the Confederate Congress to repeal the act. It did so in early 1864.[3]

It is unclear how much marauding the 56th conducted in Mississippi, and how well it operated as a more traditional unit after 1864. What is clear is that James Powell Carr chose to sign up not for the regular cavalry but for the irregulars, who were not subject to traditional military rules and discipline. He stayed with the unit until the surrender in North Carolina.

Postwar Plantation Life

James Powell Carr returned home soon after his surrender in North Carolina. We do not know what transpired between former master and former slave, but we do know that from the wreckage of war a new agricultural model emerged. At first plantation life changed little; former slaves were listed as agricultural workers in the 1870 census. Gradually the system evolved to one of sharecropping and tenant farming, both already in use but greatly expanded in the postwar period.

We have no records from the period for the Carrs, but it is possible to reconstruct a picture of life on the plantation after the war from the 1870 Census. The census enumerators gathered information by physical location. In the still rigidly stratified slaveholding regions of South, the census-takers also organized the data in hierarchal fashion. The former slaveholding families were listed first, followed by the Black sharecroppers who occupied their former slave cabins. This may be seen in Table 4.1, which depicts the Carr family and the Black families enumerated after it. This hierarchical system was repeated throughout the census records. All of the families listed below a white family were Black, until another white family was listed, followed by Black families. The break between Black and white demarcated the human boundaries between plantations.

This simple table is incredibly rich in the story it tells. Two Black families, headed by Perry Townsend and Eliza Campbell, tilled the land, and they and all of their children worked the field.

I examined a rough sample of plantations around the Carr property. The data show that wealth, whether real estate or personal, is listed with the white head

Table 4.1 Former Carr Plantation, 1870 U.S. Census, Sumter County, Alabama, Township 16

Name	Age	Sex	Race	Occupation	Real Estate	Personal	Birthplace	Cannot Read	Cannot Write
Carr,									
James P.	47	M	w	Farmer	800	800	NC		
Ann G.	39	M	w	keeps house			NC		
Robert B.	14	M	w	Student			Ala		
Susan D.	12	F	w	at school			Ala		
Betty P.	8	F	w				Ala		
James O.	7	M	w				Ala		
Agnes	4	F	w				Ala		
Ed	2	M	w				Ala		
Townsend									
Perry	60	M	b	farm laborer			NC	X	x
Sallie	40	F	b	farm laborer			NC	X	x
George	18	M	b	farm laborer			Ala	X	x
Dora	16	F	b	farm laborer			Ala	X	x
Harry	14	M	b	farm laborer			Ala	X	x
John	14	M	b	farm laborer			Ala	X	x

Continued

Table 4.1 Continued

Name	Age	Sex	Race	Occupation	Real Estate	Personal	Birthplace	Cannot Read	Cannot Write
Campbell,									
Eliza	50	F	b	farm laborer			Ala	X	x
Henry	18	M	b	farm laborer			Ala	X	x
Milton	16	M	b	farm laborer			Ala	X	x
Daniel	13	M	b	farm laborer			Ala	X	x
Mary	10	F	b	farm laborer			Ala	X	x
Carr,									
Sarah	36	F	b	cook			NC	X	x
Wallace	11	M	b				Ala	X	x
Dora	8	F	b				Ala		
Sallie	3	F	b				Ala		
Gilmore,									
Tom	34	M	b	farm laborer			Ala	X	X

Source: 1870 United States Federal Census, Alabama Sumter County, Township Range 1, 2, 3, and 4.

of household, but not with any Black family head. James P. Carr listed $1,600 in real estate and personal wealth, a great decline from the wealth he reported in 1860. Black families on his plantation five years after the war had nothing in the way of wealth.

All Black families are listed as "farm laborers." There is one exception: Sarah Carr, who listed her occupation as "cook." She probably did that job when she was a slave. She and her children bear the Carr name, whereas no other Black families do. Blacks on plantations commonly received one name and were free to adopt a last name only after they were emancipated. Former field hands often did not adopt the plantation owner's name, but house servants sometimes did. Sarah listed her birthplace as North Carolina, indicating that she traveled to Sumter with James Powell Carr in 1851 as a teenager. Sharecroppers Jerry and Sallie Townsend also listed their birthplaces as North Carolina.

The Census data also provide information about patterns of literacy and school attendance. All of the white Carrs were literate, but none of the Black families were. The older Carr children were listed as students and able to read and write while none of the older Black children were in school or literate. Consider the Townsend family. No one in the family is listed as able to read or write, and all are listed as farm laborers. Below the Townsends is the female-headed household of Eliza Campbell. Not only was Eliza unable to read or write, but none of her children could do so. All of her children were farm laborers, even little 10-year old Mary. Neither cook Sarah nor her oldest child could read or write.

The Carrs did not educate their slaves, nor did they make provisions for educating their plantation workers. The Federal Government's Freedman Bureau was active in Sumter and was instrumental in building Black schools there and all over the South, but apparently workers on the Carr plantation did not have access to them in 1870. There was no sense of noblesse oblige on the part of the Carrs, nor on the part of other planters in the area.

The Economics of the Postwar Plantations

Recent studies of the loss of wealth among slaveholders after Emancipation indicate a surprising recovery by former slaveholding families after "one of the largest episodes of wealth compression in history." They were able to recover because of the resilience of the accumulated human and social capital and state governments that became increasingly infiltrated with influences from the landholding class.[4]

The James Powell Carr family is an exemplar of this resilence. In 1860, James Powell Carr assessed his wealth as $16,896. At the time, the average wealth of a free white male in the United States was $2,500.[5] Ten years later, he reported his wealth as $1,600.

It is difficult to compare the figures before and after the Civil War, for two reasons. First, the war itself was highly inflationary (estimated at 14.5% per year nationally), and the period between 1865 and 1870 was deflationary. Second, these trends were exacerbated for the South because of the inflationary policies of the Confederacy and the rapidly decreasing value of its currency as the Confederacy appeared doomed. The war devastated the Southern economy, and caused a catastrophic collapse of the banking system, increasing deflationary pressures that continued until 1879.[6] Nevertheless Carr survived the war with both land and personal property even though he possibly committed crimes as a partisan ranger and had taken up arms against the legitimate government of his country. By providing for their education, Carr ensured that his children built the human capital to succeed. Robert Bryan Carr, my great-grandfather, attended medical school at the University of Louisville. The Carrs did not provide their former slaves with opportunities to build the human capital that they would need to pass at least the tools for future success to their children.

Former slaveholders for the most part felt little remorse for their participation in the brutal system of slavery, and generally felt resentful that they had lost their property. Sharecropping was a way to maintain the plantation system without slavery, but the system was much less "efficient" than one based on forced labor.

This pattern was true as well at the Ball rice plantation system in South Carolina.[7] The plantations gradually lost their economic vitality as many freedmen left, leaving a smaller workforce. There were lots of reasons for this loss of productivity, including the lack of capital investment and the decline of large-scale organization of the slave plantations. Intensive cultivation of cotton exhausted the soil, making it less and less productive and more reliant on fertilizer. Fertilizer came into widespread use in the 1880s, but cartels made it expensive.

Electoral Politics in the Gaston Beat of Sumter County

James Powell Carr returned home from the war to a region where Blacks were a strong majority and were seeking their rights as citizens.[8] Sumter County, was home to 18,400 Blacks and 4,800 whites, a 4-to-1 ratio. The Union League, initially established among white North Alabamians to promote Union interests during the war, became a major force in organizing Black freedmen in Sumter and other counties. The League specifically targeted getting freedmen registered in the Republican Party.[9]

After the war, electoral politics were shaped by Federal demands for reentry into the Union. States were required to write new constitutions reflecting the freeing of slaves. In 1865, counties sent delegations to Montgomery to write a postwar constitution. North Alabama counties sent pro-Union Republicans or mixed delegations, while South Alabama sent conservative, pro-Confederate contingents.[10] The resulting document did not include voting rights for Blacks and was rejected by Congress as insufficient for readmission to the Union. It was superseded by an 1868 version, incorporating Black suffrage.

The Alabama electoral law passed in 1868 included several measures to deter voter suppression by whites. One provision allowed citizens to vote in any county precinct, permitting Blacks to vote in the safest precinct. A second measure prohibited challenges to the legitimacy of a citizen's vote, ensuring that whites could not use challenges to deny Blacks the right to vote. In county seats, the state provided overseers, and federal troops often were called on by local Republicans to minimize fraud and violence.[11]

As the 1868 election approached, it was clear that Sumter Blacks enthusiastically supported the Grant-Colfax ticket. Although the electoral system included protections for Black voters, it did not eliminate violence and intimidation. A few days before the election, three Republican candidates spoke to a large group of Blacks in Gaston, in the southern part of Sumter County. Six or eight whites stood nearby. Another group of whites joined them and began to shoot. Some shots hit the carriage, endangering the candidates. The candidates escaped by driving as fast as they could out of town and called on the Alabama governor to send troops, commenting, "without troops many of our friends will not vote."[12] It is likely that whites in Gaston coordinated the event to intimidate potential Black voters. If so, it worked. Democrats won 85 to 0 in the Gaston Beat. This episode became known as the Gaston Riot.

The Carr and Larkin plantations were near Gaston. Soon after returning there
from his stint in the Confederate cavalry, John Powell Carr resumed his civic
duties, including sessions on the county grand jury and as a county commissioner. He served as an election manager or inspector for several elections in
the Gaston area. Carr served at least in 1872, 1876, 1878, 1882, and 1884.[13]
He also acted as an election manager for Choctaw County when he moved
there after his wife died.

The *Livingston Journal*, the newspaper of record for Sumter's county seat
Livingston, printed the table below on the day after the 1868 election. Republicans carried the county by over 1,000 votes—63% of the vote (Table 4.2), but
the reported vote included vast variation among the precincts.[14]

Table 4.2 The 1868 Election Result in Sumter

Precincts	Democratic	Radical
Livingston	224	1,104
Jones' Bluff	55	101
Cuba	108	0
York	80	0
Belmont	75	309
Black Bluff	14	47
Sumterville	102	0
Gaston	85	0
Intercourse	75	0
Bluff Point	23	33
Brewersville	83	169
Preston	45	0
Earbee's	18	16
Lacey's	60	40
Paneyville	42	0
Rosserville	55	0
Gainsville	290	728
Warsaw	83	0
Hare's	No results	No results
Totals	1,517	2,547

Source: *Livingston Journal*, 08/06/August 6, 1868.

The table shows two kinds of precincts: those whose votes were split between the Democratic-Conservative Party (as it was then known) and the Radical (Republican) Party, and those in which voters supported only for the Democratic Party. Democratic Party officials claimed that Blacks had voted for the Democrats to escape the corruption of the Radicals and because Blacks were "perfectly willing to be represented by the intelligent white men among whom they live."[15] This interpretation is highly unlikely. It seems impossible that in half of the precincts no Blacks voted for the political party that freed them and ran the state Reconstruction government in Montgomery.

What could account for the pattern of precinct votes? Sumter County was three-quarters Black, and the Black population was spread out across the county, yet most of their votes were concentrated in Livingston, the county seat. In the county seat of Livingston, state election officials oversaw the process, and federal troops were stationed there. Republicans carried the town by a margin of 5 to 1—that is, 1,104 votes for the Republican ticket to 224 for the Democratic-Conservative ticket. The number of Blacks going to Livingston to vote may be roughly gauged by the fact that the town had only 500 residents in 1870.

Those districts where no Black votes were cast remained under the control of the Democratic-Conservative Party machinery, and the Black votes in those districts were either discarded or cast for Democratic candidates.[16] In a handful of precincts the election seemed to have been conducted in a more even-handed fashion, with votes for both Democrats and Republicans.

In the 1872 election, when Ulysses S. Grant ran for reelection, a similar voting pattern held. Republicans urged Blacks to vote in Livingston and Gainesville, where they could be sure of the integrity of the system. Almost all the votes for the Republican candidates were cast there. Republicans won the county by 700 votes, again about 63%. The *Livingston Journal* attributed the victory to the gathering of Blacks in Livingston and Gainesville, the efficacy of Republican speakers, and the presence of federal troops.[17]

"You Can Out Vote Us, But We Can Out Count You"

In 1874, Sumter went Republican again, but changes were afoot. That year the Alabama governor and legislature flipped from Republican to Democratic.

Alabama Republicans faced both increasing fraud by Democrats in the Black Belt and an unfavorable national sentiment due to the severe Panic in 1873 followed by a long recession.

In 1876, the "Redeemed" Alabama legislature enacted a new electoral law, and the unabashedly Democratic *Livingston Journal* was ecstatic. The new law required all citizens to vote in the precinct where they lived, which meant there would be no opportunity for Blacks to travel to Livingston or Gainesville to cast their votes. The law also allowed any citizen to challenge another citizen's right to vote, and the *Journal* urged its readers to exercise that right.[18]

The new system opened the floodgates for fraud. Whites could use the citizen challenge to intimidate Blacks attempting to vote. Local election managers, now unsupervised, could commit fraud freely. The new system led to Bourbon Democratic (by then the Democratic-Conservatives had acquired that moniker) success in the August election for governor, carrying Sumter County by 878 votes. The "safety in numbers" that voting in Livingston and Gainesville had provided Black citizens collapsed in 1876. In that election, Livingston produced 19 more Democratic votes than Republican.

Just before the election, the *Livingston Journal* asked in print how much the Bourbon Democrats planned to cheat. "Several days ago we received a request to forward the vote of Sumter by telegraph as early as practicable. Shall we send a good report? . . . It is for our Democratic and Conservative friends to say . . . we'll telegraph a majority that will make the wires tremble."[19]

The presidential election that autumn replicated the summer gubernatorial vote. In Sumter, Rutherford Hayes, the Republican candidate for president, received 868 fewer votes than Samuel Tilden, the Democratic candidate. Tilden and Hayes tied in Livingston, but the number of votes was only 20% of the total vote tabulated in the 1868 through 1874 elections. Gaston behaved as usual, generating only votes for Democrats—68 votes for Tilden and none for Hayes.

James Powell Carr participated in most if not all of the elections held in the Gaston region from 1868 to 1884. Was he complicit in the election fraud that occurred there? His regular participation in electoral administration in precincts where no Blacks voted suggests that he was. Fraud was limited by the centralized voting system until 1876, but intimidation was not, as the 1868 Gaston white riot indicated. At the very least, Carr knew about the fraud and tolerated it. Fraud was so common among Bourbon Democrats in the Black Belt after Redemption in 1874 that it is fair to conclude that most if not all election officials there were complicit.

The state legislature, now controlled by segregationist Democrats, passed laws to reverse Reconstruction era fair voting regulations that had empowered Black voters. Between 1874 (an off-year election) and 1876 (a presidential election) Republican votes in Sumter dropped from 3,310 to 1,370—a loss of almost 2,000 votes—while the Democratic total increased by over 500 votes, allowing the Democrats to win the county. Black Belt Democrats carried out the fraud and intimidation in the open, even boasting, "You can out vote us, but we can out count you."[20]

The Carrs Move to Pushmataha

In 1876, James Powell Carr's son and my great-grandfather, Robert Bryan Carr, married Eva Christopher, and the couple settled in Sumter County near the family plantation. Eva was the daughter of J.C. Christopher, a planter and Confederate veteran who held an enslaved a couple and their five children in 1860.

According to the 1880 Census, Robert owned and farmed 40 acres, presumably part of the original Carr plantation, and was attending medical school at the University of Louisville. There had been other changes on the plantation too. Sarah Carr, a slave who had been brought from North Carolina to Sumter, had left the plantation area and was living with her daughter and son-in-law in Choctaw County.

Between the 1870 and 1880 Censuses, the agricultural system had evolved from one based on agricultural workers on a plantation owner's land to one based on rent. Tenant farmers paid in cash; sharecroppers paid in crops. James Powell Carr farmed 100 acres, and his immediate neighbors were mostly white, small farmers who owned or rented land. Nearby were Black farmers, some of whom rented for money but most of whom rented "for shares of products."[21] Few people are listed as farm laborers, but many of the sons and daughters of the tenant and sharecropping renters labored in the fields.

When Robert Bryan Carr completed his medical school studies in 1883, he, Eva, and their children moved to Pushmataha, a small planter settlement in Choctaw County near Eva's family home. Robert and Eva acquired land, and Robert began his medical practice there. He farmed the land as well, growing cotton and raising a few cattle, but Robert was foremost a medical doctor. He and Eva had two more children, Robert and James. Robert's father, James Powell, joined them at Pushmataha after his wife, Ann Larkin, died in 1881.

Tragically in 1892, on a night call to see a patient, Robert Bryan Carr was killed in a buggy accident. Eva was widowed at 33 with five young children: Janie, 14; my grandmother Laura, 12; Ora, 10; Robert Jr., 8; and James, 6. It was an event that deeply haunted my grandmother for the rest of her life.

Upon Robert's death James Powell Carr, at 70, became the head of a sizable family and the family's primary breadwinner. He farmed the land, and was still actively doing so in 1900, at 77 years of age, dying in 1903 at 80.

Human Capital and the Remnants of Plantation Society

My great-uncle Robert Bryan Carr Jr., known as Bob, was eight years old when his father died and his grandfather, James Powell, took over running the farm. Bob attended school and labored in the fields; according to his daughter, he "plowed the fields with an old wooden plow" and "salted the beef before putting it in the smokehouse." In the midst of his chores, Bob had an epiphany. "He realized that if he didn't get off of that farm, he'd be doing this work for the rest of his life." Bob was educated in the local white Pushmataha schools, where he learned Latin—the local white Black Belt schools were clearly superior to what was provided in poorer sections of the state. Bob then alternated teaching Latin in the local school and going to college for a year "so he could get the money to pay for another year of school."

Bob later enrolled at the University of Alabama Law Department, graduating in 1917 at 33. He moved to Anniston, in North Alabama, and set up a law practice. In 1924, he ran for a seat as a judge on the Seventh Circuit, covering three Alabama counties. He'd go home after work to campaign by putting on a pair of overalls, renting a horse, and riding around handing out business cards. Bob won the election. Such was retail politics in Alabama in 1924.

In 1943, Governor Chauncy Sparks appointed Carr to an open seat on the Alabama Court of Criminal Appeals, and he served there until his death in 1955.[22]

The Carr family had fallen into difficult straits after Robert Bryan Carr Sr., my great-grandfather, died. Still they had many assets, especially compared to their family's former slaves and the Blacks living on or near the Carr farm. They owned land and other intangible property. They were educated in decent schools, and both Bob Carr and his father went to universities. Both men were ambitious and found ways to leave the old decaying agricultural system behind.

Today we would say they possessed both human and social capital. The Carr women were also educated; my grandmother was teaching school when she was 20, and living at home.

We know that the former slaves on the Sumter County Carr plantation were left in poor situations after the war, with most illiterate and none of the children in school. The situation was similarly bleak for Blacks living near the Carr farm in Pushmataha. The Blacks who were recorded on the same census page as the Carrs in 1900 were severely disadvantaged compared to the Carrs. On the farm next to the Carrs lived the Black washerwoman Rose Dubrutz, who was listed as illiterate. Rose had a 12-year-old son, Manuel, illiterate, who worked as a farm laborer. Rose was able to send a daughter, Annie, 10, to school. Rose also housed two lodgers who were listed as farm laborers and illiterate.

None of the other eight nearby Black families had literate members, save one, 12-year-old Daisy Atkinson; she was also attending school. Daisy's stepfather, Thomas Knott, was a farmer, renting his farm, indicating that he was a tenant farmer rather than a sharecropper. Jenny Horn, also listed as a farmer, owned her land, but it was mortgaged. Other Blacks rented farmland if they were farmers or houses if they were farm laborers.

Of the homesteads listed on the census page, only the Carrs owned land outright. The only other white family listed, Christopher Brown, rented. Brown's entire family was literate, and the underage children were in school.

Sarah Gilder, a Black nearby neighbor of the Carrs, was a 38-year-old washerwoman and listed as illiterate. Her 70-year-old widowed sister who lived with her was also illiterate. Her 16-year-old son, Thomas, was a farm laborer and could read and write, even though he had never gone to school.

In the census pages for houses and farms around the Carr farm, all whites were adults who were literates and their children were in school. Among the Blacks, about equal in number to the whites, only Daisy and Thomas were literate. The plantation pattern of literate whites and illiterate slaves reproduced itself in the tenant farming system, with most of the white children attending school and most of the Blacks children working for their parents as farm laborers.

Schooling served, and still serves, as a major human capital investment by parents and the state in children's future. The nature of schooling in the 19th and early 20th centuries was sporadic, especially for Blacks. The schools for the children of white planters were exceptionally good in comparison to those for Blacks and even whites in the poorer regions of the state. Although both the Carr and Brown children attended school for nine months a year, Annie

Dubrutz and Daisy Atkinson attended only for three months, probably under the tutelage of a part-time instructor who traveled from place to place to teach.

There seems little doubt that the Carrs lived in reduced circumstances after the early and extremely disruptive death of Robert Bryan Carr. His death did not end the transmission of physical and human capital to his children.

The Role of Women

Tracing the Carr family history from the early days in North Carolina to the turn of the 20th century puts a spotlight on the role of women in the period, white and Black, slave and free. The early death of James Larkin made his wife, Lady Liza, the manager of a sizable plantation, one she ran as an overlord of a domain of forced Black laborers. She bought slaves from drovers, breaking up families, and ran the plantation efficiently enough to have substantial wealth in retirement. The physician Robert Bryan Carr died young, leaving Eva Christopher Carr a widow for 42 years. She was not working outside the home in 1900, deferring to her father-in-law to run the farm. Her daughters were educated and taught school.

My grandmother Laura, a schoolteacher, married the local Methodist minister, Thomas G. Jones in 1905. He started life as a tenant farmer near the Wiregrass town of Geneva in 1905. Laura spent her adult life moving from post to post in the small towns of Southeast Alabama with Reverend Jones. Never staying at any one church longer than a year or two, she coped with poor pay and little stability, and always felt it was simply below her Black Belt plantation roots.

My grandmother's sisters both married into the well-off Brown family. Aunt Janie Brown and Ora Brown both lived long lives as widows after their husbands died in middle age. Janie lived to 102 and Ora to 95. Janie served as Pushmataha's postmaster, and managed the family farm, still of sizable acreage when we visited in the 1960s.

Most of the Black households living on and around the Carr farms in Sumter and Choctaw counties were female headed. Why were there so many female-headed households in the post–Civil War period? Slavery broke up families through drover sales such as the one attended by Lady Liza Larkin, ripping Ank Bishop's mother away from her family. Sometimes owners gave slaves to their children to help them "get started" in life, breaking up family units in the process. All this transactional economics treating humans as property led to heartbreaking newspaper advertisements after Emancipation as freed husbands frantically searched for their wives and wives their husbands; and parents sought their lost children. Most were never united. The losses through early deaths of Black men were a cause for the number of female-headed households as well. The censuses of the period list many widowed Black women; how their husbands died we don't know.

Accidents and disease left widows among both white and Black families in a manner that today is hard to conceive. There were also widowers among rich and poor. Sometimes these widows and widowers remarried and started new families; sometimes they didn't. The founder of the Carr line in America, Joseph Carr, married the widow Barbara Beverett. His son James died early, leaving his wife, Suzannah, a widow. She remarried, but lost her second husband as well. Osborn Carr lost his wife when she was 29. Two of the major characters in the antebellum Carr drama were left without spouses. Lady Liza ran her plantation after her husband died. Joseph Powell Carr outlived his wife and took charge of his son's farm when Robert Bryan died at a young age, leaving my great-grandmother Eva a widow.

Second marriages were so common that almost every family in all four of the lineages I trace involved them. Death in a family often left women on their own to run a farm or plantation, either until remarriage or until they died. That trend continued into the second half of the 20th century; at 48 my mother was herself twice widowed.

CHAPTER 5

Myth and Reality in the Black Belt

The transference of myths across generations is powerful way to uphold the existing social system, perpetuating both the fair and the unfair elements of that system. The building blocks of myths are narratives—the stories that members of societies tell themselves to justify past actions, present norms, and institutional arrangements. These narratives also transmit myths about which groups in society are worthy of respect and those that are not, maintaining status distinctions through time. If they distort history, they buttress unfair inequalities in both status and class.

Narratives have increasingly become central to our understanding of why things don't change when we think they should. Although scholars in the humanities have traditionally focused on the nature and structure of the narrative form, the focus of social scientists on narratives is more recent. Historians, sociologists, political scientists, and even economists now see narratives as important in themselves and as mechanisms that justify the existing distribution of power, wealth, and status. Such transmissions may account for what political scientists call *behavioral path dependency*, the tendency for human behavior to stay more stable across time than can be accounted for by variables such as class, gender, or race.

Transmission by myth, however, is a flawed system, because the intergenerational transference of a socially constructed ideal invariably contains errors, both factual and logical. Most members of younger generations receiving a set of narratives accept the stories and their premises because they are transmitted by authoritative figures—parents, schools, officials, and public and religious figures. Nevertheless, some of those in the receiving generation recognize the internal contradictions in the myths, taking note of conflict between the myths and the current reality. I noted earlier that tracing an ancestorial lineage can be a powerful tool for understanding changes in the myths and narratives that underpin a social structure.

Southern conservatism, based as it was in white supremacy and hostility to federal intervention, was carried forward from the post–Civil War years, through Jim Crow, through the Progressive Era and the New Deal, and into 1950s. Conservative and white supremacist attitudes rode on the back of the Lost Cause narrative that justified plantation society, slavery, and the war fought to defend them. Proponents of the lost but noble cause claimed that the reason gallant Southern gentlemen went to war was primarily to protect the Constitution and states' rights. The narratives explained the violence by the Klan and Knights of the White Camelia as honorable, because the Reconstruction was a period of rule by carpetbaggers (Northerners coming South to prey on the destitute but honorable society) and scalawags (Southern collaborators) taking advantage of simple-minded Blacks.

The Lost Cause narratives were developed in large part to unify a fractured South around the notion of white supremacy. They were perpetuated to give meaning to the non-slaveholding participants in a war, to explain to them why their losses in such a cruel war were justified, and why they were drafted to defend slaveholders. Organizations such as the United Daughters of the Confederacy, founded in 1894, worked to bolster the myths by urging cities to erect monuments to Confederate heroes and by preserving battlefields. Reunions of veterans often centered on the Lost Cause and the justification of secession.

The myths explained and justified the oligarchic Black Belt antebellum society of Sumter County, not the upland raucous and more democratic prewar society of Blount County. Indeed, the whole narrative was designed to forge a "Solid South" that brought uplanders into the fold by rallying them around the call of white supremacy and the fear of "Black rule."

It is no accident that the most intense promotion of the Lost Cause occurred in periods when the unitary mind of the South seemed to be coming apart—the 1890s during the Populist agrarian revolution and in the 1960s and 1970s during the civil rights movement. In both cases the potential of class-based coalitions between Appalachian whites and Black Belt Blacks were possible. Highlighting the unity of Southern whites through myths and ideology was a major mechanism of keeping the Solid South intact—the South of one mind organized around white supremacy.

As a boy in the 1950s, I encountered these myths. They were taught in school and even infused the games we played. I absorbed them and believed them, but I discarded them when the internal contradictions became self-evident and the reality I observed did not correspond with the myths I had digested. These myths were important to me, and were even more important when I discarded them.

Tales of the Old Plantation

When I was a toddler, my Grandmother Jones gave me a copy of Joel Chandler Harris's *Uncle Remus: His Songs and Sayings*, originally published in 1880. Uncle Remus, an imaginary former slave, tells stories about Brer Rabbit and his adventures to a boy during the Reconstruction period. Harris, an associate editor of the racially conservative *Atlanta Constitution*, reconstructed the various dialects of Southern Blacks, distinguishing in his writings between the dialects of the cotton plantation slaves and those working on the rice plantations on the Carolina and Georgia coasts. But more insidiously he used the storyteller and his avid listener to romanticize the plantations of the Black Belt South.

The stories about the Rabbit and his tormentors, the Wolf, the Bear, and especially the Fox, are allegorical, as the weak but wily rabbit triumphs over the strong predators through guile and misdirection. Harris believed the legends originated in Africa, but also notes similarities with folklore from other regions of the world.[1]

These legends may be captivating to children, and the story of the tar baby and other tales are well-known and continue to be read today. They were so captivating that Walt Disney made them the subject of an animated movie in 1947, *The Song of the South*. Nevertheless, the movement of the Remus storyline from a game of wits between the Rabbit and his adversaries toward the agonizing deaths of the Wolf, the Bear, and the Fox indicated a glee in the malign cruelty imposed by the weaker but wittier Rabbit. I don't think my Grandmother had read all those stories when she gave me the book.

The work of Harris and of his seemingly sensible character, Uncle Remus, itself carried an underlying theme of the essential necessity and moral nature of the plantation. Harris writes: "The myth-stories are told night after night by an old Negro . . . who has nothing but pleasant memories of the discipline of slavery—and who has all the prejudices of caste and pride of family that were natural results of the system . . . as he proceeds to unfold the mysteries of plantation lore to a little child."[2]

A second theme in this benign depiction of slavery by Harris and other perpetuators involved claims of an essential lack of discipline on the part of Blacks. According to the advocates of the Lost Cause, slavery instilled not only discipline, but other desirable qualities in Blacks as well.

Uncle Remus includes not just the animal legends, but also a set of seemingly real-life events that involved the imaginary Uncle Remus. Some, such as "A Story of the War," involve the intervention by Uncle Remus to save the life of his owner during the Civil War. Others involve Uncle Remus intervening to put a "Savannah Darkey" in his place for being too "uppity." For the same reason, Uncle Remus did not approve of educating Blacks.

Harris, speaking through Uncle Remus, thought that race relations would be improved through heavy-handed law enforcement against indolent Blacks.[3] He saw Uncle Remus and other "sensible" Blacks as yearning for the order that slavery required. Harris conveniently ignored the regular lashings imposed on slaves to ensure complete obedience and the use of dogs trained to chase escaped slaves through the brush.

The inferiority of the undisciplined Negro and his lawless ways depicted by Harris and other Southern authors posed against the wise Uncle Remus gave birth to the "Good Negro–Bad Negro" stereotypes parroted by whites which were carried forward into the segregated South. These stereotypes were certainly an undercurrent in race relations through the 1960s and beyond.

Scientific Racism and the Construction of a Mythic South

The Lost Cause narratives were powerful, spilling over into Northern journalism as well. They even influenced academic studies. Historians and political scientists developed theories that justified the restoration of white supremacy in the Redemption period following Reconstruction. These theories hinged on the alleged incompetence and corruption of Black rule. According to the social scientists of the era, war and Reconstruction destroyed the efficient plantation designed to bring out the best of the supposedly simple-minded Black slaves. Writing in 1905, the historian Walter Lynwood Fleming depicted slaves left on the plantation while the master went to war as "working contentedly" as a Black overseer made sure the crops were planted and harvested with infrequent desertions. How could such behavior be understood? There were few whites around to supervise slaves. Why did plantations work so smoothly? The reason for this loyalty and devotion was "the faithfulness of trained obedience rather than of love or gratitude, for these were fleeting emotions in the soul of the average African."[4]

This commentary was from a Columbia-educated professor who later in his career held a major chair in history at Vanderbilt University. Today we recognize it as untrue self-serving nonsense. Fleming's mentor at Columbia was William Archibald Dunning, who spent an academic lifetime justifying white supremacy and Jim Crow.[5]

Dunning and Fleming, along with the Columbia political scientist John Burgess, were early proponents of examining primary sources, and thought of themselves as providing careful scientific and empirical studies of social inequalities based on the evolutionary theories of Charles Darwin. Burgess, Dunning, and Fleming gave Social Darwinism, basically the notion that people were successful because they were genetically superior, a great deal of both credibility and popular success. According to the Social Darwinists, economic success was a function of genetic fitness, and they developed a moral theory justifying white supremacy. Redemption restored the natural order of things.

The Dunning school's interpretation of slavery, Reconstruction, and Redemption was accepted history until the 1930s, when W.E.B. Du Bois, Howard K. Beale, and later Beale's student C. Vann Woodward painted more accurate views of Reconstruction and Redemption. Reconstruction governments, those that incorporated Blacks and were elected during the immediate post–Civil War period, did have issues with corruption, but they paled in comparison to the corruption, voter suppression, economic pressure, and physical violence promoted by the Redeemer governments that restored white rule in 1874–1876.

A narrative is powerful not just because it influences how we understand social reality. It also influences what sources of new information we choose. It was the fallacious Lost Cause interpretation that I and so many other Southerners accepted rather than the corrected historical record. So we tended to seek out stories even in entertainment that reinforced that narrative. There were plenty of the "Old South" themes in books and movies and on television.

The Mosby Romance

The Lost Cause myth was such a powerful transmitter of white supremacy and segregation because so many different narratives buttressed the myth. One narrative centers on the deification of Confederate partisan raiders. The Confederate guerrilla became a hero during the war and an essential element of the Lost Cause myth later. Colonel John S. Mosby led what was by far the most successful of the irregular units created under the Partisan Ranger Act. Mosby became known as "the Gray Ghost" because of his ability to strike fast and quickly disappear into the local population or nearby forests. Close behind in marauding skill were Turner Ashby and John H. Morgan.

Mosby and other irregular units performed a distinct service for the Confederacy by harassing Union troop movements. Often, however, the irregulars were no better than rampaging bandit gangs, plundering from friend and foe, leaving a trail of death and destruction. Recall that one of these guerrillas was my Sumter County ancestor, James Powell Carr.

Ashby and Morgan were killed in the war. Mosby was captured in 1865, was pardoned by Ulysses S. Grant, and became a Republican working to unify the nation. Because of this heresy, it took a while for Mosby to regain his exalted status in the former Confederacy, but he did as the Lost Cause was gaining adherents after the turn of the century. Virgil Carrington Jones continued the exaltation of Mosby and the other Confederate guerrillas in two books: a biography, *Ranger Mosby*, published in 1944, and *Grey Ghosts and Rebel Raiders* in 1956.

Around 1956 or 1957, television entered our South Alabama evenings for the first time. The TV required an antenna on top of a telephone pole installed next to the house. The nearest television station was in Montgomery, 50 miles to the north, and our antenna used a rotator system to calibrate the connection to the variable signal strength. The pole was necessary because television signals, unlike radio signals, do not bend with the curvature of the earth.

One early series we avidly watched was *The Gray Ghost*, based on the exploits of Mosby. The system romanticized guerrilla warfare fought on behalf of an immoral cause. Still in my Lost Cause phase, I watched the series religiously, and read Virgil Jones's books that served as the basis of the series. The Gray Ghost was a critical part of the mythology of the Old South and the Civil War that fed my whole boyhood imagination back then—from the Trojan Wars to the knights of the Round Table to Walter Scott's depiction of Robin Hood in *Ivanhoe*, to the cowboys and Indians of the old West, all feeding into the romance of conflict and a simple good guys and bad guys conception of the world. In my boyhood world, the Confederates were the good guys and the Yankee invaders the bad guys, and nobody was more romantic than John Mosby—not even Robert E. Lee.

Marinating in the Lost Cause

I never knew the term Lost Cause growing up, nor did I ever get very steeped in the mythology of benign slavery. However I marinated in the notion of the righteousness of the "states' rights" constitutional justification for secession. Slavery was basically defined out of the myth; it was a war based on constitutional principles. Even more powerful was the notion that even if the cause was lost, the war was noble, and military leaders, particularly Robert E. Lee and Thomas "Stonewall" Jackson, were depicted as knightly figures on a quasi-religious cause.

My best friend growing up, Dick Nave, and I read voraciously the "War Between the States" novels that were available in the library, including the Reconstruction novels of Thomas Dixon such as *The Clansman*, which served as the basis of the D.W. Griffith's 1915 epic movie, *The Birth of a Nation*. The novel and the movie glorified white-on-Black violence used to restore white supremacist rule to the former Confederate states. The "redemption" of the South from the clutches of Northern occupation was the logical extension of the Confederate myths.

For a while I decorated my room with Confederate battle flags and a bayonet purchased at one of the Virginia battlefields. My eighth-grade history teacher made sure we knew at least three nicknames for Jackson—his nickname "Old Blue Light" was derived from his religious zeal, and was not intended to be complimentary, although our history teacher depicted it positively.

Interestingly, my parents tolerated my obsession with the military aspects of the Lost Cause more than encouraged it. If my father had ever told me that his grandfather served under Stonewall, and surrendered with Lee at Appomattox, what a bragging point to my friends it would have been for me! But he did not.

By my senior year in high school, I had become disenchanted with the whole Southern belief structure. It was a belief system built on a powerful edifice, an edifice constructed from the intertwining of culture, education, and plain on-the-street conversations that justified past slavery, the War Between the States (as it was known to us), and present racial segregation that existed by law, ordinance, and custom. The problem with such tightly constructed belief systems is that if one seemingly small part of that system is questioned, it invariably leads to the conceptual collapse of the entire edifice. Or so it was for me.

Many other Southerners have stories of their own wake-up calls. Ty Seidule writes about the network of myths and lies that bolstered the Lost Cause that he, as an officer in the U.S. Army, believed until later in life. Seidule, as he admits in his brutally honest book, engaged in hero worship of Robert E. Lee, a worship that was bolstered by institutions from grade school to college to the Army. The hero worship that Seidule encountered in the Army was part of a deliberate and comprehensive effort to reunify the nation, not around the vigor of a nation fighting a war to end the horrible evil of slavery but one with heroes on both sides fighting to defend honorable principles. The current attempt today to teach the correct version of that period of history has stimulated a vicious backlash aimed at restoring the old myths and the white supremacist beliefs they justify.

In the end Seidule concluded that Lee was in fact not a hero but a brutal slaveholder who put his economic interests ahead of his duty, and a poor commander who committed treason.[6]

The myths of the old plantation survive in the modern world.[7] As the debate over Confederate monuments heated up in the wake of the killing of George Floyd in Minneapolis in June 2020, Lowndes County, Mississippi, debated removing a monument in downtown Columbus. The motion failed, and County Supervisor Harry Sanders defended the action with language that could have been lifted right from Joel Chandler Harris's *Tales of the Old Plantation*: "In my opinion, they were slaves, and because of that, they didn't have to go out and earn any money, they didn't have to do anything," Sanders said. "Whoever owned them took care of them, fed them, clothed them, worked them. They became dependent, and that dependency is still there."[8]

A Visit to West Alabama

One beautiful spring Sunday morning in the early 1960s, my sister and I got in the car with my father, drove to Montgomery to pick up my Grandmother, and drove west to the hamlet of Pushmataha, near the Mississippi border.

We traveled to visit my Grandmother's sisters, Janie and Ora. Janie still lived in the family house; Ora came over from Centerville, where she lived with one of her children, Ruthie. The house, a white, two-story structure with a long front porch with ceiling fans, overlooked fields, mostly uncultivated. The family held a considerable amount of land around Pushmataha.

We were warmly greeted, and sat on the porch beneath the slowly rotating fans and drank sweet iced tea and lemonade as we visited before lunch. A well-dressed Black man served drinks and hors d'oeuvres set out on a Lazy Susan. At some point, Aunt Janie pulled a chair up close to mine, leaned in close to my ear, and began to tell family stories. I guess the story-in-the-ear approach to conversation was a Carr family trait.

The story I remember most vividly was of the beginnings of sharecropping. I recall she told me that "Colonel [James Powell] Carr," her grandfather, had returned from serving in the Confederate cavalry after his surrender with Lee at Appomattox, and found his property devastated. Most slaves had stayed, according to Aunt Janie, and when James Powell Carr returned, they asked him what they were supposed to do. He told them "you are free now, and you can do whatever you want." But, Aunt Janie recounted, they told their former master that they did not know what to do, and could he help. "I have no money," he said, "and I can't pay you." But, he continued, we could arrange it so you could work the land, and pay the rent in shares of the crops you grow. Hence, Aunt Janie said, the sharecropping system was born.

I was a sophomore or junior in high school at the time, and had already developed a sense of cynical skepticism. I figured even at the time that the story was at best questionable and probably myth. That story was told over and over throughout the plantation South such that it was incorporated seamlessly into the Lost Cause mega-myth—the magnanimous master returning from the gallant fight to bestow a method of livelihood on his former subjects.

There was more romanticism and error in the story than that, I discovered later. Carr was a corporal, not a colonel. He joined the "glorious cause" not at the outset, but in March 1863, ahead of a new Confederate draft law that changed age limits and eliminated exemptions for slaveholders with fewer than 20 slaves. And he did not serve under Lee. He was in the cavalry, but in a partisan ranger unit, and he did surrender—with Joe Johnston at Durham, North Carolina, the last Confederate army in the field.

When we were called to dinner, we moved to a large and, to us, opulent formal dining room with a sparkling crystal chandelier. We always referred to the big meal of the day as "dinner," and that was usually reserved for midday Sunday. Otherwise, we ate lunch and supper.

The well-dressed Black man served us, bringing the large plates of food from the kitchen and courteously pouring water and iced tea. After dining, we sat in the parlor and talked, and after a decent amount of time had passed, we took our leave and headed back to Montgomery and thence home to Troy.

Even at the time I found the situation uncomfortable, even surreal. It was as if the old plantation South had somehow survived in west Alabama, and I recall not liking it at all. It was a world I did not know, did not want to know, and a world I thought no longer existed.

Stability and Change between Critical Junctures

The Carrs and Larkins, and other white slaveholders like them, settled Sumter County following the Choctaw cessions in 1832, part of the first historical critical juncture that structured Southern society. The Civil War and Reconstruction, the second critical juncture, emancipated the slaves and changed the economic and social structure in a permanent way.

Substantial changes can occur in the more stable periods between critical junctures. Two of these trends were especially important in Sumter County, as well as the rest of the South: variations in the price of cotton and the undermining of interracial democracy after the Civil War.

The price of cotton was so critical to Southern economic development because the region relied on one crop for the general market. Between 1791 and the Civil War, prices experienced variability, with quite substantial ups and downs. After the war a long-term decline in commodity prices, including cotton, continued to the end of the century.[9]

Even though these economic cycles had large impacts on the state of the economy and the financial health of planters, they did not disrupt the fundamental nature of the forced labor plantation system, which existed alongside the yeoman farmers of the regions of the South that lacked the rich soil conducive to slavery. The Civil War may have destroyed the chattel slavery system, but a variant of the plantation system continued.

Emancipation eliminated much of the Carr and Larkin wealth. But the Carrs escaped relatively well-off: James Powell Carr returned from the war apparently unscathed. His land remained in his hands. He was able to resume farming through a farm-labor system based on his former slaves. His great house remained undamaged. His children went to school, and he could afford a house servant.

Although the plantation system based on forced labor was gone forever, a substitute system based on tenant farming and sharecropping emerged from its ashes. In some ways the system mimicked the old plantation system. On James Powell Carr's land, Black agricultural workers continued to live in the slave cabins doing many of the same chores as before emancipation. The children worked in the fields at 12 years old as they did before freedom, did not attend school, and were illiterate. To them, Carr was still the master. But they were free laborers. They could leave, and over time many did so—first to other plantations, and then to the towns nearby, where the skilled trades that Blacks learned on the plantations were valued.

Even after such a cataclysmic event as the Civil War, James Powell Carr could pass on advantages to his offspring. His son Robert Bryan received a professional education. He was able to establish himself on mortgage-free land with a substantial house nearby. The long-term decline in cotton prices and the disarray from Reconstruction and Redemption and its associated racist violence, propelling Blacks to leave Sumter and the region, made the plantation economy increasingly untenable. Nevertheless, relative to most of the population of the region (which was still overwhelmingly Black), the Carrs led comfortable, even prosperous lives.

The undermining of democracy in the Black Belt, illustrated by the vote fraud in the Gaston Beat, operated systematically in the slaveholding regions of the South. The politics of Redemption ensured white supremacy and left Blacks (and many poorer whites) at the mercy of a relentless economic process that ensured inequality and a political process that legalized that inequality. The myths of the Lost Cause, the paternalistic plantation master, and the inferiority of Blacks helped justify this obviously unjust system, a system that openly defied the ideals of the founding of the nation.

PART 2

Upland Uprising on Sand Mountain

It was a cold, crisp February day, and I was in Pell City, Alabama, at my sister Carol's home. I had come to attend my 101-year-old Aunt Jane's funeral in the South Alabama town of Luverne. On the way over from Texas, Carol called me with the news that another elderly aunt had died, so I extended my stay to attend a second funeral. Since we had an extra day between the funerals, we decided to drive to nearby Oneonta, our mother's birthplace, and hometown of her family, the Davidsons, for many years. We went in search of our great-grandfather Alvin Steele Davidson's grave and any other traces of the Davidsons in the North Alabama hills.

We drove the 35 miles between Pell City and Oneonta along US 231, leaving the Piedmont hills after we crossed Interstate 59 into the much more rugged Appalachian region. The long and worn mountains of the American Appalachians, which run 1,500 miles from Newfoundland to central Alabama, end 100 miles southwest of Oneonta, just north of Tuscaloosa. The mountains of Blount and surrounding counties stretch from northeast to southwest. They are long and often narrow, with deep valleys and plateaus between them, making for poor farming, inhospitable to the plantation economy.

As we traveled northwest, the snow from the day before became deeper and the terrain increasingly mountainous. We crossed 1,200' Straight Mountain and drove into Oneonta, situated on a 900' plateau backing up to 1,100' Red Mountain in a beautiful Appalachian Mountain setting. Red Mountain, which continues down to Birmingham, is particularly rich in the iron ore that facilitated the development of the steel mills that made Birmingham the industrial powerhouse of the South.

Running parallel to Red Mountain is Sand Mountain, a huge highland plateau that dominates Northeast Alabama. Sand Mountain, named for its hard sandstone base, is the southern end of the Cumberland Plateau. It served as the easiest route for 18th-century migrants traveling from Pennsylvania through Virginia, North Carolina, and the northwestern tip of South Carolina. The route was known as the Old Indian Trail or the Great Wagon Road, and it brought the Scots and Scots-Irish from the Cumberland Region of Pennsylvania, where they had first settled, into the South following the removal of the Cherokees.

Oneonta today is a thriving market town of about 7,000 people in a spectacular Appalachian Mountain setting. When Mother was born in 1914, it was but a small village of 600 souls. We stopped for lunch at a bustling local restaurant, Charlie B's, advertising "Southern Dining At Its Finest." I had a real taste for Southern cooking, whetted by the wonderful luncheon we'd had the day before at the First Methodist Church of Luverne. The luncheon was classic Deep South—fried chicken, collard greens, three kinds of peas, including cream peas and butterbeans, squash, turnips, okra, cornbread (buttermilk and no sugar!), a couple of kinds of pie, and swee'tea, as it is pronounced in Alabama. I have what they used to call a "Jones" for Southern vegetables, so I had three helpings, but no chicken and no pie.

Charlie B's was busy at lunch, but we got served quickly—good food, but by no means did it meet the standard of the Ladies of Luverne. While we were eating, I noticed that Carol seemed uncomfortable. "Notice anything?" she asked. I responded no, and she said "no Blacks." She was clearly concerned about discrimination.

I chuckled, because Blount County has never had many Blacks within its boundary. In 1860, Blount had fewer slaves than any other Alabama county except Winston—of the "Free State of Winston" fame—after it declared its secession from Alabama as the Civil War began. Today, Oneonta is but 6% Black.

Yet Carol's question was not misguided. Author James W. Loewen classifies Oneonta as a probable "sunset town," one of the white towns in the South and elsewhere in the nation in which Blacks were unwelcome after sunset.[1] He also notes that today it is "surely not" a sunset town—as it has a sizable Black community.

Northeast Alabama certainly harbored such towns. Loewen documents as many as 3,000 U.S. towns where whites expelled Blacks between 1890 and 1930.[2] Historian Dan Carter tells of his wife's visit to a nursing home on Sand Mountain in the 1980s. One of the older residents there told her that Sand

Mountain was inhospitable to Blacks and that it once had a sign at the foot of the mountain: "N—r don't let the sun set on you on Sand Mountain."[3]

The Davidsons were prime representatives of a hill country culture very different from the slaveowning Black Belt. Until the industrial development of Birmingham in the fourth quarter of the 19th century, the economy was based on subsistence farming. These yeoman farmers, both owners and renters, lacked sympathy with the slaveholding Black Belt planters, and virtually all counties in North Alabama sent antisecessionist delegations to Montgomery in 1861.

Yet as the sundown town phenomenon vividly illustrates, it was not that overwhelmingly white North Alabama was open-minded on the race issue, although the uplanders were less racist than whites in the Black Belt. Rather the economic and political interests of the region continually clashed with slaveholding South Alabama. This continuing tension reflects the culture and politics of upland and lowland Southerners not just in Alabama, but anywhere the Appalachian Mountains cut through the region—Virginia, North Carolina, Tennessee, and Georgia in particular.

In what must be seen as the classic confrontation of Southern politics, a tragedy of Greek proportions played out among white planters and former slaveholders, Black former slaves, and the poor farmers and craftsmen of the mountains and hills. Would Alabama and the rest of the Appalachian South develop a politics of competition around economic interests, or would white supremacy dominate the debate and lead to a politics of oligopoly based on racial oppression?

It would seem obvious that the politics of race would surely win out, because slavery and white supremacy were so ingrained in the Southern mentality. On the other hand, other observers sketched out what modern social scientists call "counterfactuals" of a politics not so heavily dominated by race. Could the post–Civil War period have led to a different Southern politics, one based on economic interests rather than race? The Upper South perhaps came closer to achieving that aim than many realize.

The next few chapters trace the histories of the Davidson and Dean families (Figure P2.1), their migrations to North Alabama, their war and Reconstruction experiences, and their commitments to the Populist enterprise. Populism was the last gasp of the potential to forge an interracial democracy based not on racial acceptance but on hardheaded political calculations. Its failure was a true American tragedy, and its defeat led directly to the era of Jim Crow oppression.

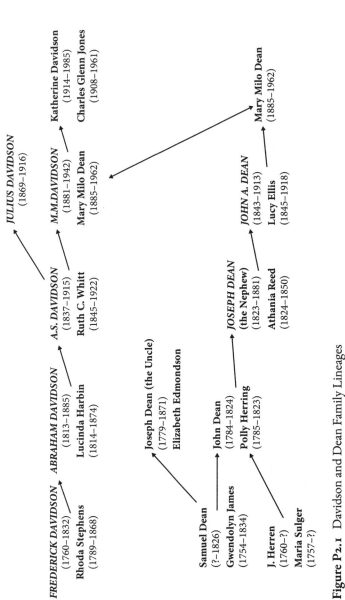

Figure P2.1 Davidson and Dean Family Lineages
Source: Author.

CHAPTER 6

Removal, Religion, and the White Republic

Three great human forces swept the South in the first third of the 19th century and shifted the path of American development. They came together in a manner that intensified all three. They combined to form the first critical juncture peculiar to Southern history.

These interacting forces were the Indian removal that expanded the American frontier from its colonial confines to incorporate the seemingly unbounded potential of a vast nation; the Second Great Awakening and the democratization of religion; and Jacksonian democracy, with its expansion of the franchise for white males and the reformation of political and governmental institutions along a more progressive path.

I have labeled Indian removal as the first Southern critical juncture, but like most critical junctures, removal did not occur in a single moment. The Indian Removal Act of 1830 was a signature moment because it ended any question about the role of Native Americans east of the Mississippi—there was to be none. Before 1830, a series of treaties involving land cessions by Native peoples moved the frontier ever westward until finally in 1830 the Indian Removal Act moved all Eastern tribes to the west of the Mississippi. This great removal of settled populations destabilized the social structure and led to a period of turbulence, change, tragedy, and opportunity. It opened the frontier for the expansion of white settlements, moved slavery and the plantation economy to the west, stimulated Jacksonian democracy and fundamentalist religion, and made political equality among white men a possibility.

Indian removal allowed for recent immigrants from Europe to move onto lands formerly occupied by Native populations. Most of these areas were hunting lands, but some most assuredly were not. Cherokees traditionally lived in a "confederacy of towns," cultivating various crops.[1]

The second force at play before 1830 was the religious fervor of the Second Great Awakening, a social movement that pulled religion out of the hands of church leaders in structured hierarchies and into the hands of the common man. Religion was adding a democratic and emotional element, as camp meetings and itinerant exhorters in the Methodist and Baptist denominations worked their followers into states of religious frenzy.

Jacksonian democracy constituted the final great force constituting the first historical disruption. The movement led to expanding the franchise for white males, eliminating property and educational requirements for voting, and adopting institutional reforms that democratized America. In the process Blacks, Native Americans, and women were excluded. Of course, wealth and status differences were not obliterated; these not only survived but generated an increased class consciousness among the slaveholding economic elites.

Jackson and the movement around him achieved more political equality in America for white males, but that highlighted the remaining glaring inequalities in the system. In 1830, the French aristocrat Alexis de Tocqueville traveled to America, and returned with a broad set of observations that set the tone for the study of American democracy for many years afterward. Tocqueville highlighted equality and its leveling quality, while nevertheless noting the contrast with slavery and the treatment of Native peoples.

Nor did the old hierarchies disappear with Jacksonian democracy, especially in the South, even among white males. Political scientist Bartholomew Sparrow examined these disparities in detail, concluding that Tocqueville overlooked "the longstanding presence of the white poor in America."[2] The white poor in the South migrated later and were steered along migration routes to the Appalachians and the sandy pine barrens, where soils were poor and plantation agriculture was not feasible.

Removal and Migration

The Carrs and Larkins had been in America long enough to build some wealth and took advantage of Choctaw removal to bring slavery to west Alabama. First-generation immigrants of lesser means, like Frederick Davidson, did not move into the Black Belt, but rather traversed in the hills and mountains, moving west. They moved not as planters, but as yeoman farmers, nonlandholding renters, and craftsmen. One generation removed from highland Scottish peasants involved in the Jacobite Rebellion, they had moved south along the Appalachian trail, where land was cheaper and populations were sparse. Then they went west out of the northwestern tip of South Carolina into Georgia and finally into Alabama following Cherokee and Creek removal. Where the Cherokees left, the Davidsons showed up, a pattern common to the uplanders who immigrated from Scotland and Northern Ireland.

The Davidsons Come to America

The name Davidson is of Scottish origin. Historically, the Highland Clan McDhai (Davidson) was part of the broader confederation Clan Chattan, known primarily for its continual feuds with Clan Cameron through three centuries. Like many Americans of Scottish descent, the particulars of the Davidsons' arrival in America are difficult if not impossible to trace. Here is the most likely story.

In the late 17th century, Clan Chattan, including many Davidsons, joined the Jacobite Revolution, which flared into open rebellion from the time James II was deposed from the English throne in 1688 until the English finally crushed the Jacobites in 1745. Many Davidsons, along with other members of Clan Chattan, were convicted and sent to the American colonies. On gaining freedom, many settled in western North Carolina, where they became a hotbed of Patriot support during the Revolutionary War.

Many of the Scots and Scots-Irish who migrated to the British colonies in North America during the mid-1700s came through the port of Philadelphia and first settled in the rocky hills of central Pennsylvania, as the better farming land was already taken. The great migration of Scots and Scots-Irish whose descendants still dominate Appalachia moved south as land was later "ceded" to the United States by various indigenous nations. The Royal Proclamation of 1763 prohibited European settlement beyond a line along the eastern side of the Appalachian Mountains, effectively dividing the original 13 colonies from lands reserved for the Native tribes. The colonists, however, did not respect the line, and continually encroached on Indian Territory.[3]

Genealogists' attempts to trace the Alabama Davidson line go no further back than Frederick Davidson, who was born around 1764. His rough hand-carved tombstone at Mossy Creek Methodist Church cemetery in Georgia, where he died, states that he was born in Buncombe County, North Carolina (the Asheville region). There is some question about that, as the tombstone was placed there many years after his death. Family tradition holds that Frederick's father was named John and came directly from Scotland and that Frederick was born in Virginia, around Staunton.[4] Apparently he moved to Buncombe as a young Revolutionary War veteran.

If so, Frederick's father traveled down to Virginia from Philadelphia, following the Great Wagon Road, America's first interstate highway. The Wagon Road followed the Warpath Trail, a trail used by the Iroquois in their attempts to unify southern tribes with the Five Nations' Confederacy. That trail followed the Great Appalachian Valley, a highland valley stretching northeast to southwest from Quebec in the North to Alabama in the South. It is known locally as the Shenandoah Valley in Western Virginia, and the Cumberland Plateau in Georgia, Tennessee, and Alabama.

Frederick probably moved from Virginia to Buncombe County, North Carolina, after his participation in the Revolutionary War. This journey exemplified the Scottish-American pattern of traversing the Appalachian spine tracing the removal of native tribes. The Buncombe County region was brutally cleared of Cherokee by General Griffith Rutherford and the North Carolina Militia in 1776 because the Cherokee had sided with the British in the Revolutionary War. The Cherokee dropped out of the war, and ceded lands in the region to North Carolina.

The Treaty of Paris ended the Revolutionary War in 1783 and ratified the land arrangements. Frederick subsequently moved to what was then the Pendleton District of South Carolina, the western tip and only mountainous region in that geographically plantation-friendly state. The western tip of South Carolina was part of the land ceded by the Cherokee in 1776. The region served as a gateway to Georgia and Alabama as Native tribes were subdued, their lands taken, and their people later forcibly removed to the west.

For many Scots and Scots-Irish immigrants, including Frederick, Pendleton was but a stopover as they moved into the wilder frontier regions of north Georgia and Alabama. In 1812, Frederick married Rhoda Stephens there. Frederick would have been in his 50s at that time, suggesting that Rhoda may have been a second wife. In 1813, his oldest son, my second great-grandfather, Abraham Burdine Davidson, was born.

The Georgia Borderlands

The story of the Georgia Borderlands, that region between colonial America and the Cherokee and Creek lands, is a story of settler incursions on regions inhabited by native tribes, treaty violations, subsequent recognition of the reality of the permanence of those incursions, and more incursions.[5] Although the federal government sporadically tried to stop the incursions, the State of Georgia encouraged them.

To replace a land distribution system that had become corrupt, Georgia devised a system of lotteries to distribute land from the repeated Cherokee and Creek cessions, basically democratizing the land distribution process for white Georgians. Widows were eligible, but not single women. Georgia conducted land lotteries in 1805, 1807, 1820, 1821, 1827, 1832, and 1833. The 1820 and 1821 lotteries involved primarily former Creek lands. The 1820 lottery also dispensed Cherokee land that was added to Habersham County, later organized into White County.[6]

As a Revolutionary War veteran, Frederick was eligible for extra draws, and he and his family may have moved to Georgia to participate in the 1820 lottery. In any case, the Davidson family pulled up stakes in South Carolina and moved to Habersham County, Georgia in 1820. By then he was around 60, but with a young family. Some family members of Frederick's wife, Rhoda Stephens, moved to Habersham County as well. There at Mossy Creek he and several other pioneers founded a Methodist Church.[7]

Habersham County straddled the area between the Pendleton District of South Carolina and Cherokee Lands to the west. It formed part of the "Borderlands" adjoining the Cherokee Nation (Figure 12.1). Scots and Scots-Irish immigrants like Frederick settled these borderlands; most of them eked out a living as small farmers on the limited arable land in this mountainous region. They also placed themselves between the more settled regions of South Carolina and Georgia and Cherokee and Creek Territories.

Habersham County's pioneer families consisted predominantly of subsistence farmers and simple craftsmen. Of the 74 families dwelling in and around the Mossy Creek community, only three families held slaves in 1820.[8] Each of these slaveholders held one slave each, and all three were female. All were probably house servants.

The Borderlands, although ceded by the Cherokees in treaties, were by no means settled or secure. Georgia rushed to create counties, establish governments, and draw settlers to the region. Cherokees and whites moved back and forth across the border. Both engaged in violence throughout the region, but historians tell us that whites were by far the greater abusers on that front.[9]

Frederick bought and sold land around Mossy Creek, including lots from land lottery winners.[10] He engaged in subsistence farming, produced simple pottery jugs and bowls, and was a prime founder and preacher at the Mossy Creek Methodist Meeting House. Frederick probably found religion in the Pendleton District of South Carolina, and was already referring to himself as a preacher. He likely "heard the calling" and converted from his heredity Presbyterian religion, caught up in the religious excitement of the Second Great Awakening.

Frederick passed on his religious commitment to his descendants; his son Abraham, his grandson A.S. Davidson, and his great-grandson, my grandfather, M.M. Davidson, were all Methodist ministers.

It is not surprising that Methodism found fertile ground in Georgia borderlands. The Scots and Scots-Irish branch of Presbyterianism was a structured and orderly denomination that required its ministers to be professionally educated. The rough-and-tumble Georgia frontier was far more amenable to the open and free-flowing "preach the Bible" Methodism that had captured the imagination of Americans during the Second Great Awakening.

Methodism in America was based in the notion of itinerant ministers who were circuit riders into the unruly frontier regions. They rode from place to place to minister to the local congregations and ad hoc gatherings, and reported back to an annual state conference on their accomplishments before being assigned another circuit. Local preachers like Frederick kept the religious community together between visits from the circuit-riding preachers.

Methodists, Baptists, and other "subversive" sects gained strength during the turbulence of democratization driven by the expanding frontier and large-scale immigration. From the 1790s well into the 1830s, itinerant preachers traversed the country, holding revivals and preaching simple messages to the throngs of farmers and craftsmen. Many of those gatherings were held at the campground at Mossy Creek, where large crowds spent days in the rapture of preachers and mass conversions often occurred. As politics became democratized, so did religion.

Methodism was not the only thing that Frederick passed on to his descendants. He was a potter, producing crude utilitarian jugs and bowls, perhaps learning the craft in North Carolina. Mossy Creek, beginning in the 1820s, was a center of primitive pottery, probably because of the quality of the clay.[11] Urns, jugs, butter churns, and the like were essentials in small communities. Finding a proper source of clay and setting up the kiln for pottery could be difficult, and the throwing process required continuous power, either horse or water. As a consequence, the craft was not normally practiced on a single farm. Rather farmers turned to the community potter for the essentials they needed.[12]

Clearly the craft captivated the Davidson family. Three of his sons, including Abraham, were potters, and Abraham listed his primary occupation as potter on census forms in 1850 and 1860 (earlier censuses did not ask occupation). Abraham's son, my great-grandfather A.S. Davidson, listed his occupation as potter in 1860 and 1870.

Jacksonian Democracy in Georgia

Alexis de Tocqueville originally traveled to America to study prison reform, but broadened his observations to many aspects of political and social life, which he reported in his masterful *Democracy in America*. The South, while lagging behind the dynamic governmental reforms in the Northeast, still bubbled with democratic proposals, particularly in the Appalachian hills and mountains where Andrew Jackson was born. Georgia revised its constitution and many policies (such as the land lotteries) to fit the new democratic ethos. Habersham County was no exception to this trend.

Frederick served in 1822 on the Habersham County Grand Jury, which discussed county public policy issues as well as legal ones. The body discussed items concerning infrastructure development, particularly road construction as well as broader issues. In 1832 the Habersham County Grand Jury recommended a statewide penitentiary system be established with a set of principles that strikes today's reader as forward-looking reform. "We do not believe that it is the severity of punishment as much as the certainty of it that will operate as a preventative to the perpetration of crime in our country." The Grand Jury also objected to the corporal punishment that was inflicted on criminals by the patchwork of county judicial systems, as it exhibited no "tendency to reform but rather augment and harden them in crime." The Grand Jury called for a system of experienced managers to run the system and wanted a system of punishment directly related to the severity of the crime.[13]

In its recommendations, the Habersham County Grand Jury followed the general policies being established in other states. Criminal justice reform in New York and Pennsylvania moved policies in those states toward a stance of rehabilitation rather than retribution. Other states followed their lead. One modern observer wrote in 1995, "Nothing indicates more tellingly the difference between Tocqueville's America and ours than the decline of our penitentiary ideals."[14]

In the 1820s, a great fervor for the expansion of democracy swept the nation, exacerbated by the 1824 presidential election. The popular war hero, Andrew Jackson, won a plurality of the popular vote, and won a plurality but not a majority of the Electoral College vote. The election was decided by the House of Representatives, as dictated by the Constitution in the case that no candidate receives a majority of the electoral vote. Jackson lost there when presidential candidate and House Speaker Henry Clay, who despised Jackson, supported John Quincy Adams.

The Jacksonian movement to expand democracy stimulated positive reforms, such as criminal justice reform and the expansion of the franchise. But there was a dark underside of the movement as well, and the Georgia borderlands exposed it more clearly than anywhere else in America. Jacksonian policies of Native removal highlighted the fundamental principle that the ideal of equality applied to white (and male) Americans, even if some whites were desperately poor.

In 1825, Georgia began an expansion of the electorate that effectively empowered the small farmers of the hills of North Georgia. Jacksonian democracy was strong in Georgia, and Jackson's adamant desire to open up native lands to allow the expansion of opportunities for poor white immigrants was popular. According to historian Adam Pratt, the democratization of Georgia led to more aggressive removal policies, along with policies that legalized white supremacy over Natives in law and in its implementation. These policies included a law prohibiting Indians from testifying against whites in court.[15]

Challenging the Single Mind in the Borderlands

Fundamental to the governing arrangement in Georgia in the early years of the 19th century was a consensus among political and economic elites on the "white republic." The underpinning was a sociracial hierarchy in which white supremacy distinguished between all whites, on the one hand, and Blacks and Natives on the other. A strict hierarchy existed within the white community as well. At the top were the true elites—the wealthy land owners and slaveholders—followed, after a substantial gap, by yeoman farmers and craftsmen, then tenant farmers, and finally the rough frontiersmen who trapped and hunted and engaged in trade with native tribes.

Deference to the upper classes by Blacks, Natives, and poor whites was essential to maintaining the hierarchy. A consensus on this socioracial hierarchy cemented by deference yielded a single Southern mindset. The consensus did hold in the more settled areas of Georgia with its rich soil and plantation economy. At the same time, the Borderlands were experiencing an outbreak of social and political democracy, putting the deference system at risk.

Interracial democracy pushed against the rigidity of the white supremacist hierarchy to some extent in North Georgia. "On the border between the Cherokee Nation and the state, white settlers and Natives interacted in ways that put the superiority of whites in flux."[16] Christian missionaries entered to bring the Gospel, and trade flourished. Although white violence was serious, many whites in this lawless region cooperated with their Cherokee neighbors, and substantal two-way acculturation occurred. Even more threatening to the white oligarchy were the successful efforts by whites and Cherokees in solving cross-border problems, such as controlling the extortionist gangs that plagued the region.

The key question for planters and politicians was how to put the genie back into the bottle—restore consensus on the white supremacist oligarchy. Oligarchs everywhere have two methods: co-optation or suppression or a combination of the two. Democratic institutions make suppression difficult, so the co-optation route is usually the preferred path.

In pursuit of a unified white republic, Georgia politicians deployed the typical white supremacist dialogue and policies. In 1817, the Georgia legislature rewrote its penal codes to impose heavier penalties for slaves than for whites convicted of identical crimes. These and other provisions signaled through the majesty of the law that racial status mattered, not the nature of the crime.[17] When a governor tried to repeal the provision that Indians could not testify against whites in 1831, he was defeated in the next election as his opponent highlighted the issue in a campaign that focused on racial resentment.

White supremacist politicians had a second powerful tool to encourage incorporation of the unruly uplanders into the oligarchic system: distributing Cherokee land titles to land-hungry Jacksonian whites.[18] The land distribution system conflicted with federal policies aimed at encouraging Native people to abandon their traditional ways and settle into farming and commerce, but Georgia pursued the policy anyway.

The discovery of gold in the Georgia Borderlands and the Cherokee Nation in 1828 destabilized the already-uneasy relations among Cherokees, Georgia, and the national government. It set off a stampede of white prospectors, a movement of whites onto Cherokee land known as The Great Intrusion.[19] The Borderlands were already wild and unruly, and the State of Georgia struggled to maintain order. Most of the trouble came from whites who seized Cherokee land unlawfully or prospected for gold there without permission. In an attempt to stabilize an out-of-control situation, the federal government removed whites from Cherokee lands, stimulating an antifederal states' rights reaction from Georgia.

White Borderlands behavior of alternating patterns of violence and cooperation threatened both order and the stable oligarchy of the coastal regions. The Federal Government strove to maintain order to salvage a policy of white-native incorporation, but that was threatened by white violence. The State of Georgia struggled to impose order as well, but the endgame of the State was radically different. It strove to assert domination and ultimately more-or-less peaceful removal, not incorporation.

The key to grasping Southern politics is to view the spectacle of the Georgia Borderlands through the dual lenses of class and status. Elites struggled to maintain a broad single structure to politics and governance in which status dominated, an order in which the established rankings of ethnic groups prevailed over any cross-ethnic class commonality. The planter elite distrusted the unruly new immigrants pouring into Georgia, especially when they were empowered by Jacksonian values and a more extensive franchise. Could the upcountry Scots and Scots-Irish be enticed into joining an oligarchical society in which elites accumulated wealth through the plantation economy and the poor farmers and craftsmen of the hills and mountains were kept in line through the unifying notion of white supremacy? Could distribution of Cherokee lands be used to channel poor white demands while maintaining the plantation oligarchy?

The 1832 Georgia Land and Gold Lotteries

The 1832 Georgia Land and Gold Lotteries were the last of the schemes run by the State of Georgia to distribute native land. Much of the gold found in North Georgia was on Cherokee lands, whose nation centered on its capital at New Echota in Northwest Georgia. Georgia had already laid claim to Cherokee lands in violation of federal laws, and now was distributing it.

Frederick Davidson was listed on the "eligible" list for the 1832 Cherokee Land Lottery, a list that included his sworn claim to have served in the Revolutionary War. Frederick received four draws, two of which were due to his Revolutionary War service and two of which were due to his family status (married with minors in the household). His son Abraham also entered the lottery as a 19-year-old single male, entitling him to one draw. Although his father won a plot of land in the Gold Lottery, Abraham did not.[20]

The State designed the 1832 Georgia lottery to control the "Great Intrusion" in the Georgia gold rush. No person who had mined gold in the Cherokee Territory, or who lived in that Territory, was eligible for the draw. Georgia also prohibited "any person who is a member of or concerned with the "horde of thieves known as the Pony Club."[21] The Pony Club was a crime ring that formed during the gold rush. Settlers and members of the Cherokee tribe formed a vigilante group called the Slicks, and used violence to restore order.[22] The Slicks, representing Borderlands cooperation between whites and Cherokees, was a serious threat to the concept of a "republic" based on white supremacy.

White lottery winners quickly took possession of the homesteads of Cherokee families on Cherokee lands. Although the lottery law prohibited them from evicting Cherokees themselves, winners found "creative" ways to accomplish their purposes, including force. Gold fever drove the lottery winners to scour every streambed on their allocated plots, doing great damage to the land.[23]

Abraham Davidson and the Tragedy of Cherokee Removal

As a young boy, Abraham Davidson, my second great-grandfather, moved with his family from Pendleton to Habersham County, Georgia, and lived there in his early years. Under the tutelage of his father, he became both a Methodist preacher and a potter. He married, and could have settled down at Mossy Creek, farming and working with his father as a potter. However, Abraham was a restless soul, and joined the U.S. Army during the disputes with the Cherokees. Afterward he uprooted his family and moved to former Cherokee land, and then from place to place in Georgia and Alabama.

Why this restlessness? It certainly was a characteristic of the Davidsons during the period; Frederick followed Indian removal through treaty cessions down the east side of the Appalachians into South Carolina and then over to Georgia. Abraham wandered back and forth across the Georgia-Alabama boundary, as did Abraham's sons, who similarly relocated again and again. Many of these moves involved searches for better seams of pottery clay.[24]

Tocqueville noted this restless unhappiness as characteristic of Americans even in the midst of what he saw as prosperity. In comparison to European peasants, who exhibited happiness with their station in life, he saw Americans as "forever brooding over advantages they do not possess."[25] Men like Abraham were desperately poor, and lived in a highly unequal society.[26] That relative deprivation was harder to bear when riches were so close by. Seemingly underused Cherokee land was tempting, and the discovery of gold there intensified the Great Intrusion, as these unhappy white men took what they wanted from their Native neighbors.

Georgians were particularly aggressive in claiming and seizing Cherokee land, causing both a policy issue and a federalism issue for President Jackson.[27] Jackson was simultaneously immersed in the nullification controversy with South Carolina over tariff issues. Perhaps as a consequence, the federal role turned toward recognizing the "facts on the ground" established by Georgia's aggressive land distribution schemes.

With the Great Intrusion, gradual integration of the Cherokee and the white pioneers living in the Borderlands was failing. Removal was on the national agenda. After President Jackson was reelected in 1832, the Cherokee opposition divided into two camps. One, led by Major Ridge, Speaker of the Cherokee Council, supported negotiation of Cherokee removal on favorable terms before the intrusion become so severe as to serve as "facts on the ground." The other, led by Principal Chief John Ross and including a majority of Cherokees, rejected removal and developed a careful legal strategy to compel the United States to enforce existing treaty rights. The Ridge group signed the Treaty of New Echota, and, despite Ross's legal and moral arguments against the treaty, Congress ratified it by one vote in 1836.

Abraham responded to this Borderlands disarray by signing up for service in the Army. Between 1835 and 1838, Abraham served as a first lieutenant in the tragic Indian Removal Wars against the Cherokees.

It quickly became clear that the Cherokee were almost uniformly opposed to the Treaty of New Echota, and generally refused to leave their lands willingly. In late May of 1838, President Van Buren enforced the deadline for removal by sending General Winfield Scott to conduct the process forcefully. The Cherokees were rounded up and, until they could be removed, put in internment camps where they suffered terribly. From there, Chief Ross led the exodus along the "Trail of Tears" to Indian Territory (current-day Oklahoma).

Abraham, assigned to the New Echota area, doubtless took part in this action, participating in the final removal to internment camps in 1838, right before he left the service on July 2.

What caused Abraham to participate in the cruel wars against the Creeks and Cherokees? Abraham was not a land lottery winner. He seemingly had no direct material stake in the removal operations. His father's will made him a partial owner of his estate, which presumably would include Frederick's lottery lot, but not until Frederick's youngest son reached the age of 21. That would not happen until 1851.

Historian Adam Pratt's description suggests Abraham was not unique:

Of the 600 men who enlisted into federal service from Hall, Habersham, Carroll, Campbell, Gwinnett, or Rabun counties [the North Georgia counties bordering the Cherokee Nation], only 71 (or less than 12%) had won a gold lottery and only 55 (9%) won a land claim. . . . The border county militiamen, mostly young, poor yeoman, perhaps sought to expel the Cherokee to create space for themselves and their families. Others may have seen it as their duty as citizens in the republic. Certainly some saw it as an adventure that would cure their boredom and curiosity about the wider world.[28]

Racism was a component of the motives of many of the nonslaveholding yeoman farmers. "The zeal with which many Georgians sought to use violence as a way to intimidate, coerce, separate and, finally, remove the Cherokee, at its core, was based on a philosophy of white superiority."[29] Racism so aroused through deliberate actions or because of a volatile situation generally leads back to oligarchic rule as poor whites see themselves as superior to Natives and Blacks. Add to this the greed stimulated by the gold and land rushes, and the poor yeomen increasingly saw themselves through the lens of skin color. The Georgia planter elites reestablished the endangered white republic as yeoman farmers benefited from the State's land distribution policies directed at whites alone.

Abraham's life spanned two great Southern distruptions, or critical moments. The first was Native removal and the opening of the frontier, generating the great interlocked social movements of Jacksonian democracy and the Second Great Awakening. The second was the Civil War and Reconstruction. Both of these great tidal waves centered on struggles over status rankings among racial groups. The first sealed the fate of the role of Native Peoples in America. The second emancipated Black slaves and ushered a period of struggle over the integration—or rather the lack thereof—of the newly emancipated Americans into the political, social, and economic lives of the nation.

CHAPTER 7

Sand Mountain People

In Blount County and the Appalachian region generally, the reality of antebellum life was far different from the cruel reality of slaveholding regions. Blount was hardscrabble farming on small plots, with a smattering of craftsmen scattered among the subsistence farms—blacksmiths, potters, and the occasional self-educated medical doctor. There were no serious plantations; slaveowners were few, and the average slaveholder held one slave. This was the antebellum South of the Davidsons and Deans and families like them. Unlike the oligarchic hierarchical political system generated by the slaveholding regions of the South, the uplanders continued a Jacksonian-style raucous democracy based on white male political equality. The political landscape there was quiescent much of the time but could also explode in resentment against the planter oligarchs of the Black Belt.

Sand Mountain Pottery

Taking advantage of the newly available land (to whites), Abraham Davidson relocated from Habersham County to former Cherokee lands in the New Echota region.[1] In the 1840 Census, he listed himself as both a farmer and a tradesman, certainly a potter. His family at this point consisted of a wife, Lucinda Harbin, and their six children. They moved from New Echota to Chattooga Valley, south of Chattanooga, Tennessee, after the lands were made available to whites by Cherokee removal. The census taker left the color column blank, indicating that the Chattooga Valley area had no Blacks. The land was on the side of a mountain, suggesting that Abraham moved in search of good sources for clay for his pottery. In the 1850 census, Abraham listed his occupation as potter, with real estate worth $100. For a man in his late 40s, Abraham was a poor man. Compare him with James Powell Carr in the same year; Carr, a much younger man, had real estate worth ten times that amount.

Around 1858, Abraham moved his family to Alabama. The 1860 Census lists Abraham and his family in DeKalb County, Alabama—in northeast Alabama not far from Chattanooga Valley and also previously part of the Cherokee lands. He listed his occupation as potter, and reported real estate worth $300 and personal property at $1,200. Again his property was a mountainside, and that mountainside included a rich seam of clay valued by potters.

The region was far from the slaveholding regions of the Black Belt and across the mountains from the handful of slaveholding counties along the Tennessee River; the entire county was only 8% Black. The region where Abraham had moved according to the 1860 Census was a rugged one of white yeoman farmers and a few blacksmiths. There were no slaves there. The census also showed that some of the farmers listed no value for real estate, indicating that they were tenants.

Living on land adjacent to Abraham's was his oldest son, Alvin Steele (A.S.) Davidson, my great-grandfather. He too listed his occupation as potter, and reported $300 in real estate and an equal amount in personal property. On the nonpopulation schedules, Abraham reported that only 20 acres of his 90-acre farm was improved, that is, under cultivation. A.S. Davidson also listed 25 acres of his 160-acre property as improved. Other farmers grew Indian corn and oats, and produced very small amounts of cotton, but Abraham and A.S. report only some livestock on the property. The Davidsons were potters almost exclusively, apparently doing little subsistence farming.

Sand Mountain, the large sandstone plateau in eastern Alabama, is about 800 feet higher than the surrounding hills. The lots purchased by Abraham and his son A.S. were on the southeastern slope of Sand Mountain near the settlement of Belcher's Gap. Azel Davidson, Abraham's brother, joined Abraham and A.S. there.[2]

Unlike the rudimentary items made by Frederick Davidson at Mossy Creek, the Davidsons' Sand Mountain pottery was of high quality, and remains highly collectable folk pottery today. Other potters congregated in the region, and the line of pottery they produced is now known as "Sand Mountain Pottery."[3] The Davidsons exported their jugs and storage jars throughout the region, but whether they made it to Sumter County is unknown, so the "mystery" of whether the Davidsons' pottery was ever sold in Sumter County must remain unsolved.

Religious Zeal in the Mountains

Abraham was extremely religious, deeply influenced by his father and the tenor of the times. His son A.S. wrote in an obituary of his father, "In early life, he was a class leader, then for some years an exhorter, then a local preacher" until he was finally ordained in the Methodist Church. "I do not remember any time when the fire was not burning upon the family altar both morning and evening. I think I can point to one place where I have heard him pray more than six thousand times."[4] Abraham preached in a primitive, fundamentalist style; his messages were "simple and earnest" and relied mostly for evidence on "quotations from the Scriptures."

Abraham was constantly in poverty. "So far as the possession of the world's goods, he was always poor, but numbers of itinerant and other preachers lodged under his roof."[4] Poverty did not stop Abraham from sharing home and meals with others. A.S. noted, "Traveling preachers often visited [Abraham's] home, and with their holy conversations, counsels, Bible reading and prayers they could not fail to make indelible impressions for good."[5]

Methodism was democratic in philosophy and organizational form. Its theology centered on rejecting the Calvinist doctrine of predestination and emphasizing the responsibility of individuals for their own salvation. In that sense, it was centered in the democratic notion of personal responsibility.

Its organizational form focused on establishing small local societies connected by itinerant nonordained evangelists. Each local Methodist society was divided into smaller groups of about 12, called classes. Class leaders linked members to the local society and itinerant preachers linked local societies to each other and the broader church. American Methodism was built to generate social connections that fostered the flow of ideas and news, accelerating democratic as well as religious ideals.

During the 1820s and 1830s, Jacksonian democratic ideals and religious revival swept through the Appalachian hills like wildfire, igniting passions among the white underclass. These intertwined social movements were imperfect; they excluded Native Americans, women, and Blacks from leadership positions and in most cases even membership. The most troublesome issue was slavery.

When Methodism was established in America in 1784, it officially opposed slavery. During the Great Awakening the new fundamentalists, both Methodists and Baptists, argued for better treatment of slaves.

The bourgeoning slave society led both denominations to a crisis born of the demands of the national churches that ministers and bishops not own slaves. In 1844 the Methodist National Conference voted to prohibit such ownership outright. That was not much of an issue in Southern Appalachia, but, as we've seen, many church leaders in the Black Belt held slaves. Southern slave-owning states withdrew from the national church, forming a southern branch. The branches reunified only in 1939, forming today's United Methodist Church.

One perhaps overlooked element of the democratization of religion during the Second Great Awakening was the promotion of literacy. If anyone could be called to God, and "preach the Bible," then clearly being literate enough to read the Bible was necessary. This was no easy task. The religious calling perhaps led Frederick Davidson to provide for "the maintenance and education of my children" in his will.

The hill-country Davidsons had modest wealth, and were relatively fortunate for hill folks. They never owned slaves, and held limited land which was on the poorly producing soils of hillside Appalachia. The keys to Davidson success over the generations were the availability of lands from treaty cessions from Native Americans, the power of religion, and the craft of pottery.

Social Connectivity in the Mountains

Startling differences in wealth and social organization divided the yeoman and tenant farmers of the North Alabama mountains and South Alabama Wiregrass region from the planters of the Black Belt. Initial migratory patterns brought wealth to the Black Belt from the outset. Geography reinforced these migratory patterns, economic life followed geography, and the cultural differences between North and South Alabama intensified. Class and wealth disparities followed geography, with the Black Belt counties becoming startlingly rich while the mountains and pine barrens were rooted in the simple life of the yeoman small farmer.

The economic differeces were truly enormous between regions. In Black Belt Sumter County, where the Carrs settled, 76% of white families were slaveholders. In Blount County, home to the Davidsons and Deans, 7% were. Taxes followed wealth; per capita taxes paid in Sumter County in 1861 were $4.45; for Blount they were $0.26. These figures are comparable to other counties in the regions they represent.[6]

The mountain and Black Belt regions were isolated from each other in a way almost unimaginable today. No railroad connected North and South Alabama, and it took several days of travel to get from one section of the state to another. Commercial activity was minimal, with the northern section more linked to Tennessee and North Georgia than to the southern sections of Alabama.[7] The topography worked against railroad construction and road-building connecting the regions.

In 1865, A.S. Davidson's first wife, Julia Waldrop, died, and the next year he married Ruth Whitt. A letter from her father, and my second great-grandfather, William Whitt, to one of his sisters in 1877 gives us an insight into life among the mountain whites, or Sand Mountain people, as they were known. William, a small farmer in Etowah County, writes, "Times is very hard here," describing losing hogs to cholera, poor crop yields, and that "everybody is in debt. Right smart of sickness and a heap of death." He writes of religious decline even in the new fundamentalist churches challenging the Methodist and Baptist mainline churches, writing "I contend that the Primitive Baptist is the only true church of christ there is." But "the church seems to be going down" and "the churches has been in a cold condition this year everywhere."

William writes in closing, "I am in my 59 year. I never have had to buy a bushel of corn nor a dollar's worth of bacon yet never was I more than a day's travel from home yet. I live at the same place yet."[8]

William Whitt speaks to the self-sufficiency, isolation, poverty, and lack of integration into the broader economic and social systems of the region. Life was hard, families were large, and many of the young did not survive. Whit himself lost two sons in the Civil War and one young child to diphtheria. William writes that one of his friends has suffered even greater losses—"Lost one daughter that was married. Left 2 little children. Lost another girl nearly grown, Got two children left out of 16. He wrote that he was agoin to Texas."

The planters in Sumter County lived privileged lives indeed, but the slaves on their plantations could not have dreamed of the life of relative privilege that William Whitt had in North Alabama. He owned land and farm animals, could read and write, and had the ability to move even if he did not take the opportunity to do so. But his life was hard.

This story of poverty, isolation, and a general sense of alienation and disconnectedness from a broader community is a typical recounting of Appalachian life, even today. However, there was another side of Appalachian life in the antebellum period. Tocqueville noted the vibrant civil society in America, a set of intermediary organizations between the individual and the state.

The Great Awakening and democratization of politics led to camp meetings, networks of itinerant preachers, and general political activism, leading to the building of social capital. Mossy Creek in Halberstam County, Georgia, the home of Frederick and Rhoda Davidson, was the locus of a busy campground used by various sects. A.S. Davidson writes of his father that his poverty did not prevent him from lodging itinerant preachers and other transient visitors coming through the region. These itinerants carried information and commentary from place to place, serving to knit isolated communities together more than the letters of William Whitt might imply.

After the Civil War general decline in agriculture led to malaise and outmigration. These hard times also led to a vibrant agrarian reform movement that experimented with various forms of collective action to supply farmers with more reasonably priced seeds, tools, and fertilizers. The Grange, founded in 1867, brought more efficient agricultural methods to farmers, white and Black, and its chapters formed collectives to buy seed and other necessities in bulk. The itinerant proselytizers of the more political Farmers' Alliance spread out from its birthplace in Texas throughout the South and West, preaching the evils of corporate barons, railroads, and the nation's hard money policies. These traveling agrarian reformers served to build social capital and knit together communities of like political interests across the region. They emerged as parallel networks to the religious networks that already existed and interacted with them. Small farms meant shorter distance to the neighbor's home, making attending political and religious meetings simpler than the mountain isolation perspective implies. Group life in the backwoods was vibrant and dynamic, not dreary and isolated.

Regional Politics in Southern States

While there is abundant evidence of the Davidsons' activities in upland crafts and religion, there is scant evidence that the Davidsons or the Deans participated in politics before the Civil War. Nonetheless, the political milieu bubbled from the same sources as religion and economic expansion, and they doubtless participated in political dialogue along with their religious activities. After the war, and particularly during the agrarian revolt, both the Davidsons and the Deans became deeply involved in the political process.

Upland Southerners worshiped at the feet of God and Andrew Jackson. The Second Great Awakening and Jacksonian democracy freed the uplanders from the strictly hierarchical colonial social structure. Indian removal was key in this new white freedom, and the uplanders recognized that both the Indian wars conducted by Jackson and his removal policies as president provided them with the land they craved.

It was not just his policies, but his presence as a mountain man as well. He symbolized what the immigrant poor could attain. He rose from poverty to great military, political, and economic success. He spoke the language of the rural frontiersmen that inhabited the hills of Tennessee, Georgia, and Alabama. He acquired great wealth along the way, and held numerous slaves. This route of upward mobility meant that many mountain yeoman farmers saw slavery as a route to wealth, but most, like the Davidsons, seemed contented with their upland lives. The stark division between economic elites and yeoman and tenant farmers made the wealth divide too large to bridge.

The families of many Southerners claimed to have lineage to Jackson. Members of my maternal Davidson family thought that we were so related, although there is no evidence of any such connection. I am not sure where this untrue rumor came from, but when I learned of it as a boy, I asked my father, "Do you know who I'm kin to that you are not?" "Your mother?," he responded.

Uplanders rewarded Jackson and his Democratic Party successors with huge electoral majorities in their runs for president. In 1832, all Alabama, Georgia, and Tennessee counties voted for Jackson. By 1836, however, distinctive sectional patterns had emerged in Georgia, Alabama, and to a lesser extent Mississippi, with Democrats carrying the hill and mountain counties and the Whigs carrying the Black Belt regions of these states. Martin Van Buren, President Jackson's vice president, won every North Alabama county save one. The Black Belt counties voted solidly for the Whig William Henry Harrison. The elections of 1840, 1844, 1848, and 1852 replicated these patterns.

The two parties were reasonably competitive for most of the period, with the Whigs winning in 1840 in more settled Georgia with its established plantation economy, but losing in Alabama, which was more frontier-oriented at the time. In 1848, the Whigs won in close elections in both states (Figure 7.1). The sectional pattern followed a class politics, with the poorer mountain and hill regions voting for the Democrat Lewis Cass, and the Black Belt areas voting for the Whig Zachary Taylor. A generally similar pattern held for Mississippi,

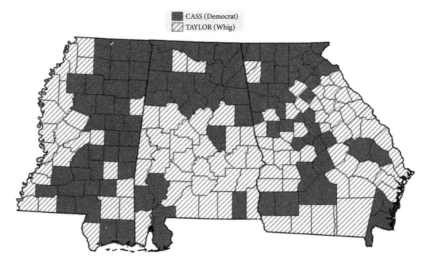

Figure 7.1 Election of 1848, Georgia, Alabama, and Mississippi

Source: Modified from Wikipedia Commons, "1848 Presidential Election" [https://en.
wikipedia.org/wiki/1848_United_States_presidential_election].

with the rich Mississippi Delta region voting Whig. While slavery was always an
issue, the South was not a one-party bastion, and during the 1840s a class-based
politics emerged that was reflected in the sectional patterns.

As the Civil War approached, the within-state sectional divisions faded,
but they were still in evidence. In 1856, the North Alabama mountain
counties went most solidly for the Democratic candidate, James Buchanan,
while votes for Millard Filmore, the Whig candidate, were concentrated
in a handful of southern Alabama, mostly Black Belt, counties. Wiregrass counties in the state's Southeast voted for Buchanan at higher
rates than the Black Belt counties, but not as high as in the mountain
counties.

The variations in lifestyles between slaveholding counties and the yeoman
farmers and craftsmen of the mountains, along with the vigorous interaction in upland meeting halls, churches, and visits to each others' homes
led to starkly divergent political cultures in the two regions. The separate
regional cultures led to different political preferences and party choices. These
stark cultural differences built different mindsets, with the hierarchical slaveholding counties turning to oligarchical rule and the mountain counties
adopting a vigorous democratic style reinforced by religion and regular social
interaction.

Regional Identities

As the Civil War approached, the South was becoming an increasingly unequal society, with wealth concentrated in the Black Belts. Slavery of course was the great unequalizer, but inequality among whites was increasing as well. The Black Belt regions of the antebellum South had become regions of planters and slaves, with fewer and fewer yeoman farmers and white craftsmen. The logic of what might be called monopoly slavery was the accumulation of more and more land and slaves, with the most prosperous slaveholders buying out small farmers and minor plantations during the recession of 1857. In the mountains, the recession drove yeoman farmers into tenancy, contributing to the sectional inequality.

The sectional patterns rooted in differences in migration, cultures, and economics had all of the hallmarks of developing class-based politics based in sectional differences. Viewing county-level election data during the antebellum period shows clear-cut divisions between poor and rich counties throughout the South, but party identifications differed from the simple Democratic-Whig divisions because of candidate loyalties and other local factors. Nevertheless, this pattern is clear in the lower tier of Southern states. As long as the Whigs existed, they had great appeal in the Black Belts. The Democrats held sway in the regions of Cherokee, Choctaw, and Chickasaw removal, even well into the 1850s, but the more settled mountain regions of Virginia, North Carolina, and Tennessee felt free to vote for Whig and Kentuckian Henry Clay in 1844 and war hero Zachary Taylor in 1848.

Party choice was affected by migration patterns as well. The Sand Mountain People were part of a distinct east-to-west migration pattern disproportionately composed of Scots and Scots-Irish. They moved down the Old Wagon Road from their entry points into the United States, following the Indian removals through western Virginia and North Carolina, the Pendleton District of South Carolina, into Tennessee, North Georgia, and Alabama. The migratory trace did not stop there; these hill folks and their offspring moved through the Ozarks in Arkansas and into central Texas, where they settled into the Texas Hill Country.[9]

These Scots and Scots-Irish moved west as Natives were removed, occupying the space between the settled lowlands and piedmont regions and the frontier. As they did so, they adopted a broad cross-state identity—hillbillies, hill folks, mountain men, and crackers in the east; cedar choppers in the Texas Hills; Sand Mountain People in Alabama. They developed a class identity as well, characterized most notably by hostility to the rich and entitled planters and country gentlemen in the rich coastal lands and Black Belts. They typically voted Democratic.

Historian Keri Merritt notes how early in Southern development this distinction occurred, and how potentially threatening it was to the entitled classes.[10] Within the Southern states major class divisions reflecting geography emerged, especially after the election of 1824. Was a class-based Southern politics emerging in the middle years of the antebellum period? Were sectional divisions strong enough to generate an alternative historical path other than the one taken? Or did slavery and white supremacy always have the upper hand? The story of Native American removal in Georgia would seem to support the single-mind thesis, one that unified Southerners of different classes around the idea of white supremacy. Regional politics following native removal revealed a stark class divide between the white small farmer and the landless poor, on the one hand, and the rich planter and business class, on the other.

The Davidsons can be viewed as archetypical North Alabama whites, never leaving the hills through three generations. These were the people of the hills, farming poor-quality land on hillsides, pursuing simple crafts, showing no interest in slave-holding, and consumed by religion. Abraham Davidson could be the poster child for these Sand Mountain People. He lived a life of rural poverty. Starting life in the hills of Georgia he engaged in Indian removal; moved from place to place incessantly; developed Davidson pottery from a rudimentary basis to near-art; and joined the Confederate home guard during the Civil War. He carved his own tombstone out of local sandstone as he approached death. He was buried in a former campground between Blountsville and Cullman.[11]

CHAPTER 8

Yeoman Farming in the Mountains

In 1847 in the rugged hills of North Alabama a young man named Joseph Dean supported himself and his growing family on a 100-acre farm, 35 acres of which were under cultivation or pasture. He labored on the farm with 2 working oxen and 3 horses. He had 5 cows that produced milk and butter, and he grew 800 bushels of Indian corn, both to feed the swine he owned and to sell to other farmers in the region. Joseph grazed a few beef cattle and sheep but he produced none of the premier antebellum cash crop of the Deep South—cotton. Neither did any of his neighbors; the land was simply not amenable to growing cotton.

Joseph, my second great-grandfather, at 27 was a reasonably successful yeoman farmer, growing vegetables and corn and husbanding animals in a manner typical of the mountain counties of Alabama. Being unable to grow cash crops meant limits on his income flow. Joseph held a single slave—a male Black man about his age.

Even though large plantations, concentrated in the Black Belt regions, produced most of the wealth in Southern societies, some slaves worked on small farms. Joseph's one slave allowed him to clear and cultivate at least twice as many acres of his land as would be possible with him working alone. Landowner and slave worked side-by-side, at least during planting and harvesting seasons, but there was no doubt who worked hardest and who was the owner. Subsistence farming allowed Joseph to feed his slave at low cost. The slave may have shared a modest cabin with the Deans, or he may have had an even more modest shack for himself. Both patterns were common among slaveholding small-time farmers.[1]

Joseph, the Orphaned Son

Just how Joseph got to the mountains of Walker County in Alabama is somewhat of a mystery. Joseph was born in Tennessee in 1823, the son of John Dean and Polly Herring. Polly died in 1823, probably in childbirth, and his father, John, died the next year. Joseph and his orphaned siblings were put under the guardianship of John's older brother, Joseph, whom he was perhaps named after, a well-off farmer.

It is unclear when the Deans arrived in America, or from where, but they followed the classic Appalachian trail to the South in a manner like the Davidsons. Samuel Dean, the father of John and Joseph, served in the Revolutionary War while living in Cumberland, Pennsylvania. In 1786, Samuel, and his wife Gwendolyn (Gwinny) James, traversed the Great Wagon Road with their children, including John, my third great-grandfather, and Gwinny's family. In a familiar pattern of migration, they settled on land ceded by the Cherokees after the Revolutionary War, in the hills of the Pendleton District of South Carolina near Anderson.

In South Carolina, John married Polly Herring. Sometime after their second child was born in 1812, they moved to Lincoln County, Tennessee, joining John's brother, Joseph, there.

Joseph the Uncle Gets Rich

Joseph, the brother of John, became guardian of John and Mary's children after John died in 1824; Joseph the nephew was but a year old. Joseph the uncle seems to have been focused and aggressive in his desire to make himself a rich man. He began building his wealth in Lincoln County in a systematic fashion. He built his wealth first through business (he ran a tavern out of his house), land speculation, and farming on a small-scale plantation. He held 9 slaves in 1820, but 10 years later had expanded that to 22. This former Pennsylvanian had become deeply involved in the slave economy.

It is unlikely that Joseph the uncle fulfilled his responsibility as guardian of his younger brother's children. Some strange patterns emerge out of a careful study of census records. An analysis of the ages of Joseph the uncle's dependents in the Census of 1830, where only sex and age are listed, indicate that Joseph the nephew was not in his uncle's household. Joseph the nephew would have been 7 or thereabouts, and no male dependent of that age was reported by Joseph the uncle. It is possible that the Census was in error, or probably more likely, Joseph the nephew was sent to live with another family.

Joseph the uncle moved his family to Marshall County, Mississippi, in 1837, establishing himself on land near the town of Holly Springs. He named his holdings Cuffawa Plantation. Marshall County is wedged between the rich black soil of the Mississippi Delta and the red clay hills of what is known as the Mississippi Hill Counties in the northeast corner of the state. Mississippi has none of the Appalachian Mountain regions characteristic of Alabama and Georgia, but the hill counties of northeast Mississippi are less hospitable to the economies of the plantation than the Delta and other regions of the state. Nevertheless, all of Mississippi's hill counties, and especially Marshall, had significant slave presence, especially in comparison to the nearby Alabama mountain counties.

Census figures for 1840 indicate that Joseph, the son of John Dean and the nephew of the slaveholder Joseph, did not move with the family to Mississippi, as he is not listed as a member of his uncle's household in that year, the first Census that lists families by name.

Marshall County was part of a Chickasaw forced territorial cession after President Jackson's Indian Removal Act of 1830. The Choctaw Nation to the south had signed the Treaty of Dancing Rabbit Creek that year and were forcibly removed to Indian Territory. After the removal, the Chickasaw were the only nation remaining in Mississippi.

The Chickasaws ceded their lands in two treaties, with the Mississippi hills ceded in 1836. The Chickasaw removal took place a year or so later. The United States had already surveyed and platted the territory by then, and the first land sales took place in January of 1836. Joseph Dean the uncle must have taken advantage of one of the early land sales, moving into the region because of the availability of land suitable for plantation economy.

In moving to Mississippi, Joseph the uncle was tying himself more tightly to the slaveholding economy. In 1850, Joseph held 49 enslaved people, had $4,400 worth of real estate, and listed himself as a farmer. He was 71 at the time, but he did not stop the slave-accumulation business. In 1860, on the eve of war, the 81-year-old Joseph held 70 people in bondage worth $53,000 and held land worth an estimated $19,000. No longer a "farmer," Joseph listed himself as a "planter." A "blind" inflation calculator estimates his worth at over $2,000,000 in today's dollars. Not only had Joseph gotten wealthy, but so had his offspring. His 47-year-old son, Russell, also a "planter," held six slaves worth $16,000 but listed no real estate. He was probably farming his father's land. Russell's 23-year-old son Aaron was the family plantation's manager, or overseer.

Joseph the uncle had amassed enormous wealth, made possible by Chickasaw removal, and that wealth was being transferred to his son and grandson. This pattern resembles closely that of the Carrs and Larkins, but at a much grander scale. Joseph had assembled great wealth by moving quickly when Chickasaw land became available, and by investing aggressively in increasing his slaveholdings and in land. These valuations for slaves and land in 1860 reflected the high point of worth for these assets.

Joseph the uncle died in 1871 at the age of 93 and was buried at a cemetery on the old plantation. At the end of his life, with his formerly enslaved people freed, Joseph still owned real estate with an estimated worth of $4,600, of which $4,500 was in land. Although much of his wealth was gone with emancipation, that which was left had been accrued through his immersion in the plantation economy. After the Civil War, his extensive land holdings were likely leased, most probably through the sharecropping system. In any case, the family retained enough wealth that in 1871 Joseph's son purchased an elegant home in Holly Springs. The intergenerational transfer of wealth from Joseph the uncle to his heirs, wealth based on involuntary servitude, had transcended war and Reconstruction.

One might see Joseph's life as a series of choices that led to economic gain and the potential for extraordinary wealth, but the choices for the most part were morally repugnant. Each of his moves—from the hill country of South Carolina to south-central Tennessee, from Tennessee to North Mississippi led to more opportunities to accumulate land and slaves. Each move led to land with better agricultural potential. As the soil improved, so did the potential to exploit Black slaves to increase white wealth. Pickens County, South Carolina (Pendleton District when Joseph was there), was 23% slave at the outbreak of the Civil War; Lincoln County, Tennessee, was 30% slave; and Marshall County, Mississippi, was 60% slave. Joseph moved where the land was good and slaves were plentiful, and consequently he built enormous wealth.

Joseph the Nephew Makes Different Choices

By 1842, at age 19, Joseph the nephew had left Tennessee and was in Alabama. He first shows up in the public record in 1842, when he married Athenia Reid in Jefferson County (later the home of Birmingham) Alabama. His son, my great-grandfather, John Albert Dean, was born in Walker County, Alabama, in 1843. Joseph the nephew spent his entire adult life, save the years in a Union prison during the Civil War, in the mountains and hollows of Appalachian Alabama.

Surely Joseph knew the ways of the rich planter from his uncle, and either couldn't master them or didn't want to do so. The deliberate choice of the hills and mountains of Walker County suggests the latter. Perhaps his tormented married life contributed to his devotion to farm life—he married four times. Joseph's first wife died in 1850, and his last wife died after him, but it is unclear if his two other wives departed through death or divorce, though death is most likely.

Two Alabama Counties, Two Different Worlds

Slaveholding upcountry farmers were rare in the North Alabama county of Walker, where my great-grandfather John Albert Dean was born. There were a handful of slaveholders and they each held very few slaves. Tax records from the late 1840s show that there were only 208 slaves held by 56 out of a total of 876 landowning families in the county. Ninety-four percent of the landowners owned no slaves.

The distribution of slaves among the slaveholders may be gleaned from the 1850 Census Slave Schedules. The typical (modal) slaveholding family held one slave, and the richest slaveholder in Walker County held 13 slaves. Most farmers who held slaves in the mountains of Alabama, Georgia, and Tennessee used them as house servants or to produce subsistence crops. Joseph's single slave was doubtless a farm laborer, perhaps until Joseph's children were old enough to guide the plow behind the family mule. The slave was not present in the household by 1855 in an Alabama census of that year. It is likely that the slave was more like a hired hand than a permanent fixture on the slaveholding map. Unlike on the plantation, yeoman farm slavery was a substitute for a robust free labor market.

Little had changed by the outbreak of the Civil War, as the population of Walker County was 6.5% slave in 1860. That year there were 567 slaves in Walker County. At the same time in Sumter County, 100 miles south in the Black Belt, 122 families held more than 40 slaves each. One slaveholder,

Jerrit Brown, held more slaves than the entire number of slaves in Walker County.

These vast differences did not simply reflect population differences. Indeed, the number of whites in the two counties was similar. Sumter County, where 24,000 people lived, was home to around 6,000 whites, while Walker was home to over 7,000 whites. The differences in the compositions of populations of these counties reflected great differences in geography, social organization, and political power. Whites in Sumter were far wealthier than whites in Walker, and far more politically powerful, both due to wealth and the structure of representation. The U.S. Constitution provided representation based on free and slave populations, with one of the latter counting as three-fifths of the former. For the purposes of electing U.S. House Representatives, Sumter County had a population for apportionment purposes of around 6,000 whites + (18,000 Blacks x .60) = 16,800, even though only the whites could vote. Walker's apportionment population was a little over 7,000.

The same system was not in place for the Alabama state legislature, which apportioned seats only according to whites. Walker had similar representation as Sumter. As a consequence, Whigs seldom held majorities in the state legislature. Democratic legislators taxed wealth, and most tax revenues came from a tax on slaves, although the tax was low.

Intermittent Slaveholding

Why engage in slavery at all, as Joseph the nephew did, where a plantation-style economy was not feasible? One key was the underdeveloped farm labor system. It was difficult to hire seasonal labor in the isolated hills, except for the farmers' teenage sons who hired out to other farmers. Large families could provide labor as the boys grew to young men, and in some sense that explains the tendency of farm families to be so large.

The system of chattel slavery allowed the slaveholder to hold an investment for a number of years, selling the investment later. The small scale of slavery in Walker County probably generated an informal neighbor-to-neighbor sales system, but it is also possible that the landowner traveled to Huntsville or Montgomery, where slave markets existed. A downside for the modal slave-holder was that it was doubtless easier for a single slave to escape into the deep forests and steep valleys of Alabama's mountain counties than from plantations with overseers and packs of dogs to hunt down escapees. Indeed, of the 266 slaves listed on the 1850 slave schedules for one of the census districts for Walker County, 4% were fugitives.[2]

Historians have engaged in some spirited but limited debates on the existence of intermittent slaveholding, in which a slaveholder would get out of the slavery business at some point, perhaps to engage again in the future.[3] Business downturn could account for such patterns. Certainly, Joseph Dean followed the path of intermittent slaveholding; when he moved from Walker to Blount County in the early 1850s, he held no slaves.[4]

If a farmer could afford the initial investment, holding a slave for a short period of time could yield a solid investment return. Between 1840 and 1860, the price of a slave in current dollars appreciated significantly—from about $300 for the average slave to almost $800—but that period followed a boom/bust period in the 1830s.[5] When Joseph moved from Walker to Blount County, he gained wealth by selling his improved property and his slave, still well within working age. The slave economy even where it was virtually nonexistent could benefit some yeoman farmers to some extent, as it probably did Joseph Dean.

Joseph in Blount

Joseph's wife died around 1850, and he remarried in 1853. He moved to Blount County, near the hamlet of Summit in the far north of the county. Joseph the nephew was never a wealthy plantation owner, nor does it seem he ever desired to follow his uncle's footsteps by acquiring slaves. His farms in Walker and then Blount were similar to those of the nonslaveholding farmers around him, and he certainly never got wealthy through the classic plantation mechanism of slaves and land. He seems to have done slightly better than other nonslaveholding farmers, indicating that slaveholding even for an intermittent time could lead to the financial betterment of the white yeoman farmer.

The slave that Joseph held is lost to history. The Census Slave Schedules produced in 1850 and 1860 list the sex and age of slaves, but not their names. A census conducted by the State of Alabama in 1855 listed only the number of slaves, presumably for tax purposes. Where did the enslaved male go when he left Joseph's Walker County farm? We know what happened to Joseph, thanks to the federal and state censuses, and other records such as county tax records, but there is no record of the slave.

Joseph Dean's life, like Abraham Davidson's, brings into question the common lore that the nonslaveholding whites in the South supported slavery because they hoped to get in on the action at some point. Joseph was considerably better off economically than Abraham, and his uncle was an aggressive slaver. Yet Joseph the nephew never sought such wealth, and held his only slave for a brief period.

It is true that most uplanders were content with the existing order based on slavery. One reason nonslaveholding upland farmers supported the slave-based political system was that taxes fell most heavily on planters, not them, for what little revenue the state collected.[6] Taxes in Sumter County raised $445 per capita in 1861, but only $30 from the poor yeoman farmers in Walker County.[7]

Joseph and John Albert Dean Go to War

On August 12, 1861, Confederate recruiters came to Blountsville in search of volunteers. Confederates in Virginia had defeated the Union Army at Bull Run just a few weeks before; excitement was in the air all over the South. Would the war be over before Alabama soldiers saw action? Joseph Dean traveled the 10 miles from his farm near Summit, and signed up as a private in Company K, the "Blount Guards." Less than a month later, Joseph's son and my great grandfather, John Albert Dean, enlisted in Company C, the "Jefferson Warriors" at Huntsville.

Two men, neither of whom owned slaves and who lived in a region hostile to secession, signed up for a cause that seemed a remote one. All North Alabama counties, including those along the Tennessee River with substantial slaveholding, sent delegations to the January 1861 secession convention in Montgomery opposing immediate secession. They favored continued negotiation with President Lincoln. Outvoted by South Alabama counties, the North Alabama counties joined the Confederate cause, but harbored draft resisters,

Unionists, and deserters from the War's outset. The numbers of these "hide-outs," as they were called, increased as the Confederacy collapsed. Winston County, next to Blount and Walker, declared itself "the Free State of Winston," and raised a regiment that served in the Union Army. Even though most moun-tain counties were loyal to the Confederate cause, the lack of enthusiasm for the Confederacy among upland Southerners in Alabama, Georgia, Tennessee, North Carolina, and Virginia was an important reason for secession's failure.

The 19th Alabama Infantry Regiment that the Deans had joined was not a good regiment for a soldier to serve in. It took disproportionate casu-alties in many of the battles in Tennessee and Georgia, starting with the Battle of Shiloh in April of 1862. John Albert Dean was badly wounded there, and the 19th lost a third of its soldiers killed or wounded on that bloody battlefield. John Albert Dean was listed among the soldiers who lost their rifles, but his commanding officer ruled that as justifiable. John Albert was able to rejoin his unit, and requested clothing in mid-1864.

The 38-year-old Joseph Dean was assigned to hospital duty as a nurse. He had the misfortune of being captured and serving time as a prisoner of war two different times. Joseph was first captured at the Battle of Stone's River in January of 1863, which bears the "distinction" of being the battle with the highest percentage of casualties on both sides. Joseph, along with the wounded and other hospital personnel, were sent to Fort McHenry in Mary-land, where he served as a cook. He and other prisoners from the 19th were exchanged and sent to Virginia in June 1863 after a pledge not to rejoin in the fighting.

Joseph, however, violated his pledge and went back to his medical unit. He was captured again on May 15, 1864, during the Battle of Resaca, part of the Confederate retreat toward Atlanta. Sent to the Louisville Military Prison and then to the Alton, Illinois, Military Prison, Joseph was discharged on June 14, 1865, after he gave an oath of allegiance to the United States. I'm not sure get-ting captured twice was exactly common in the Civil War, but lest we be too critical of Joseph for managing this feat recall that he was a nurse responsible for the wounded in field hospitals. To abandon the wounded in the face of the enemy would have been gross negligence.

John Albert Dean continued with his unit until the end of the war. He surrendered at Durham, North Carolina, with the remnants of General Joe Johnston's army.[8]

Home to Blount

After the war, Joseph and John Dean returned to Blount County. Joseph remained a farmer the rest of his life, living on a farm of around 500 acres, with 100 of those acres in cultivation in 1880. He grew a few acres of corn and wheat, but no cotton, and kept cattle and swine. Probably most of his income came from the animals. Joseph's younger sons provided the labor needed on his farm. Joseph died in 1881.

John Albert returned to a life of farming as well. In 1868 he married Lucy Ellis. Lucy's father, Stephen, had migrated with his family from the Pendleton District of South Carolina in the classic pattern for hill folks.

John and Lucy acquired a small farm of 100 acres in Blount County; by 1880 they had 40 acres in cultivation. It seemed that his life would resemble his father's, as he grew mostly for subsistence, with 7 acres of corn, 10 of wheat, and a few cows and pigs. Like his father, he grew no cotton or other cash crops. In 1880 Dean paid a white laborer for 20 weeks of work.[9]

John's seemingly settled life was about to change dramatically. In a contested election that took the Circuit Court to resolve, he got himself elected as Blount County Tax Assessor in 1878, in a period of political turmoil and change.[10]

CHAPTER 9

North Alabama in War and Reconstruction

In 1949, V.O. Key wrote, "Two great crises have left their imprint on southern political behavior: The War of the 'sixties and the Populist revolt of the 'nineties."[1] These are two of the great critical junctures that divide Southern history into rough eras. The Civil War separated the Antebellum South from Reconstruction and Redemption. Then the defeat of the Populist Revolt divided the possibilities for cross-racial democracy from the period of white supremacy and Jim Crow, with its system of apartheid and oppression of Blacks.

Today the Civil War looms powerfully in the minds of many, with Confederate flags flying as symbols of white supremacy and white Southern identity. As vibrant as the symbolism of the Confederacy remains, the Populist Revolt has faded in memory. Why would the narrative of a war fought to continue and extend slavery be honored, while the narrative of a robust effort to challenge the oligarchic power structure through democratic means, using an alliance of whites and Blacks, farmers and workers, urban and rural, be forgotten?

The Civil War in North Alabama

In the 1850s, national politics in the United States became increasingly sectional. Slavery became an overridingly salient issue, and because of the dominance of the plantation economy in the Southern states, slavery dominated Southern positions in national politics. The tension became so great after Lincoln's election that eleven Southern states, led by Black Belt planters, seceded from the Union.

After the 1860 election and the secession of South Carolina, Alabama called a convention to consider secession. Each county sent a delegation to Montgomery, and two factions emerged. One, the secessionists, wanted immediate secession. The second, the cooperationists, were divided; most were willing to consider secession but not immediately. They wanted to institute negotiations with the Union and with other slave states prior to any rash actions.

Secession did not cause intrastate sectionalism to disappear. In Alabama and Georgia, as well as the rest of the South, lowland slaveholding regions were more supportive of secession than upland regions. Figure 9.1 displays the concentration of slavery and the composition of county delegations to the Montgomery secession convention, January 1861. The differences divided high slaveholding regions from those with few slaves, but geographic sectionalism

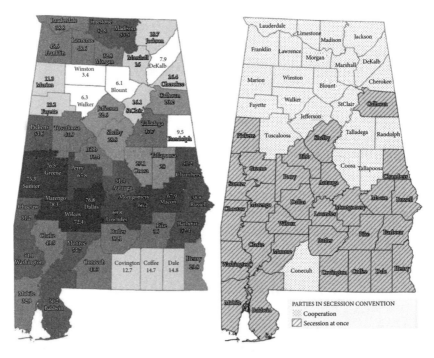

Figure 9.1 Percent Slavery in 1860 and Delegation Composition to the Alabama Secession Convention, 1861

Sources: Slavery: U.S. Coast Survey, "Map of the Distribution of the Slave Population of the Southern States of the United States"; the map was drawn from data from the U.S. Census. Convention: Walter Lynwood Fleming, *Civil War and Reconstruction in Alabama* (New York, Columbia University Press, 1905), 29.

was clearly evident and seemed to have divided the delegations as well. The delegations from the low slaveholding regions of Southeast Alabama supported immediate secession, whereas the high slaveholding regions in the Tennessee Valley sent delegates committed to cooperation. Indeed, the positions on secession divided North from South Alabama almost perfectly—only one North Alabama county voted for immediate secession while only one South Alabama county voted for cooperation.

Northern counties were just not as concerned with slavery, nor were they interested in fighting a war on behalf of rich planters. The convention debate focused almost solely on the issue of delay, with the cooperationists seeing no harm and plenty of benefits in negotiations. The cooperationists, like the Blount delegation, felt secession was unwise, but they were not fond of the idea of "Black Republican Rule," the specter that hovered over the convention. In the end the secession ordinance passed 69 to 31, with 15 cooperationists joining the 54 secessionists.[2]

The secession vote did not end the sectional controversy. For many North Alabamans, the decision to fight for the Confederacy was not an easy one. In some cases men joined the Confederates because of the increasing closeness of the fighting to their homes; for others it was a stringent draft law enacted in 1863.

Sectionalism emerged not only over secession, but during the war as well. Desertion was a massive problem for the Confederacy, much more so than the Union—a fact conveniently ignored by purveyors of the Lost Cause. The desertions came primarily from conscripts or "hideouts" avoiding conscription from the poor mountain and Wiregrass counties.[3] Most deserters left because of privations at home. Wives of Confederate soldiers from the mountain counties traveled to the Black Belt to beg for food from the prosperous plantations there. During 1863 more than one-third of families in all counties except those of the Black Belt received aid as indigents. Forty-eight percent of families in Blount County received aid, while 59% of families in Walker did so. In Sumter County, only 13% received aid.

The Davidsons Join Late

We've seen how the Deans joined the Confederate army early in the war, but the Davidsons took different paths. Abraham enlisted late in the war (August 1863) in a Georgia militia unit. He was 50 years old at the time, and fit enough to join the home guard. Abraham enlisted during a period when Union forces were conducting a major offensive in southeastern Tennessee and northwestern Georgia. Union troops moved into Alabama seeking to sever the supply lines to Confederate General Braxton Bragg, operating in Middle Tennessee. The Battle of Sand Mountain occurred in April, a prelude to the great battles around nearby Chattanooga in September. Abraham joined because the war came to him, and he signed up for a six-month period.

Abraham's son Alvin Steele (A.S.) Davidson, my great-grandfather, enlisted in April 1863 as a private in the Alabama 7th Calvary (later known as the 9th due to military reorganizations). It is not clear why A.S. enlisted when he did, but his late entry into the war effort probably indicates that he volunteered under the threat of conscription. The Confederacy passed a series of conscription acts, and A.S. had been subject to conscription for a year when he volunteered. The mountain counties of North Alabama contributed a disproportionate number of "volunteers" facing conscription.[4]

By the time A.S. joined the fight the war had become terrible, killing thousands of Americans in each battle, and desertion by North Alabama soldiers had become widespread. When A.S. finally signed up, he apparently was committed to the cause, for he served throughout the rest of the war. The Alabama 9th participated in Confederate General James Longstreet's campaign in Tennessee in 1863, was in the front lines at the Battle of Atlanta, and harassed Sherman's army as it moved through Georgia. A.S. and the remnants of the Alabama 9th surrendered with General Joe Johnston in North Carolina in April of 1865.[5]

My family apparently was made up of stubborn men, committed to a false cause that was not to their economic benefit. Most surrendered at the end of the war. A.S. Davidson, John Albert Dean, and James Powell Carr surrendered at Durham. Charley Jones (my paternal great-grandfather) surrendered at Appomattox. The sole participants who did not surrender formally at the end of the war were Joseph Dean, a prisoner of war, and Abraham Davidson, whose enlistment period had expired. Yet only one, James Powell Carr, had any economic interest in the cause.

One of A.S.'s brothers was killed during the Battle of Atlanta, as was an uncle. Another brother was terribly wounded, and A.S. suffered a less grievous wound. These losses reflect a heavy toll for a war never desired by the inhabitants of North Alabama yet fought on behalf of the slaveholding planters in the faraway Black Belt.

Did the War Make Republicans?

Although my ancestors were Jackson Democrats at the start of the Civil War, many of the Davidsons and Deans became Republicans, and at least two, my great-uncle Julius Davidson and my grandfather Marvin McCoy (M.M.) Davidson were very active in the Republican Party (See Figure 16.2). Did the war make them Republicans?

In 1949, political scientist V.O. Key wrote, "Mountain Republicans in all southern states have a common origin. Before the war, the yeomen farmers of the hills were reluctant to abandon the Union for the cause of the planter and his slaves . . . the highland yeomanry did not want to fight a rich man's war."[6]

Many of the Unionists in the mountains moved to the Republican Party after the war. However, Union sympathizers in the mountains are by no means the entire story. Many mountain farmers fought with the Confederacy. Once committed, they likely remained Democratis, both because of the experiences of their early years and the reinforcing experience of the war.

The evidence for the Davidsons is clear: The war did not make them Republicans. They were Democrats after the war. A.S. even spent a term in the House of Representatives in 1878 as a Democrat. How and why did they make the switch to the Republican party? The Populist Revolt was the key.

Reconstruction and Redemption

After the Civil War, Southern legislatures set to work to impose a set of rules that would ensure white supremacy. Required to replace the secession constitution of 1861 with one reflecting the freedom of Blacks, to re-join the Union, Alabama state political leaders called a constitutional convention in 1865. Blacks could not vote, and all North Alabama counties sent Republican anti-Confederate or divided delegations to Montgomery, while all South Alabama counties save one Wiregrass county sent conservative, pro-Confederate delegations. The Federal Government rejected the 1865 constitution.[7] Undeterred, the legislature passed Black Codes in 1866, limiting the freedom of former slaves. Determined not to lose the peace after winning the war, the Union intervened forcefully in the politics of the defeated South on behalf of Blacks, including demanding voting systems that were in compliance with the Fifteenth Amendment. White Southerners were recalcitrant, and the imposition of a democratic society proved difficult.

While the Republican Reconstruction government empowered Blacks and established other democratic and economic reforms, its idealism was tempered by corruption. Democrats, labeling themselves Redeemers, depicted Republican corruption as worse than it was. They downplayed the reforms and the empowerment of Blacks, which the white supremacist Democrats wanted to undo. In addition, they engaged in a campaign of intimidation and violence, which the federal government thwarted using constitutional amendments and implementing laws enforced via the occupation by federal troops.

Many historians and political scientists treat the presidential election of 1876 as the critical juncture in which Union attempts to build a reformed South collapsed, allowing the construction of a Jim Crow regime and the virtual reenslavement of Blacks. Republican supporters of their presidential candidate, Rutherford B. Hayes, and Southern Democrats forged an informal agreement that mandated the withdrawal of the remaining federal troops from the South in return for Southern support for Hayes. Reconstruction ended.

Black historian W.E.B. Du Bois saw the juncture occurring between the election of 1866 and 1873 and in more comprehensive terms. "For a brief period—seven mystic years, the majority of thinking Americans of the North believed in the equal manhood of Negroes."[8] Unionists determined that the basic structure of Reconstruction would center on the integration of Blacks as equals into the political and social life of the nation. Republicans held large legislative majorities and moved swiftly to impose a strong Reconstruction on a resistant Southern elite.

Du Bois also saw the end of Reconstruction as less a result of sectional tensions and more a loss of faith brought about by the Panic of 1873. Economic hard times made it easier to blame Republicans, and they suffered large Congressional losses in 1874. "Then came in 1873–76 sudden and complete disillusion not at Negroes but at the world—at business, at work, at religion, at art. A bitter protest of Southern property reinforced Northern reaction; and while after long years the American world recovered in most matters, it has never yet quite understood why it could ever have thought that black men were altogether human."[9] America had awakened from the economic turmoil of the latter part of the 19th century into the long period of Jim Crow, during which racial issues were "settled" based on the understanding of the inferiority of Blacks in a rigid racial hierarchy.

Democrats regained control of the state legislature in Alabama and other Southern states in 1874. As we saw in the Gaston Beat in Sumter County, the Southern Democratic "Redeemers" engaged in massive intimidation, fraud, and violence against Black voters, enough to regain control of many Southern governments, including Alabama's.

In 1875, as soon as Reconstruction in the State was terminated, the Alabama Legislature passed a new Constitution that Auburn University history professor Wayne Flynt called "a reactionary document designed to overcome what whites perceived as the excesses of radical Republicans."[10] It segregated schools, constricted the franchise for Blacks, prohibited interracial marriage, and limited taxation by local units of government to reduce funds for schools and other state services, especially for Blacks. With the new constitution in place, the 1878 legislature was reduced to only eight Republicans and by 1880 only one Republican remained.

Reconstruction in Blount County

The postwar Appalachian landholding patterns differed in kind from Black Belt arrangements we explored for the Carrs and Larkins. The Black Belt postwar social structure in Sumter County consisted of educated whites such as the Carrs, and illiterate Blacks working as house servants or as tenants and field hands. There were few white tenants or yeoman farmers in the region. The county remained highly unequal in wealth and education after the war.

The restless Abraham Davidson had moved to Blount County during the war, taking up life as a farmer. A.S., his son, moved there as well, perhaps because of his wife's death in 1865. In the 1870 Census A.S. still listed himself as a potter. His life resumed as it would have been absent the war.

The residents of the region were far more equal economically than the inhabitants of Sumter and the Black Belt. A.S. Davidson's Blount County neighbors were farmers who generally owned their small farms. Tenant farming had become less common. The Blount County economic structure consisted of white yeoman farmers, both literate and illiterate, craftsmen such as blacksmiths and potters, and a smattering of better-off residents. The rural neighborhood could be classified as middle and working class, with substantial poverty and illiteracy.

A.S. Davidson's neighbors were almost all white. There were few Blacks listed in the Census, and those listed worked as house servants, living with a white family. A Black woman with a baby was listed as part of the household of Lynn Williams, a physician. A well-off farmer, Hiram Vaughn, listed a Black family with his household. That household was female-headed and consisted of a teenager and two infants. None of the Black house servants were listed as literate, and many of the white farmers and their wives could not read or write.[11]

Reconstruction violence in Appalachia took a different form from the process in the Black Belt. In the Black Belt, the Ku Klux Klan was an instrument wielded on behalf of planter elites to control Blacks. The Klan and other hate groups were active in Blount, with harassment and violence directed at Unionists as well as Blacks. The Blount Klan consisted of many former Confederate soldiers, most of whom acted as an unruly group of thugs, who gained control of the Blount County political machinery. Blount County Unionists requested aid from federal troops in Huntsville, and the governor of the state sent an investigator to examine Klan activity there. Nothing much changed, so citizens established anti-Klan vigilante groups and went so far as to threaten known Klan members. Klan activity declined in the 1870s after Congress passed the Anti-Klan Act and law enforcement improved.[12]

The Civil War and Reconstruction disrupted A.S. Davidson's life, but it was not the kind of disruption that affected planters and slaves in Sumter. The latter were forced to free slaves and screamed about the fear of "Black rule." A.S. owned no slaves to free and had no extensive landholdings to tend. He was a simple but highly skilled potter and returned to that trade after the war.

A.S.'s first wife, Julia Waldrop, who bore three children, died in 1865. Two years after Julia's death, A.S. married Ruth Whitt (1845–1922), and had 12 children with her, 2 of whom died in childhood of measles and croup. The last child born was my grandfather, Marvin McCoy (M.M.) Davidson.

A.S. expanded his pottery operation into a vibrant business, employing two other men. Students of folk pottery know the specific location of his pottery factory today. The site "is scattered with a wide assortment of ash-glazed pottery fragments."[13] A.S. lived in a settlement of craftsmen surrounded by yeoman farmers. Four nearby neighbors were potters. Others include a basketmaker, two blacksmiths, a carpenter, a gunsmith, and a grocer.

By 1880, A.S. listed his occupation as physician, although he never had formal medical education. He had earned a certificate from the county medical board sometime before 1878, when he served as president of the Blount County Medical Society. Success in pottery led A.S. Davidson to move from the yeoman farmer/craftsman class to the professional class, such as it existed in rural and sparsely populated Blount County.

Increasing Tensions between North and South

After "redemption," differences between the largely stagnant agricultural South Alabama and the more dynamic North began to spill over into political tensions. In the postwar period North Alabama experienced an industrial boom. The mineral belt, centering on the new town of Birmingham, was growing fast as the iron and steel industry developed.

The state constitution of the era provided at least one representative for each county. One of the mechanisms for increasing the representation of the interests of the north of the state was increasing the number of counties, important in both the State Senate and the House of Representatives. More population meant the potential for more representation, which became a major sore point between the Black Belt and the mountain region. In 1877, the legislature created Cullman County out of several North Alabama counties, mostly Blount and Winston. At the time of the Civil War, modern-day Cullman County was one of the wildest parts of the state, filled with squatters, poor farmers, Union supporters, and deserters. After the war, the area had begun to attract immigrants from Germany, Northern states, and from within the state. These new residents often settled on land granted to railroads; the railroads sold the granted land to immigrant location companies, who subdivided it. This system added to the increasing hostility of farmers toward railroads, seeing the scheme as one enriching the railroad barons at the expense of the locals.

The fortuitous location of iron ore and coal in Alabama's mineral belt led to an industrial boom centered on Birmingham. The boom brought new industrialists—owners and operators of the mines, iron smelters, and steel mills, who came to be called "Big Mules." The Big Mules naturally allied with Black Belt planters—the Bourbons—and both objected to the new county. It would add representation for the small farmers and craftsmen that inhabited the region. These poorer citizens were likely to be hostile to the emerging planter–industrialist alliance. One of the better-off opponents commented on the poverty in the county by haughtily claiming, "It would be better to build a poorhouse at Cullman instead of a courthouse."[14]

A.S. Davidson served in the Alabama State Legislature in 1878 as a Democrat, dealing with the spillover effects of the new county, with most controversy centering on moving the Blount County Seat further from the boundary of the new county.[15]

Although Blount remained mostly an agricultural county in the postwar period, the southern part of the county was increasingly drawn into the industrial and mining orbit centering on nearby Birmingham. Southern Blount County was ripe for mining booms.

The new industrialization also brought labor as a new force in North Alabama politics. Labor issues infused new energy into the controversy surrounding the convict labor system. Mine owners leased convicts, usually Black, who were often convicted on flimsy evidence. These men were sent from their home counties to work in mines in appalling conditions. Blacks were deeply opposed to the system, which was cruel, inhumane, and abused.

The mostly white free labor system joined Blacks in opposition to the convict labor system. Companies used the system to keep wage rates low and discourage unionization of the mines. Some local papers in Blount reacted with a distinct prolabor stance. In 1888, the *Blount County News-Advocate* described the town of Warrior, on the boundary between Blount and Jefferson Counties, as a boomtown with rapidly increasing real estate prices. The town was shipping great amounts of coal down the Black Warrior River to the mills in Birmingham. "All the mines are working full time, except the Warrior Coal & Coke Co., and the only reason it is not is the fact that the company is working convicts. All the free laborers have left the company."[16]

A.S.'s son, Tyre Harbin Davidson served as a Blount County state representative in 1890–91. In alliance with his uncle, Silas C. Davidson, publisher of the *Warrior Enterprise*, Tyre Harbin and a fellow legislator tried to get two new counties created.[17] They argued that population growth and diverging interests of southern Blount County justified the move. Southern Blount was increasingly industrial, while northern Blount County was still strongly agricultural in outlook. South Alabama legislators objected to adding representation to the north, and were able to kill the bill.

In the 1880s, North Alabama was growing, while South Alabama stagnated, leading to a shift in the balance of representation over time. Industrial free labor was confined almost exclusively to North Alabama, except for the shipyards in Mobile. South Alabama remained almost exclusively agrarian. In 1890, South Alabama Democrats ran on a platform of leaving the number of counties unchanged because any additional counties, hence representatives, would be added in the North Alabama mineral belt. Given the power of the Black Belt, it is not surprising that Tyre Harbin and Silas failed.

CHAPTER 10

"The Blowhard of Blount"

In 1878 John Albert Dean was elected as Blount County Tax Assessor in a close and contested election. He served in that office for 14 years, between 1878 and 1892. Dean regularly traversed the county to aid landowners in determining their land assessments necessary for calculating tax bills. It was a period of increasing hardships for Southern and Western farmers, with crop prices declining and loans for land and tools expensive.

No local official knew more about the plight of yeoman and tenant farmers than the county tax assessor. Between February and April of each year, Dean traveled to 33 different county locations, advertising in local newspapers where he would be. How better to understand the financial plights of farmers than to calculate the value of their property?

Across the West and South, the quickly monopolizing railroads had become targets of a coalition of interests harmed by their price-fixing policies. This discontent led to the Interstate Commerce Act regulating railroads in 1887, the first major regulatory act by the federal government.[1]

Usually, tax assessors accepted the estimates of the land values claimed by the railroads without serious questioning. In 1885 Dean assessed land owned by the Louisville and Nashville Railroad (L&N) at an exorbitant $1.00 per acre for rugged rural land worthless for agriculture (Figure 10.1).[2] The value of agricultural land in Blount County at the time averaged $4.00 per acre.[3] Assessed value was much less—today it is 20% of market value ($0.80, in this case).[4] It was lower in 1885 due to limitations set by the 1875 "Redemption Constitution," which kept taxes low and government weak. L&N was used to even lower assessments because of its political influence. The railroad challenged the assessment because it meant higher taxes. The Blount County Commissioners' Court, doubtless grasping which way the winds were blowing, upheld Dean's judgment.[5]

Figure 10.1   The Louisville and Nashville Railroad Traverses Sand Mountain
Source: Wade Hall Postcard Collection, Troy University Libraries [https://digital.archives.
alabama.gov/digital/collection/troy2/id/1938/].

With that action, Dean made a politically useful corporate enemy, and became the leading proponent of economic and agrarian reform in Blount County. He was by no means the only advocate, but he was a central figure in the agrarian revolt.

Agricultural Turmoil and Discontent in the Upcountry

The agrarian turmoil in the upcountry was a consequence of the close relationship between the Conservative or Bourbon faction of the Alabama Democratic Party and the national "Gold Democrats." The Gold Democrats were conservative on monetary policy, with little distance between them and the conservative business-oriented Republican Party. The hard money policies of the Republicans and the Gold Democrats led to tight money and deflation that harmed the farm economy in the West and South because so many farmers were debtors.

The Bourbon faction came to power by "redeeming" the South from the alleged corruption of Blacks, carpetbaggers and the despised scalawags, traitors to the Southern cause in the minds of the Redeemers. Whatever the epithets coming from the Redeemers and their allies in extralegal organizations such as the Ku Klux Klan and the Knights of the White Camellia, many "scalawags" were Unionists who had never joined the Confederate cause. Carpetbaggers, also Republicans, came from the North both for opportunistic and idealistic reasons, hoping to bring prosperity and democracy to former slaves. Generally representing planters, the Bourbon faction did little to alleviate the growing crisis on the farm.

Post–Civil War America was a period of rampant speculation, especially in railroads, resulting in a series of economic bubbles, and severe economic recessions in 1873, 1887, 1891, and 1893. During the Civil War, the national government had issued paper money—generally called greenbacks—that was not backed by gold. Postwar monetary policy was based on returning to the gold standard, a policy that both political parties backed. This strategy of tying the issuance of money to gold in the time of an expanding economy as the industrial revolution proceeded caused the value of money to increase over time. Indebted farmers were particularly hard-hit by both the trend of increasingly valuable money and the repetitive speculative crashes.

Hard times in American farm country generated a broad movement of discontent, and a series of organizations devoted to the improvement of the conditions of farmers proliferated. The first of these was the Grange, which started in the Midwest in the 1870s and spread outward. The Grange was a self-help organization for farmers featuring local branches. It served somewhat as a think tank with a mass membership and decentralized information delivery system. It circulated newsletters, sponsored regular periodicals, and hosted lecturers. Through its local branches the Grange sponsored cooperative buying and selling to lower the prices of supplies and the oligopolist fertilizer market. It was decidedly apolitical, and it sponsored both white and Black local cooperatives.

As effective as the Grange was at transmitting agricultural information and setting up cooperatives to avoid merchant price gouging, it did not solve the many farm problems that could only be addressed through politics. As a consequence, farmers turned to more political and more radical organizations, the Agricultural Wheel and the critically important Farmers' Alliance.[6]

The Farmers' Alliance formed in Lampasas, Texas, in 1876; by the late 1880s the Alliance had developed a program of regulatory and monetary reform including an end to the gold standard. Like the Grange, the Alliance developed a network of cooperatives to buy farming supplies and seed wholesale. Its subtreasury plan to store agricultural output and sell it when prices increased was a precursor of New Deal agricultural policies.

The Alliance swept out of Texas, sending lecturers across the country. Alliance lecturers were filled with the zeal of itinerant preachers backed up by the knowledge of the capitalist system's effect on the impoverishment of the yeoman farmer. It carried with it an activist political philosophy and a willingness to engage in the political process.

The Texans found fertile ground in the North Alabama hills and in the Wiregrass. They created local affiliates and parallel Colored Farmers' Alliance chapters that exchanged ideas with the white chapters and opened the possibility of Black-white alliances around class politics.[7]

Unlike the nonpartisan Grange, the Alliance was not fearful of engaging in politics, and endorsed candidates at both the national and state levels. As political scientist Elizabeth Sanders writes, the political movement that grew out of the Alliance cooperative network "required broad collaboration across occupational lines. Alliance officials now urged an outreach to the Colored Farmers' Alliance Members, and in 1891–92 it was possible to envision a new era in southern race relations, one based on a politicized movement of *farmers* as a class."[8] The Alliance put aside racial demagoguery for an ideology based on class, advocating for farmers and laborers and attacking the planters, bankers, and railroads.

In Alabama the Alliance formed a faction within the Democratic Party and called themselves Jeffersonian Democrats. The Jeffersonians were a direct challenge to the Regular Bourbon Democrats. In 1890 they endorsed for governor Reuben Kolb, former state agriculture commissioner and a participant in the Grange and the Alliance. The Jeffersonians fielded a slate of candidates within the Democratic Party for state legislature as well. Going into the convention, Kolb had a large lead, but after multiple ballots Bourbon Thomas G. Jones won the nomination and the governorship. Even though the balloting process at the convention was corrupt, Kolb played good sport and endorsed Jones but began to make plans to run in 1892; Jones planned to run again as well.

As the leading scholar on the agrarian revolt in Alabama summarized, "The farmers [in 1890] had made a frontal assault on the entrenched bourbons" and "the conservative Democrats had resorted to desperate political maneuvering—unprecedented since Reconstruction—to maintain their power structure."[9] Alliance-endorsed candidates won a majority in the State House of Representatives and did well in the Senate.

In December of 1890, the Farmers' Alliance, having done so well in endorsing candidates in numerous states in the election of that year, gathered in Ocala, Florida, and issued the "Ocala Demands."[10] The Alliance transformed itself into the Peoples' Party (also known as the Populist Party), and fielded candidates under that banner in 1892. In Alabama the Jeffersonian Democrats fused with the Peoples' Party for electoral purposes while remaining within the Democratic Party. This would prove to be a temporary resting position.

The Populist Blowhards

On May 1, 1892, the Blount County Democratic Convention convened at Blountsville. The two contending Democratic factions, the Conservative or Bourbon faction, which held the party machinery in the county, and the insurgent Jeffersonians, were there in full force. These two factions sparred for control of the county delegations to the State and Congressional District Conventions. The Bourbons supported aristocratic Thomas G. Jones (no relation; our Joneses were anything but aristocratic) for governor, while the insurgents supported Reuben Kolb in his second try for the governorship.

The question for the County convention centered on the allocation of delegates from eight contested electoral beats (precincts). The factions had won approximately equal delegates in the uncontested beats. The boisterous convention ran late into the night of May 12, resumed the next day, and continued through until 3 the next afternoon.[11] The Jeffersonians, led by John Albert Dean, vigorously challenged Bourbon Regulars and their corrupt precinct-level practices.

The *Birmingham News*, a staunch supporter of the Bourbon regulars, wrote, "The straight-out Jones (Regular) Democrats control everything and are willing to make all fair concessions, but John A. Dean and Lawyer [J.P.] Lockwood are kicking up a fuss. The blowhards of Blount are dying hard, but die they must."[12]

But the blowhards did not die. Working against the odds, the Jeffersonian blowhards were able to achieve an equal division of the delegations to the State and Congressional District Democratic Conventions between the supporters of Kolb and Jones. Dean was selected to attend both the District and the State Conventions; Lockwood went to the State Convention.

The Election of 1892

If there was confusion over the nature of the 1890 election, the same was not true of 1892. The race would be a repeat of 1890, with Jones representing the planters and their new allies from the Birmingham industrial class, the so-called Big Mules. Jones made clear that the clarion call of white supremacy would again be the Conservatives' main theme. In a well-circulated speech before the State Convention, Governor Jones emphasized that "the walls of our civilization . . . can be guarded only by a unified white race."[13]

Kolb was no flaming liberal on the race issue, but he did recognize the advantage of appealing to the Black voter. The Jeffersonians, expecting Bourbon shenanigans at the upcoming convention, prepared a platform that involved not only liberal economic policies but also included Black voting rights and educational improvements, a direct appeal to enfranchised freedmen. Similar interracial coalitions were forged in other Southern states, threatening Bourbon rule throughout the South.

In September, county delegates traveled to the state Democratic Convention in Montgomery. Fresh from the vigorous Blount County Democratic delegate fight, John Albert Dean and J.P. Lockwood joined a Blount delegation split equally between Conservative Regulars and Jeffersonians. Statewide, the county conventions sent more Kolb than Jones delegates, setting the stage for a Kolb victory. Instead, using a set of corrupt procedures, the Regulars engineered a credentials convention fight that excluded enough Kolb delegates to ensure Jones's renomination.

At this point, the Jeffersonians left the Democratic convention and met separately, nominating Kolb for governor. They would run as a separate political party in the August general election, in alliance with the Populists and Republicans.

The Bourbon Regular Democratic Regular Bourbon faction wrote a typical Bourbon white supremacist platform that explicitly included the aim of voter suppression. The Bourbons made no secret of their desire to make it difficult for Blacks (and the poor and illiterate upland Jeffersonians) to vote, adopting a plank that urged the passage of election laws that would "secure the government of the State in the hands of the intelligent and the virtuous."[14] The "intelligent and virtuous" were none other than the Black Belt planters. According to the Bourbons, the planter oligarchy would represent the interests of the state, and would not succumb to the whims of the uneducated poor farmers and Blacks.

Kolb's acceptance speech to the Jeffersonians was a clear attempt to shore up the Populist coalition based on agrarian reformist whites and Blacks. It included:[15]

• Protection of Negroes in their legal rights
• A liberal public school system;
• Equitable taxation on property;
• Opposition to trusts;
• Prohibition of competition between convict and free labor;
• Expansion of the currency and the unlimited coinage of free silver;
• A graduated federal income tax.

Many of these elements were from the national Populist program, but some were specific to Alabama and the South, such as the protection of Black rights and the protection of free labor by ending the convict leasing system. The platform included the "Negro Plank," which is worth stating in full: "We favor the protection of the colored race in their political rights and should afford them encouragement and aid in the attainment of higher civilization and citizenship, so that through the means of kindness, a better understanding and more satisfactory condition may exist between the races."[16] There were limits however to the equality. The platform also proposed a primary system to break the control of the Democratic Party by the Regulars but limited it to whites. A major reason was to keep Bourbons from winning primaries using the voter suppression techniques of the Black Belt, but racism played role as well.

The Republicans and Populists endorsed Kolb and the Jeffersonian candidates in a "fusion" ticket, and they did so around a strongly progressive platform that appealed not only to white yeoman farmers, tenants, and sharecroppers but also to Blacks and the incipient labor movement in the industrial belt.

The Populist label of the 1890s carried few of the connotations of the term today. Its supporters were culturally religious, prohibitionist, and anti-immigration. At the same time, they stood for fair elections and better treatment of Blacks, and offered a strongly progressive economic program. Their rhetoric and platform included language attacking the moneyed classes and spoke directly to the "common man." Populists in the 1890s rejected conservative economic policies, racism, and white supremacy.

Bourbon Democrats continually waved the bloody flag of the Confederacy, reminding the yeoman farmers of their sacrifices in the war. For most small farmers, Redemption seemed far in the past; the immediate issue was the farm crisis. The Bourbons insisted that party loyalty was necessary to ensure white supremacy, reserving special ire for the Negro Plank.

During the campaign, the Jeffersonian Democrats and their Populist and Republican allies pursued a politics of economics, stressing the hard economic times and programs to alleviate it. The Populist coalition was diverse—it was cross-racial and preached racial toleration and even kindness. It appealed to the economic interests of small farmers, miners, and city laborers. It was, however, anti-immigrant. To the Jeffersonians, white supremacy was insufficient to keep the Democratic Party intact, and it proposed reforms that would limit Democratic dominance. The one-note Democratic Regulars responded with a politics of race, urging the recalcitrant reformers to return to the white supremacist fold.[17]

For a brief period during the 1890s, class interests trumped status politics and white supremacy. Perhaps it was the hard times of the deep depression, and the primacy of white supremacy would have returned as normal afterward. Or perhaps a different trajectory would have been possible had Kolb been elected. But that did not happen.

The reported election results were much closer than the major Alabama newspapers had estimated on election night. The *Birmingham News*, which spoke for the "Big Mules" faction of the Democratic Party (and continued to do so into the 1960s), trumpeted before the count was finished, "Jones' Majority Will Hardly Fall below 30,000." Even that was a smaller majority than the newspaper had predicted earlier.[18] The official results were a 10,000-vote plurality for Jones.

The results were highly suspect, and the prevailing view of historians is that the election was stolen from Kolb. As historian William Rogers put it, "It seems certain, on the basis of available evidence, that Kolb was the legitimately elected governor but was counted out in the black belt."[19] The evidence of fraud comes from field reports, the implausibly large Black vote for Jones in the Black Belt counties; the correspondence between Regular Democratic control of the county election machinery, and the improbably large Democratic majorities.

The 1892 election was a classic class-based confrontation: the antidemocratic oligarchs of the plantations and the industrial corporations on the one hand, and the raucous unstable democracy of the Populist cross-race coalition on the other. Underlying this class clash was the grievance politics of white supremacy and the Lost Cause used effectively by the Bourbon oligarchs to undermine the Populist coalition. Even this was not enough: only blatant election cheating brought the Bourbons victory.

Kolb Comes to Blount County

In late August 1893, Reuben Kolb came to the village of Oneonta, the county seat of Blount County. Kolb came at the invitation of his friend John Dean to give a speech at a political rally in the courthouse. Dean had recently been elected County Circuit Court Clerk as a well-known Jeffersonian, and had asked Kolb to stay with him for several days. Dean served on the Jeffersonian State Executive Committee, and the committee was to meet in September. Doubtless the two discussed strategies for the upcoming 1894 gubernatorial and legislative elections.

John Dean was a natural host for Reuben Kolb, as he was still the most strident Jeffersonian in Blount County. His political career was intimately bound with Kolb's and it followed the rise and fall of Jeffersonian Democracy and Populism in Alabama.

In 1892 Kolb had carried the county by a solid majority, and was enormously popular there. He still was in 1893, and Kolb addressed a large crowd at the courthouse, with "every seat being occupied, and the aisles were filled with those who couldn't find seats," wrote Kolb's overtly hostile hometown newspaper, the Eufaula *News-Dispatch*.

Kolb's speech, part of a statewide tour to build support for a run for governor again in 1894, was a set of complaints about the corrupt conduct of Democratic Party leaders in the election of 1892. Kolb was denied the Democratic Party nomination for governor in 1890 even though he had the largest number of delegates. Then he was defrauded in the Democratic Convention and electorially in the 1892 governor's race. The Bourbon cheating in the count of county delegates in the State Convention led to the Jeffersonian-Populist-Republican fusion ticket, which was subsequently defrauded in the general election.

Kolb supported his complaint with a table of votes for each county showing his estimates of the cheating that took place in the counties where the Conservative faction controlled the election machinery. His Bourbon-supporting hometown newspaper had little patience with his argument. "Honest, God-fearing people on both sides are sick and tired of political juggling and fratricidal strife, and desire its cessation."[20]

The Jeffersonians Persist

In the aftermath of 1892 businessmen hoped that the state would forget the wounds that the election had laid bare.[21] However, the political conflict was too deep to be dismissed easily. The Jeffersonians had offered as liberal a platform for Blacks as they thought possible, although it did contain elements that were not favorable to Blacks, especially the white primary. The Populists added a strong call for "free and fair elections" to their policy priorities, and indeed it was election reform that more than any other single issue held the diverse coalition together. Moreover, the steep recession of 1893 and the coal miners' massive strike that year would add to the Populist economic critique of the Bourbon Democrats.

Bourbon Democrats, seeing a continuing Populist threat because of the potential of fusion between Populists and white and Black Republicans, called for a new constitution based on the 1890 Mississippi segregationist constitution. Jeffersonians and Populists opposed legislation designed to call a referendum on the matter and blocked it. The Conservative Democrats then enacted the harsh Sayre Law in 1893, a complex piece of legislation designed to discourage voting. It required registration in May, which was difficult for farmers because it was planting season and was usually rainy, making the poor roads muddy and often impassable. The law required the adoption of the Australian ballot, which was secret but listed candidates for an office alphabetically, without party affiliation and without party symbol. The earlier party list ballot put party symbols above lists of candidates to designate party affiliations of candidates. These symbols served as guides for voters who could not read. The Australian ballot precluded the party list system, effectively eliminating many illiterate Black voters and a good number of white potential Populist supporters.[22]

Was Kolb Cheated Out of the Two Elections?

On December 30, 1893, the Jeffersonian Democrats of Blount County held a mass meeting to select delegates to the State Convention to be held in February

1894 in Birmingham. In that meeting my great-grandfather A.S. Davidson, the chair of the meeting, presided over the appointment of his son, Tyre Harbin Davidson, and my great-grandfather John Albert Dean as delegates to the State Democratic Convention. The convention instructed that the delegation "vote for the old State ticket, known as the 'Kolb ticket.'"[23]

The convention then heard from a visitor from Texas about the reform movement in that state. The Texas visitor, an Alliance man, was part of the generalized reform movement spreading across the nation. Reformers were interconnected across the country through pro-reform newspapers and traveling representatives, building a powerful movement to challenge the businessmen and Southern planters of the Gilded Age.

In the February Jeffersonian State Convention in Birmingham, the Jeffersonians met, fused with the Populists, jointly nominating Kolb, with the enthusiastic support of the Blount delegation. The Jeffersonians and Populists had hoped for a fusion with the Republicans, but the Republicans wanted to maintain themselves as a distinct party. Nevertheless, they endorsed Kolb as well.

In both 1892 and 1894, the Conservative Bourbon Democrats faced serious social upheaval and a unified front of allies agreeing to oppose almost everything for which the Bourbons stood. In 1894 they returned to the same playbook as in 1892: campaign on white supremacy and the threat of Black dominance. When that was not enough, the Conservatives cheated by all ways possible: "fraud, intimidation, bribery, violence, and terror."[24] Bourbon activist, Civil War hero, and future governor William Oates urged electoral cheating in 1892. He acknowledged, "I told them to go to it, boys, count them out. . . . We had to do it. Unfortunately, I say it was a necessity. We could not stop ourselves."[25] The Sayre Law proved effective in allowing the Democrats to win with legalized voter suppression techniques and less corruption.

In 1894 Oates was the Democratic candidate for governor. He won the election with huge majorities from Black Belt counties, with a bigger majority than the Democrats achieved in 1892. Turnout was considerably lower, doubtless due to the Sayre Law and continuing election fraud. As in 1892, Kolb won in counties where whites were in the majority but lost in counties where Blacks were in the majority. This did not indicate lack of support for Kolb in those counties; rather it demarked counties where Bourbon cheating was rampant, as election officials such as James Powell Carr of Sumter County counted out Black votes.

I've examined the figures for the elections of 1892 and 1894, using newspaper reports, and indeed the results are suspect.[26] In the election of 1892, if one were to believe the reported results, many Black voters in Black Belt counties seem to have voted against their own interests by supporting the Bourbon Regular Democrats so heavily. This pattern indicates voter intimidation, suppression, or Oates-style counting out ballots in a pattern similar to the Redemption votes in the 1870s.

This inference is bolstered by an examination of which faction controlled the election machinery. Where the Bourbon Regular Democrats held firm control of the party machinery in 1892, that faction did better than expected. In urban Montgomery County, the fusion ticket could muster only 15% of the vote; in Wilcox County, 12%; and in Lowndes County, 30%.

On the other hand, in 1892 the Populist-Jeffersonian fusion ticket did exceptionally well where the Bourbon Regular Democrats lost control of the election machinery. In particular, in heavily Black Macon County, where Tuskegee Institute is located, Kolb won 64% of the vote. Populists were strong in Black Belt Choctaw County, and won an identical 64%. Some other heavily Black counties managed to produce strong votes for the fusionists, even in Sumter, which offered up 43% of its voters to Kolb.

My analysis indicates that the cheating continued into 1894, but voter suppression through the Sayre Law made direct cheating less necessary. Figure 10.2 compares the percentage received by Kolb in 1894 with those received in 1892, by county. The line on the graph represents the best-fit line, which predicts the 1894 county results from those tabulated in 1892. Overall turnout declined, likely due to the Sayre Law designed to discourage Blacks and poor whites from voting. The important element of the graph is the disproportionate number of Black Belt counties falling below the line—the expected percentage based on the 1892 vote.[27] Nine of the 13 Black Belt counties fell below the line. Over two-thirds of Black Belt counties *reduced* the percentage of voters supporting the candidate most favorable to Blacks. That could only happen with increased suppresson and intimidation of Black voters.

A second feature is once again control of the election machinery. Where the Bourbon Regular Democrats controlled the election machinery, Oates did better, even adjusting for 1892 votes. In Macon, the Bourbon Regular Democrat seized control of the county, and the percentage voting for the Populist fusion ticket that year plummeted from 64% to 17%. In Sumter County, Kolb's percentage dropped from 43% to 18%; in Lowndes County from 30% to 7%. In

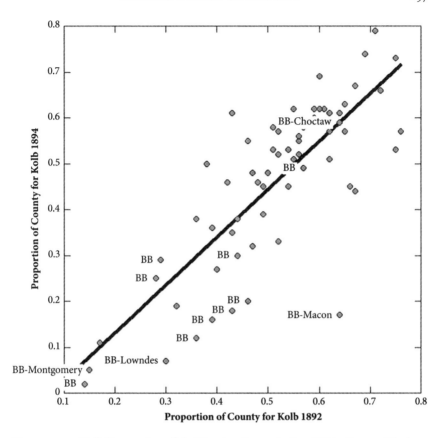

Figure 10.2 Kolb Proportion of the Vote in 1892 and 1894. BB indicates a Black Belt county.

Source: Author's graph; data sources: "The Official Vote," *Livingston Journal*, August 24, 1894.

Choctaw, where the Jeffersonians remained in control of the election machinery, Kolb won the county easily, dropping only from 64% to 59%. In the mountain counties, Kolb held a similar percentage of the votes as in 1892, but with fewer votes cast.

Even where voting was already suppressed, the Bourbon Regular Democrats were able to suppress it even more. In populous Montgomery, the support for the Populists fell from 15% to 5%. In Dallas County (Selma) reformers went from a paltry 14% of the vote to a vanishingly small 2%. Little wonder that the Populists and Republicans called for free ballots and an open count as a fundamental part of their platform for 1896.

The incidence of blatant cheating in the Black Belt was astounding. In the election of 1892, 11 of the 12 Black Belt counties where the Black population exceeded the white, the votes for the Bourbon Jones exceeded the white male population.[28] Bourbons claimed this was because Blacks wanted to be ruled by whites, but this is highly doubtful.

How Voting Suppression Works

For some time, political scientists have recognized that high turnout elections do not benefit one party over the other, because the factors that mobilize one party's supporters also mobilize the other party's supporters.[29] Mobilization may not work as well as parties think, but this well-supported observation does not rule out voter suppression if it can be aimed at targeted groups.

Voter suppression works cumulatively—in the 19th century and today. The first rule of voter suppression is to shrink the electorate to make it more manageable. The second rule is to put as many roadblocks in the way of the opposing party as possible. One roadblock may not suppress opponents, but a cumulative set of roadblocks may well do so.

The Sayre Law was crafted to suppress votes of Blacks without running afoul of the 15th Amendment. That meant and still means finding factors that are correlated with race to limit Black voting—such as requiring a ballot that is very difficult for illiterate citizens to master. This was the case for freedmen who seldom attended school due to farm duties and lack of access. Vote suppression via the Sayre Act did lower voting among Blacks and poor whites. In particular, the adoption of the Australian ballot, with its failure to list candidates by party affiliation, confused voters intending to vote for Kolb. A Blount County newspaper reported that many "Kolb people through a misunderstanding and ignorance of the new election law voted the first name on their ticket and failed to mark the others."[30] This led to "roll off," in which voters fail to mark their ballots for offices further down the ballot, behavior encouraged by the Australian ballot.[31] Apparently, voters thought they were voting a party-line ballot as they had before. As a consequence, the Republican-Jeffersonian fusion ticket did worse on down ballot offices than otherwise would have been expected.

Even if suppression had decreased all votes similarly, that would have favored the Bourbons *because they needed to cheat on fewer votes.* Governments that suppress votes, even if that suppression affects both parties equally, have needed to cheat less in counting the votes because fewer ballots must be changed or discarded. Measures that expand the suffrage, such as same-day registration, make successful fraud more difficult. When states introduce measures that shrink the electorate, even if the measure is fair, fraud is more likely to succeed should it occur.

Even with the vote fraud in 1894 the fusion ticket between Populists and Republicans won two North Alabama Congressional districts and gained control of some county governments in the North Alabama hills and the Wiregrass in Southeast Alabama. It was not enough, and Populism went into decline.

CHAPTER II

"Our Demosthenes"

On July 4, 1896, John Albert Dean, chairman of the Blount County People's Party Campaign Committee, sponsored a big barbeque to celebrate Independence Day: 1,800 pounds of beef, kid, and mutton were barbequed the day before, stands were erected, and a band from a local college was engaged.

Some 2,500 were in attendance to hear the reform party of Blount, again in allegiance with Republicans, to heap "abuse, slander, and vilification" on the Democratic Party. According to the *Blount County News-Dispatch*, which supported the Democratic Party, the speakers were "third class," except for Julius W. Davidson, "our Demosthenes."[1]

Julius, my grandfather's older brother and my great-uncle, was fast becoming a political star in the region. A talented orator, he was already one of the region's best lawyers, and he was politically ambitious. Having read law with an uncle in Birmingham, he opened a law practice in Oneonta with a Birmingham judge in 1892, when he was 23.

"A Free Vote and an Open Count"

Dean's barbeque celebration was a follow-up to the Populist County Convention that had occurred a month before. Some 900 enthusiastic Blount County residents had gathered at the courthouse in Oneonta to approve a fusion slate of county officials and to choose delegates to the State Senatorial Convention who would select a candidate for the state senator for the region.

The Blount County residents attending the County Convention had made a firm break. They had left the Democratic Party; they no longer called themselves Jeffersonians. They were now Populists.

The not entirely objective correspondent from *Peoples Weekly Tribune*, Birmingham's Populist newspaper edited by Reuben Kolb, was ecstatic to see the enthusiasm of the crowd. He described it as a "grand political meeting [with] the spacious halls of her Court house filled to over-flowing." At 10 o'clock the members of the Convention assembled while a band "made melodious the occasion, the whole band was composed of farmer boys of [the] North Alabama Hills."[2]

Two of the leading Populist families of Blount, the Davidsons and the Deans, dominated the convention. Former Oneonta mayor and A.S.'s brother, John Wesley Davidson, gave the welcoming remarks to the crowd.[3] The convention appointed Tyre Harbin Davidson, who had been the County's state representative in 1890–1891 and was currently Probate Judge of Blount, to the Senatorial District Conference Committee. Tyre Harbin was half-brother to Julius and my grandfather, M.M. Davidson. He was older half-brother to A.S. Davidson's sons and daughters. His nieces and nephews (my mother and aunts and uncle) called him "Uncle Judge."

E.O. Dean, John Albert Dean's younger brother and a justice of the peace, was instrumental in organizing the Convention and was chosen as secretary. The Convention chose John Albert Dean as its delegate to the Senatorial Convention to be held a week later to choose the fusion candidate for state senate. The convention selected up-and-coming Julius Davidson as Chairman of the Blount County's delegation to the Populist State Senatorial Convention and as the county's candidate for state representative.

Alabama Populists had agreed to fuse with the Republicans in an effort once again to defeat the Bourbon Democrats. The Populists nominated candidates for some offices, and the Republicans for others. Representatives from the County Republican Party recommended a slate of candidates to the Populists. It was clear that the two parties had developed a county fusion slate beforehand, and the Blount Populists accepted the Republican slate without dissent.

In his closing speech, John Wesley Davidson urged unity with the Republicans. The Republican County Chairman, who was in attendance, reciprocated, pledging that Blount Republicans would support the Populists. In an obvious reference to the massive vote suppression and outright fraud of the 1892 and 1894 elections, he guaranteed that the party's members "are heartily into the fight for a free ballot and an open count."[4]

The 1896 Election

Before 1896, the national Democratic Party hewed to economic policies that resembled those that the national Republicans advocated. Represented by Grover Cleveland, the "Gold Wing" of the party stood for locking the dollar to the gold standard. This hard money policy resulted in a continuing deflation that was good for bankers but hard on borrowers and consumers, especially farmers. Both parties supported internal Hamilton-style infrastructure investments, particularly for railroads.

Even as business gained enormous power, neither party pushed very hard to regulate convict labor or conditions in factories, and neither pushed to end the monopoly power of the industrial magnates in iron and steel, oil, tobacco, and fertilizers. When there was movement, it involved both parties—the Cleveland administration passed the Interstate Commerce Act regulating railroad rates, and the Republican Benjamin Harrison administration enacted the Sherman Anti-Trust Act. Then stasis returned; it took 10 years before the Sherman was used against trusts.

These economic conditions and the lack of interest by either party to respond to agrarian and labor discontent led to vibrant social movements in the West and South. The Greenbacks argued for the issuance of paper dollars not tied to gold; the Silverites demanded bimetallism, with both gold and silver backing the currency; the Socialists demanded a series of regulatory reforms and social benefits centered on the working-class misery in cities. The Populist Party emerged from the agricultural reform movement and integrated the bubbling issues left unaddressed by the two-party system into a wholistic reform agenda.

A political system as unrepresentative as the two-party system was in the 1890s was ripe for change, and Populism was the vehicle for that change.

Political scientists see 1896 as a critical election—"a type of election in which there occurs a sharp and durable electoral realignment between parties."[5] The notion of single realigning elections has not held up to extensive empirical scrutiny, partly because electoral change is spread out over time and among states.[6] The churning politics that had been occurring in the states, especially the West and South, in the years before the realignment is a case in point. There is little doubt, though, that the 1896 presidential election was a major component of the complex process.

These were confusing times, with shifting alliances that appeared in different guises in the various Southern states but had similar underpinnings. The party system in the United States was far more fragile than it seemed. Late in the game, the Democrats nominated the bimetallist William Jennings Bryan in an obvious attempt to attract Populist votes. This was a serious dilemma for the Populists, who had to decide whether to support the Democrats or field their own ticket.

Among the as they had planned most committed Populists there was a great deal of hostility toward the Democrats, but the pragmatists wanted to fuse with the Democrats nationally, endorsing the full Democratic ticket. At their national convention the Populists endorsed Bryan but refused to endorse the vice presidential candidate, Arthur Sewall, a Gold Democrat, and nominated instead the Georgia Populist Tom Watson for vice president. Alabama and Georgia Populists followed suit.

This led to a revolt by the two leading Populists in Alabama, Reuben Kolb and P.G. Bowman, who vowed to support the full Democratic ticket. On October 24, the Populist State Executive Committee met, replacing both Kolb and Bowman on the Executive Committee with M.W. Howard, a Populist congressman, and Julius Davidson. The already-strong anti-Democratic sentiment among Populists exploded at the State Convention; Alabama Populists wanted a continued fusion with the Republicans.[7]

The nomination of Bryan made the Populist-Republican fusion impossible for the national ticket. In state politics, Populists fused with Republicans in the South, but in the North and West they allied with the Democrats. In national politics, the Populists chose a separate slate featuring the Democrat Bryan and Populist Watson.

In Alabama, Georgia, and other Southern states Populists ran a fusion ticket with the Republicans at the state level but not at the national level. This caused considerable confusion for both Populists and Republicans. The two parties could agree primarily only on two issues, electoral reform and Black rights, but bimetallism was key at the national level. On this issue, the Populists differed profoundly with the Republicans.

One committed Democrat wrote his local paper about this confusion:

> I have asked at least a dozen Populites [term used for Populists, as was Pops] about their platform, and all they can tell me is "a free ballot and a fair count." A very reliable old negro in this beat told me that "Pops" were telling the negroes if Johnston [Democratic candidate for governor] won they would never be allowed

to vote again. He said they told him if the Democrats got in power this time, they would disenfranchise the "poor white folks and the negroes."[8]

The Populist message as interpreted by the reliable old Negro turned out to be quite astute. Led by the Bourbons Democrats, the full disenfranchisement of Blacks in Alabama elections would be accomplished in just a few years.

Defeat of the Populists

By 1896, the Alabama Jeffersonian Democrats had moved to the Populist Party, which went into fusion with the Republicans; both groups appealed to Blacks but still lost with huge majorities supporting Democrats in the Black Belt due to massive vote fraud. Turnout in the August governor's race was lower than in 1894 as the Sayre Law and voter fraud in the Black Belt discouraged participation by upland farmers; the Populist strongholds of Blount, Walker, and Winston even went for the Democrats. Joseph Johnston, who had participated in the machinations of the Democrats in the earlier elections, ran for governor as a reformist Democrat. He cherry-picked a few parts of the Populist platform to attract Populist votes, but he kept intact the white supremacy of the traditional Democrats.

The national Democratic-Populist ticket lost soundly in the presidential election of 1896. The white supremacist Democrat Johnston won the governorship and won reelection easily in 1898 against a Populist-Republican fusion ticket. The fate of Populism both nationally and locally was sealed.

The big election news in 1898 was not from Alabama, but from North Carolina. The Scottsboro, Alabama, *Citizen*, using language from an earlier period, blared, "North Carolina Redeemed," writing, "Every patriotic citizen in Alabama will be rejoiced at the gratifying news that North Carolina has been redeemed from negro misrule, caused by 'the white people dividing.'" The Democratic-supporting paper blamed the Populist-Republican fusion ticket there, warned of the dangers of fusion for Alabama, and called for a constitutional convention to disenfranchise Blacks.[9]

After 1896, as Populism declined, Populist and agrarian radical papers disappeared, leaving few voices to oppose Bourbon Democrats and white supremacist views. The Oneonta *Southern Democrat* was always a Democratic paper, but in 1898 it doubled down on white supremacy: "History never has and never will record the permanent ruling of a superior race by an inferior race."[10]

By 1900, the fusion arrangement had collapsed. In the general election for governor the Populists finished third, behind both the Democrats and the Republicans.

Fusion in Strong Populist States

I've focused on Alabama because of the importance the movement played in the lives of my mountain country ancestors. It is worthwhile to take a brief look at other Southern states and their experiences with the agrarian movement. Populism was the most important attempt at constructing a viable interracial governing coalition in the South—indeed, in the United States, until modern times. It failed. We can gain some insight into whether this failure was inevitable by looking at other Southern states where Populism was strong. North Carolina is particularly instructive.

Fusion politics in North Carolina very much resembled fusion politics in Alabama. In 1892 in North Carolina, as in Alabama, the Democrats barely won, and acted quickly to suppress potential Populist votes. In 1894, as in Alabama, North Carolina Republicans and Populists endorsed a single slate, but in North Carolina the slate won, and quickly passed a pro-voting law. That led to a second win in 1896, and the ticket included numerous Black candidates who subsequently won office.

North Carolina Democrats responded in 1898 with a vicious racist campaign, waving the bloody flag of white supremacy and engaging in considerable voter intimidation. The culminating event was a successful coup in Wilmington, where a white mob violently expelled an interracial coalition which had won control of city government. What the North Carolina Democrats could not win by the ballot they took by violence. Once in power, the Democrats instated disenfranchisement policies to ensure continued rule.[11]

In Texas, the strongest Populist movement emerged, and indeed it was born there. Even though Texas had a relatively low percentage of Blacks in the population, and the Democrats had won both the 1892 and 1894 elections, the closeness of the latter election showed that if the Populists could fuse with the Republicans a majority would be clearly possible. In 1896 they did so. As in

North Carolina and Alabama, Texas Democrats ran a deeply racist campaign and Populist leaders who had fused with Republicans failed to rally enough whites to their cause. They faced the same barriers as in North Carolina and Alabama. Two historians of the period wrote, "Populist success depended on persuading black Republicans to support fusion, overcoming voter fraud, and conquering their own racial prejudices."[12] The two authors rank the commitment to white supremacy as most crucial in undermining interracial democracy.

As in North Carolina and Alabama, interest in Populism declined after 1896. Texas did not use a new constitution to disenfranchise Blacks, but did enact a poll tax in 1902, and instituted a white-only primary in state law in 1923.

Throughout the South, following the Populist high-water marks, voter suppression laws were cutting deeper and deeper. The decline in the Populists' appeal was also due to the adoption of some of their issues by the national-level Democrats and the Progressive wing of the Republicans. Populism's greatest failure was the inability to create a vibrant new political party and structure that incorporated white reformers and Black Republicans.

Populism as a Vehicle for Changing Parties

As I noted in Chapter 10, V.O. Key characterizes the Civil War as a stimulus for many yeoman farmers of the hills to change politicial parties. He argues that the antisecession feelings in the mountains led to a move toward the Republicans after the war.

This is true but incomplete. Like many mountain voters, the Davidsons did not switch parties immediately after the war. A.S. Davidson continued to identify as a Democrat. His brother, Silas, was a Jeffersonian Democrat, serving as justice of the peace in Warrior, Alabama, and as a state representative from Jefferson County (Birmingham) for one term, 1898–1900.[13] Across the region, mountain men and women like A.S. and his wife, and especially men who had fought for the Confederate cause, found a direct switch to the Republican Party difficult. The aftermath of the upland uprising made the switch to the emerging progressive wing of the Republican Party far easier.

The Davidsons' switch to the Republican Party occurred in the early 1900s. The switch was through the intermediary vehicles of the Jeffersonian faction and the Populist Party. The young Davidsons did the switching—the sons and daughters of A.S. Davidson. Three or more of A.S.'s children—Tyre Harbin Davidson, Julius Davidson, and Marvin McCoy (M.M.) Davidson—all joined the Republican Party, but only after identifying as Populists.

John Albert Dean and his brother E.O., who was also a committed Jeffersonian-Populist, took the same path as the Davidsons: from Democrat to Jeffersonian to Populist to Republican. The Deans, however, seemed to have lost interest in the political process.

Progressivism

As Populism waned, another reform ideology, Progressivism, was on the rise. Republicans moved first as Teddy Roosevelt pushed the movement inside the party and then as president. Progressivism focused on reform, including strengthening the civil service, instituting municipal governmental changes, and addressing the corruption that plagued both urban machines and Southern states. Progressives also demanded labor reform and wanted more equality of opportunity for urban workers and rural poor.

Did Progressivism stem from Populism? Progressivism was distinct from Populism because of differences in policies and differences in supporters. The Progressive emphasis on institutional reform and deference to experts had great appeal to middle-class Americans, whereas Populism was a reform movement by and for the poor. This led Progressives to a focus on middle-class values at the expense of working class and minority power due to a disdain for society's "undesirable" elements. Progressivism also brought with it a downplaying of race relations as a major problem for government to address.

Some observers depicted North Alabama Populists as isolated on small farms in the mountains, driven by alienation from developing society. In this view, Populism was built on ignorant and resentful poor dirt farmers toiling on marginal lands.[14] A *Mobile Register* editorial claimed that the Populists "were found in the mountain coves, where ignorance and superstition, suspicion and envy reigned."[15] I've depicted a different political upland, one saturated with networks of religion, self-help organizations such as the Grange, and politics. Small farmers may have led isolated existences in the hills and mountains, but they could be mobilized by village and rural elites networked though business, political, and religious ties. The rural poor may have been isolated but they were capable of turning out in great numbers for political and religious gatherings, such as occurred in the Populist County Convention of 1896.

The Farmers' Alliance and other reform associations produced serious and complex policy solutions to the problems facing the nation. The connection from "politically motivated farmers" to later policy solutions using modern bureaucratic means is not farfetched.[16] The connection can be traced by the transfer of Populists to Republicanism through the Progressive Roosevelt wing of the Republican Party. Populist reformers carried their ideas into Progressive Republicanism as they left the Bourbon Democratic Party in droves.[17]

This would not have been possible if mountain farmers were isolated and alienated. Only if farmers were networked in a broader reform movement could the social capital be generated to address the difficult problems of agriculture in the industrializing society. They were linked to collective networks via earlier agricultural reform organizations. These networks were ripe for activating, which is what community elites did via the Populist Party.

The Davidsons and Deans were tightly integrated into these networks, and many held political offices or were community leaders. Meetings like Kolb's speech in 1893 to Blount County Populists and the People's Party County Convention in 1896 illustrate these connections. John Albert Dean's networking as county tax assessor also reveals the social ties throughout the county. Farmers had regular relations with merchants to acquire the funds needed for seed and implements. Religion was an important part of life in the 19th century, and many farmers met their neighbors in the churches in the villages and crossroads. Schools were part-time, but they served to link people in the mountains, as did the taverns. Even though the poor farmers of the mountains were isolated for days and even weeks, they nevertheless had regular contact with each other. These networked features of even an isolated rural society made strong social movements possible.

As their movement faded, according to historian Sheldon Hackney, Populists "had four basic options in 1897. They could join the Democrats, join the Republicans, withdraw from politics altogether, or remain with the Populists."[18]

Withdrawal

By the late 1890s, Populism was a spent force. Many Populists tried to reinvigorate the movement, but the energy was gone. The Alabama Democratic Party put forth a weak reform platform, attracting some former Populists. Nationally the Democrats renominated Bryan in 1900, but Republican President William

McKinley won easily. There were increasingly low odds that Populism would succeed due to the suppression of Black and poor white votes. Why vote if the cause was lost?

The Deans and Davidsons took different routes out of the destruction of Populism. Dean chose withdrawal, but he was no dispirited farmer. In1897, the outspoken John Albert Dean led a delegation from North Alabama to Texas to explore business and agricultural opportunities. Anyone could join them for train fare and two dollars.[19] Apparently his son Sidney was attracted to those opportunities and moved there.

Reading the handwriting on the wall, John Albert did not run for reelection as circuit clerk in 1898, rather he continued his exploration of Texas opportunities. In early 1899, Dean and a companion, J.P. Roberts, went on an extended trip to Texas. The *Southern Democrat* commented, "We have not observed any visible change which the trip made upon Mr. Roberts, but not so with Mr. Dean, for he had horns fully four feet long when he landed at home," apparently in reference to longhorn cattle.[20]

John Albert and his wife, Lucy Ellis, settled their affairs late in 1899 by hosting the marriage of their daughter, Sallie, and headed for Texas.[21] With him was his teenage daughter, my grandmother, Mary Milo Dean. They were part of a vast westward movement of Southerners abandoning the thin and depleted soils of the Southeast for the prairies of Texas.

The Dean family first located near their son Sidney, and in the 1900 Census John listed himself as a farmer on rented land near the town of Crockett. Then on January 10, 1901, the great gusher of oil exploded at the Spindletop salt dome near Beaumont, the biggest the world had ever seen.[22] Along with thousands of others, John Albert, his family, and his grown son Eugene, moved to Beaumont. Both John Albert and Eugene listed their occupations as truck farmers, and apparently did very well.[23]

John Albert Dean died in 1913. There is no evidence that he pursued politics after leaving Alabama. John Albert had left Alabama, Populism, and politics behind, throwing himself into farming and business.

Rejoin the Democrats

The second option for Populists according to Hackney was to rejoin the Democrats. That is the route that Reuben Kolb took. Many of the Wiregrass Populists also rejoined the Bourbons, perhaps successfully pushing the Bourbon governor Joseph Johnson to adopt more reformist policies. Some older

North Alabama Populists also returned to the more moderate face of the Democratic Party as well. Brothers A.S. and Silas Davidson chose that route.

Stay with the Populists

Hackney calculates that most former Populists who had not dropped out moved to the Republican Party.[24] Yet many were not quite willing to give up on the Populists after 1896. Certainly, Julius Davidson did not, or so he vowed. At the Populist Seventh Congressional District Convention in September of 1896, Julius was elected chairman, stating that he "had entered the Populite Party to stay, and as long as the flags float he would follow them."[25]

Julius held true to his word for a time. He attended the Populist State Executive Committee in Birmingham in December of 1897. The Committee offered a general address putting the issues of fair elections and better schools front and center for the coming 1898 elections, and appealed for Republican support.[26]

Join the Republicans

The succession of Vice President Theodore Roosevelt to the presidency following the assassination of the McKinley brought a new vigor to the office and a new set of forward-looking policies. These more progressive policies made the transition from Populism to Republicanism more palatable. Many former North Alabama Populists made that move in the early 20th century as it became clear the Populist coalition could not be restored.

The Populist-Republican fusion arrangement made it easier for members to move to the Republican Party. Within a year of his pledge to the Populists, Julius became a Republican. In September of 1898 Republicans held their convention for the 9th Congressional District. Julius attended as the representative from Blount. The *Birmingham News* wrote that Davidson made "the speech of the convention. He electrified the audience by a splendid outburst of patriotic eloquence."[27] Julius was rewarded with a seat on the district's executive committee. His party change was cemented when President McKinley appointed him as assistant district attorney of North Alabama.[28]

At the 9th District Convention, Ad Wimbs, a Black man, announced that he was a candidate for the District's Congressional nomination. The district had been gerrymandered to dilute Black votes, so Wimbs was a likely loser. He withdrew, but he was offered the chairmanship of the 9th's Executive Committee. Wimbs's moves are classic ones within political coalitions in which politicians have some power based on the number of votes they may be able to generate for the party. Ralph Bunche saw these "votes for jobs and services" negotiated by Black politicians in the North as one of the major reasons for better benefits Black citizens there.[29] Within three years the racist 1901 Constitution would negate these kinds of opportunities for Wimbs and Black Alabamians more generally.

Other Davidsons moved in the Republican direction as well. A.S. Davidson had 15 children—3 by his first wife, Julia Waldrop, and 12 by his second wife, Ruth Whitt. Tyre Harbin was the first child of A.S. and Julia, and he had moved to the Republican Party by the late 19th century. Julius was the 4th child; my grandfather, Marvin McCoy (M.M.), was the 12th. Julius was born in 1869 and M.M. was born in 1881, 12 years later. My grandfather was too young to be an active participant in the Populist actions of the early and middle 1890s. Later he followed in the steps of his older brother Julius, studying the law and becoming active in Republican Party politics.

M.M. Davidson ran as a Republican for several offices. In 1906 he ran for and received the Republican Party nomination for the State Senate in a district that was composed of three mountain counties. Apparently, he too was capable of rousing speeches.[30] He was nominated for solicitor (district attorney) in his judicial district in 1908.

Most of the Davidsons crossed over from Jacksonian Democrats to Jeffersonians to Populists to Republicans, mirroring the pattern of Julius and M.M. They were joining a party that held to a more racially inclusive set of policies and continued to capture most Black voters until the New Deal. A major reason for higher allegiance among Blacks for the Republicans was the lower level of white supremacist consciousness in the counties where Republicanism was strong. The sectional pattern that had defined the differences between the upper and lower South also defined areas where Republicanism was a natural and accepted part of the social environment and where it was viewed as odd and even threatening—the old slaveholding South. The pattern was not unique to Alabama—former Populists joined the Republicans in most Southern states.

Confederate Reunion in Blount

In late September of 1903, Blount County Confederate Civil War veterans gathered for a reunion. A.S. Davidson gave the major address, "The Right of the Southern States to Secede, or States' Rights." A newspaper correspondent wrote that Davidson "clearly proved that the principle was a justifiable one and that our government has ever maintained that principle during all of its existence."[31] Davidson had been a committed Populist, as had his brother, W.S. Davidson, and other attendees. This type of argument was characteristic of the emerging Lost Cause mythology, perhaps strange coming from a man whose family never owned slaves and who did not rush to join the Confederate cause.

As strange as it may seem today, apparently A.S. saw no conflict between the legitimacy of the Confederate cause and the class-based politics of Populism. Sympathy with states' rights and the Confederate cause was not a barrier to joining the Populist cause, at least for the Davidsons, the Deans, and many other families in the upper South.

A.S. could hold both the Lost Cause and the ideal of interracial democracy in his mind simultaneously. Few Southerners today know of the upland uprising, certainly in comparison to the Civil War. A.S.'s speech suggests that the states' rights theme could have co-existed with the more ennobling narrative of the Populist alliance between the yeoman farmer, the laborer, and the Black sharecropper carrying forward the ideal of interracial democracy.

The Great Disenfranchisement

The disenfranchisement of Black voters after the Civil War occurred in two stages. The first stage, Redemption, used economic and physical intimidation and outright violence to restore white rule. Redeemed states passed voting restriction acts, such as Alabama's Sayre Law, to eliminate Black (and generally poor white) voters, and to test the limits of what federal courts would tolerate. It was not unusual for local election boards to manipulate the administration of these laws to remove even more Blacks from the rolls.

There was one problem for Redeemers with Black disenfranchisement: if Black voters were off the rolls, then they would be unavailable to Black Belt politicians to use in their regular fraud and ballot-stuffing schemes. If the fraud were eliminated, then the Black Belt planters and their business allies could not prevail in state politics. So long as whites voted as a block on the premise of white supremacy, the Bourbon Democrats would prevail, but if there was a split in the white votes, and if Blacks voted with the anti-Bourbon whites, then the planters and their allies would face a losing situation.

So the Bourbons developed an alternate plan, one that would similtuanously disenfranchise both Blacks and poor whites through constitutional revisions and changes in statutes. Mississippi had already accomplished this by instituting a "pay to vote" scheme known as the poll tax and a literacy test with an understanding clause required of citizens attempting to register to vote. The Supreme Court upheld that scheme unanimously in *Williams v. Mississippi* (1898), stating that since all citizens were subject to the literacy test and the poll tax, the scheme did not violate the 15th Amendment. The case encouraged other Southern states to pursue the same route, and pursue they did. South Carolina in 1895, Louisiana in 1898, North Carolina in 1900, Alabama in 1901, Virginia in 1902, and Georgia in 1908 wrote new constitutions or amended their old ones to disenfranchise Blacks. Texas, Florida, and Tennessee legislated the poll tax rather than embodying it in their constitutions.

The regional consensus on the removal of Blacks from political life was tolerated and even encouraged by a shifting national political climate. Many northern politicians had tired of addressing race relations. Southerners had rejoined Congress and had formed a solid block against reform. The press and opinion magazines, save for the vigorous Black press, generally painted a racist view of Blacks. Academic scholarship buttressed the prevailing white supremacist ideology. The new era of Jim Crow had become the new normal.

The Effects of the Southern Constitutions

Was the Great Disenfranchisement due to corruption on the part of "Bourbons and Big Mules" or because of racism on the part of upland whites? Or both? There is little doubt that upland whites were less racist than whites in the Black Belt, so the real question is whether they were racist enough to support the Bourbons in disenfranchising Blacks.

Poor whites in the mountains and Wiregrass well understood that devices like the poll tax and literacy test would disenfranchise them. Or at least their leaders did. But they also understood that so long as Blacks remained dependent on plantation owners in the Black Belt, they would be subject to the vote buying, intimidation, and ballot box stuffing that Black Belt politicians had used since Redemption. Ballot stuffing (or ballot removing, depending on what the preferred candidate needed) had become so pervasive that even Black

Belt Bourbons had become uneasy about it. A major argument in favor of dis-
enfranchisement was a kind of "stop us from sinning" plea—disenfranchise
Blacks so we will stop cheating. That was also on the minds of Populists and
Republicans, who had seen three elections stolen by Black Belt Bourbons.

Even some reformers supported disenfranchisement based on a pragmatic
if unethical reason. They thought that they could win elections on the basis
of their reformist and economy-centered ideas among white voters if Blacks
were taken out of the mix. This would also allow them to neuter the white
supremacist campaigns of the Bourbons—by adopting the banner of white
supremacy as well. The problem was that the provisions envisioned by the
Bourbons for the constitution would disenfranchise Populist voters, so there
was considerable resistance in the mountains and Wiregrass to both calling the
constitutional convention and ratifying it after the document was drafted.

Alabama was unique among southern states in holding elections both to call
a constitutional convention and in ratifying it in 1901. The same north-south
sectional pattern emerged on both. Blount, Cullman, Winston, and most of
the rest of the mountain counties all voted against both, as did three Wiregrass
counties. All Black Belt counties voted to hold the convention, and most voted
for the proposed constitution. Dallas County (Selma) had 1,800 white voters
and over 9,000 Black ones, yet the county voted for the constitution which
disenfranchised Black voters. Sumter County had five times as many Black voters as white ones, yet seemingly the Blacks went to the polls to disenfranchise
themselves. As in the elections of the 1890s, the massive cheating in the region
carried the constitutional vote.

Even though the constitution lost in most North Alabama counties, many
mountain country whites voted for the constitution, generally because of their
fears of "Black rule." However, their representatives had been able to secure
provisions that would permit them to register and vote. These provisions
included grandfather clauses that allowed registration if the applicant had a
direct ancestor who was a veteran and "good character" clauses that authorized
registrars to sign up people who were respectable members of the community, as determined by the registrar. In addition, the constitution established
a temporary system that in effect registered many white voters but no Black
ones.

The provisions of the constitution first came into play in the election of
1902. In the Black Belt, the new suppression system resulted in eliminating
virtually all Blacks from the electorate, but almost no whites. For example, in
Sumter County, no whites were disenfranchised, but 5,321 of the 5,408 Black
voters were eliminated.

In the mountains and the Wiregrass, most Blacks were disenfranchised, but many whites were as well. In Blount County every one of the 356 Black voters was disenfranchised while 24% of the 4,367 white voters were disenfranchised. Wiregrass patterns were similar. In my Grandfather Jones's home county of Geneva, a Populist stronghold, 34% of white voters could not meet the criteria for voting; again all Black voters lost the right to vote.[32] A fair system of voting was transformed into a system unfair to both races, but far less fair to Blacks.

Recent research by three political scientists on disenfranchisement in Louisiana confirms the collapse of Black voting after the state ratified its new constitution in 1898. Registration for Black voters declined from a percentage that was both high (80% to almost 100%) and equal to white voters in 1896 to almost zero in 1900. White registration fell to around 40%.[33]

The result of the 1890s and the 1901 constitution in Alabama were twofold. First, Blacks were almost totally removed from politics. Few Black voters survived the massive purge. Second the voting universe, the size of the electorate, shrunk overall, even accounting for the suppression of Black votes. The white electorate shrunk as well, and it did so differentially. Poor whites in Blount and Geneva and demographically similar counties dropped off the voting rolls in significant numbers, but the white better-off electorates in the Black Belt counties continued to vote.

Disenfranchising measures are cumulative. They are multiple barriers that must be crossed. A prospective voter must register, the most onerous part of the process for Blacks and poor whites due to literacy and "good character" requirements. Then they must pay the poll tax. Voters then go to the polls, where the Australian ballot system, in which candidates were listed without party affiliation, was confusing, particularly to less educated voters.

In such circumstances, a discouragement factor can set in. Voting is hard and expensive, and the rules are set against the agrarian and laboring classes. If the Bourbons don't win, they cheat. Why vote?

Figure 11.1 shows the cumulative effects of these measures. The downward trending line depicts the total number of voters in Alabama's gubernatorial general elections between 1890 and 1906. The two vertical lines represent the Sayre Law of 1893 and the Constitution of 1901. The 1901 Constitution clearly had a significant and permanent effect on the size of the electorate, while the Sayre Law may have been part of a long-term discouragement effect. As Populism declined and Alabama moved toward being a one-party state, most of the action shifted to the Democratic primary election. In 1902, Alabama adopted a white primary, prohibiting Blacks from voting in

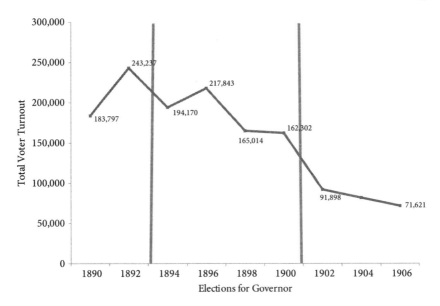

Figure 11.1 Size of the Electorate in Alabama Gubernatorial Elections, 1890–1906

Source: Author's graph. Data: Wikipedia, various pages.

Democratic primaries. The competitive party system and any possibility of it disappeared.

The Bourbon Democrats had achieved their aim.

Julius Davidson—Demosthenes or Cassius?

There was another consequence to the Great Disenfranchisement. The incentives for winning office changed. By excluding Blacks from civic life, the strategic calculations of white politicians shifted from constructing or opposing cross-racial alliances to simply adopting the inclinations of their white constituents devoid of Black voices. Because such a large proportion of Blacks lived in the South, where they were disenfranchised, the incentives were not only regional, they were national.

Republicans in the South in the years after the Civil War had factionalized. One faction, the "Black and Tans," under the general influence of Booker T. Washington, was integrated and tied to the national party. The second faction, the "Lily Whites" was a racial purity faction which sought national Republican policies supporting segregation. The Lily Whites were usually denied national patronage.

Julius, having left the Populist Party for the Republican Party, associated himself with the segregationist "Lily White" faction.[34] Here was a man who was a leader in the Populist cross-race coalition; he had also intervened aggressively to save a Black man from being lynched. He was likely a white supremacist, but one with chameleon-like qualities. Above all, he was ambitious.

Prejudice is not the only reason for the destruction of a period of promise for universal democracy that perhaps could have turned out differently. Some people may harbor deep prejudices but are nimble creatures; they can change sides as their interests require. They serve as intermediaries between the rich and powerful and the governing institutions they wish to use for their benefit. These intermediaries are transactional. When incentives change, they change. They are ambitious men, and are, in Madison's words, checked only by men of ambition with other incentives.

One such man was Tom Watson of Georgia. He was a strong Populist, an advocate for the poor, and a proponent of cross-race alliances in pursuit of reformist goals. Watson may have been motivated by higher goals, but as an ambitious politician he saw the Black vote as necessary for his election on an agrarian reform platform. In the elections of 1892 and 1894, running as a Populist, he was defeated by a conservative Democrat in an election characterized by fraud and intimidation of Black voters.

Watson became a national figure in the class struggle and was nominated as vice president on the Populist ticket in 1896. Over time Watson transformed into a racist demagogue.[35] Driven by his disgust at the manipulation of Black votes by conservative Democrats, he demanded Black disenfranchisement. Watson's ire over the electoral successes of the Bourbons made possible by the manipulation and suppression of Black votes seems to have initiated his spiral into dark racism from which he never recovered.

Great-Uncle Julius Davidson found himself motivated by similar electoral calculations when Alabama Bourbons succeeded in constitutionally disenfranchising Black voters. He opposed both the calling of the constitutional convention and its ratification, as did the majority of voters in Blount County and North Alabama more generally. Julius never fell into the dark hole of racist demagoguery that Watson did, but his electoral calculations changed with Black disenfranchisement.

Julius's ambition fostered his ability to align his self-interest with the emerging incentives generated by the disenfranchisement of Blacks. He was brilliant and conniving, throwing off the Populist coat he swore to wear forever for a Republicanism that offered him political advantages. When he acquired leadership in the Lily White faction of the Alabama Republican Party, his clear commitment to universal democracy as a Jeffersonian Democrat and then a Populist fell by the wayside. Although I found no evidence of the racist public language that Tom Watson used, Julius nevertheless felt comfortable with excluding Blacks from participation in the State Republican Party Convention.

As I put together my reconstruction of Uncle Julius, I could not help recalling Julius Caesar's characterization of a senator in Shakespeare's play: "Yon Cassius has a lean and hungry look; he thinks too much; such men are dangerous." Cassius epitomized the complex mixture of personal ambition on the one hand, and a deep commitment to democracy and the Roman republic on the other. Southern politicians like Julius Davidson and Tom Watson could almost seamlessly change from democratic stalwarts to defenders of the white supremacist political order when personal gain required it, and the route to interracial democracy seemed permanently closed.

As Populism declined, Republicanism rose, with President McKinley carrying 12 Alabama counties in the election of 1900. Clearly an opportunity presented itself: if Blacks were disenfranchised, could Republican policies based on the Progressivism advocated by President Theodore Roosevelt prevail in an election battle against the Bourbon Democrats? Julius surely was making this calculation.

The Davidsons had encountered such an idea when Georgia planters and politicians conceived of a white republic to integrate the uplanders flowing into the status system of the Georgia oligarchy. The result was unfavorable to the uplanders as policies became more conservative leading up to the Civil War.

Southern Republican politics after the Civil War were plagued by tensions between the Black-and-Tans and Lily Whites. The economic policy distinctions between the factions overlapped quite a bit.[36] As a consequence, it became all too easy to for the Lily White faction to appeal both to the reformist notions of "free vote and fair count" and a "white man's party" simultaneously. As an emerging leader of the Lily Whites, Julius Davidson was a facilitator of the dual approach.

The *Birmingham Times*, a strong Republican newspaper, reported on the state Republican convention held in September 1902, the first convention since the adoption of the white supremacist Constitution of 1901. Former Congressman T.H. Aldrich, a coal baron who had broken a strike by hiring Black workers, addressed the convention. He accused the Democratic press of a "campaign of misrepresentation," stating that the Republican Party did not endorse the new constitution. Aldrich decried the disenfranchisement of thousands of white men by the constitution. He complained of the overrepresentation of Black Belt counties compared to North Alabama counties, where Republicanism was strongest.[37]

The statewide Republican convention, after choosing Julius Davidson as state chair, ratified a strongly progressive platform that condemned the 1901 Constitution, supported organized labor, called for an end to child labor in cotton factories, demanded an extension of education with free tuition, and endorsed Roosevelt for reelection.[38]

The convention may have staked out a position more favorable to Black participation than the Democrats, but that did not mean they welcomed that participation. The executive committee refused Black delegates admission to the convention, leading to several hours of raucous debate. The debate featured appeals to democratic ideals by both white and Black delegates. J.O. Thompson, a white delegate, demanded a return to the cry of "free vote and fair count," and restoration of the plank of equal rights. Another said, "I speak for the negro because I am a Jew."

Other delegates supported the measure for pragmatic reasons. Counties with large percentages of Blacks would lose representation in the party. Julius Davidson understood the massive structural change the new disenfranchisement constitution had wrought, making a plea for putting aside the old regime and building a new party.

In the end the Black-and-Tan faction was excluded, and leading newspapers reported the implications in identical words: "This means henceforth the Republican Party in Alabama is to be a white man's party."[39]

The ambitious Julius Davidson had anointed himself leader of the Lily White faction through a campaign of speeches and pronouncements and led the exclusion of the Black-and-Tans at the 1902 convention. Julius, however, had made a major miscalculation. He was serving as acting district attorney of North Alabama and wanted the permanent appointment. He thought he had President Roosevelt's support for his move to fight the Democrats within an increasingly white electorate on policy grounds. Roosevelt refused Julius the appointment, instead appointing a Gold Democrat recommended by Booker T. Washington.[40] The split between the Lily Whites and Black-and-Tans across the South was becoming an increasing headache for the national Republican Party, and Roosevelt hoped to rein it in.

The Alabama white press saw this as a slap in the face. One paper bitterly noted that "the brilliant young Davidson" was turned down because he "failed to pay his respects to the chief mogul at Tuskegee. If Alabama Republicans want anything from the matchless Teddy, they must see Booker [Washington] about it beforehand."[41]

In 1906, Julius's craven political ambition surfaced in a factional patronage fight. At first economic ideology did not divide the factions, but over time the Birmingham industrialists drew closer to the conservative wing of the national party, and Julius went with them. In the mountains, though, most Republicans were still progressives, opposed to the planter-industrialist alliance that came to dominate the state as voting participation declined. Julius lost the patronage fight.[42]

In 1908 Julius made another mistake—his faction fought the presidential nomination of William Howard Taft, anointed by Roosevelt.[43] J.O. Thompson, who headed the Alabama Republican Party regulars and had made the impassioned plea against excluding Blacks in the 1902 Republican Convention, led a delegation to the Republican National Convention that supported Taft. Julius assembled an irregular anti-Taft faction of active and committed Republican Party workers and challenged Thompson's delegates. The Davidson faction was soundly defeated after pleading its case to the National Committee.

Julius remained active in Republican Party politics until he was killed in Birmingham in 1916 at the age of 46, when his skull was fractured by a rock. The county coroner ruled it an accidental death, but back home in Blount the locals were sure it was murder. Certainly Julius had made plenty of enemies over the years.

My grandfather M.M. Davidson continued his activities in the Republican Party as well. He ran for several different offices and served as the chair of the Blount County Republicans in 1914. He was an active antiprohibitionist; he campaigned against ratifying a state prohibition constitutional amendment in 1909, which was defeated. He did not have the ambitious drive that his older brother did and moved away from politics over time.

"The Tragedy of American Prejudice Made Flesh"

Were other paths than the Jim Crow white supremacist era possible? Perhaps. Historian C. Vann Woodward noted the increasing acceptance of Blacks in many areas of life during Reconstruction, even though much of the segregationist regime remained. Boundaries were not rigid, and many were crossed freely. There was horrendous violence, but also considerable acceptance of the new social system.

Woodward quotes abolitionist Colonel Thomas Wentworth Higginson's observations from a trip he made through the South in 1878: "The Southern whites accept them (Blacks) precisely as Northern men in cities accept the ignorant Irish vote—not cheerfully, but with the acquiescence in the inevitable. . . . Any powerful body of voters may be cajoled today and intimidated tomorrow and hated always, but can never be left out of sight."[44]

Any cross-race alliance between upland whites and Blacks would not require purity and morality in race relations; indeed, that was not possible in post–Civil War America. The alliance would and did resemble Northern city political machines, full of ethnic tensions and outright hostilities held together by common political objectives. The only requirement, according to Higginson, would be the vote. Lose the vote, and the faction loses its leverage.

One does not have to agree with one's coalition partners on all issues. Purity is the enemy of good politics. The urban political machines of the late 19th and early 20th centuries managed great ethnic hostilities between immigrants and Yankees and among ethnic groups to establish powerful if often corrupt governing mechanisms.

The fusion tickets of upcountry Populists and Black Republicans did not rely on an absence of racism, but it did require the "acquiescence in the inevitable." The Southern regime laid out in the 13th, 14th, and 15th Amendments to the U.S. Constitution envisioned a society in which upland whites, the Black Belt Blacks, and Bourbon planters would accept an imperfect regime treating emancipated slaves as political equals. Uplanders accepted the new regime, but Bourbon planters and their political allies were willing to institute a regime based on massive intimidation and fraud rather than acquiesce to the seemingly inevitable. Aided by a Supreme Court refusing to enforce the Civil War Amendments and a Congress moving toward a clash over economic power rather than pursuing racial inequalities, oligarchs in Southern states were able to establish a constitutional order that disenfranchised Blacks and rigidly enforced newer versions of Reconstruction's Black Codes.

Other scholars have seen white supremacy as always undermining class-based reform. Du Bois writes of President Andrew Johnson in words that could apply to Tom Watson or Julius Davidson: "This change [from advocate of the poor laborer to refusing to embrace universal democracy] did not come by deliberate thought or conscious desire to hurt—it was rather the tragedy of American prejudice made flesh."[45]

Many poor whites in the mountains and especially in the Wiregrass could not set aside white supremacy to defeat the Bourbons; consequently, neither could their leaders. White prejudice, according to these scholars, was the major factor destroying the attempt at interracial democracy in the 1890s.[46]

The flirtation of the Southern Populists with a cross-race coalition makes one wonder whether another historical pathway could have been possible, one incorporating Blacks into Southern politics. At the individual level, surely so. John Dean left for Texas because the prospects for progressive policies had evaporated in Alabama; he likely would have stayed with a Populist victory. The ambitious Julius Davidson would have stayed with the Populist Party if there had been a chance for success. His refusal to move to the Democratic Party suggests a limit to his chameleon-like quality when it came to politics. My grandfather M.M. Davidson also was amenable to a cross-race alliance as a Populist and then as a Republican. So were Tyre Harbin Davidson and most if not all of the rest of the sons and daughters of A.S. Davidson, as was A.S. himself. The Davidsons and the Deans are exemplars of uplanders whose distaste for the corruption, planter control, and over-the-top racism caused them to be unwilling to move back to the Democratic Party. Even the white supremacist hysteria of the era did not cause the upland Republicans to move back to the unabashedly white supremacist Southern Democrats.

At the structural level, however, the path to interracial democracy was less favorable. As historian Glenn Feldman put it, "Populists, independents, and anti-Democrats of all stripes in the late-nineteenth and early-twentieth-century Alabama made an attempt at mounting biracial political challenge to the entrenched, conservative, oligarchical rule. Various successes were achieved, but no lasting change was [accomplished]."[47]

Ever since Redemption, the Bourbons had governed the state from the perspective of planters, not the yeoman and tenant farmers. They did so through a corrupt system that involved economic and physical intimidation, vote fraud and suppression, and payoffs to political allies with state government contracts. The Bourbon oligarchs waved the flag of white supremacy, romanticized the war, and warned of federal imposition of Black rule.

The Populists were less interested in the specter of federal oppression than the then-current economic damage of the day. The symbols of white supremacy and romanticized war had worn thin as the rural farm crisis proceeded. Therein lay the danger for the Southern oligarchy.

In the end, however, it did not matter much. The Planter–Big Mule alliance, after realizing how close they came to losing power, moved to change laws and state constitutions to disenfranchise the Black man, and the poor man, a move that was region-wide. The Great Disenfranchisement meant that both major political parties would have to compete for the votes of the white man (women could not vote for 20 more years). The disenfranchisement of Blacks, a movement led by conservative Democrats, and the acceptance of that state of affairs by Republicans were instrumental in creating a "solid South" built on white supremacy.

INTERLUDE

A Populist Narrative

Two friends about my age and I left Austin on a warm February morning, off on a barbeque crawl in central Texas. Our aim was to compare the quality of Texas BBQ in the towns of Luling and Lockhart, south of Austin.

As we headed toward Luling's City Market, I asked my Texas-reared companions whether they had received the dousing of Lost Cause mythology that I had. They responded that they had little knowledge of the Lost Cause, but had been fire-hosed with the romanticism of the Alamo and independence won by Sam Houston at San Jacinto. Cowboys tending cattle on the open prairies, roundups of longhorn cattle, and cattle drives to the railroad lines in Kansas, not plantations where gallant owners gently oversaw compliant slaves, came to stand for Texas.[1]

In some ways this divergence from the Deep South was true: the dynamism of the Texas economy compared to those of Alabama, Georgia, and Mississippi led to different economic and political structures. Many deep Southerners, including some of my ancestors, left the weak economies of their states for dynamic Texas. But slavery was an essential part of Texas, and the classic Southern plantation economy could be found in much of eastern Texas. And the different foundation myths did not save Texas from the hate-spewing white supremacist politicans who run the state today—perhaps aided and abetted by the romance of the Alamo that depicted Tejanos as the enemy.

The narratives critical to how a society views itself and passes those understandings down to future generations are unifying forces, but not for all citizens. Because most societies are diverse, the myths that somehow get chosen for the central theme emphasize some elements and exclude others. The Lost Cause narrative envelops the white deep South "like a fog that refuses to lift," as the Congressman Carl Elliott put it. Embedded as it is in slavery, war, and an agricultural oligarchy, it naturally leads its adherents to a defensive crouch, defending the indefensible, a story-line that is not in evidence in Texas. It is also exclusive, a unifying narrative for whites only.

Many and probably most Southern Blacks are quite familiar with the Lost Cause, but they can turn to a much more positive narrative: that of liberation and resistance to a government that excluded them from full participation. The Liberation narrative emphasizes resilience, resistance to evil, and democracy. It is positive and welcomes allies, whereas the Lost Cause is negative and eschews cross-racial cooperation.

The desperation to reimpose the old order after the Civil War brought on the Lost Cause story, and the Bourbons largely succeeded in doing just that. But there were forces afoot that could have led to a different outcome. And could have led to a different more positive narrative—one based on the Populist uprising.

The Populist movement had everything that the Lost Cause lacked. It looked to the future rather than grieving about the past. It lauded democracy rather than adoring oligarchy. It reached toward political equality rather than wallowing in the haughty stench of status rankings. Populism was not confined to the South. It unified the disadvantaged across the nation— farmers, laborers, craftsmen—and set them against the monopolists, industrialists, and bankers. It offered a David and Goliath parable of good versus evil.

As a boy, I was deeply steeped in the mythology of the Civil War, with the storyline of the romanticism of the outmanned, outgunned South still managing to challenge the Union "invaders." After the war we learned of the alleged honor of redemption from the clutches of carpetbaggers and scalawags. It was in schools, books, movies, and even the games we played as children. I knew nothing of Populism and its attempt at democratizing an increasingly oligarchical South. These positive elements were pushed out by the slavish worship of a corrupt and immoral system of slavery, and the justification of the legal system put in place with the white supremacist constitution of 1901.

Acquiring Knowledge of the Suppressed Past

I got interested in politics when I was 11 or 12, motivated by Dwight Eisenhower's reelection campaign. My mother picked me up from an event and in the car headed home I recall saying "Eisenhower just *has* to win, doesn't he Mom?" I have no idea where my support for Eisenhower came from, but she didn't answer. Then I asked, "Are you a Democrat or Republican?" I was shocked when she said "a Republican." I thought everyone in Alabama was a Democrat. We were a one-party state! At the time I had no idea why that was the case, just that was what we were. My father was a Democrat, calling himself an "Independent Democrat." I think that meant he did not always agree with the national ticket on civil rights issues but supported the national party over the Dixiecrats.

I stored that back in my memory, and never raised it with Mother—she hated talking about politics. Later I began to wonder why she was a Republican in a one-party South.

The story of how the Davidsons, not just my mother, became Republicans turned out to be far more interesting than I could have imagined. The story is intertwined with the Populist attempt to construct class-based alliances between Southern whites and Blacks. It is also intertwined with a family story of a renegade marriage between my grandfather M.M. Davidson and his bride, Mary Milo Dean, daughter of the Blount Blowhard John Albert Dean.

A piece of the family puzzle emerged when my Aunt Mary Elizabeth Davidson, known as "Woo" from the usual source—her baby brother could not pronounce her name—told a family story that hinged on John Albert Dean losing his position as circuit clerk of Blount County because he was a Populist. "They were all Populists," she exclaimed, referring to the Blount County Davidsons and Deans. The Populist cause led them to shift their partisan allegiances to the Republicans and accounted for my mother's answer about her party affiliation.

When my Aunt told me the story of our Populist ancestors, I knew the importance of Populism in Southern politics; I was studying the phenomenon in political science classes at the University of Alabama. So I listened intensely.

And indeed the story did not end there. According to my aunt, my grandfather M.M. Davidson boarded a train, traveled to Beaumont, and brought John Albert's youngest daughter, Mary Milo Dean, back to Blount County over the opposition of his future father-in-law. Traveling by train back to North Alabama, M.M. and Mary found a minister on the train, who married them as they traveled through east Texas.

My aunt continued the story by claiming her father had experienced what I guess one would call an immaculate conversion. Suddenly, in 1918, walking down the sidewalk in Gadsden, M.M. was called to preach, dropped his law practice, and was ordained in the Methodist Church, South. Apparently he acquired a reputation for leniency among younger congregants who wanted to marry despite their parent's opposition. In my aunt's telling, M.M. would take couples across the state line and marry them when he was convinced that they had made good choices. Having pulled the same kind of stunt, I suppose he was sympathetic to their plights.

Aunt Woo was an instructor of history at West Texas State University (now West Texas A&M) for many years. After earning a master's degree in history at Alabama, she did graduate work at Penn in the 1950s, where her PhD advisor called her "little lady." She did field work in England before taking her position in Texas in 1957.

Aunt Woo apparently inherited the golden tongue of her father M.M. and her Uncle Julius. She was a riveting lecturer given to stories that mesmerized students, and was renowned for dropping deliberately absurd and incorrect statements to be sure students were attentive. Or so she claimed. I suspect she just liked to tell stories. Attentive students would take notes furiously as she cranked up the story, only to end with a clearly absurd ending. That led one student to ask, "Miss Davidson, for the test, are we responsible for all that stuff you tell us that isn't true?"

While I assumed the family stories she told me were true, I could not be completely be sure. Maybe she was just testing my attention. My first inkling that all this might be true was my mother's comment after the tale of the renegade grandfather's adventures: "Oh, Woo." Sounded to my ears that this was a true story that should not be shared.

Indeed, I was able to verify most of the key points of the story, and here are the facts as I ferreted them out. M.M. was born in Blount County in 1882, graduated from Birmingham Southern College, studied law as an intern with his uncle, and practiced law in Oneonta in Blount County and in the larger nearby city of Gadsden. He was by reputation a gifted trial lawyer with golden courtroom tongue. "He could outdo William Jennings Bryan in oratory," commented one of his friends.[2] After a promising career as a lawyer, he did feel the calling of the ministry in early middle age, was ordained, and spent the rest of his life as a minister or in church administration.[3]

John Albert Dean did not lose his Circuit Court position by electoral defeat. He did not run for reelection in 1898. He likely saw the handwriting on the wall for his prospects as Circuit Clerk of Blount as the Democratic-Conservative Party regulars gained control of the county and as the voting suppression provisions of the Sayre Law cut into his constituency. John did move his family to Texas, and after a brief stint farming in east Texas near the town of Crockett, he headed to Beaumont.

What about the rest of the story—my grandfather engaging in a renegade Christmas-time foray into Texas to run away with a willing fiancé? M.M.

obtained a marriage license in Texas on December 26, 1907. He married Mary Milo Dean, John Albert's youngest daughter, the same year, after December 26 but before January 1. By then Mary was 22, a little old for the storyline.

The "smoking gun" could be an item from the *Attala (Alabama) Mirror*. "M.M. (Coy) Davidson made a trip to the Lone Star State during the holidays and returned Monday with one of Texas' most beautiful and accomplished young ladies as his bride. Mr. Davidson is a young lawyer of ability and has a good practice in this and adjoining counties. His bride is one of Texas' fairest daughters."[4]

I can find no announcements of their upcoming marriage in the local Beaumont nor Blount county papers, nor an item after the marriage except in Alabama. Sure sounds unplanned. The weight of the evidence supports my aunt's tale.

Had the agrarian revolution not swept North Alabama, had John Albert not seen the suffering on local farms as the county tax assessor, had he not been Blount County's most outspoken Populist reform advocate, perhaps he would not have lost his position as Blount circuit clerk. Perhaps the marriage between Mary and M.M. would have been a standard affair. It is not a stretch to argue, as my aunt did, that Populism caused my grandparents' renegade marriage. After all, "they were all Populists."

The tale was important in a second sense. I began to see the deep differences between the Sumter County slaveholding line of my paternal ancestors and my maternal North Alabama line. That North Alabama line could be traced from my great-grandfather A.S. Davidson, a Populist; to his son and my grandfather M.M. Davidson, a progressive Republican; to my Mother, a Republican, and her brother, my Uncle Mac, a labor-liberal lawyer in Tuscaloosa. And maybe to me, an outspoken racial liberal as I entered college. Much later I began to grasp that the difference could be used to highlight the diverse forces that forged the modern South, and that might be a story worth pursuing.

It is clear that a Populist storyline of southern development based on democracy and interracial alliances would have benefited the South and the nation as a whole. Even knowing this history today would help Southern whites deal with the issues of inequality in a more productive manner by allowing them to recognize that prodemocratic forces were a strong element in Southern history. The "Solid (white) South" was not as solid as the defensive Lost Cause narrative demands. As the term "populism" takes on a new meaning today, stripping it of many of its historical virtues, restoring them would also help Americans understand the difference between the encompassing upbeat populism of the 1890s and the hate-ridden populism of today.[5]

PART 3

Traverses of the Common White Man

All theories of Southern politics that see an oligarchic ruling system also postulate a follower class, the "common man." The Georgia "white republic," the Secessionist convention, and the 1901 segregationist constitution all reflect a white oligarchy posing as democracy. As historian Jefferson Cowie has highlighted, the oligarchy used the pretense of democracy to unify the common white folk around a "freedom" based in racial politics and defined as resistance to federal intrusion.[1] That ideology left Blacks unfree and poor whites impoverished.

W.J. Cash saw these men and women as part of a hierarchical society in which leadership had once been a "moral right" of the rich and entitled. Over time the system became a "prescriptive [imposed] right of the captains of the upper orders to tell the people what to do and think—the whole notion of society as divided into such captains on the one hand and willing and eager followers on the other." It was not just the captains but the "vast majority of the people themselves, who had always subscribed and still subscribe to the hierarchic idea and system."[2] Such a system was aided and abetted by churches, once raucously democratic, now preaching the conviction that "God had called one man to be rich and master, another to be poor and servant."[3]

Broader theories of autocracies rely on the simple dichotomy of rulers and ruled as well. "The question is not whether there will be ruler and ruled, but only who will rule and who will be ruled."[4] Southern oligarchs claimed to rule by right, but Jacksonian democracy ensured that the oligarchs could be challenged on the premise of popular sovereignty. Hence the Southern ruling class relied on whites in a Solid South to promote a sense of regional solidarity and victimhood among both rulers and followers.

The sandy coastal soils of the Wiregrass and the associated pine barrens of Southeast Alabama were inhospitable to plantation agriculture, and economically the region was more like the uplands than the Black Belt. Politically the yeoman and tenant farmers of the region were swing voters. At the high point of Populism in the election of 1894, 7 of the 10 Wiregrass counties sent Populist representatives to the state house, but the region experienced a weakening of class consciousness across time. The Wiregrass became more aligned with the Black Belt than one would expect from the economic circumstances of the common whites there.

My paternal ancestors, the Joneses (Figure P3.1), represent the common white men and women of the Wiregrass, but politics was only a sideshow to them. They seemed to have been networked into the Bourbon faction through friendship and war remembrances rather than through ideology or deference. Generally they gravitated toward Methodist camp meetings and away from politics. I see nothing of the genuflecting to a revered upper class in the Joneses, although they did not challenge the ruling class by participating in the Populist uprising. Rather they were consumed by religion, prohibition, and the struggle to earn a living.

Around 1816, small-time South Carolina planter, slaveholder, and my fourth great-grandfather, Charles S.V. Jones, got out of the business, gave up his slaves, and went out into the wilderness to preach the Gospel. Brother Charley Jones, as he came to be called, was already over 50, but was brimming with the enthusiasm of the Second Great Awakening and the democratization of religion.

Brother Charley's choices led to generations of downward mobility for his family, wracked by sickness, death, war wounds, and illiteracy. His surviving sons and daughters spent their lives on the frontier as explorers, small farmers, and tradesmen—the white common folk of the day.

My great-grandfather Charles Cade Jones and his half-brother were severely wounded in the Civil War, both disabled for life. After the war they forged social networks with former soldiers and officers centered around William Oates. Oates had parlayed his war hero status into a political career that led him to the federal House of Representatives and the governorship of Alabama. These networks moved many Wiregrass farmers such as Charles Cade Jones toward the Bourbon faction of the Democratic Party.

Charles Cade's son, my grandfather Thomas Jones, was an illiterate farm laborer who worked menial jobs until he was able to get an education and was ordained as a Methodist minister. He married Laura Carr of the Carr slaveholding line, which led to a long and productive marriage, but one with some tensions over the status differences between the Carrs and the Joneses. He was a prohibitionist, and moved toward the progressive side of the Democratic Party, becoming a strong supporter of woman's rights.

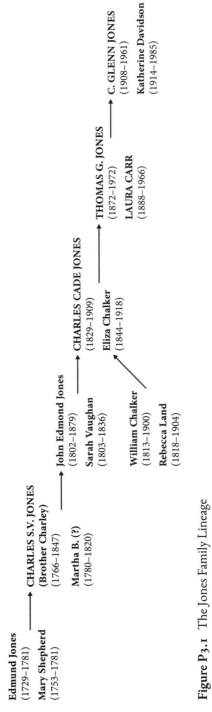

Figure P3.1 The Jones Family Lineage
Source: Author.

CHAPTER 12

The Two Faces of Brother Charley Jones

Charles S.V. Jones's life was a play in two acts, one of which represented the hierarchical American Colonial society, the other the mobile and more open Jacksonian America. In the first act, Charley was a small-time planter in the South Carolina Low Country, with a few slaves that he likely worked alongside on his rice plantation. In the second act Charley was a schoolteacher, a minister, and a subsistence farmer moving restlessly to the frontier as the frontier moved west through Georgia, South Alabama, and the Florida Panhandle.

Associated with the forced removal of native tribes—in the Southeast, the Choctaw, the Chickasaw, the Creeks, the Cherokee, and the Seminole—was a change in the American mindset. For white males, politics and religion converged to empower the common man. Both politics and religion became more democratic, and hence more open to the voices of common men.

Indian removal and the expansion of the frontier offered opportunities to relatively new immigrants, like the Davidsons and the Deans. It also drew migrants from coastal settlements, like the Carrs of North Carolina, who took their slaves to Sumter County, Alabama. Charley Jones and his family abandoned slavery to move, and therein lies a very different story.

Around 1817, when he was 50 years old, former small-time planter Charley Jones and his family left coastal Carolina, taking no slaves. From the time he left South Carolina, always moving on former Creek lands, Charles S.V. Jones never owned slaves again, nor did any of his offspring in my direct lineage.

Why was Charley's life sundered in the middle? It would seem he accepted a downward move in the white status hierarchy of the day to pursue a more interesting but more dangerous life. Although we can never do more than speculate about the "why," we can trace the "what next." While many of the consequences were exciting, more were devastating.

Brother Charley Jones Gets Out of Slaving

As Cornwallis was surrendering at Yorktown, Edmund Jones lay dying near Charleston. On November 14, 1781, Edmund wrote, "I, Edmund Jones, being very much indisposed and weak in Body, though of sound Mind and Memory, do make my last Will and Testament. . . . I leave my four Negroes, Daniel, Lucy, Elsey, and her child Annie to my loving wife Mary . . . if she chuses to live on my Plantation with my children, it is my Will that she should (while unmarried) enjoy an equal Share of the Produce . . . for her Support."

Edmund's will continues, "I give and bequeath all my real estate to my two Sons Charles Shepherd Vincent Jones, and Robert Jones, the same to be equally divided between them."[1] Charles, born in 1766, signed his name CSV Jones, carried two middle names, one from his mother Mary Shepherd, the other from his father's mother, Patience Vincent.

Edmund left but scant traces of his life in the historical record. Perhaps he immigrated from Glamorgan, Wales, as some family records note, but it is more likely that his immediate ancestors did. He volunteered in a local militia, the Colleton County Regiment, at the start of the Revolutionary War, but the unit saw no action and disbanded in 1776.

Edmund had established a small plantation in what became Colleton District (later County), west of Charleston. The region primarily grew rice at the time, so it is likely that Edmund's small plantation was invested in that crop. His wife, Mary, died at about the same time he did, and his two sons, Charles and Robert, were minors. Presumably they took control of the slaves and the property on reaching age 21.

Charles seemed set in life as a small-time Carolina planter. In the first U.S. Census in 1790, he reported living in the same area as his father had, perhaps on the family farm, owning five slaves. In 1810, he and his wife, Martha, had five children and held seven slaves. Charley was in his mid-40s, had been a plantation owner since he was a young man, had lived in the same region southwest of Charleston for all of his life, probably farming the same plot of land.

He did not seem to be particularly ambitious. He was certainly a small actor in the slaveholding hierarchy. As historian Julia Floyd Smith points out, "The planter hierarchy extended downward from the planter aristocracy through the middle-class to the small-scale planter." Planters owning a few slaves, as Charley did, "remained farmers, working side by side with their slaves in rather informal relations."[2] Many small-scale planters aspired to join the slaveholding aristocracy by acquiring more slaves and land. But Charley just did not seem to be that interested in acquiring enough land and slaves to move up into the higher ranks of the slaveholding class in the way James Powell Carr did. Carrs left coastal North Carolina and moved to Black Belt Sumter County Alabama to build wealth through slaves and land. Charley Jones left coastal South Carolina to carry the gospel to the frontier.

Networks Replace Hierarchy on the Frontier

The decade from 1810 to 1820 was a turbulent one in America. The decade started with war with England and the Creek War, which made vast lands in Georgia and Alabama available to white settlers. The decade ended with the Depression of 1819. The decade brought the peak of the upheavals of the Great Awakening, which was not solely a religious movement but also a social movement carrying with it an emphasis on equality, at least among white males.

Historian Donald Scott captures the movement between the signing of the Constitution and the turbulence of Jacksonian Democracy and the Second Great Awakening.

> For the most part, eighteenth-century Americans lived their lives within hierarchically ordered institutions. They were oriented primarily to place, and they valued order and stability in their families, work lives, and communities. Communities were composed of a recognizable set of "ranks and orders" in which the higher orders governed and the lower orders were expected to defer to the greater wisdom and virtue of their betters.
>
> By the early nineteenth century, however, Americans increasingly had become a people in motion, constantly moving across social and geographical space. Under the force of this fluidity, families, towns, and occupational structures lost much of their traditional capacity to regulate individual and social life. Instead, Americans devised a different kind of institutional order as they turned to an increasingly dense fabric of new organizations—religious sects and denominations, voluntary societies of various sorts, and political parties—to give needed structure and direction to their lives.[3]

During the Second Great Awaking, Methodists spread the Gospel through revivals and later camp meetings, where on the frontier families came with tents for camping out and sat on split log benches arranged as an outdoor church. Families shared meals, sang hymns, socialized with each other, listened to speakers, and regularly engaged in wild enthusiasm, spontaneous conversions, and general mass hysteria. More established churchmen frowned on camp meetings but had to admit that they were highly successful in converting the unfaithful.[4]

Charley was caught up in the frenzy of the period. By 1813, Charley had become deeply involved in Methodism as a lay preacher or exhorter.[5] Because of his devotion he had become known as Brother Charley Jones.

In 1817, Charley and his family moved to Talfair County, Georgia.[6] There he lived and worked as a small farmer (without slaves), a schoolteacher, and Methodist exhorter. He lived a simple life in Central Georgia, and it was not easy. Schools were open only part of the year, and the ministry paid little if anything. He and Martha very likely led a life that was much more rugged and difficult than his life in settled lowland South Carolina.

Although it is difficult to reconstruct the exact pattern of events that led Charley Jones to give up the life of a lowland planter for school teaching and preaching in central Georgia, it is likely that his intense commitment to religion was a large part of the story. Leaving South Carolina gave Brother Charley an opportunity to make a new start, to forge a new life, one based in evangelical religion. It was a life less ordered and hierarchical than the one he left behind, one that offered more mobility and more equality for the white man.

In 1820, Brother Charley's wife, Martha, died in Talfair County. It was apparently time for Charley to move on.[7] He headed to the village of Geneva, Alabama, and then on to the Panhandle of Florida, likely encouraged by a Scottish Presbyterian, John MacKinnon (Figure 12.1).

Charley met MacKinnon in Georgia as MacKinnon passed through Talfair County, heading southwest to join a community of Scots Presbyterians in Spanish Florida.[8] The Scots Presbyterian community MacKinnon aimed to join migrated from North Carolina and settled in Florida's Euchee Valley on the Escambia River, hoping to build a better future there.[9] The story goes that the leader of the group, Neil McClendon, met a friendly Uchee chief, Sam Story, who invited the Presbyterians to settle in the Euchee Valley area.

The Scottish Presbyterians had moved into an unsettled region. By 1818 the Spanish had lost control over Florida. The Spanish colony had become a cauldron of adventurers from the United States and Europe, Seminoles, a tribe of Creek origin that had recently moved from Georgia and Alabama, and Black escaped slaves seeking freedom. Settlers from Georgia and Alabama were mostly squatters in West Florida, causing consequent boundary disputes and land claim issues.[10] In 1821 the United States took possession of Florida after Andrew Jackson invaded, allegedly to stop Indian intrusions into the United States but instead forced the Spanish to surrender at Pensacola.

Charley moved to Florida in 1821 with his children, including his oldest son, John Edmund Jones, and daughter-in-law, Sarah Vaughn, and members

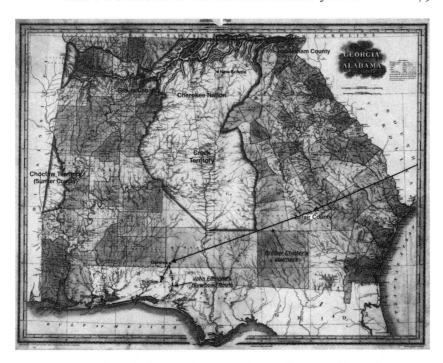

Figure 12.1 Brother Charley Jones's Journeys Imposed on 1823 Tanner Map
Source: H.S. Tanner Map of Georgia and Alabama, 1823. By Henry Schenck
Tanner—Historical Maps of Alabama Collection, University of Alabama Department of
Geography, Public Domain [https://commons.wikimedia.org/w/index.
php?curid=7162394].

of her family. Charley came with Methodist missionary work on his mind.
By 1822 the MacKinnons, the Vaughans, and the Joneses had established
homesteads in the Alaqua-Euchee area. There Charley established a new life,
marrying Nancy McCaskill, one of the Scots Presbyterians who had migrated
to the region from North Carolina.

Reverend Portier's Travels

In 1827 Michael Portier, the Catholic vicar of Alabama and Florida, sailed from
Mobile to Pensacola, where the small parish was in disarray. He tried unsuc-
cessfully to remedy the situation, and left Pensacola, traveling by land across
the territory to the healthier parish of St. Augustine. For the journey he joined
up with a mailman, Thomas Jones, the son of Alaqua postmaster C.S.V. Jones.

Charley had been appointed postmaster the year before.[11] Thomas had picked up the mail at Pensacola and was heading back to Alaqua.

For the first day of the journey a farmer rode with Portier and Jones, along with the Pensacola Parish priest, and the talk turned to religion. The farmer professed strong religious beliefs, but refused to talk further, as he conveyed that he was deciding between sects. Portier, who respected religious hierarchy, thought this indecision was a reaction to the religious reform of the Second Great Awakening, which "submits religion to the personal interpretation of a skeptical and blind reasoning." The bishop conjectured that this lack of sect preferences was due to the amazing mobility of American farmers during the period. Portier wrote that

> The American husbandman is a wanderer. Providence seems to urge him incessantly toward the wilderness ... Vast territories are crossed; the children are carried in farm wagons with the provisions; many weeks are spent in camping out; at night the wagons are turned into beds; yet everyone is happy.
>
> The result of all this moving is that to-day one encounters a Methodist exhorter; tomorrow an Anabaptist; and with each successive day new doctrines and new practices, of the most contradictory kind are offered to the choice of a shifting people. How can one become fixed among this confusion of opinions?[12]

Portier continued riding with Thomas Jones, repeatedly trying to engage him in conversation with little luck. After learning that Thomas was the son of a Methodist minister, he concluded that Jones's austerity was a consequence of his Protestant religion. More likely, Thomas just did not want to engage in a religious disagreement with the Catholic prelate.

Riding through the Florida Panhandle, Portier describes two different ecologies. On the range of hills running from Pensacola to Tallahassee stood pine barrens, a pine savanna standing on sandy soil that does not hold water, and hence is of little use for cultivation. Fires were common in the Wiregrass region of southwest Georgia, Southeast Alabama, and the Florida Panhandle. Fire does little damage to the native longleaf pines but restores the wiregrass (*Aristida beyrichiana*) and removes the underbrush that could compete with longleaf seedlings.

The second ecology Portier described, creek and river bottoms, are fertile and covered with magnolia, oaks, laurel and cypress, various vines, and underbrush. The Alaqua Settlement was in such a setting. The vast stretches of pine barrens and fertile land only along the creeks meant that the region was not particularly suitable for plantation agriculture; Walton County, where Alaqua is located, was 14% slave at the time of the Civil War. In 1824, a congressional report to clear up land claims of squatters who had moved into the panhandle while it was still governed by Spain reported that almost all of the claimants had fewer than 15 acres under cultivation.[13] The 1830 Census figures show that the region had a number of free Blacks, because the region served as a refuge for escaped slaves during its chaotic years.

When Reverend Portier sought sustenance at a farmhouse in Alaqua, a "Scotch Methodist" informed him that most of the family had gone to a meeting, where a new preacher was "to try his powers that day, and by dint of lung force and length of sermon" the new preacher kept the family engaged for such a long time that Portier moved on to find sustenance elsewhere.

Tragedy Strikes Brother Charley Again

The period of Portier's travel corresponds to the founding of the Alaqua Methodist Church by Brother Charley. It is likely that Brother Charley was the mesmerizing preacher to whom Portier was referring; it was certainly his congregation. He had been preaching occasionally at the welcoming Euchee Presbyterian Church, but he had attracted enough Methodists, by conversion or from new settlers to the region, to form a congregation. Brother Charley and his congregation, doubtless including the Vaughans, built a one-room log building, originally called Steele Church. The church still operates today.

Then, in 1834, tragedy struck—all of Charley's children with Nancy died of an unspecified fever. The next year, Nancy and her father, Alexander, died as well. Charley was a widower once again.

Brother Charley remained in the Alaqua-Euchee community, preaching at the church and engaging in other community activities. In 1837 he joined the local militia raised to counter Seminole Indian threats as a private—he was 70 at the time.[14] He died in 1847 at the age of 80. He was buried in an unmarked grave in the Euchee Valley Presbyterian Church, next to his second family. Much later the congregation of the Alaqua Methodist Church added a headstone noting his role in founding that church.

Brother Charley's Life Crosses Eras

Charley's life stretched across two historical eras, one anchored in the colonial hierarchical structure of plantation Low Country South Carolina, the other based in the raucous and egalitarian frontier life of Georgia, Alabama, and Florida.

When Charles S.V. Jones began his planter life he conformed to the 18th-century Colonial hierarchy. The hierarchy included a planter aristocracy; middle-class and small planters; yeoman farmers; and indentured servants and slaves at the bottom. But the 19th century brought new sets of social relations, relations that were as horizontal as they were vertical. Charley could have transferred his slaveholding operation from the Carolina Low Country to the frontier, as did James Powell Carr, but he did not. He chose a different path, one made available during the Second Great Awakening, interacting in horizontal networks of religious, political, and cultural ties that had replaced the more rigid social order of the Colonial period.

Charley could be described as two separate model white Americans, one for the 18th century and one for the 19th century. The Charles S.V. Jones of South Carolina was a settled minor slaveholder, likely secure in the Low Country hierarchy but toward the bottom of the landholding class. He was *Colonial Charley*.

The Brother Charley Jones of Georgia, Alabama, and Florida was the frontier man, full of religious vigor, restless, unsettled, and eager to recruit others. In Methodism, one's salvation was in one's own hands. One's relationship with God was direct, not through some intermediary. Similarly man's relation with his government was direct, not mediated by a political upper class. He was *Jacksonian Charley*, a full participant in the new open society—again for white males.

For many Americans, the new trajectory did not open new doors. Slaves toiled as they had in colonial society. Frontier life may have given white women more agency, but it was limited. And the new trajectory carried with it many elements of the old hierarchy. Charley lived long enough to see his Methodist Church ripped asunder over the issue of slavery and white supremacy. Even though he left plantation life and moved to a region of few slaves, the Southern structure of society remained in place, and would plague his offspring in the coming years.

John Edmund Jones Navigates the Choctawhatchee

John Edmund Jones, Brother Charley's oldest son, and his wife, Sarah Vaughan Jones, were part of the Alaqua community, and there they had seven children together. One of them was Charles Cade Jones, my great-grandfather. Sarah died in 1836, perhaps of the same fever that plagued Brother Charley's second family.[15] Following her death, John Edmund moved with his children up the Choctawhatchee River to Geneva, Alabama, where he had set out to start life with Sarah Vaughn 15 years before. After getting established in Geneva, John married Elizabeth Albertson; they had six children together.

The Choctawhatchee River flows gently southwest from near Ozark, Alabama, past the town of Geneva, into the panhandle region of Florida. Instead of flowing directly south into the Gulf of Mexico, the river takes a sharp westward turn, flowing into the Choctawhatchee Bay, where today Fort Walton is situated on its western bank. The populated area of Pensacola lies on the next bay over, also named Pensacola. A series of barrier islands between the two bays makes the river navigable from Geneva to the towns of Milton and Pensacola [Figure 12.1].

John Edmund saw the potential for ferrying cargo from Geneva to Pensacola, and decided to explore the route for himself. He made the first attempt to navigate the Choctawhatchee River from Geneva to Choctawhatchee Bay and found a profitable route. He then established a transportation business taking goods up and down the Choctawhatchee. John Edmund and his crew made the journey with a raft of logs, drifting downstream and having the crew pole back upstream on the shallow river bottom.

John Edmund generally carried down cargoes of hides and wood from the backwoods of Geneva, and brought back finished goods, such as tools, salt, and other essentials not available inland. The journey took four weeks. A few years later, steamboats from Pensacola began making the journey upriver, putting John out of business.[16]

John Edmund moved back into the farming business, which he had pursued in Florida. By 1850, John, 49, was working a 120-acre farm (80 improved) with his son, Charles Cade, my great-grandfather, then 21. John and his son likely hacked the farm out of the longleaf pines and fertile creek bottoms that disected the savannah.

In 1850, the property was estimated to be worth $600, or $20,000 in today's dollars (applying an inflation calculator). John and Charles Cade used a horse and two oxen to work the land. He had both milk and beef cattle, and grew corn, beans, sweet potatoes, and peas, but no cotton.

In 1860, John Edmund reported to the Census Bureau that he was a physician, although he had no formal training. He reported no real estate holdings, and a personal estate of $1,000. Apparently he retired from farming and sold his land, and lived in a rented house. He continued to hold livestock, perhaps renting a modest amount of land to support subsistence farming. Many of his children still lived with him, and two listed their occupations as farmers. John Edmund had hacked out a modest but successful life from the piney woods on the brink of the Civil War.

The Dual Edges of the Frontier Character

It is worth contrasting John Edmund Jones's life with that of James Powell Carr. John Edmund was a a frontiersman. He was a small-time farmer in Florida. He was a boatsman, ferrying freight up and down the Choctawhatchee River. He cleared and worked a small farm near the village of Geneva in Alabama. He somehow acquired medical skills, and billed himself as such. He never owned slaves, nor did he seem to have any desire to acquire them. James Powell Carr, my grandmother's grandfather, was a slaveholder until Emancipation, and worked two different farms, renting to Black former slaves. In 1860, the 59-year-old John Edmund Jones reported his net worth as $1,000 up from $600 in 1850. The 26-year-old Carr reported land worth $1,000 in 1850, which had grown to around $17,000 in 1860. Young Carr's net worth was 17 times what Jones's was. The 36-year-old James Powell Carr built his wealth through slavery, holding 13 Blacks in 1860. Carr brought the old colonial hierarchy with him from coastal Carolina. Jones lived in a more egalitarian world, at least as far as white males were concerned. That society allowed John Jones to experiment and innovate, trying life as a farmer, a boatsman, and a self-made doctor.

John Edmund Jones, James Powell Carr, and Carr's slaves represent the stark differences in how these three strata of Southern antebellum society lived. John Jones and his families lived comfortably, if simply. Carr lived well, maybe even lavishly, on a plantation worth four times what Jones's small farm was worth. Yet the plight of Carr's slaves was categorically worse—different in kind not degree. They could accumulate no wealth and felt the sting of the whip instead of the freedom of occupational choice that Jones experienced.

In 1893, historian Frederick Jackson Turner wrote his seminal but controversial essay, "The Significance of the Frontier in American History." Turner thought that historians of the day spent too much time on political institutions, missing the factors that shaped those institutions. He argued that the key was free land on the frontier.[17] The frontier was opened again and again, providing a setting in which the primitive met the front lines of civilization, promoting democracy and individualism. "So long as free land existed, there was always opportunity for a man to acquire a competency, and economic power secured political power."[18]

Turner's thesis has been roundly criticized, and rightly so, especially for its ignoring of other factors in the development of American democracy. Richard Hofstadter, arguably America's most influential historian in the mid-20th century, saw the ideas as emerging from class conflict and notes that cities were cauldrons of democratic ideas even more than the frontier.[19]

The opening of the frontier in Georgia, Alabama, and Florida did bring men like Brother Charley Jones out of the settled and stratified South Carolina Low Country, and opened possibilities to him not available there. Even as the South Alabama and North Florida frontiers closed, the process offered choices to John Edmund Jones not available in the stratified East.

The continually opening frontier also brought the slaveholding Carrs and Larkins (of Lady Liza fame) from eastern North Carolina. They brought their slaveholding ways to the rapidly closing frontier, essentially mimicking Eastern stratification. Although the Joneses (and the North Alabama Davidsons and Deans) lives follow the Turner theme, the Carrs and Larkins definitely did not. The Black Belt was as much frontier as the Wiregrass or the mountains, yet it did not yield democracy and individualism. Rather it led to a caste system based in race, topped by a class system for whites in which planters were supreme.

CHAPTER 13

Charles Cade Jones Goes to War

In 1850, 21-year-old Charley (Charles Cade) Jones (my family seems to have had little imagination when it comes to naming) lived with his father, John, his stepmother, Elizabeth, four of his sisters, and six of his stepbrothers and sisters. He worked on his father's farm. Charley acquired carpentry skills, and by 1860 he lived in the nearby village of Westville, earning his living as a full-time carpenter.

Charley's world was substantially different from the world of his father and grandfather. His grandfather, Brother Charley Jones, left a staid Colonial society to follow a rapidly opening frontier. His father, John Edmund Jones, experienced the culture and politics of the frontier at its apex. Charley Cade Jones experienced a closed frontier. Farmers were pouring into South Alabama, and villages and towns grew. The Second Great Awakening waned as the Baptist and Methodist churches became the mainstays of the elites of many towns and villages. The Methodist lay minister and circuit rider systems by no means disappeared, but established churches became more common. Jacksonian democracy was firmly established, and early Alabama constitutions reflected a clear democratic tendency for white males.

The temper of the national times was rapidly moving toward sectional divisions over slavery. That tension was exacerbated because of the unfortunate decision of the U.S. Constitutional framers to include the three-fifths clause, which led to overrepresentation of the planter classes in national politics.

While the tumult of Indian Removal, the Second Great Awakening, and Jacksonian democracy was subsiding, a Cash-style hierarchy was emerging in the Black Belt. Elsewhere intrastate differences remained strong, pitting the upland and pine barrens common men against the planter class. Horizontal networks of religious, political, and trade groups operated against an all-encompassing hierarchy with slaveholders at the top. Although some commoners hoped to join the planter class, the economics of large-scale agriculture was pushing in the opposite direction: large plantation owners were buying out many small-scale slaveholding farmers. Many inhabitants of the Wiregrass, including the Joneses, exhibited no interest in becoming slaveowners, and indeed had little of the necessary capital to do so.

In January of 1861, Charley Cade Jones married Eliza Jane Chalker at her father's farm near Westville. Eliza's father and mother, William Chalker and Rebecca Land Chalker, had moved from Georgia in 1848 to homestead their Westville farm. William Chalker, my second great-grandfather, was the illegitimate son of Georgian Samuel Chalker, also a yeoman farmer on a small plot.[1] Neither William nor his father in Georgia were slaveholders.

The westward movement of the Chalkers was made possible by the removal of the Creek Indians from Georgia and Alabama. The removal was particularly brutal in Alabama, where an uprising in 1813–1814 by a Creek faction known as the "Red Sticks" inflicted considerable damage on white settlers. Andrew Jackson raised a militia in Tennessee and marched into Alabama to suppress the uprising. At Horseshoe Bend, on the Tallapoosa River east of present-day Montgomery, Jackson, joined by Cherokees and Creeks opposed to the uprising, defeated the Red Sticks, killing many and leaving the Creek tribe destitute. The Treaty of Cusseta (1832) resulted in the forcible removal of many Creeks to Indian Territory (Oklahoma). Some Creeks fled south into Florida, where they continued raids on whites for years.[2]

War Fever

In 1860, William Chalker and his wife, Rebecca Land, lived on their farm near the village of Westville with their 13 children. The local newspaper *Southern Star* depicted him as a "robust and vigorous . . . husbandman"—the very picture of a yeoman Wiregrass farmer.[3] William Chalker held 130 improved and 110 unimproved acres, worth about $2,000. He mostly engaged in subsistence agriculture to feed his growing family. Most of the farmers in his region did likewise, and most owned mules, working oxen, milk cows, and swine. Corn was the most common crop, and, unlike the farmers of the hills and mountains, many farmers produced limited amounts of cotton as a cash crop (William produced 20 ginned bales in 1860).

The Chalkers held no slaves, and the 1860 Census lists no Blacks living in the region around the Chalker farm. None of Chalker's neighbors held slaves. The Chalkers and their neighbors listed their primary occupations as farmers or farm laborers, with the farm laborers almost exclusively being the older sons.

Sixty-year-old John Edmund Jones lived 25 miles away, near the village of Geneva, in a neighborhood of small farmers. None of his neighbors held slaves, and no Blacks—hence no slaves—lived in the region. John Edmund's son, Charles Cade Jones, was building houses and furniture as a full-time carpenter in Westville. If all the slaves in the South had been freed, the effects on the Chalkers and the Joneses and their neighbors would have been minimal.[4]

On January 11, 1861, a majority of delegates in a secession conference meeting in Montgomery voted to secede from the Union immediately. Dale County, like all South Alabama counties save one, voted for a secession delegation to the convention in Montgomery in January 1861. Unlike the mountaineers in North Alabama in similar economic circumstances, the yeoman farmers and craftsmen of Southeast Alabama sided with the Black Belt planters on the issue of secession.

Confederate recruiters spread out through towns and villages urging young men to sign up and march off to war. On July 3, 1861, at the urging of one of those recruiters, Charley Cade Jones enlisted as a private in Company E of the 15th Alabama Infantry. The newlywed Charley was almost 32 when he enlisted. Charley's younger half-brother, John Edmund Jones Jr., a teacher living in Geneva at the time, also enlisted, and was elected third lieutenant of the Company. John Wesley Chalker, Charley's 21-year-old brother-in-law, joined as well. John Wesley Chalker was a single nonslaveholding farmer, living at home with Rebecca and William.

Company E was assigned to the Alabama 15th Regiment, organized by a slaveholding Black Belt planter, James Caney. The top officers of the 15th were from plantation society; they bore the cost of the volunteer regiments. The privates and corporals were tradesmen and small farmers, reflecting the emerging Southern oligarchic structure. Of the 84 enlistees in Company E on July 3, only 5 were from slaveholding families.[5]

Unlike the strong Unionist sentiment and war reticence in North Alabama, South Alabama was generally pro-war. Those who were against secession became Confederate supporters after their side lost the secession vote. There was less of the "rich man's war and poor man's fight" talk so common in the hills and mountains of North Alabama. An air of bravado and celebration prevailed.

Charley was a typical southern soldier from a county that had few slaves and produced little cotton. He faced a future of simple subsistence farming or skilled manual labor whether the South won or lost the war. Indeed in 1870, when he was almost 40, he reported only $200 in total net worth. He pursued the craft of carpentry before and after the war, building houses and furniture, but later became a tenant farmer to support his growing family.

Why Did Charley Go to War?

Why did Charley, John Edmund Jr., and John Wesley Chalker join when they were the men of modest means in a slaveholder's fight? One explanation commonly suggested is that such men hoped to own slaves in the future. Yet this is not convincing for these three men. They were not from slaveholding families. The plantation economy was becoming increasingly oligopolistic, cotton prices were rising, and slaves had become extraordinarily expensive, far beyond what carpenters and teachers could ever afford. Quite simply, it is not possible to make a convincing case on economic grounds.

It is more likely that sectional attachment, a general sense of war fever in the air, the possibilities of glory, the underestimation of the strength and endurance of the enemy, and the strong sense of adventure explains the enthusiasm of the simple men of Dale County joining the war. Mostly they did what men around them were doing—a combination of war fever and group-think sent men off to the underestimated horror of war.

The man fated to become their regimental commander and later governor of the state, William C. Oates, fully understood that men like Charley Jones would not fight for the Confederacy if they understood that the fundamental cause of the war was the defense of slavery. During the war, Oates insisted to his superiors that if the Confederate government proclaimed that the war was being fought for slavery alone, it "would have caused a disbandment of the armies . . . the men would have laid down their arms and gone home."

The thrust of Oates's argument is clear: if class divisions had become more prominent, and the ownership of slaves had been more clearly explained to the farmers and craftsmen of the regions of the South that were less hospitable to growing the major cash crops of cotton, rice, and sugarcane, they would not have fought. Oates saw a complex mix of motives on the part of nonslaveholding Southern soldiers, but a major component of why they joined and fought was the importance of status politics. Freed slaves implied a potential loss of status for poor whites. "Besides their other grievances, the apprehension those poor men had of the consequences of the emancipation of four million of negro slaves in their midst, and they to be given the franchise and elevated to political and social equality with the whites, was horrifying to their proud spirits, and those who never owned a slave fought for slavery to avoid such direful consequences." And he made the racial component of Southern status politics crystal clear: "Southern pride was offended and the blood made to boil at the idea of enforced equality of an inferior race."[6]

High Spirits

I tell the story of Charley's war experiences not because it was a story of glory; it was most assuredly not. I tell Charley's story because it was a story of a massive failure that left him permanently disabled and downwardly mobile. With death and desertion all around, and with a severe wound, Charley dragged himself through the war to its actual end in the trenches of Petersburg and its formal end at Appomattox, surrendering with a mere handful of his Company E surviving comrades.

Civil War history from the Southern side still centers too much on the brilliance of generals and the bravery of soldiers and not enough on the follies of leadership and the suffering of simple soldiers for a terrible cause. The brilliance of generals, particularly Robert E. Lee, has been vastly overrated. Lee again and again went on the attack when defensive maneuvers were called for.[7] Southern depictions of the war focus too little on the men whose lives were ruined or forever altered by the fight not just by battle but by disease—three times as many men in Company E died of disease as died in battle.

As terrible and benighted as it was, the war was a unifying experience, leaving a stronger sense of Southern unity than before.[8] The war provided an opportunity for the oligarchs leading the war effort to forge a single mind of the South out of the shared Lost Cause experience and the fear of Black rule.

War bonding started with high spirits, as early volunteers marched off to war. On July 18, the newly formed Company E assembled at Darien Church in Westville where, according to Sergeant Ambrose Newton Edwards, "we bade good bye to our loved ones and took up our march to the battle front in answer to our country's call." Lieutenant William A. Edwards picked up the narrative: "No more sumptuous feast was ever spread for departing patriots than was spread under the shade of the beautiful oaks that stood around old Darien church . . . In all my life I have never seen deeper and purer emotions or heard so tender farewells as followed that sumptuous feast."[9]

After a muster parade, the 86 men of the company, wearing new uniforms of "white Osnaburg cloth with blue stripes down the trousers and jacket sleeves" sewn by their wives and mothers, marched off toward Fort Mitchell, where they were to train.[10] Charley Jones marched out with his half-brother and brother-in-law, doubtless with his new bride, Eliza, and Rebecca and William Chalker, his in-laws, looking on.

The soldiers of E Company were in high spirits as they looked forward to a new adventure in the fight to forge a new country. Sergeant Edwards wrote, "the first night we camped on the banks of [the] Pea River and bathed in its waters and spent this our first night in joyous hilarity."[11]

The next night the Company marched to Perote, in Black Belt Bullock County, where "its best families welcomed us with royal favors." Then on to Union Springs, where the men from Dale heard the news of the Confederate victory at Manassas (Bull Run).[12] "Many thought the war was ended and some kindhearted mothers hoped their boys might see Richmond before they were disbanded," wrote First Lieutenant William Edwards in a letter to the *Southern Star* in 1915.

Lieutenant Edwards continued, "How little we knew of war and the bitter cup before the south."[13] In only a few months the war was to turn toward a much more threatening and malign force for Company E, and for Charley in particular. Only 100 of the approximately 240 men who joined Company E during the war would return home.[14]

From the Pea River, the men of Company E marched to Fort Mitchell, south of Columbus, Georgia, on the Chattahoochee River and next to James Caney's plantation.[15] There they joined other units to form the Alabama 15th Infantry Regiment, known as "Caney's Rifles." After "a few weeks of company and regimental drill we had orders to go to Virginia, and this for me was a matter of exquisite thrill and interest," noted Sergeant Edwards.[16]

The 900 men of the Alabama 15th boarded the train to Richmond. "The whole Southern country was in a state of enthusiasm," wrote Captain William C. Oates of Henry County, who had raised and provisioned G Company of the Alabama 15th. Oates continued, "Scarcely a house was passed by our train in daytime but that handkerchiefs were waved by fair hands from doors and windows."[17]

"The Worst Enemy of Our Army"

Reaching Virginia, the Alabama 15th camped near the James River, then in mid-August was moved by boxcar to the front near Manassas, setting up camp near the battlefield. There an epidemic of measles struck, killing 150 men of the Alabama 15th—a 17% death rate. Oates called measles "the worst enemy of our army."[18]

The men assembled themselves into informal groupings called "messes," usually along family and friendship ties. The messes camped and cooked together, bonding and calling one another "messmates."[19]

As winter approached, sickness again stalked the camp, taking the life of John Wesley Chalker, who died of pneumonia in November. Many of those weakened by the measles outbreak in September died of pneumonia as the weather grew cold. We can only imagine the grief of Charley, who was supposed to watch over his younger brother-in-law; the letter he had to write his new wife and in-laws must have been wrenching.

For Charley, the winter horrors of war were already supplanting the euphoria of summer. So many men of the 15th had already died, and still none had experienced battle. By spring, Charley would be in the hospital in Richmond and then in Charlottesville, suffering from acute diarrhea, a common complication from measles. He returned to duty in mid-June.[20]

In March 1862, the Confederate Army, under the command of General Joseph E. Johnston, abandoned Manassas and pulled back to the Rappahannock River in a pattern that would be repeated many times during the war. In April, the 15th was assigned to the Corps commanded by Stonewall Jackson and crossed the Blue Ridge Mountains to join Jackson's Shenandoah Valley Campaign.

Jackson and the 15th marched to Richmond in June 1862 to take part in the Peninsula Campaign. Union General George McClelland designed the campaign to capture Richmond from the east. In the early fighting, General Joe Johnston was wounded, and Robert E. Lee replaced him as commander of the Army of Northern Virginia. Charley and Company E fought at Cold Harbor on June 27 and at Malvern Hill on July 2.

Charley at Hazel River

As the fighting ended around Richmond, the Northern Virginia Campaign began. Jackson's Corps moved north and was joined by major elements of the Army of Northern Virginia. Captain Esau Brooks, who had raised Company E, resigned, and First Lieutenant William A. Edwards was promoted to captain. John Edmund Jones, Charley's half-brother, was promoted to first lieutenant.

The Union Army massed around Manassas to provide an overwhelming force to attack Richmond, this time from the North. But the Confederates struck first, with Jackson attacking the Union Army at Manassas and winning a major battle there. As Jackson's Corps crossed Hazel River, a tributary of the Rappahannock, a spirited fight broke out as federal troops crossed the Rappahannock River to capture a wagon train. During the fight Charley was shot in his left knee and severely wounded. As Oates put it, "He was a splendid soldier; was severely wounded at Hazel River, August 22, 1862, which disabled him to such an extent as to render him inefficient after that time." After his wound at Hazel River, Charley was in and out of the hospital for much of the rest of the war to deal with his shattered knee. At the second battle of Manassas, John Edmund Jones was wounded, returning to duty on September 15.

Charley was absent because of his wound while the rest of the Alabama 15th, led then by Oates, who had been promoted to colonel, moved into Maryland, only to be defeated at Antietam. The Union victory gave Lincoln the opportunity to issue the Emancipation Proclamation. Charley was admitted to the General Hospital in Charlottesville on August 27 for treatment of his gunshot wound, and he remained there until October 10, when he was furloughed. While Charley was in the hospital, his good friend, Jesse Carmichael, was wounded in the terrible fighting at Antietam, lost a hand, and was discharged. The two remained firm friends until they died, a year apart.

The 15th Alabama was at Fredericksburg in December. It is difficult to discern from Confederate service records whether Charley had rejoined Company E by then, or whether he remained on furlough until the next year. During that winter Lee reorganized his army, and the 15th was transferred from Jackson's Corps to Longstreet's.

Charley Jones Rejoins Company E

In winter 1862–1863, Charley rejoined his company. Lee sent two of Longstreet's divisions to Suffolk, in Southeastern Virginia, to block any Union invasion there, and to forage for needed supplies in North Carolina. But Charley was back in the hospital at Richmond due to continued problems with his gunshot wound in March, returning to duty a few days later. Charley's knee took him again to Richmond's Chimborazo Hospital, where he was admitted on June 23; he was transferred to another hospital on August 8.

In early May, the death of General Jackson deeply marred the Confederate success at the Battle of Chancellorsville. Nevertheless, Lee invaded Pennsylvania, engaging an entrenched Union army under the command of General Joe Hooker at Gettysburg. There, on the battle's second day, the Alabama 15th participated in an attempt to turn the Union left flank on Little Round Top. The Maine 20th, commanded by Joshua Chamberlain, repulsed the 15th Alabama's assault. The battle concluded with the famous and desperate bayonet charge by the 20th as both divisions ran out of ammunition. The toll was terrible for the Alabama 15th: 72 killed, 190 wounded, and many captured. The near disaster for the Union at Little Round Top and the successful Maine 20th bayonet charge made both Chamberlain and Oates successful politicians.

After his disastrous defeat at Gettysburg, Lee's weakened army retreated back to Virginia, and, like McClelland after Antietam, George Meade's exhausted Army of the Potomac failed to follow up on the victory. Charley left Howard's Grove General Hospital in Richmond and returned to duty on September 1, in time to catch the train for North Georgia with his company. Lee sent General Longstreet's division, including the Alabama 15th, to the western theater, and the Confederates arrived at Chickamauga in time to seize a Confederate victory in September 1863.

During the battle John Edmund Jones, by then promoted to captain, was severely wounded. Furloughed and unable to participate further, John was discharged from the service in 1864. He returned to Alabama, reduced to begging potential employers to remember the service he rendered his "country" even though he could not work at full strength.

The Federals responded in late November with a great victory at Chattanooga. Tennessee was lost to the Confederacy, and Georgia open to Federal invasion. Simultaneously Longstreet's Division and the Alabama 15th took part in the failed siege of Knoxville and spent a miserable winter camped in Eastern Tennessee. It was a cold winter; on New Year's Day, the temperature fell to −24 degrees. Longstreet's eastern Tennessee campaign had failed, and with spring, his corps crossed the mountains into Virginia and rejoined the Army of Northern Virginia.

The winter camp must have aggravated Charley's knee. On February 16, 1864, writing from Longstreet's east Tennessee camp, the 15th's assistant surgeon wrote that he had examined Charley and "found him suffering from a gunshot wound of the left knee, and that he is hereby rendered unfit for duty in the field. I therefore recommend that he be detailed for lighter duty."[21] It is likely that Charley served as a cook; Captain Edwards, then commanding the 15th, wrote, "The only three men I detailed to cook for me were John Trawick, Jess Flowers, and Charley Jones; the first two were killed and Charley Jones crippled for life."[22] Being a cook was no easy duty.

Returning to Virginia, the Alabama 15th participated in the battles of the Wilderness and Spotsylvania as Grant's superior forces forced Lee back toward the defense of Richmond. At Petersburg, Charley went back to full-time active duty. He fought in the battles at Darbytown Road on October 13 and Williamsburg Road on October 27, 1864, the last major action of the 15th.

In August of 1864, the war in the East had become trench warfare as Grant forced Lee's Confederates to defend Richmond and the important railhead supply town of Petersburg, 25 miles to the South. In the last major offensive of the War, General Grant attacked the Confederate lines south of Petersburg and north of Richmond.

Many Black Union troops participated in the Petersburg campaign, giving the Union an increasing advantage in manpower, and many Confederate units began encountering them. The presence of Black troops led to racial hostility on the part of many Confederates. The Alabama 15th had begun to encounter Black Union troops at Fort Gilmer in September.[23]

On October 27, Confederate General James Longstreet sent Field's Division, which included the Alabama 15th, along Williamsburg Road to prevent the Union forces from turning the Southern left flank. At Williamsburg Road, the all-Black 3rd Division encountered a brigade of Confederate cavalry. The Confederates managed to turn back the assault, but they murdered the wounded and captured Black soldiers after the battle ended.[24] Such actions received far less attention than the Fort Pillow (Tennessee) Massacre in April of 1964, in which Confederate soldiers under the command of General Nathan Bedford Forrest murdered 200 surrendering Black soldiers. It is not likely that the 15th was involved in the Williamsburg Road massacre, but clearly many knew about and harbored resentment toward the Black Union troops. Such actions as occurred at Williamstown Road may have emerged spontaneously from troops enraged at former subservient slaves fighting them, which is bad enough, but Confederate commanders in at least some cases also encouraged them.

Grant slowly tightened the noose around Petersburg and Richmond, weakening the Confederates as supplies became increasingly short and disease and desertion increasingly affected the troops. Increasingly desperate, on April 2, Lee tried but failed to break through the Union lines, and he was forced to abandon Petersburg and Richmond. Grant captured the Confederate capital on April 3. Lee made a desperate dash for Lynchburg, hoping to unite with General Joe Johnston's army in North Carolina. One can imagine the lame Charley struggling to keep up with his comrades. Grant encircled Lee at Appomattox, and Lee's Army of Northern Virginia surrendered on April 9.

Alongside the remaining 172 soldiers of the Alabama 15th, Charley surrendered and laid down arms at Appomattox Court House. He was among the 28,000 veterans of the Army of Northern Virginia issued parole passes by General Grant, indicating that he was a paroled prisoner of war with the right to travel home.[25] Charley was one of only 27 men left in Company E as they stacked arms.[26]

Most of Charley's comrades had been killed, had died of disease, were wounded, or had deserted. His brother-in-law was dead, and his half-brother was at home in Alabama recovering from severe wounds. William Oates, badly wounded at Petersburg, was recovering in Abbeville. Jesse Carmichael, who lost his hand at Antietam, was back home in Dale County, hacking out a living on his farm with one hand.

Memories of War

History is assembled from pieces of the past—from stories from soldiers and civilians, from whatever government records and participants' diaries historians can recover, from contemporaneous journalistic accounts, and from verbal or written accounts of participants passed down through time. The U.S. Civil War was particularly subject to contending narratives, because it represented an epic historical struggle for power, a critical clash over what the nation's constitutional values represented. Most important was the role of slavery, the original sin of the nation's founding, and the myths of the dangers of Black rule. The fundamental role of slavery has been integrated into today's accounts of the war, but still mostly missing in those accounts is that the war was a contest between a democratically led Union against a Southern agrarian oligarchy.

The Civil War, far from settling the underlying issues, had the effect of prolonging them—not because it was unclear who won and who lost the war, but because of the constructed narratives that emerged during Reconstruction. The South may have lost the Civil War but it won the battle to construct the narratives that infused meaning into the war.

In the great struggle over the South's Lost Cause mythology, individual stories took on a particular meaning. Individual soldiers and civilians were the raw material for this greatest of America's dramas, and individual reconstructions in the struggle for America's soul became critical in that drama. Charley Jones was no exception.

We don't know how much Charley brought his war experiences home, but his participation in one of the most famous regiments in the Confederate Army ensured that his story would be told. We do have surviving family accounts authored by my grandfather in a sketch of his father's life and by my grandmother, who gave a talk to an audience of "Ladies," probably the United Daughters of the Confederacy.[27] These accounts bear the heroic romanticism of a war lost for a terrible and immoral cause dressed up in the individual soldier's commitment to duty and honor. Grandmother Jones wrote that the man she called "Father" "was at the forefront of the battle line in the Second Battle of Manassas." In this engagement, "the Confederates drove the Federals to within a few miles of Washington, D.C. and threatened to take the city."

Charley did not participate in that battle, having been severely wounded several days earlier at Hazel River, a skirmish in the Northern Virginia Campaign that culminated with Second Manassas. He was part of the 14,000 soldiers of

"Stonewall" Jackson's bold lightning raid into Northern Virginia until he was wounded, but he was not at the final enormous battle of that campaign.

My grandmother continued, "Our soldier participated in many of the battles of the war: Battles of Shiloh, the Wilderness, Gettysburg, and others. He made his last stand in the siege of Petersburg." Charley was not at Shiloh. It is likely that she confused Shiloh with the Battle of Chickamauga, which took place in Eastern Tennessee more than a year later. Charley did participate in this battle. Charley also participated in the Battle of the Wilderness, and he was part of the Siege of Petersburg.

Charley's son, my grandfather Thomas G. Jones, was the source of much of what my grandmother wrote. But his recollections were also muddied. Whether that came from misunderstanding what Charley told him, or whether Charley himself exaggerated his service is impossible to disentangle. My grandfather was born seven years after Charley returned from Appomattox. One can imagine a little boy listening to the tales of Charley and his Civil War companions and reconstructing them over the years.

My grandfather wove the tales into a narrative of service, devotion, and duty. He writes that Charley "marched with his unit in the long and exhausting trek to Gettysburg, where he took his place beside his fellow patriots in that historic battle, where good soldiers fell in heaps in 'this last full measure of devotions.'" He continues, "Charles C. Jones' personal account of the march from Gettysburg back to Virginia is a story of hardships, privations, and suffering unsurpassed by all the top horror of history."

Charley may or may not have been at Gettysburg. Transcripts of medical records place him back in the hospital in Richmond because of continuing difficulty with his wound. He was admitted to Chimborazo Hospital on March 19, 1863, and released on August 8 to the General Hospital at Howard's Grove. This is a long time for a single stay in busy wartime hospitals. It is possible, perhaps likely, that the hospital records were not complete and there were two separate hospital stays rather than one. A record of muster for the battle indicates that Charley was "in hospital," but did not specify if this was a field hospital. The fact that he was on the muster role indicates he may have been there but not in the battle.

My grandfather wrote movingly of the end of the war as experienced by his father: "The rest of the history of the Confederate Cause is known to all. It was fought with fear of eventual defeat, short food supply, dispirited soldiers, and thinning ranks. Throughout all this Charles C. Jones held his place as a faithful soldier. At the siege of Richmond and Petersburg the Confederates made their last stand. They bore the strain of the siege as long as they could, then retreated southward. Charles C. Jones, faithful to the last, stood fast at his post of duty until the ranks broke and fled in confusion."

"Then the march to Appomattox and surrender to General Grant. This was the hardest march of all, the march to inevitable defeat. Here 'Charlie' mingled his tears of surrender and humiliation with those of his fellow sufferers; and turned his face toward the South."[28]

This part of my grandfather's emotional narrative is substantially true. Charley was on light duty for part of the siege, but that did not mean he had an easy time in a rough situation. He returned to full duty in October, in time for the last battles the Alabama 15th fought. He surrendered with the few remaining comrades of the 15th on April 9 and was paroled.

There is no doubt about the sincerity of my grandfather in writing of service, sacrifice, and commitment to a noble cause. Surely that reflected Charley's feelings as well. But the cause was not noble. While even the victor, General Ulysses S. Grant, shared that despondency, he recognized the evil nature of the cause: "I felt like anything rather than rejoicing at the downfall of a foe who had fought so long and valiantly, and had suffered so much for a cause, though that cause was, I believe, one of the worst for which a people ever fought, and one for which there was the least excuse. I do not question, however, the sincerity of the great mass of those who were opposed to us."[29]

The Life of a South Alabama
Tenant Farmer

After Appomattox, Charles Cade Jones returned to, as my grandfather put it, "his father's house in Geneva County, Alabama, where he found his young wife awaiting him." They returned to Westville, where Charley resumed carpentry and he and his wife, Eliza began their lives together. The war had been particularly hard on the Wiregrass region, with its mostly subsistence economy devastated and many of its men killed or wounded.

My paternal grandfather, Thomas Glenn Jones, was born in October 1872 at Westville. He was the seventh and last child of Charles Cade and Eliza. Fifty-five years later, he picked up his pen and began to write an autobiography, which he titled "Records and Recollections of Thomas G. Jones." I rely on those notes here.

Networks of War

Charles Cade Jones' network of friends gives us some indication of his social and political propensities. One of Charley's E Company close friends during and after the war, was Jesse Carmichael. Discharged after his wound at Antietam, "he went home . . . to a little farm in the piney woods. . . . . With his one hand he worked, made crops, supported his little family, and read law at nights by pine-knot fires." Carmichael was admitted to the Bar, served in the Alabama legislature, and became justice of the peace of Dale County and then circuit judge. William Oates called him a "thorough Democrat in politics," which meant that Carmichael's affiliation was with the conservative Bourbon faction of the Democratic Party.[1]

That we know as much as we do about soldiers of the Alabama 15th is due to William Oates, Charley's 15th Infantry commander during part of the war. Oates had a successful political career after his military service. Severely wounded at the Petersburg siege, Oates highlighted his wounds in his political career, and became known as the "one-armed hero of Henry County." In his book on the war, Oates compiled biographies of the soldiers under his command, detailing their battle experiences, wounds, and deaths, and what happened to the survivors after the war.

It is likely that Oates wrote many of the accounts of the soldiers in the 15th Alabama from the notes he assembled during his political years. These notes reflected Oates's networks of connections he found useful in campaigning. Oates was particularly effusive in his language describing Jesse Carmichael during and after the war. We cannot be sure, but words like "excellent soldier" and "esteemed citizen" suggest such connections. And certainly such war networks did exist. Oates referred to Charley Jones, a private, as a "splendid soldier" and "a highly respected citizen." He called Charley's half-brother, John Edmund Jones, an officer, "a very fair officer," which seems faint praise.

The "Rolodex" approach was especially characteristic of the "friends and neighbors" style of Alabama politics at the time.[2] That style carried forward to the 1960s and beyond. I recall an informal talk by gubernatorial hopeful Ryan DeGraffenried in 1965, sponsored by the Department of Political Science at the University of Alabama. DeGraffenried detailed his personalistic, friends-and-neighbors approach centering on his hometown of Tuscaloosa and moving out from there in a series of concentric circles, each contact marked with likelihood of support. Oates must have constructed something similar three-quarters of a century before. Based on his veterans' network, he was elected to Congress six times and to the governorship in 1892.[3]

Another of Charley's postwar friends was Civil War veteran Joseph Adams, founder and editor of *The Southern Star*, the town of Ozark's newspaper. Born in eastern Alabama, he moved to the "frontier country of Dale County" in 1866,[4] and established the *Star*. The *Star* was a strong supporter of Oates, regularly endorsing him and printing favorable coverage of him. The *Star* endorsed Black voter suppression, writing in 1890 its support for the Mississippi disenfranchising constitution.[5]

These kinds of networks, linked as they were to the Bourbon faction, help account for the general affinity of the Wiregrass for conservative politics after the war even though economics and the low percentage of slaves would predict a more liberal orientation and less susceptibility to racial hostility. While my grandfather discusses religion in detail in his recollections, he never mentioned politics, but it is likely that his father Charles Cade Jones hewed to the Bourbon affiliation of his friends.

Charley Becomes a Teetotaler

Charley and his war buddies regularly gathered at taverns to discuss war memories and current politics. The postwar period was one of great change and possibilities for change, so there was plenty to discuss. While the Wiregrass was a hotbed of agrarian reform pushed by various organizations, the reformers generally came up short. But one set of reforms, those of Progressivism, found a niche.

The first powerful stirrings of the coming Progressive movement came about through a union of religion, women's rights, and prohibition. Temperance and prohibition were especially strong in the Wiregrass and mountain regions of Alabama. My grandfather, Thomas G. Jones, recalls the critical moment in which his father became a teetotaler in his memoirs:

> There were . . . saloons in every town and hamlet, and many by the road-side in the country. It was [my father's] custom to drink socially at the bar with his friends. On one occasion in Ozark . . . he accepted an invitation to drink with a friend. When the two entered the saloon, the place was so crowded that they had to wait. While waiting, my father said, he was shocked and made sick at heart with the carousing, obscenity, profanity and general lewdness. This disgusting scene drove him to resolve never to take another drink. (He) was ever afterwards a strong advocate of the prohibition of the manufacture and sale of alcoholic liquors as a beverage.

And, like father, like son, Thomas was himself a committed "crusader against alcohol," active in the temperance movement to the end of his life.

For Southerners the war provided a stimulus for a resurgence of religion, and many churchmen preached against the evils of drink. Methodists held an old-fashioned Great Awakening–style camp annually near Ozark, where the evil of alcohol was a major topic of discussion. The tradition of the family altar, so important during the religious revival of the Second Great Awakening, continued, and my grandfather writes, "One of the first things I recollect was the family altar. My father would read a passage from the Holy Bible and pray at night just before we retired."

Building a Farm Out of the Wilderness

Charley relocated to Ozark in 1872, where they lived for seven years. Ozark was but a small village of a couple of hundred souls, but it was growing. That allowed Charley to continue his trade as a carpenter.

As his family grew to seven children (two other infants died), Charley moved his family from Ozark to a rented farm outside of town in 1878, when my grandfather Thomas was six. Charley was not a young man by then; he took up full-time farming at the age of 48.

The Jones family moved from farm to farm around Dale County. They always rented as leases ran out or other farming opportunities beckoned. This was the world of the Southern tenant farmer, white and Black. The tenant farmer often struggled, as did Charley and his family, but they engaged in the market system by raising enough money through cash crops, mostly corn and cotton, to repay loans offered by bankers or merchants for seed and tools. The crop-lien system that merchants deployed allowed small farmers to borrow at lower rates than from banks. That put them in a substantially better situation than the classic sharecropper, but they were held hostage by the merchants who supplied the tools and seed.

Charley never became a landowner, even of a small farm. That was a serious hardship when he and his family were forced to leave one farm for another. But his participation in the cash economy also meant that he could move; he was not locked into the landowner-dominated sharecropping system that bound most Blacks and some whites to the land in the Black Belt.

In winter 1883 the family moved to a plot they called the McGowan place, on the Choctawhatchee River near the homestead where Charley was reared. The family moved with wagons drawn by oxen, camping next to a stream under the towering longleaf pines. There a fire destroyed many of the Jones family belongings. The next day, my grandfather walked through the pines wearing "a coat partly burned at the back and made the few people we met laugh."

Charley and his oldest son, Henry, built a house, hewing trees out of the forest. His son wrote that Charley "with his ax on his shoulder, walked into the forest, and with his own hands, felled the trees and hewed the trunks into shape and built a house for his growing family . . . They called it a log cabin, but the young wife and mother said it was the most beautiful house she had ever seen." The family cleared land and built outbuildings as quickly as possible to get the crops planted. That first crop was small, but "most welcome."

River bottoms were especially unhealthy then, and in the summer of 1884 the entire family except Charley contracted malaria. At times, the whole family was in bed, leaving Charley alone to work the land. The chills and fever did not fully abate until the following spring.

Life at the McGowan place was difficult. Most of the time the Jones family was poor, living "with no real privation but at times we had to live rather scantily." After a few years, life improved somewhat, and "we had quite a plenty of wholesome food produced on the farm, and our cotton crops brought us some money." Charley continued to construct homes and outbuildings for local people, which also generated cash.

In fall 1892, the family's lease on the farm expired, and the Joneses were forced to move. They left the house they built, the outbuildings, and the land they cleared, the home that sustained them over the previous nine years. They traveled to a place 10 miles to the west, where Coffee Springs stands today.

The small farm, the Ray place, had only recently "been wrestled from the virgin pine forest with most of the dead trunks of the pines still standing in the fields." While my grandfather says that the soil produced fairly well, the piney woods, and especially the sandy uplands that likely characterized the place, were less productive than the McGowan place would have been.

The tenants on the small farm had scant interest in clearing the fields of the huge pine stumps, even though they often "insisted on falling down on the growing crops on the slightest pretext of every stiff breeze." Perhaps Charley had learned his lesson when he lost his investments in the land at the McGowan place. Clearing the enormous standing trunks of the longleaf pines would have meant a serious commitment of effort, not worth the trouble for renters.

In 1894, Charley and his family moved again to another small farm nearby. Such was the life of a tenant farmer. This was a hard life and led to bouts of poverty and difficulties in accumulating wealth.

The Transformation of the Wiregrass

During the last quarter of the 19th century, the United States experienced a period of almost unimaginable change. In the 20 years between 1870 and 1890, the population of the country doubled, from 38 to 76 million. Alabama's population grew more slowly, by a still impressive 50%. While all regions of the state were affected, North Alabama experienced industrialization and extensive mining around Birmingham, whereas the Wiregrass remained based in farm-ing and resource extraction. The great expanses of longleaf pines may have been a nuisance for farmers like Charley, but they were greatly valued in the construction trade.

Loggers and farmers cleared the great pine forests, at first slowly because the slow-flowing rivers and the small labor supply limited the lumbering oper-ations. By the 1880s, railroads replaced rivers as transportation systems, and logging occurred on a massive scale.[6] Farmers poured into the region seeking land, even the poor-quality soils of the region, as the population of the region grew.

When the logging ceased and the farms were established, the land looked nothing like what the Creek Indians had ceded to Andrew Jackson in 1814. The open forests were replaced by fields, croplands, and forests of faster-growing loblolly pines, hardwoods tolerant of sandy soils, and tangles of underbrush that had been burned in the regular fires started by lightning or by the Creeks clearing underbrush.

In this period of great change, Charley Jones spent his life as a craftsman and tenant farmer. His networks from the Civil War locked Charley into the Bourbon wing of the Democratic Party, a politics that did not correspond to his class interests. Although the radical ideas of the agrarian revolution thrived in the Wiregrass, Charley did not seem involved in them. He was preoccupied with providing for his family and his devotion to religion. His religious com-mitment did not include church attendance; the distance to town meant that the family seldom went to church. His move to farming in the wilderness meant he could provide for his family better than as a carpenter in town, but its iso-lation meant illiteracy for his younger children. The horizontal networks that had characterized the non–Black Belt south were weakening.

By 1900, 70-year-old Charley and his wife, Eliza, had moved to Enterprise, Alabama, with four of their children. There he rented a house and resumed work as a carpenter. He had owned no real property his entire life. My grand-mother remembers "Father" tending his roses in front of his house. He died at age 79.

CHAPTER 15

"I Was Greatly Embarrassed Because of My Ignorance"

Within the ossifying Southern hierarchical system, there were always some white men (and a handful of Blacks) who, as W.J. Cash put it, "could and did sometimes surmount the odds against tenants and sharecroppers, escape . . . and make their way from the bottom to riches, or to such competences and position as was satisfactory to the less vaulting ambition."[1] My grandfather, Thomas Glenn Jones, surely fits this description. He had no ambitions for riches, but he had a strong yearning for knowledge and religion.

Thomas's life spanned the construction of Jim Crow through to its end, and his incomplete biography, along with a novel he wrote late in his life, give insight into how a white man born into poverty navigated the changing economic and social structures of low-slaveholding regions in the Deep South. In that journey through life, he came to hold progressive ideas on the weaknesses of American institutions and on the role of women but failed to make the connection with the plight of Blacks. For Thomas Jones, Jim Crow was background noise seemingly unquestioned until the end of the period.

I pursue the story of Grandaddy because it is a case study of the common man struggling to get ahead and making huge mistakes in the process, all against the background of racial segregation and economic hierarchy that characterized the Jim Crow South. His writings gave me insights into the man I could not have discerned otherwise. The combination of his writings and my observations lead toward a more personal narrative, a narrative that will become more so as the book proceeds.

As a young man, my grandfather admitted to being functionally illiterate, although both of his parents could read at some level. Moving from a town life to a life in the backwoods led to the possibility of intergenerational downward mobility.

Granddaddy, as we called him, struggled through his tenant-farming childhood, frustrated with his lack of opportunities on the farm. He wrote of these frustrations, resenting the limitations that he felt kept him ignorant. But he did not have the knowledge of how to better himself, and committed unforced error after unforced error as his driving ambition pushed him forward.

Geneva County was still sparsely settled, and weeks went by in which the Charley Jones family saw no other humans. They seldom went to town, attended church only sporadically, and attending school was difficult. By the age of 12, Thomas had been to school but a few weeks. Schools in Geneva County in the 1880s and 1890s operated only three months a year, and even that was impossible to manage for the Jones children because of duties on the farm. Thomas was unable to attend the short school sessions with any regularity until he was 15.

The short school sessions were in part a reaction to the reliance of small farmers on their children for farm duties, but that is not the whole story. Reconstruction governments in Southern states funded educational systems for both Blacks and whites. Redemption brought retrenchment in state spending aimed at lowering the tax levies on landowners and attracting Eastern economic investments. Railroads, mining, and insurance were particularly successful in receiving special treatment. Rare was the tax assessor who would evaluate railroad land at a fair value—although as we saw earlier, John Albert Dean, my great-grandfather and tax assessor for Blount County did. Redeemers also limited the abilities of local governments to raise money for public services, particularly schools. The average length of the typical school term dropped around 20% during Redemption, and did not regain its Reconstruction average until after 1900.[2] Thomas was in his schooling years during the height of the Redeemer governments.

The lack of schooling did not mean that Thomas did not study. "On the farm, in the woods, on the bank of the river, in the river and up and down the brooks and creeks, nature was my university." Yet he hungered for the knowledge that he could not acquire through observation and experience. "In my university of nature I received courses in agriculture, horticulture, botany, biology and forestry. But of sociology, psychology, and business I learned almost nothing. We were too isolated to observe anything of value."

Charley and Eliza were concerned, and sent Thomas to the village of Geneva to buy a book to teach him to read. He returned with *McGuffy's First Reader*, and he learned by "studying at night by the light of a wood fire, my mother helping me."

As poor and isolated as his family was, the attitudes of his parents toward education and betterment clearly reinforced his desire to escape poverty through education. Yet again and again poverty and the demands of the farm interfered with that path.

Charley and Eliza were intensely religious, which gave Thomas a sense of direction. For Thomas religion was salvation, because what we would call today "peer pressure" led down a different path. He describes his companions as "avowedly wicked, constantly violating civil and moral law. . . . With the idea prevailing that the boldest violator was the greatest hero, I feel that I might have degenerated into an incorrigible but for the restraints and instructions of the Christian religion . . . I give credit to the Bible, my parents, and the Methodist Church. Methodist ministers were frequent visitors to our home and contributed a large share to our religious life."

Finally at age 15 he was able to attend the short 3-month school schedule more regularly. "My first real impulse and inspiration to study and look, with some degree of hope, to a future life of intelligence, was in the summer of 1891, when I entered school." There Thomas encountered an inspirational teacher, not much older than he was. Thomas entered school literally years behind the other students in the school and confesses, "I was greatly embarrassed because of my ignorance."

Thomas was a successful student, and at the end of the 3-month term his instructor, Will Campbell, moved on to teach at another location for the winter. Campbell offered to take Thomas with him and promised to prepare him to teach. "This gave me a thrill of hope for future success such as I had never known before." But Thomas's older brothers had left home, and the eviction from the McGowan place meant he was needed to clear and plant.

Thomas writes, "I worked with my father, but my mind was far away. My ardent longing for intellectual and religious expansion and culture burned within me like a consuming fire." He fumed, prayed, asked advice, and generally chafed under the constraints. He did not think those around him understood his "wing-flappings against the bars of my cage." He read everything he could find, which was not much, including the Bible, but "that was hard reading for me." He was resentful that he had not been able to take advantage of this opportunity offered by Campbell "to take a needed step upward on the ladder of knowledge." Resentful, brooding, and frustrated, Thomas was surely quite a pain to be around.

Working as the Wiregrass Transforms

In 1894, Charley and his family moved again. My grandfather, now 21, set out on his own. He first worked as a day laborer for a neighboring farmer. Then he was hired by a timberman; as he writes, "My duty, along with the other members of the crew, was to follow the floating pine logs in the creek and see that they did not stop against the bank or other obstructions until they reached the sawmill miles below."

He continued,

> I had to learn to ride a log floating loose in the water and at the same time carry a peavey weighing about twenty to thirty pounds. We had to stand on the log with our hands free to work using the peavey to push the other logs to keep them from stopping against some object. At the sawmill the logs were sawn to square timber. The timber was thrown back into the creek, floated into the Choctawhatchee River, thence to the Gulf of Mexico and marketed.

The timber camp was near enough to Coffee Springs that Grandaddy was able to attend church and attend a pop-up school engineered by the timberman employing him. He entered school for a 10-week term. Again he was a successful student, and "I began to hope for a life above that of a common laborer . . . To hope to earn my living with my brains and not my hands." His friends urged him to "buy a farm on credit and pay for it as I might be able." But "I saw only the endless cycle of another generation falling into the old groove of the past and living out its life on the same dead level."

At that point, his mother, Eliza, grew increasingly anxious about the family's future, and asked Thomas to help. She felt that moving to town would allow the women to go to work, and her husband Charley could go back to carpentry. Thomas brought in the crops and helped the family move in early 1895 to Newton, where they thought he could get work in the town sawmill. But he found no work there, so he walked the 30 miles to Geneva and caught a steamer to Holmes, Florida, where he signed on with another logging firm.

The firm "sent the men out in to the virgin pine forest to fell the trees and cut off the top. Then with oxen or mules and tall-wheeled cart, and also a steam engine for the extra-large trees, the logs were brought to a railroad track, placed on flat cars and hauled to Choctawhatchee River. Here they were measured, cut into desired lengths, and rolled into the river and floated to Caryville, Fla. to a large lumber mill" (Figure 15.1).

Figure 15.1 Lumber Mill in Geneva around 1920. Logs still floated down the river and were pulled out for sawing into boards.

Source: Wade Hall Postcard Collection, Troy University Libraries [https://digital.archives. alabama.gov/digital/collection/troy2/id/4891/rec/2].

The railroads had come to the Wiregrass, allowing lumbering to take place on an industrial scale. Companies built short lines connecting the forests to waterways; as railways were extended, they carried logs further distances. As roads improved, logging trucks became common on Alabama roads.

Granddaddy first worked on a railroad crew, maintaining the tracks, then was transferred to a logging crew at the riverbank because of his knowledge of the peavey. He sawed the logs with a cross-cut saw and rolled them into the river using the peavey. He found the work pleasant and with his robust frame handled it easily. Yet he was a puzzle to his workmates, as he did not swear.

Industrial firms from out of the region integrated Black workers into the logging teams and often gave them equal pay. This led to racial tensions, as my grandfather noted: "Both negroes and whites were working for the firm. At times the white men would grow dissatisfied with the blacks because both had to work together and received the same wage. At one time—I was not on the works at the time—there was a small riot. Rifles and shotguns were used, and one black man was shot to pieces."

Racial tensions flare when the status of previously dominant groups are challenged. No whites lost jobs because of Black workers, and the pay was good in the industrial logging operations—especially compared to the alternatives. But integration and equal pay challenged the status of working-class whites, and they sometimes reacted violently.

"What a Hard Master Is Poverty!"

Granddaddy found the work at the logging camp "not unpleasant." But he found his fellow lumber workers' horizons limited, and he found himself deeply discontented at his lack of progress in life. He still desired to be a teacher, "the State of Florida, even then, had a very fine system of public education including normal schools for the training of teachers. . . . I felt a strong impulse to drop my working tools from my grasp and hike myself to the Normal School at DeFuniak Springs about twenty-eight miles away, and seek admission even if I was without funds. But I could not nerve myself to make so daring an adventure."

The Florida experience frustrated him terribly, and he penned a *cri de coeur*: "What a hard master is poverty! And ignorance is the handmaiden of poverty. When the two working together lay hold of a poor mortal, the bondage is truly a hard one."

In 1895, the logging firm suspended operations in Holmes, probably because the area was timbered out, and Granddaddy headed back to Alabama.

Thomas entered a period of aimlessness, desiring more education and to move on from the laboring class, but unable to put together a serious plan for doing so. As the Wiregrass was settled, educators were in short supply, and in 1895 Granddaddy was able to pass a test for a provisional teaching license. He taught in a one-room schoolhouse for a three-month term. "In my school, there were no grades, no standards, and no requirements as to the work done. The children brought such books as they had and I taught them out of such knowledge as I had." This is quite a comparison with the white schools in the Black Belt, where about the same time my great-grandfather Robert Bryan Carr was learning Latin.

At the end of the term, Thomas went back to aid his parents, who had returned to the Coffee Springs rented farm. Town life in Newton had not worked out. After the crops were planted, he taught at a nearby school in the summer and fall. When the term closed in December, Thomas was again haunted with his desire to get "established in whatever calling I was to follow in life."

That is not what he did. Instead he went to the town of Ozark, where the nearest railroad was, and bought a ticket to Columbus, Georgia, returning with less money and no job. He recognized his mistake, commenting, "I was saving no money nor was I advancing in any other way. I think I must have had a vague idea that to get on a train and go somewhere would help to break my shell of limitations." So what did he do? He took a steamer ride, which was "quite a thrill."

Granddaddy headed to the new town of Enterprise, joining his brother Henry in building houses. In 1897 the railroad arrived, and the town was growing, so the building trade was booming. However Granddaddy's provisional teaching license expired, and he was unable to teach again. He says he had no time to prepare for the exam for a permanent license, but frankly that seems lame.

In spring 1898 the Spanish-American War broke out, and Granddaddy's teacher and mentor from his first stint at schooling asked him to join a cavalry company. But that fell through, and he was offered a position in the infantry. Perhaps remembering his father's difficult time in the Alabama 15th, he declined.

That summer, some cattlemen from Texas and Oklahoma came to Enterprise to buy cattle to ship back there, fattening them up on the prairies and shipping them north to the industrializing Midwest. Thomas signed on to keep the cattle on the train from falling down and getting trampled by the other animals in the car. His crew of guys from Enterprise managed to get the herd to Texas through two train changes and rode first class back.

He wrote of his impression of the open prairies of the area:

> The treeless plains of the West made a profound impression on my mind. As far as one could see the gently sloping hills covered with a carpet of green. The cowboys sitting straight in their saddles riding back and forth watching the large herds. The sky-line beyond a glimmering wave. The herds in the distance reminded me of ants crowding at my feet.

One sees a disconnect between Granddaddy's dreams and the aimlessness of his life path. He had moved from job to job with no concrete direction. While he pined for another life, there is no indication that he was making any concrete progress. He writes, "I was getting nowhere. I was not saving any money to pay school expenses. I was not reading or otherwise gaining knowledge to fit me for my work. I was in my 27th year. Something ought to be done!"

Granddaddy Pursues His Dream

According to his recollections, Granddaddy decided to devote his life to preaching on his return from the prairies of Texas and Oklahoma. He still was reticent because of his lack of formal education (an indication of how institutionalized the Methodist Church was becoming; quite a distance from the Second Great Awakening and camp preaching of his great-grandfather, Brother Charley Jones).

He apparently had no particular plan for getting there, and "I had never known a young man to do such a thing before. . . . But I had a great inspiration; I was seeking to fulfill the high purpose of Almighty God in my life." The inspiration led him to borrow money, but loaning money to a fellow who had shown no sense of direction in his life and had no assets whatsoever from his endeavors was not a good risk. Nevertheless Thomas managed to get a loan of $75 from a local money-lender—who charged 20% interest!

In January 1899 Granddaddy headed off to Troy Normal School, and although he was not qualified for admission, he persuaded the president to allow him a special admission. As usual his haphazard planning caused him to fail again, as his money gave out before the school year ended. The college president insisted that he stay until the end of the term and pay his expenses, but he left instead, apparently defaulting on his debts to the money-lender and the college.

Here was a man in his late 20s who had little formal education, who was mostly self-taught, who had had jobs as a farmer, a logger, a carpenter, a worker on a turpentine farm, a Bible salesman, and a temporary teacher. He had attended college with no plan to pay for the experience, and defaulted on the loan that got him there. While he was apparently quite good at farming and carpentry, he chaffed at the limits of these jobs. He had a burning desire to teach or preach, but no plan to qualify for either.

The Exhorter

Then Thomas' life took a turn for the better. The pastor of Troy Methodist Church told Thomas that he could qualify as an exhorter, a lay preacher in the Methodist Church. He took the examination and was licensed to preach. The Methodist Conference hired him on the spot, and assigned him a rural region, and bought him a horse, which he named "Maude." It was a mission circuit, in a sparsely settled area in Pike, Coffee, and Covington Counties. His job was to seek out Methodists among the settlers and organize congregations.

Granddaddy and Maude traversed throughout the region, frequently off the main roads in the backcountry, from logging camp to logging camp, deep in the pines. He made appointments to preach and established new churches in this large region of mostly unoccupied countryside. "I was a pioneer surveying the territory," he wrote. "I went forth as a stranger in a strange land." He and Maude relied on the kindness of strangers for food and lodging.

The next year, Granddaddy was transferred to a regular circuit, preaching in four rural churches around Greenville, north in the Black Belt region. There he suffered a severe relapse of his malaria. It lingered for weeks, but he continued his circuit duties.

He also continued his informal education. His higher salary allowed him to buy periodicals and books; he subscribed to three church papers and weekly editions of the *Montgomery Advertiser*, the *Atlanta Constitution*, and the *Atlanta Sunday South*. He was chastised for spending so much on newspapers, but that did not deter him.

Granddaddy writes of the total eclipse of the sun that occurred on May 28. He wrote that the chickens went to roost, even though it was about 10 in the morning. His circuit, firmly within the Black Belt, had plantations and many Black tenants and sharecroppers on them. He passed on the old myth of Black fear because of alleged ignorance. "There were large numbers of Negros on the plantations. It was said many of them became so frightened at the strange darkness that they fled from the fields, panic stricken."

Granddaddy Finally Goes to College

Through his involvement in the Methodist Church, Granddaddy was able to secure a position at the Methodist-sponsored College in Greensboro, the now-defunct Southern University, in 1901. A friend put Granddaddy in touch with a wealthy lumberman who was willing to lend him money to go to school.

It is questionable whether he graduated. On a form he filled out for the Methodist Church, he failed to fill in a blank for year graduated. Nor did he attend theological school. In any case, he was licensed to preach, and was assigned to the Sumter County village of York, where Laura Carr was a schoolteacher nearby. The son of a tenant farmer married the granddaughter of a slaveholding plantation owner in 1905, which led to some friction in the marriage and a storyline for the novel he wrote in retirement.

My grandfather's stubborn if inconsistent commitment led finally to both a college education and a career as a Methodist minister. He held posts in 23 churches in the 40 years until his retirement. It was common practice to rotate Methodist ministers so that they would not allow local thinking to contaminate the purity of the gospel they taught—or so I was told as a boy.

The couple rotated through villages and towns throughout south Alabama, never staying in one town more than three years, and usually one or two. Each of their children was born in a different town. My father, his oldest son, was born in Elba in 1908. Both of Thomas's daughters married men they met while Granddaddy was preaching for a short time in their towns. Granddaddy presided over the marriage of my mother and father in 1942. He never lost his commitment to education, formal and informal, nor to addressing the social problems related to alcohol. But he never included a concern for racial injustice through the period.

Dash for Freedom

Granddaddy retired in 1945, at 73. Interviewed in 1952, at 80, he said, "the last ten years have been the most interesting of my life."[3] He bought and improved a farm and sold it at a profit. He built a house, sold it, taking a mortgage to improve his pension payments. He studied alcohol addiction, traveling to Yale and New York to do so, and became a leader in the temperance movement in Alabama. He gave a talk on temperance at the University of Alabama in 1960, but I'm not sure that a university campus was the most receptive venue.

In his late 70s, Granddaddy sat down his Underwood typewriter on the small table in the front bedroom of their bungalow, and wrote a novel, *Dash for Freedom*, published in 1951. In doing the work for this book, I read it. It was a real surprise. I always assumed that the book was on alcoholism, given Granddaddy's commitment to the temperance movement.

But the book is not about alcoholism. It was avowedly feminist for its day. Set in New York during the Great Depression, its main character is a strong-willed young woman, Hortense Boling. Hortense lived her early life on a plantation in Virginia but moved to New York when her mother died. Brought up in pampered privilege, the ambitious, driven Hortense seeks a life of service, but her family, led by her successful businessman uncle, feels that these are not suitable pursuits for a woman of her status. Wealth had the effect of limiting opportunities of ambitious women seeking to improve life for others.

The book is ruthless in its social criticism of the hypocrisy of American institutions. They fail to address the needs of individuals and consequently fail to take advantage of the assets of those individuals, especially women. No representative of a major institution in American society escapes scorn. Granddaddy adroitly explores their reasoning—or rather justifications—for supporting myths that buttress institutions. The author convinces the reader that the remorseful institution-supporter—whether minister, businessman, judge, or crime boss—has redeemed himself, only to discover that he invariably slides back into his comfortable condescending role.

The minister of Hortense's well-funded church, St. Altros, acts from a position of rigid morality and is more concerned with protecting the reputation of his church than ministering to the needy. He is occasionally tormented by his failure but looks to the businessmen on the church board for guidance. They reassure him that compassion can go too far and that deviation from their rigid conception of morality is unacceptable. And he gives long, repetitive and boring sermons—which he realizes but justifies. Perhaps it is no accident that the *Greenville Advocate*, the newspaper in a town where Granddaddy served, noted, "His sermons are pleasingly brief, calm, concise, and clear."[4]

Hortense gains control of a criminal gang, and briefly becomes a crime boss herself. She uses her ill-gotten gains to set up a refuge for mistreated women forced into prostitution by corrupt men. She has fulfilled her dream of service to humankind on her own terms.

Hortense meets her old flame from her Virginia days—the son of a tenant farmer who has worked his way out of poverty and is now a physician with a New York hospital. Hortense's class-sensitive mother had prohibited their marriage back then. While his flame is immediately reignited, Hortense holds back, afraid that her career may be curtailed. Only when Hortense is assured that her suitor is supportive of her enterprise and ambitions do they marry.

While rough around the edges and centered on an improbable plot, the book is commendable in its depiction of the construction of myths in the minds of the hypocritical defenders of corrupt institutions. The author shows how strong those myths are and how they may be breached in some exceptional circumstances by strong-willed individuals, including women. Granddaddy's ability to depict how the benefactors of social stratification can think through their hypocrisy and actively justify staying the unjust course is striking. Ministers, businessmen, and government officials may make mistakes and even admit them, but they never question the system that benefits them.

The book raised all sorts of questions in my mind. I knew from his autobiography that Granddaddy had worked his way up from poverty and illiteracy to a career as a Methodist minister, and that he was strongly committed to the cause of temperance. But I was shocked at his strong social criticism of institutions and his defense of feminism. Traces of his tenant-farming upbringing show in Hortense's fiancé. Similarly, his wife, my grandmother, hailed from a plantation family, and like Hortense, her father had died when she was young.

The critique of religion is unmistakable. Maybe Granddaddy harbored some resentment from his career as a minister, seeing hypocrisy there, or resenting aspects of his assignments. In any case, it is not accidental that a justice of the peace rather than an ordained minister performed the marriage between Hortense and her lover.

I had assumed that Granddaddy held conventional views on such matters, spending his life as a minister in Southeast Alabama. Clearly I was wrong. Where did Granddaddy's supportive position on woman's rights come from? Did he support the 19th Amendment? Had it come from working with strong women in the Temperance Movement? Was it from the influence of his wife, who was apparently more independent and strong-willed than I had understood?

Then there is the issue of race. What was his position on Jim Crow and segregation, not brouched at all in *Dash for Freedom*? Churches in South Alabama were known for segregation and conservatism—the South Alabama–North Florida Conference, Granddaddy's conference, was one of only two conferences nationally to vote against the reunification of the Methodist Church in the mid 1950s, repairing the pre–Civil War breach.[5]

Indeed he did harbor the conventional white segregationist view. In an interview for the *Troy Messenger* in 1956, he called the mixing of races "not integration. It would be dis-integration not only in schools, but in our total cultural and social order."[6] Many Southerners were strong progressives but also segregationists, as seemingly he was.

Oak Park and the Coming Changes

At my parents' urging, I spent a week in Montgomery one summer with my grandparents as a preteenager. I figured I was in for a boring time with these stodgy old folks. It was anything but that. We went out every day to the Capitol, or swimming, or some other activity. I swam at the beautiful Oak Park pool, unimaginable to a small-town boy. It was so much bigger and with more diving boards than the simple Murphree Park pool in Troy. The park was spectacular, with a small zoo and ample open space with a substantial playground.

But a couple of years later, the pool was filled in and paved over, and the zoo closed. Indeed, the whole Park Department was closed. In 1958, Montgomery Blacks instituted a class action suit to desegregate the city's parks, and in 1959 the Federal District Court ordered the parks desegregated. Rather than comply, the city closed the parks, sold the zoo animals, and filled in the pool. Neither whites nor Blacks could enjoy the beautiful park, an example used pointedly by Heather McGhee of how segregation punished all citizens regardless of race.[7] But Montgomery whites weren't ready to give up public recreation programs or to share them with Black citizens. The City arranged programs with the YMCA, which promised to keep them segregated. In 1974 the case reached the Supreme Court, which upheld the District Court's ruling prohibiting the arrangement.

Evenings were quieter, but interesting. I recall nothing of the substance of the conversations, only that Granddaddy gave grace every meal. While my Grandmother talked of the Carrs in general terms, my Grandfather never mentioned his family. I have no idea why he never raised the background of his family, but he did not; for that matter, neither did my parents. We had no family stories from the war or afterward, although many could have been told. So the gaps in Granddaddy and Grandmother's lives remain unfilled, and Thomas Glenn Jones remains far more of an enigma than I understood before I picked up *Dash for Freedom*.

At 97 years of age, Granddaddy wrote to his grandchildren. He had designed a letterhead, which read: *The Alcohol Problem: Thomas Glenn Jones, Writer, Student, Researcher.* I suspect we'd all be better off if we thought of ourselves as students throughout our lives, as he did. He died in 1970, at age 98.

Montgomery 2019

In the fall of 2019, my wife Diane and I took a civil rights tour that went from Atlanta to Montgomery to Selma to Birmingham. For me, it was homecoming; I had not been in Montgomery since we drove the 50 miles from Troy for visiting my grandparents, makng occasional shopping trips and once a year to see the Ice Capades. For the rest of the civil rights tourists, it was their first view of the deepest South. Montgomery had changed from the bustling downtown centered on Court Square at Dexter and Commerce of my boyhood, before the suburbanization of white flight and malls. Before the Civil War, Court Square was the center of the town's booming slave trade.

Surprisingly for the town that was the first capital of the Confederacy and where George Wallace gave his infamous "segregation forever" speech in 1963, today Montgomery is capitalizing on that sordid past through museums highlighting the barbarism of slavery and Jim Crow, equal justice, and the civil rights movement. The City is promoting a concerted effort to redevelop the warehouses where slaves were quartered before auction at Court Square into a restaurant, shopping, and downtown living area. Montgomery is dealing with its ugly past in a frank and unromantic way, and that seems proving to be a good investment.

While there, Diane and I decided to go over to the Oakwood Cemetery to visit the grave of my grandparents. Like other cemeteries throughout the South, this one has white and Black sections; segregation continued into death. There a helpful supervisor located the grave and even drove us over to the Oakwood Annex, also known as the Hank Williams Memorial Cemetery. Behold, my grandparents are buried but a few steps from Hank's grave and memorial. Their youngest daughter, my Aunt Virginia, was appalled that her religious parents were buried so close to a honky-tonk sinner.

The minister and the sinner. The minister from humble roots who saw through the hypocracy of religion buried alongside the sinner who contributed so much to music that documentarian Ken Burns called him "the Hillbilly Shakespeare" in his series on country music. Perhaps not as far apart as one might think.

The Jones Trace

In the early 1800s, Brother Charley Jones had reached some degree of Southern respectability in South Carolina, but he threw it all overboard to pursue the calling of God. The family fell out of Southern respectability by that move, and soon joined the ranks of the common man.

In an era in which most people were religious, the Joneses were especially so. For my grandfather, a commitment to religion and the need to earn a living dominated his early years. His autobiographical notes contain no thoughts about politics—especially striking because as a young man he toiled in a region deeply split over Populism. Nor did he write much about the plight of Blacks, seemingly accepting Jim Crow while being strongly sympathetic to the plight of women. He was highly critical of the oligarchic structure of American institutions. His father, Charles Cade Jones, was connected through Civil War veteran networks to conservative Democratic politicians. Without *Dash for Freedom*, I would have put the same label on Granddaddy. But he seems to have been a fiery if segregationist Progressive, driven by his temperance commitment and his strident critiques of the operation of American institutions.

PART 4

The Long and Wretched Jim Crow

To the people of Blount County my great uncle Julius Davidson was "Our Demosthenes" because his rhetorical skills made him the best lawyer in the region. Julius was a fascinating character in the drama that unfolded at the end of the 19th century. He was a committed Populist tilting at the real dragons of Black Belt planters, was supportive of Black voting, and opposed the white supremacist 1901 state constitution. When he saw there would be no future for Populism, he moved to the Republican Party.

When he realized the futility of progressive Republican politics in Alabama after Blacks were irrevocably removed from politics, Julius acquired leadership of the Lily White faction of the Alabama Republican Party. He had come full circle from Populist radical to segregationist conservative. Yet the story of Julius's role in opposing a segregated Southern governmental system was not done.

The strategy of building a progressive, segregated Southern Republican Party was both racist and a failure. It helped ensure the one-party dominance of the Bourbon wing of the Democratic Party as uplanders were disenfranchised from participation and were disenchanted with politics. Republican politics no longer motivated them.

The state and the rest of the Deep South declined into stultifying one-party segregationist politics. The defensive nature of "our Southern way of life" discouraged entrepreneurship and helped keep the South poor and an intellectual and economic backwater for many decades.

The New South that emerged after the segregationist constitutions was built on institutional apartheid and a parallel psychology of a hierarchy of races that destroyed the vitality of a budding interracial democracy. The new Solid South was built based on disenfranchisement of both Blacks and poor whites, undermining the incentives of ambitious men like Julius Davidson to build cross-race coalitions.

The so-called New South emerged between the two critical junctures of Populism and the civil rights movement. These movements bracketed the long Jim Crow period that governed race relations in Southern states for two-thirds of the 20th century. The structure was so strong that even two world wars and a deep and long economic depression could not dislodge it. There were challenges to this race-based system of status allocation, mostly by Blacks, during the Great Depression and after both World Wars, yet the final death of Jim Crow did not occur for 20 more years after the wars. The Jim Crow structure was so resilient because so many whites acquiesced in it as the only system they knew. Progressive whites had learned that being liberal in the deep South during the period meant accepting racial segregation while being liberal on economics.

Although the system was buttressed by strong cultural norms, the keystone to the American apartheid was its legal structure. With the blessing of the U.S. Supreme Court in *Giles v. Harris*, Southern legislatures could pass laws regulating the behaviors of Blacks. They did so with abandon. Laws affecting the races equally, such as most of the criminal code, were often applied unequally. White-on-Black violence was common, not infrequently involving vigilante tactics. Southern Blacks were not passive in the face of these arbitrary laws and their unjust enforcement, both resisting and building resilience.[1]

Duties of public officials enforcing criminal justice frequently conflicted with the demands of whites for immediate and too often unjust implementation. Police, prosecutors, judges, and defense lawyers met with pressure from their communities to allow vigilante justice. Sheriffs frequently stood by while vigilantes took control of Black prisoners. Even when law enforcement officials resisted, their jails were too weak to withstand the determination of white mobs.

Defense lawyers in cases involving alleged lurid or violent actions on the part of Black defendants were in difficult situations. They were threatened with loss of their clients, and generally refused to provide counsel to Black defendants.[2] When they did accept the job, they were hounded by the local press and shunned by many in the white community.

In this section I explore three instances in which my ancestors defended Blacks accused in cases that riled the white community. These sagas are often singled out as white savior stories, and indeed they are. Given the inability of Blacks to participate in the Southern criminal law processes except as defendants, where else would salvation emerge? If salvation did emerge, were such events more common in more open North Alabama than in the more stratified South?

The classic rendition of the Southern defense lawyer who defends a Black accused of a heinous crime is Atticus Finch in Harper Lee's *To Kill a Mockingbird*. Finch's defense proved to be a failure leading to a tragedy, but not all such defenses turned out that way. As the once bright embers of the Populist uprising faded, Julius Davidson defended Henderson Tunstall, a former slave who shot and killed a white justice of the peace in Blount County. Julius saved Tunstall from an almost certain lynching and defended him successfully at his trial for murder. A few years later, my grandfather and Julius's younger brother, M. M. Davidson, saved another Black man from the gallows.

The third case involves the arc of justice that extended from the creation of unjust segregationist laws in the 1901 state constitution to the final destruction of the legal system that had enabled those unjust laws in the mid-1960s. J.O. Sentell Sr., was an important voice in the white supremacist constitutional convention, a voice for excluding Blacks from participation in politics. His son, my uncle by marriage, J.O. Sentell Jr., helped to prosecute Klan murderers of a participant in the 1965 Selma to Montgomery march—an event that President Lyndon Johnson cited in the speeches supporting the Voting Rights Act of 1965 that enforced the 15th Amendment, ensuring Blacks the right to vote.

CHAPTER 16

A Lynching Thwarted and a Brutal Murder

Gunnar Myrdal, a Swedish sociologist, conducted a monumental study of American race relations in the 1940s, producing *An American Dilemma*. He found that the economic condition of Blacks in the South was terrible because the system of segregation buttressed by white supremacy offered few quality jobs or opportunities for advancement. Consequently, Blacks were mired in poverty in both rural areas and urban ghettos.

Myrdal found that the treatment of Blacks in courts was even worse than in economic life, and that Blacks were terrified of the legal system. Blacks were at the mercy of whites there, and courts often did not protect the life, liberty, or property of Black accused. Judges and juries, invariably all white, generally believed white testimony over Black.[1] There were few Black lawyers in most of the South, and many white lawyers refused to defend Blacks, out of prejudice, or fear of loss of clients, or concern for the lack of ability of the Black defendant to pay.

As bad as courts were, there was something even worse. Law enforcement was not just meted out by officials of the state; extralegal gangs of whites often sought vengeance against Blacks accused of crimes through lynching, beatings, and other forms of violence.

My maternal grandfather, M.M. Davidson, and his brother and my maternal great-uncle, Julius Davidson, both North Alabama lawyers, played major roles in two legal dramas involving Blacks and the Southern legal system. Both were defense lawyers in murder trials of Black men. Julius was instrumental in stopping a likely lynching, and both M.M. and Julius managed to deflect the course of the legal system that would have led to the hanging of two accused Black men. Here I recount the stories of these two events; in both cases the energetic defenses of the Davidsons in a deeply flawed and biased system led to better outcomes than if they had not intervened.

While these interventions were admirable and even brave, the broader picture is the systemic unfairness of a Southern justice system that carried over from the days of these events in the first decade of the 20th century to the 1960s and even today. And they highlight the even higher bar to justice in South Alabama than in North.

A Black Man Kills a White Justice of the Peace

On July 21, 1899, Henderson Tunstall, a Black farmer and former slave, and Justice of the Peace J.K. Hamilton got into a heated argument in Blount Springs. The argument faded, and Tunstall went home.

Justice of the Peace Hamilton continued to seethe. That night, he rode out to Tunstall's farm, accompanied by four deputy sheriffs, bent on executing an arrest warrant. Tunstall saw them coming and prepared to defend himself and his family, home at the time. In the ensuing gunfight, both Tunstall and the officers opened fire. Apparently the deputies fired first, with Tunstall returning fire. Tunstall killed Hamilton, and the deputies wounded Tunstall.[2] Tunstall immediately fled the scene. He strode through the the woods and mountains of Blount County for several days, avoiding the lynch mob cobbled together by friends of Hamilton. As he thought through the matter, Tunstall decided the best course of action was to surrender to the authorities. He headed over to the residence of a deputy sheriff, where he was apprehended and taken to nearby Cullman and jailed there.[3]

Talk of lynching intensified in Blount Springs. As was customary, newspapers played down the threat of lynching in Cullman.[4] Downplaying the likelihood of a lynching was all too common in Southern papers, but crime stories in newspapers were part of the problem. When a crime was sensationalized by newspapers and passed around by word of mouth, there was always a serious possibility of a lynch mob forming.

Surprisingly, he regional press exhibited considerable sympathy for Tunstall. The Birmingham Age-Herald printed major articles that were highly sympathetic to Tunstall. The local Cullman paper feared the possibility, stating, "Some misinformed persons are declaring there was no evidence of a lynching when the slayer of Justice J.K. Hamilton was brought to this place for safe keeping. Perhaps there was not a strong probability of a 'necktie party,' but there was a possibility of a party, and it was unquestionably the sheriff's duty to take measures to protect the prisoner." It is likely that the sheriff was receiving considerable criticism for taking these measures, probably because the citizenry of Cullman had some sympathy for the would-be Blount County lynch mob.

The Cullman Sheriff issued a curious response. He admitted racism in the county almost proudly, but vowed to protect Tunstall: "The negro is not a citizen of this county, and we might add that it will be many years perhaps before he is tolerated, but our people are law-abiding, peace-loving citizens and when a prisoner, though he be a negro, is brought here to deliver him from mob violence, he will be protected. Our people have no love for the negro, but the law must be respected." The possibility of a lynching led the Sheriff to form a posse to guard the jail. He was receiving a great deal of misinformation from people posing as law enforcement officers demanding custody of Tunstall, and he observed strangers in town milling around.[5] It is clear here that "the negro" refers to the race, not to Tunstall. Cullman County, located in the mountains of North Alabama, had few Blacks, and clearly wanted to remain that way. In the early-to-mid 20th century, the city was known as a "sundown town."

Two stellar lawyers quickly signed on to defend Tunstall—U.S. District Attorney for North Alabama William Vaughn and Assistant D.A. Julius Davidson, who had recently been appointed to his position by President McKinley. The choice of defense attorneys, themselves federal prosecutors, was an intriguing development, since it is suggestive of an interest by President McKinley's Justice Department in the case.

The Role of the Press in Encouraging Lynchings

How probable was the lynching of Tunstall? It is hard to discount a strong probability, for an array of reasons. Tunstall had killed a law enforcement officer in pursuit of his duties, even if Hamilton was out for revenge rather than justice. A Black man killing a white law enforcement official was enough to inflame a community to moral outrage and vigilante violence in the 1890s.

Lynchings were common in Alabama and the rest of the South during the period. The Equal Justice Institute has verified that 361 Blacks were lynched in Alabama from 1877 through 1950. The 1890s saw the highest number of lynchings in the United States, most of which occurred in the South.[6]

The "yellow press" of the period, which valued sensational headlines over carefully documented journalism, added fuel to the lynching flame in high-profile crime cases. News reports not infrequently offered support, sometimes enthusiastic support, to the perpetrators of lynchings, especially right after the incident.

The *Atlanta Constitution*, the yellow press leader in the period, wrote about five incidents in a single day's issue in 1897 under such titles as "Swung from an Alabama Tree."[7] One of the articles, "The Thrilling Story of the Hanging," began with the statement, "No effort is being made by the authorities to discover the identities of the men who lynched Dr. W.L. Ryder last night, and there is good reason to believe that none will be made." The *Constitution* had an artist on the scene, and carried the sketch on its front page (Figure 16.1).[8]

Law enforcement officers often, but by no means always, strove to protect prisoners, and district attorneys generally sought to bring the mobs to justice. When they did, newspapers often criticized them for doing so. After an Alabama Black Belt lynching, the local newspaper attacked the county judge for convening a grand jury "to have the so-called murderers brought to justice, or rather to law. We always entertained a better opinion of Judge Carmichael than to believe he would descend to such dodges for a little notoriety."[9]

SCENE JUST BEFORE DR. RYDER WAS LYNCHED, NEAR WAVERLY HALL, GA.
(From a sketch made on the scene by a Constitution artist.)

Figure 16.1 "The Thrilling Story of The Hanging." A sketch artist captured the event as an eyewitness. The *Atlanta Constitution* published the etching on the first page.

Source: *Atlanta Constitution*, July 21, 1897; Newspapers.com [https://www.newspapers.com/image/26900943/].

This note appeared in the *Blount County News Dispatch*, which reprinted it from the *Fort Payne Journal*, which doubtless picked it up from a paper in Lee County, far from the hills and mountains of Fort Payne and Blountsville. The extensive networks of newspaper coverage, along with the availability of articles over the telegraph wires, acted somewhat as today's social media network. Passing around inflammatory news items often added to the sensationalism. In the same way social media can generate cascades of horror today, the wire services in the 1890s could share sensationalized crime accounts generating similar copycat waves.

The pure horror of one lynching technique, burning at the stake, should have generated great negative press, yet mostly the press failed to decry this atrocity. Instead, it often blamed the victim. The press coverage labeled one victim "a black fiend" and wrote of the mob as extracting vengeance.[10] Under a subheadline, "Sam Hose Meets His Just Desserts," another Alabama paper commented, "It was cruel and barbarous treatment, no more than he deserved, but we do not see how civilized people could be so cruel."[11] Such comments were apparently about the best editors could do.

Burning at the stake was a terrible torture, but not infrequently used by white mobs. In 1904, Booker T. Washington, president of Tuskegee Institute, published a letter in the *Birmingham Age-Herald* under the title "A Protest against the Burning and Lynching of Negroes." Washington noted, "Within the last fortnight three members of my race have been burned at the stake," all accused of murder. He noted that the collapse of the rule of law in these cases would not stop with Blacks but would affect whites as well.[12] The Associated Press sent Washington's letter out over its wires to papers all over the country.

The generally uncritical or even positive "got what they deserved" coverage of lynching surely encouraged the mobs and made future lynchings more likely. Most newspapers tended to accept the mob leaders' justification for the lynching regardless of whether the alleged crime would have been punishable by death even had it been proven in court.

Julius's Wire Saves Henderson Tunstall

In some cases, law officers acted appropriately, and at least some of the press supported justice. This characterized the Tunstall case, but it was close. The facts of the Tunstall case were not disputed. A Black man had a shootout with white law enforcement officers, and a white justice of the peace was killed. The tenor of the times, the encouragement of lynching by the press, and the sensationalized and easily stereotyped nature of the incident all point to a high probability of an attempted lynching. Indeed, a lynch mob pursued him through the woods of Blount County. Amazingly Tunstall was neither lynched nor sent to prison. How this could happen is a fascinating tale, and it is indicative of how the Southern justice system worked.

Any Black accused of a sensationalized crime was at risk. Tunstall was surely at great risk. The threats against Tunstall's life were extensive and came from the many friends of Justice of the Peace Hamilton. On the other hand, Tunstall was a respected member of the community, and Hamilton seems to have had something of a rogue reputation, so getting the case to a proper judge and jury could make a difference. Few lynchings took place in the mountain counties—the Equal Justice Institute has verified three in Blount and none in Cullman. However the EJI's standards are very high, and there were other reported lynchings in Cullman County.[13]

The local paper, the *Blount County News-Dispatch*, had taken strong stands against lynchings earlier in the decade—decrying one in Cullman and demanding that the lynch mob be brought to justice. A second article lauded a hanging in nearby Walker County conducted by law rather than by vigilante justice. The paper continued, "Mob law is a dangerous experiment and has a strong tendency to demoralize all who participate in it. Very often the parties who are prominent in these mobs are as great criminals as the party whom they victimize."[14]

Regardless of the reasons that Blount County papers might offer in support of the rule of law, the facts and the sensationalism made the Tunstall case ripe for trouble. And trouble was brewing. News reports warned of mobs forming in Blount Springs and elsewhere in the county.

The power of the demand for lynching left the Cullman sheriff overmatched. The ramshackle jail at Cullman was used more as a drunk tank than a place where high-profile prisoners could be held. As much as the local sheriff vowed to protect Tunstall, he and his small posse would be no match for a large mob. The typical elements leading to a lynching were in place.

Julius Davidson recognized the danger, and wired Governor Joseph Johnson, asking him to have state troopers escort Tunstall from Cullman to the far more secure jail in Birmingham. The governor rushed what today would be members of the National Guard to Cullman. One newspaper reported that a mob formed at Blount Springs and took the northbound passenger train toward Cullman. On finding out that state troopers had been sent, the mob stayed on the train and passed through Cullman. The men got off at the next stop and headed back home.[15]

Tunstall was brought to Birmingham "under guard of a company of militia for safe keeping." Prejudging the outcome of the trial, the newspaper article covering the event called Tunstall a "negro murderer."[16] There he stayed until his trial in December.

The Trial

The trial of Tunstall was set in Bangor, a few miles from Blount Springs, for December 15, before an all-white jury. The sheriff of Blount County received word that again Tunstall would be threatened with lynching. One passenger on a train through Blount County "stated that all through Blount County large crowds could be seen," and that several men said that "there would be 'fun in old Blount if the negro was brought back.'" The lynching threats led Julius to wire the governor, requesting that Tunstall be kept for trial in Jefferson County (Birmingham) rather than return to Blount. He received no response.

The transfer proceeded. The Blount County sheriff and two deputies, all armed, and defense lawyers William Vaughn and Julius Davidson, also armed, escorted the prisoner from Birmingham to Bangor without incident. Tunstall was not handcuffed, and "seemed to be an inoffensive negro," according to one of the deputies.[17]

Tunstall was an emancipated slave, and members of the family that had formerly held him attended the trial and spoke highly of him. From slavery until the breakdown of the Jim Crow consensus in the 1960s, Southern whites engaged in the gross stereotype that distinguished between "good" Blacks or "white folks' Blacks" and "troublemakers." Clearly Tunstall was viewed as a "good Black" in the community. It is likely that the family had Republican ties and had persuaded Davidson and Vaughn to defend Tunstall. On the other hand, he had killed a law enforcement officer, making the case a difficult one for the defense attorneys.

As the trial began, Davidson and Vaughn pleaded self-defense on behalf of the defendant. Defense counsel highlighted that the warrant that Justice Hamilton sought to serve was issued only after Tunstall and Hamilton had an argument in Blount Springs earlier that afternoon, making the case that the attempted arrest was a retaliatory action on the part of the hotheaded Hamilton. They played up the good character of Tunstall, and noted his stellar reputation in the county. The defense lawyers asserted that the deputies fired first, but the deputies claimed otherwise.

The trial lasted two days, and the jury began deliberation. After staying out three days the jury was unable to come to a verdict. The judge declared a mistrial, and committed Tunstall to the jail at Oneonta, the county seat. He set bond at a level that papers of the day asserted that the defendant could make. Given that authorities had received two serious threats of lynching, holding Tunstall in the local jail might be viewed as ill-advised. But Julius had no such qualms, stating to the press that the evidence presented in the trial had entirely removed all hard feeling against Tunstall, and holding him in the local jail was perfectly safe.[18]

I can find no further discussion of this case in local newspapers. Tunstall was neither executed by the State (he does not appear on a list of executions) nor was he lynched. Such a high-profile case would have attracted coverage if another trial took place, so I am convinced that Tunstall was not retried. It had already taken a week of the court's time, with no conviction. Apparently he went back to his home and continued his life as a respected Black Blount County farmer.

This does seem a surprising outcome for a Black man who killed a white law enforcement officer serving a warrant in Alabama. Tunstall benefited from his good reputation in town. National "heat" probably brought to bear on the case, and the stellar legal defense team was certainly unusual in cases like this one. The facts in the case indicated that the arrest warrant for Tunstall was issued on questionable grounds, and Davidson and Vaughn ably brought out the inconsistencies.

In any case, energetic and involved counsel likely made a difference. Few Blacks had access to such capable (and politically connected) representation. That the case took place in the North Alabama hills with a generally supportive press rather than the Black Belt prairies was clearly a factor as well.

M.M. Davidson's Controversial Cases

In 1906 my grandfather Marvin McCoy Davidson and my mother's father, known professionally as M.M. and colloquially as Coy, finished reading law with an uncle in Birmingham and became active in Republican Party politics. In 1906, M.M. was the Republican Party nominee for State Senate for the area, losing soundly to the Democratic nominee. In 1908 he was nominated for solicitor for the judicial district incorporating Gadsden, losing again. He ran a second time on the Republican ticket for the state senate; the local paper lampooned him for failing to speak at a rally "because nobody came to hear him."[19] M.M. was no favorite of the local press.

M.M. joined a law firm in the city of Gadsden and opened an office in the nearby small town of Attalla. The region was undergoing strong growth as the industrialization of North Alabama proceeded.

As a young lawyer M.M. he took the cases he could get, including several involving stereotypical bootleggers in the Appalachian hills. One case involved John Head, who located his Blind Tiger (an illicit drinking and gambling establishment) on the county line between Marshall and Etowah (locus of Gadsden). When things got too hot in Etowah, Head just moved across the line to Marshall. Finally Marshall County officials had enough and arrested Head. M.M. managed to get a verdict of not guilty, but as Head walked free he was arrested by Etowah officials.[20]

A more serious case caused a sensation throughout North Alabama. In 1906 four masked men, branded Klansmen by the Gadsden paper, boarded a train at a nearby small town, seeking to assault two U.S. revenue officers who had dismantled an illegal distillery nearby and were transporting the parts to Gadsden as evidence for a trial. Passengers hid the officers, and the Klansmen left the train, riding off toward a saloon where the barkeeper was subsequently murdered. As suspicious as the circumstances were, the evidence was inconclusive, and M.M. got conspiracy charges dropped against the four Klansmen.[21]

M.M. and his law firm handled several high-profile murder cases, including one in which the defendant was accused of killing a town policeman. The prosecution brought in Seaborn Wright from Georgia, "the great silver-tongued orator of the south . . . one of the south's greatest lawyers and one of the most brilliant men in the whole country," according to the local paper.[22] Davidson lost the case.

In another murder Davidson had such a weak case that he offered the defense that his client, a man named Elkins, was so drunk that he did not know what he was doing. Elkins was convicted but avoided the gallows. Davidson knew he was fated to lose the case, and directed his defense at saving his client's life. The local paper pointed out that the murder occurred in Mountainboro, and that "Elkins is a typical Mountainboro product, illiterate, shiftless, airless, and utterly without regard for society."[23] Several of M.M.'s liquor cases were located at Mountainboro as well; it seems to have been a haven for moonshine production and bootlegging. It also provided sustenance for a young defense lawyer.

Elkins, in a word, was the perfect stereotype of the hillbilly, the mountain cracker. Of course every community has its Elkins, but the stereotype stuck for Southern mountain men, carried forward in such literature as Cash's *Mind of the South*. In towns and cities and among the planter elite in the Black Belt, prejudice against mountain folk was strong. Press coverage often used language directed at the "hillbilly" element that was damning, revealing quite a bias against the rural mountain folk even in nearby towns; nothing like racial prejudice, but nevertheless strong. I wonder if M.M. recalled his close connection to the mountains; his father had moved from mountain potter to country doctor only 30 years before (Figure 16.2).

A Courtroom Brawl

One day in Tuscaloosa my mother's sister and my aunt, Mary Elizabeth Davidson, jumped up and went over to a bookshelf and pulled a folder out from among the books. She showed me a copy of a *Ripley's Believe It or Not* graphic, as it would be called today. *Ripley's* was a syndicated cartoon feature appearing in newspapers for many years featuring odd and unusual events. The

Figure 16.2 The Davidson Brothers. Left: Artist's Rendition of Julius; Right: M.M. Davidson

Source: Left (Julius): Permission of the Artist, Elinore English; Right (M.M.): Author's collection.

feature set up the following scenario: In a North Alabama courtroom (presumably the probate court of Blount County), a defense lawyer got into a violent disagreement with the prosecuting attorney.

The judge lost patience and asked the probate clerk to summon the sheriff to take both lawyers to jail. All four—both lawyers, the probate clerk, and the judge—were *brothers*. They were my grandfather and great-uncles. The judge was Tyre Harbin Davidson (half-brother to the other younger three), and the defense attorney was my grandfather, M.M. Davidson. I suppose the judge released the courtroom hotheads when they calmed down, but I never heard that end of the story.

"An Atrocious Crime"

M.M. was known in the Gadsden area as one of "the most astute lawyers in Alabama,"[24] but he had developed somewhat of a mixed reputation among the "reputable class." He was known for taking cases that many lawyers would have refused. He had defended Klansmen, moonshiners, and killers of local policemen. He was a strong "wet" (antiprohibitionist on the alcohol question) in a county that voted "dry." He had gotten himself thrown in jail by his own half-brother. He operated a collection agency with the motto "Give us your bad accounts and we will do the rest,"[25] probably not the most reputable business for a young lawyer to engage in. The local press had ridiculed him for his poor showing as a Republican candidate for office. He had eloped with his bride, my maternal grandmother, Mary Milo Dean, marrying her on a train without the approval of her parents.

Yet M.M. was willing to defend the less powerful who would have had difficulties in procuring competent legal representation had he not acted. Apparently, he had not escaped the aura of Populism that enveloped his and his wife's (the Deans) families.

M.M.'s commitment to competent legal representation included cases that inflamed the community and antagonized the local press. That included the defense of a Black man accused of murdering a young boy. Unlike the Tunstall case defended by his older brother Julius some years before, the defendant in M.M.'s case did not benefit from high regard in the community.

In February of 1906, George Lige, a Black man in his late 30s, was working as a section hand on the Alabama Great Southern Railroad in Etowah County, where M.M. was plying his trade as a lawyer. A young homeless Black boy, Clarence McCauley, hired to work on the railroad, asked Lige if he could spend the night with him. Lige agreed. The next morning McCauley got up early, apparently stole Lige's pistol, or his bicycle, or a pair of trousers, depending on the newspaper report, and left camp. Lige started in pursuit, and soon encountered two young white men riding bicycles. Lige offered the two men $2 to capture McCauley.

The two caught McCauley, "arrested" him, and secured passage on a hackney, a horse-drawn carriage for hire. The two whites followed on their bicycles. About a mile up the road they encountered Lige, who was armed with a shotgun. Lige angrily threatened McCauley, demanding that he get out of the buggy. The whites in the buggy and on the bicycles claimed they had warned Lige not to shoot, but Lige demanded that McCauley get out of the carriage. The frightened boy jumped to the ground and immediately began to run across a field. Lige fired his shotgun, hitting McCauley in the back of the head, instantly killing him.[26] Lige, realizing what he had done, ran away.

Four years later, George Lige had not been held accountable for McCauley's death, but he had experienced quite a few brushes with the law on minor charges. Just released from the Shelby County jail on a different charge, he was summoned to report to the Bessemer City Court to face yet another charge. As Lige entered the court, he was recognized by the bailiff and jailed.[27]

In May 1910, Lige was brought to trial in Gadsden, with M.M. Davidson serving as his lawyer. Clearly Gadsden had not forgotten the murder, and there seems to have been great sympathy for the murdered boy and a good deal of antipathy toward Lige. The Gadsden *Times-News* pushed out a series of inflammatory articles in headlines like "George Lige Must Hang for Crime." Under the headline "This Negro May Hang," the local paper commented that "Attorney M.M. Davidson is fighting to save Lige's neck and it is believed that he has a desperate fight at that." The paper wrote, "This killing was as cold blooded as any in the annals of the county, while offering sympathy for the victim, whom it called "a boyish and harmless negro tramp."[28]

Lige swore that one of the white men did the shooting but was convicted of first-degree murder. The *Times-News* demanded the death penalty. "The crime was one of the most atrocious and most brutal this county has ever known . . . There is absolutely no doubt of his guilt nor that he deserves the extreme penalty."[29]

It is hard to conceive of a more hostile environment, stirred up by the local version of the national yellow press. But the pressure seemed to have made

M.M. more determined to pursue justice for Lige; he not only did not back down, but he pursued the case through the punishment stage. Perhaps it was the rush to judgment that stirred him up, or maybe he saw something in the evidence that left him unconvinced. In any case, Lige clearly received consistent and unyielding legal representation, something rare in the South during the period.

The next day the judge sentenced George Lige to be hanged on July 8, only a month and a half away. He commented that this was one of the most atrocious cases he had ever presided over, deserving of the most severe penalty. The death penalty was rare in Gadsden then; it had been eight years since anyone had been sentenced to death in Etowah County. Lige showed no emotion. The judge suspended the sentence so that Davidson could appeal the case to the State Supreme Court.

The case remained an item of intense local interest as the *Gadsden Times-News* continued to question why Lige had not been hanged immediately. Much of the ire was directed at M.M., already not a press favorite. The editor of the *Times-News* was ready to see a hanging and was incensed that Davidson was holding up the show. Under the headline "Negro to Hang on Account of Legal Lapse," the paper claimed that Davidson had allowed the legal time limit for appeal to lapse, and hence "there is nothing for the courts to do but to hang the negro." The paper continued to fan the flames, stating, "There is no doubt that Lige is guilty of a very brutal murder. He had not the slightest defense, the evidence showing every element of first-degree murder." The paper quoted the trial judge as informing the prosecuting attorney that the time limit had expired.[30]

The paper's claim was incorrect. Davidson had filed for an appeal. On the June 6, 1911, the Supreme Court heard the appeal, affirming the decision and setting the date for execution on July 28.[31]

The threat of execution was clearly real. Between 1861 and 1911, Alabama executed 479 people, of whom only 17 were white.[32] Alabama simply did not execute whites for even the worst of crimes most of the time, but regularly executed Blacks. That is, if they survived the lynch mob.

Davidson immediately petitioned Governor Emmet O'Neal for more time to gather evidence relevant to commuting the death sentence to life imprisonment, traveling to Montgomery for an in-person audience with the governor.[33] The governor granted the extension four days before the execution was scheduled to allow the State Board of Pardons to investigate the crime.[34]

O'Neal was characteristic of Alabama politicians after the 1901 state disenfranchisement constitution. He had been a delegate to the constitutional convention, where he stood for white supremacy, disenfranchisement of Blacks, and was antagonistic toward woman's suffrage. Yet on other issues he adopted more moderate stances, supporting railroad rate regulation, increased funding for education, local option (rather than statewide) prohibition, mine safety, prison reform, campaign finance reform, and prohibition of child labor. O'Neal's administration instituted changes to the convict leasing system but did not abolish it. He called this package of policies "progressive conservatism," but it was centered on white supremacy and reform elements and could better be termed "progressive white supremacy."[35]

O'Neal supported criminal justice reform, and doubtless M.M. presented Lige as a test case. He may have had personal ties through his brother Julius, since O'Neal had served as federal district attorney for North Alabama immediately before William Vaughn, Julius Davidson's cocounsel in the Tunstall case. They were on the same side of one of the most contentious issues of the day, prohibition. O'Neal was a committed antiprohibitionist, as was Davidson, a representative of liquor interests in Gadsden. Davidson spoke strongly against laws prohibiting the production or sale of alcoholic beverages in the state at various venues in North Alabama.[36]

In any case, on October 5, Governor O'Neal commuted George Lige's sentence to life imprisonment. Davidson did indeed save George Lige's life. There is no record of an execution of Lige during the period.[37] It is unclear when (or if) Lige was released from prison, but he probably was; life without parole was just not a sentence meted out during those years.

Just why O'Neal commuted Lige's sentence is unclear. This was a high-profile case involving a Black man accused of murdering a boy. The local and even the statewide press urged execution. Obviously one key was a lawyer eager to pursue the case. Perhaps his prison reform stance made a difference in O'Neal's mind. In any case, progressive white supremacy may have tipped the balance in such single cases as Lige's.

During the Lige incident, M.M. was the Republican nominee for state senate for the region. Defending a despised character such as George Lige would not seem to be a good campaign strategy, but that did not deter M.M.'s quixotic pursuit of justice for Lige. M.M. was apparently far less the calculating machine that his brother Julius seems to have been.

Defending Black Men in Sensationalized Trials in the Jim Crow South

The story of a strong-willed and courageous white lawyer defending a Black man in the courtrooms of the Jim Crow South has reached mythic proportions in America. A major theme in Southern literature is the unfairness of the institutional racism that aided and abetted the perversion of justice. The racial bias built into the institutions of justice are most clearly seen in court dramas where white lawyers defend Black defendants. Most famous, of course, is Harper Lee's *To Kill a Mockingbird*, probably the most read book on race relations in the United States. The Tunstall and Liege trials are real-life versions of this literary theme, but the outcomes were more favorable to the Black defendant.

A similar real-life defense of a Black defendant by a white lawyer occurred in my hometown of Troy in the late 1930s. Charles White was accused of raping a white woman. Lawyers in Troy were reluctant to serve as defense counsels, and the judge had trouble finding adequate representation for White. He finally turned to a young out-of-town lawyer, Foster Beck, who defended White. Beck was from Enterprise, to the south, and known at the time as more open-minded on the race issue than Troy. The case was so similar to that of *Mockingbird* that the author of a book on the subject contacted Harper Lee to see if she molded her story around that of Beck's defense. She answered that she did not know of the case.

Present were the classic elements of an institutionally racist judicial system dealing with a likely innocent defendant. Threats of mob violence caused the Troy police to take White to Montgomery to a safer jail. Testifying for the defense was Dr. William Stewart, whom I remember from my boyhood, stating that he had done an examination of the alleged victim and he found the charge of rape unlikely. Yet the jury found White guilty. Beck's appeal failed, and White spent the rest of his life in prison. Beck ended up in Montgomery as well, because he lost his clients in Enterprise due to his defense of White.[38]

These stories are well worth telling, and I have done so for two of my ancestors. It exposes individual acts of defiance in a system that was stacked against their Black clients. In doing so it clearly shows the cruelty of the system and how often the rule of law was ignored to impose white dominance over Blacks who had allegedly violated the law.

Without the quick actions of Julius Davidson, there was a high probability that Henderson Tunstall would have been lynched. Without the stubborn persistence of M.M. Davidson, George Lige would most certainly have been hanged. And yes, these are "white savior" stories. There were no other saviors save white ones because the institutional racism built into the justice system included the absence of Black law schools in the South.

These "rescue" stories are worth telling because the Jim Crow justice system was, and in many ways still is, broken. Before 1900 the victims of Alabama lynch mobs were one-third white. After 1900, no whites were lynched.[39] After 1900 lynching was solely a mechanism of white supremacist social control. It is no accident that this change happened after Blacks were disenfranchised in the 1901 constitution.

The criminal justice system acted in that manner as well, especially when it came to the death penalty. During the period between the Civil War and the Voting Rights Act (1861–1965), the State of Alabama executed 476 people, of whom 418 were Black—88% of those executed. And the percentage executed did not change much over time—from 1861 to 1900, 93%; from 1901 to 1925, 90%; from 1926 to 1965, 80%. Whites, on the other hand, almost never got executed—only 11.5% of Alabama's executed were white.

These stark figures indicate the uphill battles lawyers had in defending accused Blacks. Similar barriers existed for the district attorneys and judges, generally elected by white electorates, when seeking to bring the violent lynch mobs of whites to justice. These were brave men and made a corrupt system better than it otherwise would have been, as did Julius and M.M. Davidson and Foster Beck.

The cases of Tunstall and Lige occurred in North Alabama as Populism faded. Was it somewhat easier for Blacks to obtain professional counsel in North Alabama than South? Probably. The experiences of Foster Beck compared to the Davidsons would indicate that difference, but of course these are only single cases. And the North was the locus of the infamous "Scottsboro Boys" trials. In our adversarial judicial system, competent and dedicated legal representation of all is likely the only potential path to justice in a racially polarized society.

CHAPTER 17

The Arc of Injustice

The beginnings and endings of historical eras generally have markers that bracket the era in between. These brackets are the critical junctures in which the rules of the game change. They may seem obvious with the hindsight of history, but they may have passed underappreciated at the time. The period of legalized Jim Crow—an arc of injustice—was opened by the white supremacist constitutions of the late 1890s and early 1900s and was closed by the federal civil rights laws passed in the 1960s.

The brazenness of the segregationist language written into laws and ordinances and the symbols of oppression signaled the opening of the segregationist era. The life and death of a racist rooster symbolically represented the brackets of Jim Crow. In 1904, at the start of the period, the Alabama Democratic Party adopted as its symbol, the Democratic Party rooster with a banner above proclaiming "White Supremacy" and one below "For the Right" (Figure 17.1).

The white supremacy banner remained on the Alabama Democratic Party emblem until January 1966, when the State Executive Committee removed it. The Committee replaced the white supremacy banner with "Democrats," an action designed to keep Black voters loyal to the party.[1] Five short months after President Lyndon Johnson signed the Voting Rights Act, the Alabama Democrats dumped their symbolic commitment to white supremacy. The era of legalized segregation based on race was over.

I was pleased when I voted for the first time, in the 1966 Democratic gubernatorial primary, not to have implicitly to endorse such a racist symbol.

Figure 17.1 The Racist Rooster, the Symbol of the Alabama Democratic Party During the Jim Crow Period.

Source: Bob Ingram, "Loyalist Faction Wins; 'White Supremacy' Goes," *Birmingham News*, January 21, 1966. (This image was shown in other newspapers, all without citation.)

A Destructive Stability for Three-Quarters of a Century

Legalized segregation empowered oligarchical rule; in turn oligarchical rule led to economic stagnation. The 14th and 15th Amendments to the U.S. Constitution made direct disenfranchisement of Blacks impossible. These amendments prohibited denying or abridging the vote and due process on account of race or color, but the Supreme Court supported abridging the vote based on variables associated with race. Since the most efficient variables to accomplish this were economic, both the votes of almost all Blacks and many poor whites were abridged.[2]

Violence and poor economic opportunities in the South, and the booming opportunities in the industrializing Midwest led to the Great Migration, in which millions of Blacks left the South for factory work in the North. As former slaves who served as cheap labor poured off the farms and plantations, elites panicked, tried to limit mobility of Blacks and lightened up on the violence used to impose white supremacy.

The industrial boom in Birmingham and the mineral belt presented economic opportunities for Blacks and poor whites, but those opportunities were limited by the extensive use of convict labor in the mines and the state government's hostility to unions. The primary aims of the steel and coal magnates were to keeping wage costs low and to limit unionization. These objectives propelled the alliance between the Black Belt planters and the Birmingham "Big Mule" industrialists to limit democratic participation and magnify the political power of these elites. The 1901 Alabama Constitution put limitations on local government—making sure that the traditional regional divisions in Alabama did not result in more democracy in the mountain or Wiregrass regions.

The basic structure of the system did not change between 1901 and 1965. By the early 1940s, Alabama was a low-turnout, poverty-stricken state that had succeeded in making itself unattractive to entrepreneurs and outside capital. The state had reached a wretched stability—racially, socially, and economically. As historian Wayne Flynt put it, "The fact that Alabama remained throughout the twentieth century one of the poorest, most racially divided, and least educated states in the South was no accident."[3]

During the period of Jim Crow, from the end of the 19th century to the 1960s, much changed in America. The country experienced two world wars, two terrible pandemics, the Great Depression, and a Cold War armed with nuclear weapons. The automobile went from a novelty to the primary mode of transportation; most working and middle-income households listened to the radio; telephone wires crisscrossed the country; medical professionals developed the first antibiotics. Yet the racial hierarchy and the social order constructed on it remained rigidly fixed. In the Deep South, Blacks could not go to theaters, swimming pools, or schools with whites in 1910, nor could they 50 years later.

The system put in place around the time that my grandparents married remained throughout most of my father's life, breaking apart only as I was reaching my late high-school years. The South to this day remains unable to break the grip of the worst residues of that period, and white grievances remain an entrenched part of the region's politics.

Did Racial Segregation Foster Progressivism?

In his book *Origins of the New South*, historian C. Vann Woodward titled one of his chapters "Progressivism—For Whites Only."[4] Progressivism sprouted from the roots that had nourished Populism, but without the agrarian radicalism of the latter. "Southern progressivism was basically urban and middle class in nature" and it endorsed white supremacy—indeed, progressives adopted many of the reform proposals of the Populists except the more liberal race measures.[5]

The white supremacy of Progressivism was most intensely defended in the South, but it characterized most of the country. The emerging national consensus on white supremacy made Progressivism more powerful by allowing white Progressives to relegate racial issues to the back of the line. By eliminating most Blacks from politics, white reformers could contest public policy issues with corporate magnates and other business elites and not lose white voters over the race issue.

Nationally, Progressivism achieved great gains in political reform and working conditions—the direct election of senators, a fairer system of taxation by allowing the income tax, woman's suffrage, civil service, and major gains in the regulation of workplaces and corporate domination. But these gains came at great costs: the failure to address the status of Black Americans. Southern whites could join the progressive movement without upending Jim Crow. As Andrew Johnson exemplified the reticence of white disadvantaged Southerners to join cause with Blacks, so Woodrow Wilson exemplified a Progressivism that made great progress in many areas, but only at the expense of Black rights, and caused great setbacks in some cases—such as Wilson's resegregation of the federal work force.

Many otherwise progressive Southern politicians, such as Alabama Senator and later Supreme Court Justice Hugo Black and Governor Bibb Graves, were Klan members or willingly accepted the support of the Klan. Graves, who as an early Progressive opposed the adoption of the 1901 Constitution, had the support of labor, women, and prohibitionists in his runs for governor. Graves was a stalwart New Dealer, and ably led Alabama through the depths of the Great Depression. His name is now coming down off university buildings— Troy University renamed Bibb Graves Hall for John Lewis, and the University of Alabama renamed Graves Hall for Autherine Lucy, the first Black to attempt to integrate the university.

Unifying Progressivism with Jim Crow did not prevent a great white backlash against perceived transgressions against the social order by Black Americans, whose hopes had been raised by Progressivism and the First World War. Black successes were met with vicious repression in urban white riots in cities all over the country, including East St. Louis, Chicago, Washington, DC, Tulsa, and many smaller towns such as Knoxville, Tennessee, and Longview, Texas.

Whites maintained racial order by explicit laws and rules, by stoking the myths of white supremacy, by engaging in both subtle and open intimidation, and through force. Like other aspects of social stability, force indicated that the mechanisms of attitudes and myths had failed. Klan groups marching in uniformed parades in major cities with absolute discipline was more effective in maintaining the consensus than furious white riots. But these riots did terrible damage to Black communities all over the nation, especially in the years following the First World War.

The settlement that allowed the caste system of white supremacy also propelled class politics to the fore. Both liberals and conservatives could simultaneously be segregationists; hence they could contend with one another about issues like government regulation of business and promoting the rights of labor and women. With conservatives always reminding common whites that "Black Rule" was possible so long as the federal government was not held in check, the debate always had a conservative bias.

The conservative tilt did not stop with economic issues. Woman's suffrage is an interesting case. The race issue split advocates from the debate over the adoption of the 15th Amendment. Some woman suffrage activists, such as Susan B. Anthony and Elizabeth Cady Stanton, argued that woman's suffrage should be prioritized over that of Black males and developed racist arguments in defending their position. Black activists Mary Church Terrell and Ida B. Wells-Barrett opposed this strategy, provoking Anthony to respond that she did not want to awaken racist impulses among Southern white women.[6]

This reasoning suggests that the border South would be more amenable to woman's suffrage than the Deep South, where racial issues were more salient.

Indeed, that was the case. In Georgia, antisuffrage groups argued that universal suffrage "wipes out the disfranchisement of negroes by State law"[7]—a strange argument, because the disenfranchisement of Black men had been accomplished in violation of both the U.S. Constitution and national law. Ratification of the 19th Amendment happened decades earlier in the border states of Texas (1919) and Tennessee (1920) than in the Deep South. Georgia formally ratified the 19th Amendment in 1970, as did Louisiana; North Carolina did so in 1971; Mississippi was last, in 1984.

Segregated Progressivism was successful, as was segregated New Dealism. Blacks broadly supported the New Deal, even though they were excluded from many of its programs or relegated to segregated versions of them. Blacks were subject to a different wage scale under minimum wage laws; were excluded from white neighborhoods in federal housing laws; were sent to segregated Civilian Conservation Corps; and did not qualify for Social Security because agricultural and domestic workers were not eligible.[8]

Deliberate segregation in housing and camps, segregated wage scales, and Roosevelt's refusal to introduce an antilynching bill were all deliberate efforts to keep in place the caste equilibrium to satisfy Southern whites. Yet Blacks for the most part enthusiastically supported these programs because they were disproportionately represented among the poor.

Family Values

My Grandfather Thomas Jones was the archetype of the Southern Progressive reformer of the period. He seems to have been an ardent feminist and was highly critical of the hypocrisies of the American institutions of the day, which he saw as suppressing the potentials of women. But his views on segregation were standard fare. He seems to have not connected the institutional structures he was so critical of to the burdens they imposed on Blacks.

My family, whom I would characterize as race moderates for the time, nevertheless bought into the post-1900 white narratives. I have no idea how or why the topic came up, but my father saw *Birth of a Nation* as a boy, and he told me that it was a "good movie." In the 1950s and 1960s, my parents saw the need to move toward a more integrated society. My father, a newspaper publisher, wrote anti-Klan editorials and broached the subject of incremental integration in the early 1950s. His newspaper editorials supported racially moderate candidates, and he rejected the Dixiecrat wing of the Democratic party. But they shared the Southern sensitivity of being criticized especially by Northerners, and as racial stances hardened, they became more sensitive.

After the Second World War the equilibrium remained in place—Black students attending historically Black colleges and universities were not eligible for the G.I. Bill, for example, but they were prohibited from attending the segregated colleges of the South. But the edifice was crumbling.

The system seeped into the lives of Blacks and whites, exhausting Blacks but also taking a toll on those whites who would bolster an oppressive system. It restrained Southern progress by limiting the human capital that could contribute to that development. My parents lived most of their lives in this system, and I saw the racial consensus crumble as a teenager. It seemed to me, as a boy, to be an unchanging society even as I read *Popular Science* and *Popular Mechanics*, built a crystal radio, experimented with telecommunications, moved from listening to the *Lone Ranger* on the radio to watching him on television and investigated other elements of a technologically changing society. But the Jim Crow caste system of ascriptive status based on race was unchanging.

The Brackets of Jim Crow

My uncle by marriage, J.O. Sentell, helped prosecute three Klansmen involved in killing a civil rights worker taking part in the 1965 March from Selma to Montgomery. His father was a key player in drafting the 1901 Constitution. The father and son were symbolic of the bookends of Jim Crow, and their stories help to define what Martin Luther King envisioned when he said that "The arc of the moral universe is long, but it bends toward justice."

When my family went up to my paternal grandparents' bungalow in Montgomery for Christmas dinner, Uncle J.O. was there with his wife, Aunt Jane. Jane was my father's sister, the daughter of Thomas Jones and Laura Carr Jones. It was Jane who had noted the tension between my grandparents because the Joneses did not own slaves while the Carrs did.

Aunt Jane was a strong-willed and outspoken woman; Uncle J.O. was reserved and judicious in temperament. Or so my teenaged brain inferred at the time. At a family reunion many years later, Aunt Jane told me that she greatly admired my father, her older brother Glenn Jones. The admiration was so deep that in her youth she brought home a young man to meet the family, in part because he reminded Jane so much of her older brother. After that encounter, she remembered the arguments that she and my headstrong father had engaged in over the years, and realized that she probably had not chosen the right potential mate. She tried again, and found the person she saw as a perfect match—Uncle J.O.

Uncle J.O.'s father, James Oscar, was deeply involved in constructing the final act of "redeeming" Alabama. He was a major participant in writing the 1901 Alabama Constitution, pressing the cause of white supremacy. Sixty years later, James Oscar's son, Uncle J.O., joined the federal government's Office of the District Attorney for Middle Alabama, the office most involved in prosecuting Southern violations of federal civil rights laws. In this position, he helped to convict Klansmen who had murdered Viola Liuzzo, a civil rights activist taking part in the Selma-to-Montgomery march. Two Sentell generations bracketed the long Jim Crow, and this is the story of those bracketing events.

Luverne, 1890: The Railroad Comes to Crenshaw County

Although Uncle J.O. seemed to be on the mild-mannered and judicious side, his father, James Oscar, was not. Born in 1863, he was restless and ambitious. His father, a schoolteacher, encouraged James Oscar to follow a similar path, so he attended Florence Normal School and Southern University. James Oscar started his teaching career, but quickly found it too confining, and began studying law.[9]

Crenshaw County lay in the Wiregrass or "piney woods" region, and by the late 1880s had developed a booming timber industry.[10] At that time, a railroad company planned a line running south from Montgomery to serve the timber industry there. Three land speculators formed the Luverne Land Company, purchased land on the Patsaliga River, and convinced the railroad company to locate the terminus to a prospective town on the Land Company's property.[11] A river location had strong economic advantages because of the ability of timbermen to transport the freshly chopped logs to the river and float them to sawmills downriver. Then the logs could be easily transported to sawmills, and thence to the rail line nearby. By 1890 the growing town of Luverne boasted several sawmills and a population of around 1,000.

Working with the Luverne Land Company, James Oscar Sentell surveyed and platted the property, and the town of Luverne was incorporated in 1889. Sentell was elected the first mayor.[12] As mayor, he employed prisoners in the city jail to remove the huge stumps left by logging.[13] The use of prison labor on a grander scale was becoming part of a system of exploitation as the State leased convicts to planters, builders, factory owners, and coal mining companies, where the cost to health and life was horrific. A large part of the State's budget came from convict leasing during the 1890s.

Sentell was politically active in the Democratic Party, serving on the county executive committee and as campaign manager in several campaigns. In 1901 Crenshaw County selected him as a representative to the Alabama Constitutional Convention of 1901.[14] And there the tale takes a darker turn.

Disenfranchisement, Alabama Style

In 2001, distinguished Auburn historian Wayne Flynt wrote an article for the *University of Alabama Law Review* titled "Alabama's Shame."[15] Flynt's target was the 1901 Alabama Constitution. The Alabama disenfranchisement effort was "the most advanced, extreme, and comprehensive" effort at whitening Southern politics. As another historian of the period, Glenn Feldman, wrote, "If southerners were notorious for going to extremes, then Alabamans were among the most southern of all."[16]

The result "would be the "biggest and most important downward readjustment in the long and bitter process of redefining the Negro's place in Southern life."[17] The informal system that was emerging, including norms of segregation and the ad hoc corruption of the voting process, economic intimidation and violence, "would be replaced by legal, static, and uniform methods of treating Negroes."[18] The 1901 Constitution would lock in the inferior position of Blacks, raising white supremacy as the organizing principle for political contests.

Populism had shaken the Bourbon alliance to its core. The clear defeat of the Populists in 1900 and the return of better economic conditions gave the Bourbon–Big Mule alliance an opportunity to cement power in a new constitution by disenfranchising Blacks while punishing the Populists and their allies, who had been willing to sacrifice racial solidarity and white supremacy for an economic alliance with Blacks.

The way forward for the Conservatives was to stress white supremacy and racial solidarity while at the same time convincing the representatives of poor whites that their constituencies would not be affected, or, if they were, such white disenfranchisement was worth the price of restoring white supremacy. But the Populists of the mountains and Wiregrass were not entirely on board with the disenfranchisement efforts, suspicious that they would lose power as their white non-property-holding and often illiterate base would be excluded from the franchise as well.

The Bourbons themselves were split into two factions. A hardline faction wanted to punish both Blacks and Populists for challenging the prevailing power structure by suppressing the votes of both. A second faction, termed the Paternalists, was led by former governor and Civil War hero William C. Oates. Oates argued for allowing well-qualified Blacks to vote by using franchise criteria that relied on property and education—effectively a class-based exclusion system that would remove many whites and almost all Blacks from the electorate. Oates stressed the need to forestall federal intervention based on the 15th Amendment by making sure the suppression of Black votes was not too obvious.

Oates further argued that it was wrong to exclude Blacks by fraud, as they were doing; rather disenfranchisement should be accomplished by law. As one Paternalist put it, "If you teach your boy that it is right to steal votes, it is an easy step for him to believe that it is right to steal whatever he may need or greatly desire. The results of such an influence will enter every branch of society."[19] The Paternalists argued that it was fine to steal votes so Blacks could not participate, but if stealing spread further, then that would be harmful. In the campaign to get the referendum on the ballot, one leading crusader stated the purpose of the convention baldly, "The negro was . . . disfranchised years ago by fraud and the purpose was now to do it by constitutional enactment."[20] The argument boiled down to a desire to remove Blacks from the voting rolls so the oligarchs could stop themselves from cheating.

Many Populists and Jeffersonian Democrats returning to the Democratic Party wanted to exclude Blacks but not whites, and they themselves were conflicted on which to prioritize. Some were so distrustful of the Bourbons that they would stick with the status quo, allowing both Blacks and poor whites to vote. Others wanted a guarantee that poor white votes would be explicitly protected. In April of 1900, the State Democratic Committee by one vote approved a guarantee that "no white man shall be disfranchised" in the constitution.[21] It did not work out that way.

In 1901, the legislature approved a referendum to call a constitutional convention. The referendum provoked the old regional controversies. Clearly the reservations of the Populists had not been assuaged. Blount County and the mountain counties generally rejected the convention call. Most Wiregrass counties voted in favor of the call. The usual massive vote totals from the Black Belt supporting the Bourbon positions carried the day.[22] Black Belt politicians had manipulated the votes of Blacks to call a constitutional convention whose main purpose was to disenfranchise them, and used the same techniques to ratify that disenfranchisement.

James Oscar in Montgomery

By the time that James Oscar traveled the 50 miles between Luverne and Montgomery to take his seat at the Constitutional Convention the major fault lines were already clear. As a representative from a majority white poor county, he would emerge as a major spokesman for the preservation of white suffrage while supporting the suppression of Black votes.

As the convention gathered in Montgomery, the intention of its organizers became quickly clear, because it was so boldly announced. John B. Knox, the Convention president, opened the gathering by announcing that the purpose of the meeting was to replace the system of "force and fraud" with the establishment of white supremacy by law.[23] He and other leaders denied that they also wanted to disenfranchise the upland Populists, but after the convention Knox acknowledged that the plan of convention leaders all along had been to target both Blacks and poor whites to "place the power of government in the hands of the intelligent and virtuous."[24]

In the convention hall, rhetorical excesses flourished as delegates competed to prove their fealty to the doctrine of white supremacy. They lauded the Lost Cause and decried the often-mythical horrors of Reconstruction for whites. The patrician Bourbons sought to fortify racial solidarity, bringing the often-reluctant representatives of poor whites into the fold while reminding the Populists that they had deserted the cause of white superiority for the expediency of economic gain. The former Populists were just as determined to embrace white superiority and the Lost Cause, reminding the Bourbons, in the words of one mountain county delegate, "The rank and file of the Confederate army was made up of poor men . . . who owned no property . . . and never owned a negro in their lives, but they fought for principle and conscience's sake . . . When these men were called to arms from their homes, they left the plow standing in an unfinished furrow upon the hillside farm."[25]

Indeed, said the mountain and Wiregrass delegates, protecting the white franchise would promote the cause of white supremacy and ensure that no "second Reconstruction" would occur. Sentell threw his rhetorical weight behind this argument, claiming emotionally that the 15th Amendment, which prohibited the federal and state governments from denying or abridging the right to vote based on "race, color, or previous condition of servitude," was "an abominable crime . . . a crime against the civilization of the age and against the white people of the South." It had been organized in prejudice, the sole purpose . . . to humiliate our beloved Southern people who were already crushed beneath the iron heel of war." Sentell concluded with a vow of loyalty to the cause of white supremacy: "the white man is destined to rule, and he will rule . . . the inferior race as well."[26]

The structure of the franchise was the major issue for the delegates, and the critical convention floor fight occurred in the debate over the Suffrage Committee's report. Historian Glenn Feldman writes, "The battle over the majority and minority reports [of the Suffrage Committee] was the titanic confrontation, the deciding moment of the convention and, in fact, the disfranchisement movement in Alabama." The committee produced two reports, a majority report that focused on Black suppression alone, and a minority report, championed by the Black Belt planters, that excluded poor whites as well. The committee's majority report proposed the most elaborate, exhaustive, and intricate scheme of disenfranchisement ever concocted by any state.[27]

Once again the sectional divisions appeared, but the interracial elements of the incipient Populist democracy had vanished. The majority report appealed to white supremacy to exclude Blacks, whereas the minority report envisioned excluding poor whites as well, on the general grounds of incompetence of all Blacks and most common whites.

Sentell and other Wiregrass and mountain country delegates realized the dire stakes in the suffrage reports; he stated to the Convention that "all other questions . . . fade into mere minor matters compared with the great question of suffrage and elections. We were sent here almost solely for the purpose of settling this one great question."[28]

The Suffrage Committee members strongly reflected the Bourbon faction, and the majority report was not particularly favorable to white enfranchisement. The majority recommended severe measures to curtail the franchise along class lines: a property requirement; a literacy test, a cumulative poll tax, and education and employment requirements. It offered only a few spare bones to poor whites, and then only in a temporary plan—a soldier and fighting grandfather clause, allowing those who had fought in the Civil War or had fathers or grandfathers who had done so to vote; a good character clause; and an understanding clause. These latter provisions allowed electoral boards to rule out Blacks while ruling in whites. It also allowed those boards to exclude illiterate whites who could vote against the prevailing power structure.[29]

For Sentell and other delegates from poor counties, the minority report was far worse than the majority report, but they were not happy with the majority report either. Unable to derail the majority report without destroying the work of the Convention, these delegates faced two bad options. Most chose to support the majority report, and Sentell and other delegates vigorously attacked the minority report. Sentell assured his colleagues that his constituents in Crenshaw County were "intensively interested" in the question of suffrage because the Black man had become "a menace to good government."[30] "I represent my people of the Piney Woods when I say . . . that the negro has not the capacity for exercising any control in the government . . . the power to vote is the power to control."[31]

Sentell noted his disapproval of elements of the majority plan but said it was the best that could be achieved given the circumstances. It gave the white counties what they needed "to disfranchise the negro . . . because they are not fit to vote." Sentell argued that the grandfather, character, and understanding clauses were enough to offset the property and educational requirements. "So that lets in every white man." Making sure all white men voted, whether educated or with property or not, was essential because "the laws of nature" demonstrated that "the white man is superior and . . . is the only race that has ever shown the capacity to govern himself and . . . others. The negro has his place and the white man has his . . . the white man is destined to rule. . . the inferior race."[32]

The white supremacist language used by Sentell and the other delegates to the Convention was offensive, hurtful, and, unfortunately, politically effective. It was effective because it was strategic. It unified enough white delegates to carry the majority suffrage provisions that would ultimately disenfranchise almost all Blacks and a substantial number of whites. Delegates like Sentell, representing "plain whites," voted to disenfranchise many of them.

The Alabama Constitutional Convention of 1901 represented a nadir in the use of state laws to suppress the rights of Black citizens, and a low point in American history. The convention was part of a broad American backlash to the movement to guarantee Blacks the right to vote. The movement reached "its most advanced, extreme, and comprehensive form" in Alabama's constitutional convention.[33] Unfortunately the language of the convention continued to echo down the ages, and its traces are clearly evident in today's political discourse.

The Ratification of Hate

The State submitted the draft constitution to the voters, as it had the call for the constitutional convention. The mountain and Wiregrass counties faced the same dilemma: many of their voters supported Black disenfranchisement, but feared they would lose their voting rights despite the reassurances of Black Belt politicians and their allies that they would be unharmed.

A second real concern of plain whites was the rampant corruption of white Black Belt politicians, who had almost entirely eliminated Black voters from their electorates yet reported vote totals with Black voters included anyway. Black Belt fraud proved the margin of victory against the Populist-Jeffersonian Democrat-Republican Fusion Ticket in the 1892 and 1894 gubernatorial elections and had influenced every statewide election during the 1890s. The corrupted Black Belt pro-vote in the call for the constitution convention overwhelmed the mountain and Wiregrass anti-vote.

The final referendum tally showed a solid majority in favor of the constitution. But the geographical divisions were stark. Twelve Black Belt counties voted for ratification with huge majorities; outside these counties a majority of voters cast ballots against. All of the Wiregrass counties except Crenshaw voted against ratification. The mountain counties except Walker voted against ratification as well.[34] Because the margin of victory came solely from the Black Belt counties, it is almost certain that fraudulent votes provided the margin of victory.[35]

In their churches, in black-owned newspapers, in church meetings, and by taking whatever legal action they could, Blacks in Alabama objected to the 1901 Constitution. Many Blacks still voted freely in most non–Black Belt counties, and they voted solidly against the Constitution, rejecting the arguments of the Paternalists that they would be better off under their tutelage than the allegedly more overtly racist plain whites.

A group of Black ministers warned that disenfranchisement would cause the country great trouble in the future, and like a "cancerous sore," would rise to the surface in a dramatic eruption.[36] Educator Booker T. Washington, president of Tuskegee Institution, raised money for lawsuits, one of which reached the Supreme Court in 1903. In an opinion in the case *Giles v. Harris*, authored by one of the Court's most distinguished jurists, Justice Oliver Wendell Holmes, the Court announced that it would not enforce the 15th Amendment rights of appellant J.L. Giles to register and vote. This was a political question, Holmes wrote. "Unless we are prepared to supervise the voting in that State by officers of the court . . . relief from a political wrong . . . must be given by the people of the State or by the political department of the Government of the United States."[37]

With *Giles*, the U.S. Supreme Court, and with it the full federal government, assumed Alabama's shame as its own. Alabama Blacks were for all practical purposes prohibited by law from exercising their Constitutionally guaranteed right to vote. The denial lasted sixty-four years, until Congress passed, and President Johnson signed, the Voting Rights Act of 1965.

The disenfranchising constitution was brutally effective. In 1900 more than 180,000 Blacks were registered to vote; by 1903 there were less than 5,000. The white vote declined by 40,000 during the same period. A study based on the 1940 Census estimated that by then the 1901 constitution had disenfranchised 600,000 whites and 520,000 blacks. Only 440,000 Alabamians were registered to vote.[38]

After his role in the convention, Sentell did not seek nor hold public office again. He devoted much of his time to his law business and handling of real estate. He represented both white and Black citizens. His son J.O. told of his recollection as a boy that during the Ku Klux Klan revival during the 1920s, Klan members visited the Sentell family home. They objected to James Oscar's defending a Black citizen in a visible court case. The Klan left dissatisfied. He died at the age of 91 in 1954.

As Bryan Stevenson reminded us, "Each of us is more than the worst thing we've ever done."[39]

The Arc of the Moral Universe Bends toward Justice

The son of James Oscar Sentell, my Uncle J.O. Sentell, was born in Luverne in 1909, earned a law degree at the University of Alabama, and in 1933 returned to Luverne to practice law with his father. Starting a law practice in the Great Depression was a difficult proposition; in the law firm's first month the three lawyers split $15. In 1937, he married the minister's daughter, my Aunt Jane.

During the Second World War, J.O. was a price attorney for the Office of Price Administration in Montgomery, which was responsible for setting prices during the war. After the war, he returned to Luverne to private practice. He moved permanently with his family to Montgomery in 1951 to serve as counsel for the Office of Price Stabilization, which set prices during the Korean War. In 1953, J.O. returned to private legal practice in Montgomery.

In the 1950s, Montgomery was heating up as a center of activity concerning civil rights. Soon after J.O. restarted his private practice, three monumental events converged to make Montgomery the epicenter of early civil rights activity: the Supreme Court case of *Brown v. Board of Education* announced in May 1954; the appointment of Frank M. Johnson as federal district judge for the Central District of Alabama in October 1955; and the Montgomery bus boycott that began in December of that same year.

"The Most Hated Man in Alabama"

Frank Johnson was no ordinary Southern judge. The interaction of person and place, Montgomery and Judge Johnson, changed the course of American history. The typical federal appointee at the time was hostile to federal intervention on civil rights. As one former official in the Civil Rights Division of the Justice Department commented, "The major problem with the Civil Rights Act (of 1957) that we then were enforcing was the fact that we had to try our cases before judges in Alabama and Mississippi."[40]

But Johnson was cut from a different cloth. He was born and raised in North Alabama's mountainous Winston County, with few slaves in the antebellum period and strong Unionist sentiment during the Civil War. As did many North Alabama families after the war, Johnson's family became Republicans. He and George Wallace became friends at the University of Alabama, where both attended law school. Johnson worked in Eisenhower's campaign in 1952 and served as district attorney for the Federal Northern District of Alabama afterward. President Eisenhower appointed him as federal judge for the Middle District of Alabama in 1955.

Johnson quickly established his credentials as "the most hated man in Alabama," a moniker promoted by the Ku Klux Klan, due to his civil rights decisions. While that epithet may have rung true for many white Alabamians, Johnson became an icon of justice for Blacks.

During the 1955 bus boycott, Black civic leaders challenged Alabama's segregation laws in federal court. In *Browder v. Gayle*, Johnson, as part of a three-judge panel, ruled Alabama's bus segregation law unconstitutional under the 14th Amendment's equal protection clause, and ordered the immediate desegregation of Montgomery's bus system. The U.S. Supreme Court dismissed the state's appeal, upholding the panel's decision. The enraged head of the Alabama White Citizens' Council labeled Johnson a traitor, and Johnson immediately received a stream of hate mail and telephone calls that lasted for years. A cross was burned on his lawn, his mother's house was firebombed, and he and his family lived under federal protection for two decades.[41]

Johnson went on to require that the Barbour County voter registration records be turned over to the Civil Rights Commission in 1958, threatening County Judge George Wallace with jail in the process. He ruled against Alabama's poll tax, and to issue the first statewide desegregation order in *Lee v. Macon County Board of Education* in 1963.[42] In 1961 he issued an injunction against the Montgomery Police and Ku Klux Klan from perpetrating violence against the Freedom Riders riding through the South to integrate interstate bus service.

In 1962, President John Kennedy appointed Ben Hardeman as U.S. district attorney for the Middle District of Alabama. Hardeman met with his good friend, J.O. Sentell, and asked that he serve as first assistant U.S. attorney. Uncle J.O. accepted, knowing full well that the docket before Judge Johnson would be jammed with civil rights cases. This mild-mannered man contained a tough interior.

Bloody Sunday

If the 1901 Constitution marked a real and symbolic nadir in Alabama, Southern, and American history, it also marked the start of a long and painful move toward righting the wrongs wrought by the convention and what it represented. The final violent push toward the zenith occurred 70 miles to the northwest of Luverne, in Selma, a Black Belt city of some 28,000 residents at the time, three-quarters of whom were Black.

By early 1965, the voting rights efforts mounted by the Student Non-Violent Coordinating Committee (SNCC) in Selma had stalled. The city, like most

in the Alabama Black Belt, was notorious for excluding even the most qualified Black citizens from voting. SNCC had been working with local activists
to register voters for year and a half, with scant results—only 300 local Blacks
were registered to vote among Dallas County's some 15,000 eligible Black citizens. Most had not even tried to vote, deterred by violence, intimidation, and
economic sanctions. If they did try, registrars gave them an extraordinarily difficult literacy test with an "understanding" clause giving registrars complete
discretion in deciding whether the applicant could "read and understand" a
passage from the Alabama State Constitution. These and other voter suppression devices had been established by the 1901 Alabama Constitution. They
were not used in many Alabama counties, but they were invariably used in
Black Belt counties.

The impetus for the infamous march on "Bloody Sunday" was the killing
of Jimmy Lee Jackson by out-of-control police and highway patrol officers
in nearby Marion. Voting rights activists decided to organize a march from
Selma to Montgomery to confront Governor George Wallace over the death
of Jackson and the associated injustices in Selma and Marion.

Governor Wallace ordered his director of public safety Al Lingo, to stop
the march, so the march organizers expected a confrontation and mass arrests.
What they encountered, in the words of John Lewis, was "a sea of blue-
helmeted, blue uniformed Alabama state troopers . . . the troopers and posse-
men swept forward as one, like a human wave, a blur of blue shirts and billy
clubs and bullwhips. We had no chance to run and retreat. And then they were
on us."[43]

A trooper hit Lewis in the head, fracturing his skull. The troopers pressed
on, with white bystanders attacking as well, pursuing the marchers as they
retreated into the Black churches of Selma. The churches were full of the
injured. Hospitals treated over 90 wounded.

In Atlanta, Dr. King and the Southern Christian Leadership Conference (SCLC) immediately filed for an injunction prohibiting state interference in a new Selma-to-Montgomery march with the Federal District
Court for the Middle District of Alabama, Judge Frank M. Johnson
presiding.

Civic and religious groups, students, and citizens offended by the events
of "Bloody Sunday," poured into Selma, seeking to volunteer and join the
upcoming march. In the confusion, a group of Selma whites who were hanging around the Silver Moon, a café and bar popular with local Klan members,
murdered a Unitarian minister, James Reeb.

Among the activists heading for Selma was Viola Liuzzo of Detroit. Liuzzo had attended Wayne State University, a center of Jewish and Black political activism. Both Charlayne Hunter (Gault), who integrated the University of Georgia, and James Hood, who integrated the University of Alabama, studied there.

When she learned of the SCLC plan to march from Selma to Montgomery, Viola decided to join the march. Her friend Sarah Evans pleaded with her not to go, as did her husband and daughter Penny, who said in a voice filled with emotion, "Mom, I have a terrible feeling I'm not going to see you anymore." Yet Viola, determined to get involved, packed her bag and drove to Selma in her 1963 Oldsmobile right away.[44]

On March 15, President Lyndon Johnson introduced the Voting Rights Act to a joint session of Congress. In his finest speech and the strongest defense of civil rights by any president, Johnson ended with "Their cause must be our cause too. Because it is not just Negroes, but really it is all of us who must overcome the legacy of bigotry and injustice. And we shall overcome."

When Judge Johnson issued his ruling enjoining the State of Alabama from interfering with the march he did so in stinging language, noting the real discrimination Blacks had endured and the lack of violent actions on the part of the demonstrators. In his broad injunction, Johnson prohibited "[George Wallace, Alabama Public Safety Director Al Lingo, and Dallas County Sheriff Jim Clark], members of their class and others who may join with them . . . from arresting, harassing, threatening, or in any way interfering with the efforts to march or walk . . . or obstructing, impeding or interfering" with the march.[45]

On Sunday, March 21, 3,200 people, including civil rights leaders, celebrities, religious leaders, and John Doar and Ramsey Clark of the Justice Department, set off for Montgomery, 54 miles to the east. On March 25, the protestors walked the final few miles to the steps of the Alabama State Capitol. While Wallace cowered in his Capitol office, peeking out of the curtains, Martin Luther King gave his rousing Arc of the Moral Universe speech. "How long? Not long, because no lie can live forever . . . How long? Not long, because the arc of the moral universe is long, but it bends toward justice."

Klansmen Murder Viola Liuzzo

Viola arrived in time to join the marchers in Selma as they started out to Montgomery. After the march, Liuzzo ferried exhausted marchers back to Selma in her Oldsmobile. Then, with civil rights activist Larry Moton as a passenger, she headed back to Montgomery to pick up more march participants for the return journey to Selma. On the lonely section of two-lane highway in Lowndes County, as legal documents described in sanitized language, "(a) car overtook the Liuzzo automobile, shots were fired, and Mrs. Liuzzo was killed."[46]

Given new life after the 1954 Supreme Court decision *Brown v. Board of Education of Topeka Kansas* and bolstered by the election of George Wallace in 1962, Alabama membership in the Ku Klux Klan peaked in 1965 at more than 30,000 members. During the 1950s, the Klan consisted of a loose network of local organizations, called Klaverns, with no central authority. In the 1960s Robert Shelton of Tuscaloosa, founded the United Klans of America, and centralized activity around an Imperial Wizard, Shelton himself. It was, at the time, the largest Klan organization in America.[47]

On orders from Imperial Wizard Shelton, four Klan members from Bessemer, an industrial suburb west of Birmingham, traveled to Selma on March 25. William Orville Eaton, Collie Leroy Wilkins Jr., Eugene Thomas, and Gary Thomas Rowe Jr. went there to attack civil rights activists. Rowe, however, had joined the Klan at the FBI's request and was a long-time informant.

The three went directly to the Silver Moon, arriving around 7:00 PM. There Thomas pointed to a man that he identified as the accused killer of James Reeb. As the Bessemer Klansman walked out of the cafe, the accused killer came over, clapped Thomas on the back, and said, "God bless you boys . . . You go do your job, I have already done mine."[48]

The Klansmen drove through downtown Selma, and at the Pettus Bridge saw Viola Liuzzo's Oldsmobile with its Michigan license plates with a white woman and a Black man (Moton) inside. They followed the Oldsmobile out on Highway 80 toward Montgomery. Liuzzo sped down the highway, with Thomas pursuing, reaching speeds of 80 to 90 miles per hour. On the dark, lonely stretch of two-lane highway in Lowndes County, Thomas pulled his car next to Liuzzo's Oldsmobile, and the Klansmen fired into the car. Liuzzo was killed, but Morton, who had bent over to adjust the radio, survived.

FBI agents arrested Thomas, Wilkins, and Eaton on March 26. The Klansmen faced overwhelming circumstantial evidence, one eyewitness, Gary Rowe, who knew the three murderers and their motives, and a second eyewitness, Leroy Moton, who could describe the events and the automobile chasing Liuzzo and him.

President Johnson went on television to announce to the nation that the three Klan suspects had been arrested. Johnson described the murder as a lynching, saying that "Mrs. Liuzzo went to Alabama to serve the struggle for justice. She was murdered by the enemies of justice, who for decades have used the rope and the gun and the tar and feathers to terrorize their neighbors."[49]

With Martin Luther King, Rosa Parks, Ralph Abernathy, and John Lewis observing, President Johnson signed the Voting Rights Act of 1965, probably the single most important statutory victory in the long struggle for civil rights.

The Difficulty in Trying Civil Rights Cases in Southern Courts

Southern courts were notorious in their willingness to acquit obviously guilty white defendants in civil rights cases, and the Liuzzo case was no exception. In 1965, rural Lowndes County was 80% Black, yet not a single Black voter was registered. The county was already known as "Bloody Lowndes" for its violent treatment of Blacks. Now it was the location of Viola's murder. It was soon to be known as the birthplace of the Black Panther Party.

The State of Alabama brought murder charges against the Bessemer three in Hayneville, the Lowndes County seat. In 1965 Hayneville was an unincorporated village of less than 500 people, deep in the rural Alabama Black Belt where neither Blacks nor women could serve on juries. The Justice Department representative at the trial, James P. Turner, viewed "the likelihood of success there as slim."[50]

The State chose to try Wilkins first. His Hayneville trial was pure spectacle. The defense lawyer Matt Murphy, who called himself the "Klan Kounsel" strutted round the courthouse square with Imperial Wizard Bobby Shelton, admiring the Confederate statue and telling reporters that "These boys are heroes and no jury in the State of Alabama will ever convict them."[51] At the trial, Murphy called no witnesses, and based his defense on pure, unadulterated white supremacy and blunt racism. Speaking to the white male jury of five farmers, two mechanics, an electrician, a machinist, a county foreman, a night watchman, and a bookkeeper, Murphy focused on white prejudices. "One white woman . . . Riding right through your county . . . Communists, and niggers, and white niggers, and Jews."[52]

The State of Alabama put LeRoy Moton on the stand, who described the high-speed chase and its tragic ending. Then informant Gary Rowe stepped the court thorough the entire sequence of events. Klan Kounsel Murphy cross-examined Rowe, reciting part of the Klan oath in which Klansmen swore to die rather than divulge secrets. He asked Rowe if he had sworn such an oath, and Rowe said he had.[53]

Murphy's diatribe almost backfired. Many of the jurors were visibly uncomfortable with Murphy's racist antics, and 10 voted to convict. But two steadfastly resisted, saying they distrusted the testimony of Rowe, since he "swore before God [when joining the Klan] and then violated his oath, leading to a mistrial."[54]

Alabama Attorney General Richmond Flowers, a racial moderate running for governor and hoping to gain the support of Black voters newly enfranchised by the Voting Rights Act, personally led the retrial. Before the second trial could begin, a young white seminarian was killed in Lowndes County when he lunged in front of a bullet intended for the Black woman accompanying him. A local white man was charged and quickly acquitted of manslaughter.

The second trial in October of 1965 led to outright acquittal for the defendants. A less flamboyant lawyer, former Birmingham mayor Arthur Hanes, defended Wilkins. The final jury included 10 former or present members of the White Citizens' Council. The jury found Wilkins not guilty in less than two hours.[55]

Making a Federal Case

James P. Turner, the senior career lawyer in the U.S. Justice Department's Civil Rights Division, later commented, "Now, it was crystal clear. The only remaining possibility for justice in the Liuzzo case was to prosecute the outstanding federal indictment for conspiracy to violate civil rights." The Division brought a criminal indictment against Wilkins, Thomas, and Eaton "in Montgomery, in a real trial before a real Judge, Frank Johnson."[56]

The case was tried on December 3, 1965. Representing the government were Assistant Attorney General Doar, U.S. Attorney Ben Hardeman, and Assistant U.S. Attorney. Now he was prosecuting a critical case in the 1960s struggle for Black voting rights—a struggle that resulted in vitiating the disenfranchisement mandated in 1901 so vigorously defended by his father.

The U.S. Attorney's office in Montgomery became a beehive of activity as Doar and a team of lawyers and researchers from the Justice Department's Civil

Rights Division worked alongside Uncle J.O. to assemble the case. The team knew this was the last chance to convict the perpetuators of a brutal premeditated lynching stemming from a Klan-based conspiracy to "harass, threaten, pursue and assault citizens of the United States in the area of Selma and Montgomery, Alabama, who were participating in or had participated in, or who were lending or had lent their support to a demonstration march from Selma to Montgomery, Alabama," as the prosecutor's indictment put it.

The prosecutors' legal theory of the case was centered on the Enforcement Act of 1971, also known as the Ku Klux Klan Act, codified as Section 241 of Title 18 of the U.S. Code. Congress passed the act as part of its repeated attempts to enforce, the 13th, 14th, and 15th Amendments, which prohibited slavery, ensured citizenship by birthright, and guaranteed the right to vote.

The section provided that "if two or more persons conspire to injure, oppress, threaten, or intimidate any person . . . in the free exercise or enjoyment of any right or privilege secured to him by the Constitution or laws of the United States" they would be subject to not more than 10 years in prison. The acts slid into disuse as Southern resistance intensified in the 1870s and 1880s, and the federal courts proved unsympathetic to the legislation.

Justice Department lawyers resurrected the civil rights conspiracy statute, as well as others of the Reconstruction civil rights acts, in the 1950s and 1960s as Southern state courts proved resistant to punishing white perpetrators of violence against Blacks. They became important tools in enforcing the 14th and 15th Amendments almost a century after they were enacted, but the Justice Department always faced uphill fights.

As the trial proceeded, defense attorney and former Birmingham Mayor Arthur Hanes once again used the previously effective strategy of reading part of the Klan oath and asking Rowe if he had taken that oath. But the federal defense team had done its research. At the government's urging, Judge Johnson ordered Hanes to read the entire oath. Hanes reluctantly read it, including the passage that "knowledge of rape, treason against the United States, [or] malicious murder" voided the vow of silence, requiring Klansmen to "help, aid, and assist" law enforcement officers.[57]

After a day of deliberation, the jury returned and told the court that they were hopelessly deadlocked. Judge Johnson ordered them to continue deliberating. At Doar's request, Johnson gave the jury an Allen charge, known colloquially as the dynamite charge. It requests minority jurors to examine why they differed from the majority—that is, to defend their minority positions.

Four hours later, the jury returned guilty verdicts against all three defendants, "the very first guilty verdicts in a civil rights death case in modern American history."[58] Judge Johnson told the jury, "In my opinion, that is the only verdict you could possibly reach in this case and reach a fair and honest verdict."[59] He sentenced the defendants to the maximum 10 years in prison.

The Appeal

On April 27, 1967, the U.S. Court of Appeals for the Fifth Circuit in the case of a three-judge panel affirmed the verdict against the two living Klansmen (soon after the first trial, William Eaton died of a heart attack).[60] The legal team of Doar, Hardeman, and Sentell again represented the federal government. On June 22, the full court affirmed the decision of the three-judge panel.

After the Civil War, the federal government passed three constitutional amendments to rid the nation of the curse of slavery, and several acts to enforce these amendments. Federal intervention failed in the face of sustained backlash by white Southerners. James Oscar Sentell was part of the vitriolic reaction of Southerners to the federal intervention. At the 1901 Alabama constitutional convention, he fulminated against the 15th Amendment and federal enforcement of it. The 1901 Alabama Constitution and its subsequent validation by the U.S. Supreme Court in *Giles v. Harris* (1903) were markers in a critical juncture in Southern political development—the de jure establishment of Jim Crow.

Sixty-four years later, James Oscar's son was part of a legal team that resurrected those acts to convict men engaged in a conspiracy to undermine through violence the rights guaranteed by the Constitution. They relied on the very laws that had failed in the federal government's post–Civil War intervention. The Liuzzo trial was a marker of the end of the era of legal voter suppression that James Oscar had urged on Alabama.

In 1967, Uncle J.O. accepted the position of deputy clerk of the Alabama Supreme Court. He was appointed to the position as clerk of that court in 1968 and served in that position until his retirement in 1982. He was one of the founders of the National Conference of Appellate Court Clerks, and through that organization he helped to professionalize the court clerk position throughout the United States. In 1979, the organization established an annual award in J.O.'s name and chose him as the first awardee.

On his retirement from the Supreme Court Clerkship, the still modest and unassuming man commented, "I don't have any words of wisdom to say today. But I will always carry fond memories of you."[61] Clearly he had plenty of words of wisdom, but his modesty and decency led him to focus not on himself, but those around him.

He passed away in 1985. In 2022 he was inducted into the Alabama Lawyers' Hall of Fame.

PART 5

The Tragic Failure of
Southern Moderates

In mid-April 1963, Martin Luther King Jr. was imprisoned with Fred Shuttlesworth for disobeying an Alabama state court injunction to halt the demonstrations they and civil rights leader James Bevel were leading in Birmingham. On the day of the imprisonment of King and Shuttlesworth, eight white church leaders from all major denominations—Catholic, Jewish, Methodist, Episcopal, Presbyterian, Baptist—published a letter in the *Birmingham News* imploring King and other Black leaders in Birmingham to cease their demonstrations, maintain law and order, and engage in good-faith negotiations with city officials.

King pulled together pieces of old newspapers and scrap paper after being denied writing paper while incarcerated and penned his monumental "Letter from the Birmingham Jail." He defended nonviolent protest, explained the difference between just and unjust laws, and went on to express his disappointment with the failure of white moderates to bring about serious social change, writing,

> I must confess that over the last few years I have been gravely disappointed with the white moderate. I have almost reached the regrettable conclusion that the Negro's great stumbling block in the stride toward freedom is not the White citizens' "Councilor" or the Ku Klux Klanner, but the white moderate who is more devoted to "order" than to justice; who prefers a negative peace which is the absence of tension to a positive peace which is the presence of justice.

There is no doubt that by 1963 the course of moderation in civil rights in the Deep South had failed. The Birmingham clergy united once again to raise the tattered flag of moderation in a region that had continued and even intensified its program of massive resistance to ending segregation. The toughness of the civil rights leaders and the commitment of the Black community, exemplified by James Bevel's children's crusade, and the intensifying hate mobilized by Southern white racist demagogues had left no room for the moderates.

The course of that failure is a tragic story, a failure of white community leaders to seize opportunities to build a path to equality for Blacks after the Second World War. The "Greatest Generation" had united to defeat fascism but could not unite to roll back Jim Crow. Many writers see the period after the war as one of Black demands for equality and an immediate rejection of those demands by white Southerners. When Black soldiers returned from the war, they met resurgent racism and unchanged segregation. It was visible and deplorable.

There was, however, a second current—a group of moderate white civic leaders who recognized both the injustice of the resurgence of white supremacy and the necessity of changing the Southern system. Some found it morally indefensible. Most thought that the existing system would not survive the modern world, especially as the federal government was becoming increasingly active in enforcing the rights of Blacks. All underestimated the power of the white backlash that was to come.

Throughout the 1950s it became increasingly difficult to maintain a moderate stance as a Southern editor or publisher on the race issue. There were three kinds of editors during the period: the staunch segregationists who refused to budge on the issue, and indeed became more incendiary; the moderates who dreamed of a slow but steady set of changes that could work; and the realists, who understood that moderation without a real plan and real action would never yield justice for Blacks.

I examine the careers of three editors, all of whom described themselves as moderates in the late 1940s. In the 1950s the three editors faced ferocious backlash from whites resentful over the civil rights movement and the federal government's increasing support for it. Politicians, most vividly George Wallace, but many more as well, rushed to get in front of the issue.

By the late 1950s, the three editors had parted company. One, Grover Hall of the *Montgomery Advertiser*, moved more and more in a conservative direction until he became a strong ally and speechwriter for Governor George Wallace. Another, Buford Boone of the *Tuscaloosa News*, became one of the courageous racial progressive publishers of the era. My father, who had bought a controlling interest in a small-town newspaper in South Alabama, the *Troy Messenger*, became less and less convinced that a moderate stance was feasible. The editorials in the *Messenger* became more racially conservative.

The backlash that moderate editors faced increased in its ferocity over the 1950s and into the 1960s. It was unmistakable, and surely affected advertising

and sales. And something else was happening at the same time, almost unrecognized by national observers. The white South was unifying—a 'Mind of the
white South' was emerging out of the breakdown of the segregationist order.
Mountain whites were unifying with lowland whites around the status politics of segregation. This transformation that began in the mid-1950s reached
its peak in the mid-1960s; whites in Southern Appalachia increasingly adopted
the attitudes of white lowland Southerners when it came to race.

CHAPTER 18

The Greatest Generation

Journalist and television newscaster Tom Brokaw labeled the generation that came of age in the Great Depression of the 1930s and participated in the Second World War "the greatest generation any society has produced."[1] Brokaw assembled compelling stories of those who participated in the war to support his thesis. The stories all center on the war experiences and subsequent lives of the subjects of the stories. My mother's younger brother Mac Davidson, a D-Day veteran, would have fit easily into Brokaw's stories. Perhaps so would my father's younger brother, James Bryan, who served in an ordnance division during the war.

Brokaw does not examine the lives of Americans who lived through these times but were not participants in the war or served on the home front. Yet these people faced depression and war, and their lives were disrupted as well. He does give a nod to the shortcomings of the generation, such as the failure among most whites to address the evils of segregation and the failure to recognize the differences between serving your country in the great moral struggle of the Second World War and the deeply benighted misadventure in Vietnam. These are not minor failures to be swept under the rug; indeed they shaped America profoundly.

I am skeptical of the entire notion of "generations" and labeling them. A nation's population is a continuous stream of individuals born every day, so the concept of generation is an arbitrary construct. It is true that people experience different streams of events over time, and that some of those events are large-scale and memorable, such as depression and war. So the concept of generations can be a useful heuristic, although the term cohort is more fitting.

I don't want to denigrate the accomplishment of this American cohort, nor to forget that it was composed of white, Black, yellow, and brown; male and female; poor and rich; rural and urban. To be able to mobilize against the deep evil of fascism was an incredible accomplishment, and Americans of all stripes should justly be proud of this. But the Greatest Generation sat astride the Long Jim Crow, a period of injustice and justification of it. It involved an America at least tolerant of the practices of Southern segregation and in many cases complicit in them.

Mac

In the first set of informal photographs in my family's photo album is a picture of a young man in uniform holding a toddler (Figure 18.1). On the back of the photograph is inscribed, "Mac, back from Europe with Bryan 1945." The uniformed young man, 20 years old, was my mother's younger brother, my Uncle Mac.

Mac had enlisted in July of 1943 at 18, and was assigned to the 4th Infantry Division, the first infantry unit to reach French soil at Utah Beach on D-Day.[2] He participated in the battle through the hedgerows of the Cotentin Peninsula, the breakthrough at St. Lo, and the Liberation of Paris. The restoration of democracy in France is surely one of the landmark events in world history. The 4th fought in the series of battles in Germany's Hurtgen Forest in September through December of 1944, immediately facing the Battle of the Bulge, where it successfully defended the City of Luxembourg. As the German lines broke, the 4th pushed southeast into Bavaria, where it liberated one of Dachau's satellite subcamps, Haunstetten.[3]

On his return, Mac went to college at the University of Alabama, and attended law school there, finishing in 1950. He married Joan (pronounced JoAnn) Newell, and they took up residence in Tuscaloosa in a small apartment around the corner from where my grandmother lived. He was called up again during the Korean War, spending a year in Germany. He established a normal life as a lawyer in Tuscaloosa, practicing until he retired, and staying active in the First Methodist Church. He died in 2011.

The Mac I knew was a quiet, almost reserved man. I can remember few extended conversations with him, and the most extensive had to do with serving as executor of my mother's will. He was a firm New York Yankees baseball fan, unusual, to say the least, among Southerners back then.

Figure 18.1 Bryan with Mac [along with Mom], Home from Europe, 1945.
Source: Author's collection.

A North Alabama Liberal's Last Campaign

Mac practiced law with E.W. Skidmore, a fellow veteran. Both Mac and E.W. had received battlefield promotions to Lieutanant. Skidmore served as a labor-liberal state senator for several years in the 1950s. Mac was deeply involved in his campaigns, serving as his finance chair for his senate races. Skidmore was a solid liberal; he promoted a corporate income tax to support education, led the opposition to the "right to work law", and was moderate on the race issue (for the day). He was a floor leader for Governor James "Big Jim" Folsom, a liberal and race moderate who claimed a direct link to the Populists of the 1890s. Skidmore's campaigns made explicit appeals to Tuscaloosa Black voters and as finance chair Mac ran ads for Skidmore in *The Alabama Citizen*, Tuscaloosa's Black newspaper.[4] The paper was generally supportive of Skidmore, tolerating but not condoning the senator's nod to segregation during a period when the issue was becoming increasingly paramount.

During the 1950s, legislative politics increasingly revolved around race and segregation. A prime example was the continued and ultimately successful efforts to outlaw the NAACP in the state. The attack on the NAACP was relentless. In 1955, the Alabama Legislature passed a bill that outlawed the NAACP in Wilcox County, a Black Belt county where no Blacks could vote. Folsom vetoed the bill, and the State Senate had a rousing debate on the override. Despite Folsom's floor leader E.W. Skidmore's pledge that the veto would be upheld, the Senate overrode Folsom's veto.

The veto fight was soon moot; Attorney General John Patterson banned the organization from operating in the state a year later. It took three pro-NAACP Supreme Court decisions and eight years before the right of the organization to operate in the state was restored.[5]

Skidmore ran for lieutenant governor in 1958 on a strong pro-labor platform. Mac ran his Tuscaloosa County fundraising committee, and he placed ads in newspapers throughout the state.[6] As head of the Tuscaloosa Bar Association, Mac got a unanimous endorsement for Skidmore from the association, probably not an easy task given the number of conservative lawyers in the association. Skidmore had filibustered the state's anti-labor right-to-work law when it was passed in the early 1950s and proposed an end to the state's right to work law in 1957. "It's a bad piece of legislation. If anyone can show me where it helps the working man in any way" he would be happy to change his position.[7] The *Birmingham News* noted that Skidmore "has long been a champion of public education, public health, welfare, and labor."[8]

A few years earlier, Skidmore traveled to the state Congress of Labor Organizations (CLO) convention with Governor Folsom, telling the delegates that they had friends in Montgomery and attacking the right to work law as the "bleakest page" written by Alabama lawmakers since the Reconstruction era.[9] This strong labor stance reflected a relatively large, unionized workforce in Alabama compared to other Southern states. Skidmore was a firm Loyalist in the continuing battles against the states' rights or Dixiecrat wing of the Alabama Democratic Party and ran as a Loyalist in 1962 for the State Democratic Committee.

Skidmore's advertisements were titled "A Message to the Men and Women Who Do NOT Have a Million Dollars." Yet the segregation issue could not be avoided by 1958, and politicians like Skidmore tried to assure white voters that he was firmly for segregation but opposed mistreatment of Blacks. Politicians could advertise racial moderation in the early 1950s, but by the late 1950s to do so was a short route to oblivion.

In his 1958 advertisements Skidmore called himself "a spokesman for segregation, a partner of the people's interest, and a friend of the common man."[10] Tuscaloosa County administered Alabama's harsh registration laws in a reasonably fair manner, and the city did have a contingent of Black voters. More liberal local politicians such as Skidmore walked a fine line between being a segregationist and being a racist, a common distinction in the South of those times. In his campaign, he sidestepped the issue with the old plea of racial moderates of the era to let us "work out our own solution."

In his campaign for lieutenant governor, Skidmore explicitly tried to revitalize the Populist coalition of Folsom, consisting of labor, small farmers, pensioners, supporters of better schools and roads. His strategy was to build out from his North Alabama liberal support, hoping to make the race about class rather than status. In a strategy meeting to mobilize the labor vote, Skidmore claimed that a group of anti-labor, anti-farmer utility companies and Birmingham Big Mule corporations opposed him for his pro-labor positions in the legislature. Attending the meeting were the senator's state campaign chair, Tuscaloosa Mayor George Van Tassell, Uncle Mac, his Tuscaloosa County campaign chair, and other North Alabama political leaders.

Skidmore's strategy failed, as race became the key issue in both his race and the contest for governor, featuring John Patterson and George Wallace. Seeing that Patterson had the upper hand on the hot button issue of segregation, Wallace tried to appeal to North Alabamians on the class issue by promoting education, better roads, and less virulent segregation measures. But his appeals were too little and too late, and Patterson easily won.[11]

Skidmore faced two opponents, Sam Englehardt, a white supremacist, virulent racist, and leader in the White Citizens' Council, and Albert Boutwell, the darling of the Birmingham Big Mule industrialists.[12] Boutwell was substantially more segregationist than Skidmore, and he had authored many of the state's laws to preserve segregation. Boutwell was known as segregation's legal craftsman but spoke softly on the issue.

Skidmore hoped to mobilize the labor vote against the Big Mule support for Boutwell and the Black Belt vote expected for Englehardt. The first round Democratic primary eliminated Englehardt, but Boutwell won the runoff against Skidmore easily. After serving as lieutenant governor, Boutwell went on to become mayor of Birmingham during the Students' Crusade of 1963; Martin Luther King's "Letter from a Birmingham Jail" was addressed to Mayor Boutwell.

Tuscaloosa's Black newspaper, *the Alabama Citizen*, regretted Skidmore's loss and saw the white backlash against civil rights building. "Campaigning as the leading segregationist in Alabama, State Sen. Albert Boutwell of Birmingham won over State Sen. E.W. Skidmore of Tuscaloosa with a thumping . . . Skidmore had labor's endorsement and was not looked upon as a rabid foe of the doctrine of equality under the law."[13]

In hindsight, this race may have been the last gasp of the old Populist coalition reconstructed by Folsom a platform that was pro-small farmer, pro-labor, moderate on race, facing the Bourbon faction that itself was fracturing. The vitriolic racist Englehardt was increasingly unpalatable to the Birmingham industrialists trying to keep labor peace and profits flowing.

Mac's political views generally matched those of his senior law partner. He was known as a moderate on the race issue, instructing his children explicitly to treat Blacks with respect—as equals, his son JD related. Tuscaloosa Blacks knew Mac as a lawyer who would take their cases regardless of their ability to pay, and not infrequently he accepted produce in exchange for legal services. Apparently collards were a common medium of exchange in season, and his son JD recalls dreading this form of payment because he was assigned the duty of cleaning the collards in a metal washtub. I recall Mac dropping by our house with an armful of collards for us as well; there is little better than Tuscaloosa-grown collards and buttermilk cornbread.

In this regard Mac was carrying on the North Alabama family tradition of his uncle, Julius, and his father, M.M., in their willingness to accept Black clients and represent them competently. While using collards as a medium of exchange surely indicates the generous spirit of my uncle, it also points to the vast inequality between white and Black residents of Tuscaloosa. Unfairness permeated the system, and human decency could not overcome the stranglehold of Jim Crow.

Remembrances of France

Years later, on a family visit in Florida, where both my sister and one of Mac and Joan's two sons lived, suddenly Mac and I were engaging in an extended and personal conversation. I was taken aback—it was not his style to be so personal. In his 70s, Mac and Joan traveled to Europe, visiting the memorial at Utah Beach. He was surprised at the changes in France, which was still, in his words, a peasant society in 1944 but which had become a modern country.

The biggest surprise came when he engaged with a docent, and Mac noted during the conversation that he had been there on D-Day. The docent's only comment was "Interesting. Will you be staying for the movie?" He said that they indeed would. In the theater, the same docent stepped up to the micro-phone to introduce the film. She began her introduction with "Before we start the movie, I want to recognize Mr. Davidson, who came here in 1944 to help us." He was deeply touched.

Ordinary Lives in Turbulent Times

My mother, hailing from North Alabama, and my father, from the South, was the union of the two ancestral lines I've been following. Ironically, their union represented a turn toward a more unified sectional South—the mountain versus prairie, democratic versus oligarchic division began to shrink.

During the Jim Crow regime, the Southern racial caste system was back-ground to most white Southern families. They did not think much about its toll on Blacks nor its morality, nor whether they benefited from it. Most were white supremacists without consciously thinking they were (or were not), because they operated within a social system of law and custom that did the structuring for them.

That system began cracking in the late 1940s, as we see in the subsequent section. But for the Greatest Generation, depression and war were in the past, and the future looked more stable, perhaps a return to the Roaring Twenties.

My parents were members of this generation, and in some ways fit the Brokaw mold of engaging in the great moral struggle of the war and returning home. Brokaw depicts a cohort of workaholics feverishly bent on reestablish-ing normality to a stressed if victorious America. My father certainly fit that pattern. He worked long and hard, taking on more tasks as he aged. He seldom ate dinner at home and worked on most weekends.

For my mother, the disruptions were far more personal than the upheaval of war. She had a tough personal life, with both of her parents dying in her home and becoming a widow for a second time few days after her 47th birthday.

Her father, M.M. Davidson, who had saved George Lige from the gallows, had become a Methodist minister after a legal career of almost 20 years. Like all Methodist ministers, he moved his family from place to place in in the North Alabama Circuit. She graduated from high school in Florence, in the Tri-Cities region in the far northwest region of the state, but had spent only one year there in her Methodist nomadic existence.

In college at the University of Alabama, my tall (for the day) and slender mother was, naturally, known as "Stubby," a nickname that stuck. She graduated in 1935, and announced her engagement to Robert D. Lanford of Anniston soon afterward. A week later they were married at home in Tuscaloosa with her father presiding. The couple moved to Anniston, Robert's residence, where he worked as a life insurance agent. Falling suddenly ill, Robert Lanford died of a brain tumor in an Atlanta hospital August 2, 1939.[14]

After leaving Florence, M.M. was transferred to Anniston, where he remained until 1933 then moved to the Tuscaloosa District. In 1940 he was delighted to find that his next position would be in Gadsden, where he had worked as a young lawyer. He planned to serve there until retirement, and make his permanent home in the region.

After Robert's death, Mother moved to Tuscaloosa and lived with her parents until they left for Gadsden in 1940, taking a position as an elementary school teacher and moving in with a friend, when her parents left town. Unfortunately M.M. fell ill with throat cancer and did not serve long in the post he was so anticipating. So ill he could not continue his pastorate, he returned to Tuscaloosa, dying in January 1942.

Mom Meets Dad

According to Mother's scrapbook recording the relationship with my father, he noticed her a couple of times at Pug's Café, an eatery near the university that was still around when I attended school there. Finally, I guess, Dad got his nerve up and walked over and introduced himself, collecting a phone number as well. Their first date was in April 1941. Soon they began to date regularly, attending the then-popular wrestling matches. On the fourth date, they again went to a wrestling match, then left and went to a street carnival, where Mother writes that she "Had more fun." From the scrapbook, it seems that Dad wisely stopped taking her to the wrestling matches soon after.

Mother spent the summer in Gadsden with her parents, returning to continue teaching and resumed dating my father. At Christmas he gave her "a beautiful silver comb, brush, and mirror—I was really thrilled." I recall that set, which she kept in her bedroom until she died.

Mother's scrapbook contains events that could characterize any love affair—movies, drives in the country, Alabama football games—and no more wrestling matches. They worked crossword puzzles and cryptograms, and created some of their own. The one in the scrapbook, when solved, reads, "My Love, for you transcends the brightest stars—Glenn."

Finally in October of 1942, Dad asked Mom to marry him—a year and a half after they started dating. "We were both so thrilled and excited that neither of us had good sense," Mother wrote in her scrapbook. They were married at the end of the month in Montgomery with my Grandfather Jones officiating at Dexter Avenue Methodist Church.

My father was known as a hot-headed guy, but he sure was slow to get around to this. When I fell in love with Diane, I didn't last two months.

My Father's Road to Tuscaloosa

In a similar fashion to my mother, my father lived a rootless youth, moving around south Alabama with his minister dad. The state of parsonages in rural and small-town Alabama were certainly not sumptuous; churches were not well-funded in the early quarter of the 20th century, and minister's salaries were meager. An early photograph of my father as a boy was taken next to what was probably the parsonage of one of Granddaddy's churches. The house is clapboard on pier-and-beam, unpainted and without skirting.

After graduating from high school in Opelika, Dad attended Birmingham Southern College, graduating in 1928. After working briefly at the *Birmingham News*, he joined the *Anniston Star* in advertising, leaving in 1930 for the *Tuscaloosa News*. He always worked on the business side of the newspaper, serving as advertising manager, and was business manager when he left the *News* in 1949.

Tuscaloosa

In April of 1943, my future parents (Figure 18.2) moved from a small apartment to 2207 Glendale, a neighborhood later destroyed by the tornado of 2011. I remember little of Tuscaloosa, except the hardwood floors of the comfortable house we lived in. And my mother said little of her life before we left Tuscaloosa for Troy in 1949. However she spoke of a Christmas when, according to her, my father went over to a gathering at a neighbor's house and overstayed, "eating oysters and drinking beer." When he came home late it was time to construct the tricycle and wagon that were to be my presents. That did not go well, and apparently he turned the air blue with some colorful words. I hope my family, friends, and students will see no connections here between father and son.

I do not think my mother was pleased with the move, leaving her family in Tuscaloosa and the familiar environs of North Alabama for the more racially conscious South Alabama. Her scrapbook includes a couple of articles about it

Figure 18.2 Mom and Dad in Tuscaloosa
Source: Author's collection.

from the local papers. She makes no comments about the move, and the scrap-book entries stop at that point. As I got older, I had the feeling that she had trouble feeling accepted in the small-town community in South Alabama, and very soon after my father's death in 1961 she gathered Carol and me at the kitchen table and told us we were moving to Tuscaloosa. That is when she revealed to us her prior marriage, because she thought it might come up.

The stoic parenthood of that era carried the mantra "don't tell the kids." We had not been told of Dad's earlier heart attack. I had not been informed about our trip to the cardiologist in Montgomery when our Troy doctor had detected my heart murmur. I'm sure there is much more; ours was not a communicative family—except for my straightforward Aunt Mary Elizabeth. I for one, as a parent and grandparent, am glad that secretiveness belongs to a bygone era.

CHAPTER 19

Three Southern Editors

In the late 1940s, three young white men took over the as publishers or editors of three daily newspapers in Alabama. Buford Boone of the *Tuscaloosa News*, Grover Hall Jr. of the *Montgomery Advertiser*, and Glenn Jones, my father, of the *Troy Messenger* all held their positions throughout the intense flames of the civil rights movement and the brutal white backlash that buffeted their newspapers. This chapter, and the next, trace the careers of these men and how they and the organizations they ran responded to what was probably the most difficult time to be an editor in the Deep South. Each responded differently to the turmoil.

Although we can never reconstruct the internal motives and reactions to external events of these men, we can trace the stances they took in their editorials during the period. For obvious reasons, I concentrate mostly on the activities of my father, but anchor his actions in the positions taken by Boone and Hall.

Managing a Small-Town Daily

In 1948, my father was business manager of the *Tuscaloosa News*, where he had worked for 17 years. He pulled together his assets and purchased a controlling interest in the *Troy Messenger*, assuming the positions of editor and publisher on the first of the year 1949. The former publisher, Eldon Hoar, wrote a rather strange editorial about the management change, admitting that he had not done a particularly good job of running the paper because he was consumed with other business interests.[1] Hoar kept a financial interest in the paper.

My mother overcame her reservations about the move and took over as the bookkeeper of the paper. I have no idea where Mother learned double-entry

accounting—most likely on the job in Troy. Like any small business managers, they were strapped for cash—the Troy house was less spacious than the
Tuscaloosa house.

The *Messenger* was as I recall the smallest circulation daily in the state. The
staff, including news production, office management, business and advertising,
and print shop totaled only 15 in 1957. Well actually 16, because my mother
kept the books at home.

Small-town papers in the United States during that period often had local
owners who also served as publishers and editors. That period was beginning
to end; larger papers were buying up smaller papers in the classic pattern of
consolidation. By the mid-1950s both radio and television news put even more
pressure on small-town papers.

There are always two sides of any business—the revenue-generating side and
the product-producing side. There are generally tensions between these two
sides, but in the case of periodical publishing these tensions are more intense
than in other businesses. Raising revenue involves selling papers and selling
advertising. That means the content must appeal to subscribers and advertisers. This situation puts pressure not only on the news content carried in the
paper but also on the nature of the opinions offered by the editor. The 1950s
presented an especially difficult environment for Deep South editors to navigate, particularly after the U.S. Supreme Court struck down legal segregation
in *Brown v. Board* in 1954.

My father referred to himself as editor and publisher, although on the masthead he was listed only as publisher, and his editor was sometimes called the
"news editor" on the masthead. The publisher took control of the content of
the editorials and policy stances of the paper, while the editor managed the
news content for the paper. There was high turnover in the editorship during
the first several years, but after 1954 there were only two different editors, both
women.

Dad's career in publishing was solidly on the business side rather than the
editorial side. He was advertising manager in Anniston and business manager in Tuscaloosa. The *Tuscaloosa Graphic* wrote on his death, "He was one
of the best newspaper advertising men in the business."[2] He was also a master at trading advertising in the paper for various items ostensibly intended
for the newspaper. These trades included the car that our family drove and
our vacation stays at a development in Daytona Beach, Florida, called Ellinor
Village.

Resurgence of the Klan

Less than six months after the transfer of management in 1949, my father met his first challenge. How should the *Messenger* respond to a resurgent Ku Klux Klan and copycat groups in the Deep South?

The original Klan was formed after the Civil War explicitly to restore white supremacy after slaves were freed. Klan chapters quickly popped up all over the south, joined by other such racist organizations including the major "competitor," the Knights of the White Camellia. The Klan's vicious and gruesome actions against Blacks and their white allies helped to bring about the end of Reconstruction and ushered in Redemption. The Klan faded afterward.

But the Klan was not finished and reinvented itself after a movie glorified it. In D.H. Griffith's 1915 blockbuster racist movie *Birth of a Nation*, the reinvigorated Ku Klux Klan burned a cross during a lynching scene. Soon after, a reenergized Klan burned a cross atop Stone Mountain in Georgia. This version of the Klan was composed of newly radicalized men using the same name and methods of the Reconstruction Klan. Racial tensions were exacerbated when Black First World War veterans returned, expecting if not equal treatment with whites at least better treatment. Instead the opposite happened. The tensions set off a series of violent confrontations, riots, and lynchings throughout the nation. The surge peaked with a huge march of Klan members in white robes and conical hats in Washington in 1926.

Klan activities petered out in the late 1920s nationally, but the group remained powerful in Southern politics. Governor Bibb Graves, a committed New Dealer, readily accepted Klan endorsements. Graves's action provoked the *Birmingham News* to complain editorially about his "Klan-nominated, Klan-elected, and Klan-controlled administration."[3]

While the vigorous Black press continually covered and criticized the Klan as well as the segregationist practices of the period, most white Southern editors either made no editorial comments on the Klan or approached the subject gingerly. Some white editors took courageous stands against the Klan, and particularly its infiltration of government. Newspapers played an important part in communicating disgust with its activities, and editorial courage increased as the power of the Klan faded in the late 1920s .[4]

Still, the Klan was not done. Returning from the Second World War, Black veterans increased demands for desegregation, which stimulated another Klan resurgence. In March 1946, eight crosses burned in Birmingham, which had become a center of Klan activity.[5] In May 1946 more than a thousand robed Klansmen burned a huge cross atop Stone Mountain Georgia to announce that the Klan had returned.[6]

"Big Jim," the Dixiecrats, and the Resurgence of the Klan

At a Klan rally in December of 1949, an Alabama pastor and Klan leader praised the governors of Georgia, South Carolina, Mississippi, and Louisiana for their white supremacist stands. He attacked Alabama's governor James "Big Jim" Folsom and Florida's governor Fuller Warren for their stances on civil rights, claiming that they "had sold out to the Truman Crowd."[7]

It is not possible to understand fully Southern politics at midcentury without appreciating the role of Folsom. Other white Southern politicians were liberal on the race issue, but they lacked Folsom's charisma. Other Southern politicians were charismatic demagogues, but they were racists. Huey Long is held up as the epitome of the nonracist demagogue, but he neither faced the racial divisions that Folsom did nor did he come out forcefully on behalf of Blacks as Folsom did, although his programs did provide benefits to Blacks.[8]

Folsom was born in the Wiregrass town of Elba in 1908—the same year and town where my father was born. By the time he ran for governor in 1946, he had moved to Cullman, the heart of the North Alabama hills. As Folsom biographers Carl Grafton and Anne Permaloff note, "Folsom was able to run a statewide campaign from essentially two politically and economically similar but geographically separated homes. Both the Wiregrass region of southeastern Alabama and much of North Alabama were characterized by small farms, relatively few African Americans, and strong populist traditions."[9] For a brief moment, Folsom brought to fruition the Populist dream of unifying Alabama's poor white voters north and south of the Black Belt.

In the 1946 Democratic Party primary for governor, Folsom defeated segregationist Handy Ellis for governor. "The Folsom victory demonstrated that a more liberal appeal to a biracial alliance of blacks and plain whites could result in victory," a historian of the period wrote.[10] That alliance reconstructed the old 1890s Populist alliance and was subject to the same stresses it had faced. Whites would have to focus on economic issues while Blacks would have to be able to return to the electorate; the latter was dependent on the success of the NAACP's legal attack on Black disenfranchisement.

Big Jim refused to play the white supremacist race card. He also supported woman's rights and advocated a broad and ambitious economic program. He relished his few rallies in the Black Belt, where he would get few votes from the conservative whites who inhabited the region. Blacks eagerly attended Folsom's rallies to hear his criticisms of the politicians of the region, but few Blacks could vote for him.

Big Jim looked around the crowd, noting that the Blacks there were almost as white as he was, and commented, "I want you to know the sun didn't bleach 'em." In his 1962 campaign he told a crowd that despite Black Belt politicians opposition to integration, "There's a whole lot of integratin' going on at night."[11]

In his first term, Folsom had to deal with a resurgent Klan and the States' Rights Party. In 1948, half of the Alabama and all of the Mississippi Democratic electors walked out of the Democratic National Convention over President Truman's civil rights program. Along with delegates from several other Southern states, they formed the States' Rights Party, called Dixiecrats and held a nominating convention in Birmingham. The splinter party nominated South Carolina governor (later Senator) Strom Thurmond for president. The Dixiecrats got the state Democratic Party Committees in Mississippi, Alabama, Arkansas, South Carolina, and Louisiana to declare the Dixiecrat slate the official Democratic Party ticket, and the Truman-Barkley national ticket did not appear on the ballots in those states. The Dixiecrats won all those states. In Alabama, the Dixiecrat slate, under the banner of the Democratic Party, won every county save Winston, which went Republican. Most of the few Republican votes were cast in the mountain counties, where the Republican vote was around 30%.[12]

The Dixiecrat revolt intensified the factional division in the Alabama Democratic Party between the Loyalists, who supported the national party, and the States' Rights faction, which reflected the Bourbon Conservative Democrats of old. Governor Folsom, a firm Loyalist, forcefully rejected the States' Rights Party, and voiced support for the national Democratic ticket and did so again in his second term as governor in 1955–59. He maintained a moderate stance on civil rights and was closely allied with the Truman administration. In Montgomery he initiated an ambitious economic and civil rights program. He met resistance from the alliance of planters, industrialists, and bankers in the legislature every step of the way, making less progress than he had hoped.

Folsom biographers Grafton and Permaloff rate his civil rights record "a distinguished one." Mostly his program was preventing or at least delaying attempts by the Big Mules to tighten their control over Black Alabamians.

"With far less success but amazing audacity, he attempted in many ways large and small to extend the bounds of freedom for blacks, poor whites and women."[13]

Klan violence and intimidation continued sporadically throughout the immediate post–Second World War period, often directed at Black veterans. The activities were mitigated to some extent by better law enforcement than in previous Klan outbreaks and by intense squabbling among various Klan factions. News coverage and apparently public attitudes concerning the Klan were changing as well.[14]

Klan activity spiked in 1949, and it was severe. In 1948, the *Troy Messenger* published 14 articles focusing on Klan activities; in 1949 that leaped to 84.[15] Events during the spring and summer of 1949 in the Birmingham area caused news coverage to rise. The wire services characterized the attacks as "mob violence" led by "night riders." Although many incidents went unreported, much coverage focused on two floggings, the punishment of choice of the postwar Klan.[16] All the victims were white, accused of morals violations. The hypocritical Klan viewed itself as an enforcer of morals.[17]

While white floggings attracted press coverage, Blacks were the primary targets of the Klan. Distrustful of law enforcement, aware of Klan infiltration of police, and fearful of a Klan return, Blacks did not report many of these crimes. Newspaper coverage occurred nevertheless. Two courageous Methodist ministers uncovered three acts of Klan floggings in a county south of Birmingham where numerous cross-burnings occurred. All the victims moved away from the area in fear of their lives, losing their businesses in the process.[18]

The Editors Respond to Klan Violence

At first the postwar Klan seemed weaker than in its earlier incarnations. Grover Hall Jr., editor of the *Montgomery Advertiser*, claimed that the Klan of the late 1940s was far less effective than the Klan of the 1920s. "Today the organization is but a gutter into which contemptible dross flows in fetid eddies."[19] Hall underestimated the power that the Klan would accumulate during the postwar years of strife over desegregation and voting rights. He ceased criticizing the organization as time went on.

Buford Boone, publisher of the *Tuscaloosa News*, took the lead in addressing the Klan resurgence. The paper slipped an informer into the local Klavern.

The reporter wrote front-page stories all week, one of which involved an applicant whom the Klavern rejected but didn't tell him lest he spill the beans on the group, which was happily accomplished by the *News* reporter. Boone published a steady stream of anti-Klan editorials as well.

In 1947, Georgian Buford Boone had moved to Alabama to assume the position of publisher of the *Tuscaloosa News*. A native of Macon, Georgia, he worked for and briefly edited the Macon *Telegraph and News*. There he was influenced by Mark Etherege, "widely recognized as the dean of the handful of liberal editors in segregated states," and T.W. Anderson, socially progressive publisher of that paper.[20] Boone would later become a Pulitzer Prize–winning editor and a leading voice for reason and moderation on race in a state that was anything but a moderate. He took his first giant step into that role in 1949.

When Boone took over as publisher, my father was business manager at the paper, and continued to work under Boone for two more years. He was familiar with Boone's stance on issues, and probably shared most of them. Like his friend and former boss, my father wrote a series of scathing anti-Klan editorials in the *Messenger*.[21] The *Messenger*'s first comment on race relations in the late 1940s was an editorial on a police brutality case brought by a Black woman, Gertrude Perkins, against two white Montgomery policemen. Muckraking columnist and author of the renowned "The Washington Merry-Go-Round," Drew Pearson wrote critically of Montgomery's unfair treatment of her case. The *Messenger* saw the local court's poor handling of the case as having a serious detrimental effect: "racial relations in that city have been badly damaged."[22]

Then came a commentary on race focused on a Georgia lynching. A mob broke into a local jail and lynched a young Black man accused of shooting at a white man. "The State of Georgia has added another infamous blot to the history of the South and the Nation. . . . It is difficult to believe that there are Americans who deliberately take the law into their own hands and commit unmitigated murder . . . lynching[s] only stir up racial hatreds and tear down many years of constructive work of solidifying friendly white-Negro relations," the editorial said.[23]

Most moderate white editors and publishers in the South, such as both Boone and my father, were segregationists as the 1950s began, and incrementalists as it became clear that race relations had to change. Editorials during the period had dual purposes. For example, Dad's editorials highlighted the views of racial moderates who were offended by the Klan's activities and who were eager to forestall more draconian action by national political leaders. These editorials confronted the worst parts of Jim Crow and offered a defense of states' rights regarding potential intervention by federal officials.

In mid-June, the *Messenger* published its first anti-Klan editorial, a passionate critique directed at the failure of law enforcement to bring an end to "terroristic raids on citizens." Calling the Klan and its ilk "sneaking, secretive orders," the *Messenger* compared the successes of law enforcement in bringing to justice "thieves, gangsters, vagrants, murderers" with the lack of arrests of Klansmen. "Daily we hear of new outbreaks of violence, bigotry and hatred in Alabama. 'Negro Taken from Jail and Lynched.' 'Hooded Men on the March.' 'Klan Burns Fiery Cross.' 'Woman Beaten by Robed Men.' It is a rare occasion when we hear of the hoodlums being apprehended and brought to justice. Why?"[24]

Two days later the paper returned to a theme of criticizing a South that would not solve its obvious problems, in particular the failure of local law agencies to arrest Klansmen wreaking havoc on the state. Because of "flagrant violations of human rights such as flogging, threatening to kill, and the like . . . our people are in danger; the future of the state and its children's future are at stake." The *Messenger* went on to highlight the failure of Alabama to solve its obvious problem with the Klan: "The States' Rights party [the 'Dixiecrats'] claims that each state should be allowed to handle its own affairs. This should be enough to ensure the passage of the anti-mask legislation in the legislature."[25] The anti-mask legislation was a Governor Folsom initiative to prevent Klansmen from hiding their faces in their gatherings. The editorial was a reminder to states' righters that the antifederal stance they had taken carried with it the responsibility for enacting relevant public policies.

At the *Montgomery Advertiser*, Grover Hall's response was less critical of the Klan, and less supportive of Governor Folsom's anti-mask legislation. Hall initially referred to the Klan as "albino swine" but wrote that the Klan atrocities were not as bad as those committed by United Mine Workers' "labor goons" who attacked non-union Alabama miners ignoring a UMW call for a strike. He went on to praise earlier versions of the Klan, but criticized the 1940s version, stating "The Klan performed a great service to the South in the beginnings; it performs a great disservice three generations later."[26]

Animosity toward the overtly racist States' Rights Party was another marker of moderation on the race issue. Grover Hall, already moving away from his claimed moderate stance, called their movement "a worthy undertaking" and "an honorable cause." He applauded the Dixiecrats' bringing states' rights to the fore of the national debate. He trumpeted the claim that "the Dixiecrats thus won untold numbers of non-Southerners over as sympathizers." But Hall argued that the split in the Democratic Party enabled Truman to adopt his civil rights plank in the Democratic Party's 1948 Platform. He called for the demise of the movement, and reunification into the national Democratic Party. While he had little taste for the Democratic Party Loyalists Senators Lister Hill and John Sparkman, Hall thought their status in national politics could help deflect the more objectionable (to Southerners) parts of the president's civil rights program.[27]

The *Messenger*'s condemnation of the Dixiecrats was straightforward. The paper took a strong Loyalist position, advocating support for the national Democratic Party. Dad called the Dixiecrat effort in 1948 "a flop," and said they "had no record to be proud of. . . . The people of Alabama know full well that the Dixiecrats have little or no representation in Washington. And they realize how important representation in Washington is."[28] He linked the Dixiecrats to the Klan, and excoriated them: "Only the vicious, the contemptible, the traitors to the cause of upstanding, decent living, can condone such an organization and what it stands for."[29]

Even though the 1948 Dixiecrat effort was a flop at first, it nevertheless transformed the politics of the Deep South. In Alabama the Dixiecrats burrowed into state politics after the loss in 1948, trying to gain control of the Democratic State Executive Committee, displacing the Loyalists. The struggle between the Loyalist and States' Rights factions continued throughout the 1950s and 1960s, when the Voting Rights Act of 1965 reinvigorated the Republican Party as an alternative to the Dixiecrat wing of the Democratic Party.

In summer 1949, a large cross was burned in the nearby village of Goshen, the first such incident in South Alabama. It was common for many to dismiss cross-burnings as pranks, downplaying their racist intention. "Whether the burning of a cross was performed by pranksters or organized groups, the act is cowardly and contemptible," wrote the *Messenger*.[30]

The Alabama Klan activity attracted national attention, and on June 23, the U.S. attorney general ordered an investigation into the situation.[31] On the same day, the Alabama Legislature demanded that Congress keep its "hands off," while a congressman from a district where many of the floggings occurred claimed, "Lawless elements thrive on outside interference."

A few days later the *Messenger* continued its attack on law enforcement for its failure to make arrests in "the violence which spread through the state, bringing terror to thousands of innocent men, women and children. . . . It is a disgrace that not a single arrest has been made in connection with the beatings and floggings." Most of these innocent citizens were Black, so the critique of the lack of law enforcement was a sharp criticism of the dual Southern system of justice. The editorial closed by referring to "the 'despicable few' who have brought humiliation to our great state."[32]

The most powerful editorial during the *Messenger*'s anti-Klan campaign was a passionate indictment of the increasing intertwining of religion and racism entitled "Klan in the Pulpit." Many ministers were Klan members, and some were also leaders. "How ministers can stand up before their congregations on Sunday after donning white robes and masks at Ku Klux Klan meetings, is something which is difficult to comprehend. There is no place for bigotry in the church. Many so-called 'Disciples of God' . . . have openly supported an organization which holds the contempt of the decent citizenry . . . And from the pulpit there is talk of sinners."[33]

The nightrider violence continued, but opponents of Klan activity mobilized as well. In July of 1949 the Associated Press reported floggings of an iron miner and a Black farmer in Clay County. These were uncovered by two Methodist ministers who continued their work to ferret out terrorist acts against Blacks in that county.[34] The American Legion, which had demanded that action be taken against the terrorists, met in Mobile with the hooded mob on its agenda.[35]

Decrying the masked mobs, Governor Folsom signed the anti-mask legislation on June 27 (Figure 19.1). The attorney general of Alabama, a Folsom ally, demanded that the Klan charter be lifted, while a grand jury in Birmingham incarcerated a Klan leader for not producing records for their investigation. The Klan was under pressure, and Klan violence, or at least coverage of it, declined. The *Messenger* carried 23 articles mentioning the Klan in 1950 and only 3 in 1951.

The Stirrings of Integration

In 1948, President Truman ordered the desegregation of the Armed Forces. Pursuant to his executive order, Maxwell Air Force Base in Montgomery was integrated. Grover Hall at the *Montgomery Advertiser* called Truman's order a "reckless, moronic ukase," and asserted, "Rendering the nation's military bases laboratories for social experiments is the act of a dunce."[36] Hall's opinion

Figure 19.1 Newspaper Cartoon on Governor James Folsom's Anti-Mask Legislation Targeting the Klan.

Source: *The Montgomery Advertiser*, June 22, 1949. Newspapers.com [https://www. newspapers.com/image/415068820/?terms=%22The%20Business%20Before%20the% 20House%22&match=1].

was not an outlier. In response to the executive order, former governor Frank Dixon wrote to the then current governor, Chauncy Sparks, "It is a heartbreaking thing for those of us in the South who realize what the destruction of segregation would mean . . . to have all our plans wrecked by the type of very dangerous thinking which produced this order."[37]

The *Messenger* took a different view, lauding "the military personnel of Maxwell Field, white and black, and the people of Montgomery . . . for their calm and disciplined reaction to the surprising order." Following the gradualist approach advocated by white progressives, the *Messenger* saw the quiet integration of Maxwell as part of a slow and deliberate process that "can be achieved only by decades of patient education."[38]

Again, the *Messenger* carried a more positive view of integration than the *Advertiser*, even if one would rightly be appalled at the support of the slow pace of integration, and then only after "decades of patient education." Nevertheless the *Messenger* and the *Tuscaloosa News* saw the integration of Maxwell as a small step in the right direction, not a dire bellwether of disaster.

The *Messenger* displayed some classic Southern sensitivity in an editorial called "Let Them Clean Up Their Own Yards." Dad wrote, "The Eastern 'reformers' seem to be more interested in correcting Southern conditions they know nothing than about than in cleaning their own yards."[39] The piece was written after a town businessman, Roy Crow, owner of the Buick dealership in town, gave a Rotary Club presentation on deplorable conditions in the slums of New York City. Again, Southern regional sensitivity shows through.

In the Matter of Folsom

Hall of the *Advertiser* and Jones of the *Messenger* had serious differences of opinions about Governor James Folsom. Hall delighted in excoriating Folsom's hayseed manner and his appeal to the common man. The critiques of Folsom the hillbilly seemed to outweigh any admiration of Folsom's moderate racial position that Hall may have harbored.

My father, on the other hand, was a strong Folsom supporter. It is unclear how and why he became such an avid fan of Folsom. Folsom's appeal to the common man involved what former Congressman Carl Elliott called "backslapping antics" and fondness for drink, making more staid Alabamians embarrassed at the hayseed show.[40] Certainly the image of hillbillies invading the Capitol at Montgomery led to vicious criticism from the well-groomed Grover Hall, who had great affinity for the Black Belt gentry of Montgomery.[41]

Folsom appealed to the tenant farmers in the hills and the Wiregrass, and at his rallies played the music of the honkytonks that Hank Williams made famous. It was not just the rallies and policies that were targets for criticism; Folsom's lifestyle gave editors a great many targets as well. He was too sympathetic to Blacks, even shaking hands with them as equals. He had a serious alcohol problem that worsened as time progressed. As was standard in Alabama politics, he used patronage and government contracts to reward his allies.

As a part of the Wiregrass region, Troy and the rest of Pike County voted solidly for Folsom, especially in the more populous rural precincts. The *Messenger* reflected many of its readers when the paper savaged the legislature for its refusal to push forward the Folsom agenda. "By [the legislators'] failure, utter and complete, to face the real issues at stake, rather than to allow the personality of a man whom, (foolish though he may appear at times reveals an amazing sense of foresight at others), they should endeavor to work with, they are responsible for impeding the progress of this state."[42]

In a second editorial the *Messenger* again excoriated legislative leaders while praising Folsom: "He has been ridiculed and plotted against; scorned . . .," and "has been the butt of many a crude joke on the backyard fence." Yet "he has tried to bring about a spirit of cooperation between the administration and the legislature, to no avail." The editorial attacked the leaders of the opposition in the Senate and House: "If there was a 'do-nothing' bunch in the capitol or anywhere, it's there now." The editorial ended, "Folsom, by comparison, is an able, efficient, broad-minded administrator."[43]

Hall, on the other hand, supported the legislature and ridiculed Folsom for having such little influence with the legislature. Hall wrote, "Only in the Reconstruction period was there ever such an administration as that of Folsom."[44] Was this a slap at Folsom's patronage system or his moderate position on race? The editorial could have involved both, given the prominence Folsom's 1949 platform had given the race issue. Hall was becoming increasingly conservative.

An Endangered Species: Moderate Editors in the South

At the start of the 1949 legislative session, Folsom had offered a strong civil rights platform, pointedly highlighting that "Restrictions imposed by prejudice and intolerance have been declared unconstitutional." He noted progress in opportunities for Negroes, called it a "cornerstone," and called for more. Folsom ended on a note that resonates down through the years: "We must remember—that which is built on prejudice or ill will cannot survive in a democracy."[45] The governor had cast his die with the future. Did Southern editors?

In their Pulitzer Prize–winning book, *The Race Beat*, Gene Roberts and Hank Klibanoff write that "a small band of liberal white southern editors would become the region's conscience ... while many southern journalists, and virtually all of the region's politicians, decried the northern press for hiding its own racial problems while laying bare the South's."[46]

Many, and probably most, Southern editors were sympathetic to the Klan or the White Citizens' Councils. Some, like Roy Harris, publisher of the *Augusta Georgia Courier*, were Citizen Council members. Others, such as Douglas Southall Freeman, James J. Kilpatrick, both of the *Richmond News-Leader*, and Thomas Waring of the *Charleston News and Courier* staunchly defended white supremacy and segregation.

It was easier to call out the Klan in the late 1940s than earlier (or than it would be later). Even the deep Black Belt paper *Selma Times-Journal* remarked on this tendency—on page 16.[47] There was a naïve belief that gradualism would solve the problems—to the extent that the editors thought they needed to be solved.

The *Tuscaloosa News* carried a nationally syndicated column by segregationist newspaperman James Kilpatrick well into the 1960s. As a student at the University of Alabama going through the pains of integration, I found his cleaned-up versions of states' rights reprehensible. Kilpatrick advocated massive resistance and closing schools to avoid integration in the 1950s, all justified in the 1950s language of wrongheaded constitutionalism.

By the early 1950s, there was little to distinguish the *Messenger* from the race moderate editors who provided "the region's conscience." All knew many elements of the Southern system were flawed, and criticized them freely. All were in favor of serious progress for Blacks, economically and even politically, and decried the mistreatment of Blacks while white supremacist editors were defending all aspects of the system. My father's stinging anti-Klan editorials and calls for moderation in integration put him in the center of those moderate editors and publishers who realized that change was coming. The only question was if that change could be accomplished peacefully and gradually. Among these moderates, the call for local problem-solving was serious, not a ploy to delay, defer, and defeat desegregation.

Parallel to this moderation was a defensiveness about the region and the tendency to point out the flaws of critics from the North. The same editors arguing for Black progress and against the increasing resistance to integration among whites also inveighed against Federal Government activism on behalf of desegregation.

Even modest moves toward improving the lives of Blacks were viewed within the narrow lens of local problem-solving among overly optimistic Southern moderates. In 1949, segregated Southern states formed an educational compact allowing Black students from one segregated state to enter professional schools in other states. "Alabama Negroes, for example, may attend the Meharry Medical College in Nashville, which will become the center of education for Negro doctors, with expenses paid by the State of Alabama." The *Messenger* was highly supportive of this arrangement, clearly designed to inch forward on the race issue without violating the principle of segregation.[48] The trouble with the plan was that the state was playing catch-up; seemingly the U.S. Supreme Court had outlawed such schemes in a Missouri case a decade before, saying they did not fulfill the state's "separate but equal" commitment.

Throughout the early 1950s the *Messenger* took a moderate-to-liberal stance on controversial issues. It remained stridently anti-Klan, solidly pro-Folsom, consistently National Democratic Loyalist, and anti-Dixiecrat. Grover Hall of the *Montgomery Advertizer* moved steadily to the right on the race issue, while Buford Boone of the *Tuscaloosa News* declared himself a moderate, one who offered positive problem-solving to an increasingly resistant white readership.

Brown v. Board

During the early 1950s, it became clear that if Congress did not act on the race issue in the South, the Supreme Court would. The Court had both voting suppression and segregation in its cross-hairs. In the late 1940s the Court decided several relevant cases pointing to the future, including cases requiring integration of the law schools at the Universities of Missouri, Oklahoma, and Texas. Then in the 1950s the Court began oral arguments on *Brown v. Board of Education of Topeka, Kansas,* a consolidated case about school segregation challenges from five different sets of plaintiffs.

Courts were active on the voting front as well. In 1944, the Supreme Court invalidated the white primary, which excluded Blacks from voting in the Democratic Party primary. In 1949 the Supreme Court ruled that the Alabama constitutional amendment on voter qualifications requiring voters to explain the U.S. Constitution to registrars was unconstitutional. The amendment discriminated against Blacks by allowing registrars to select more difficult questions for them.

At an old-fashioned crowded courthouse rally in Troy, Governor Folsom commented that he was pleased the amendment had been struck down. He also took the opportunity to blast the Klan, calling for its dissolution. Folsom was marketing his ambitious 1949 program, which included a thorough revision of the state's antiquated 1901 constitution, and the elimination of the voter qualification amendment fit in with his plan to make the state constitution more democratic.[49] He was unsuccessful at the time, and Alabama today labors under the same constitution with much of its racist language remaining but inoperative because of federal court decisions.

Prohibited from succeeding himself in 1950, Folsom ran again in 1954. The tension surrounding the coming school desegregation decision did not derail his campaign; he won easily. Again he ran "the little man's big friend" campaign (Folsom was 6'8" tall), emphasizing what he would do for the working men and women in the state, mostly avoiding raising the segregation issue. Loyalist Senator John Sparkman, also running for reelection, followed the same strategy. A full-page advertisement in the *Messenger* blared in its headline "Smash the Attempt of Birmingham 'Big Mule' Republicans to Hand-Pick Your Senator." Sparkman focused on his record "of doing things for farmers, small business, and rural electrification," but he also emphasized his support for segregation. It simply could not be ignored anymore.[50] The *Messenger* endorsed racial moderate Jimmy Faulkner in the first round,[51] and Folsom in the runoff primary for governor. Both Faulkner and Folsom were racial moderates and both appealed to voters on economic interests. The paper endorsed Sparkman for Senate. Both Folsom and Sparkman won Pike County and their respective races.

The 1954 election was a landmark. It was the last election for a very long time in which class interests dominated race relations in an Alabama election.

As tensions rose in the South and in Troy, the tone of the *Messenger*'s editorials changed. The dreaded decision came down on May 14, 1954, overturning *Plessy v. Ferguson*, the 1896 case that had ruled "separate but equal" constitutional. The Court delayed the implementation of the decision for a year in order to hear arguments about how to proceed.

Throughout the South the initial reaction was calm. Displaying the hope for gradualism characteristic of moderate editors, Grover Hall wrote, "Even while the decision itself is dramatic and revolutionary, the results of the decision may be undramatic and merely evolutionary." He highlighted indicators pointing to "weakening of the foundations of segregation," and eventual acceptance of a desegregated world.[52]

Immediately after the *Brown v. Board* decision was announced, the *Messenger* asked local educational leaders to comment. First the paper quoted the principal of Troy High School, who said, "I think this thing can, over a period of time, be worked out satisfactorily." A dean at Troy State called for abiding by the law, commenting that he was not greatly disturbed by the decision. The principal of the Laboratory School, the elementary school associated with Troy State and where I was a third-grader at the time, noted that segregation was already breaking down but was clearly supportive of trying to keep the segregated system in place on an informal basis.

The paper summarized the approaches of the local education leaders: "Most of them voiced the opinion that time would take care of the issue and advised slow, intelligent thinking is all that is needed at the present time."[53] The tone of the locally written piece was in keeping with the *Messenger*'s earlier stances, but the changing times would soon challenge the moderate course.

The next day, the *Messenger* also stressed a slow approach: "The mighty impact of the Supreme Court's outlawing of segregation in public schools may not be fully realized for years." The paper advocated a "freedom of choice" approach with "attendance at either optional, either by white or Negro."[54] That solution would, in small towns like Troy, keep both high schools open, likely leading to less integration and probable de facto segregation. Yet this was a step beyond the status quo, and moderate compared to the perspective of the "massive resistance" that was to come.

In the period after *Brown v. Board*, people of good will did struggle to find appropriate solutions to the issue. The governor at the time, Gordon Persons, sent out a general solicitation for suggestions for handling the State's response to school integration. One Black minister suggested a "bi-racial, non-political" committee to advise the Department of Education—which assumed a well-intentioned process of implementation. An editor from heavily white Geneva County wrote that "this newspaper is unalterably opposed to segregation in any form."[55] Unsurprisingly, Black Belt legislators advocated doing nothing.

It was becoming increasingly clear that white community sentiment was more similar to the Lab School principal than to the other educators. A *Messenger* reprint from a nearby paper pointed to Northern hypocrisy in practicing segregation de facto.[56] Perhaps responding to increasing ire among locals, the *Messenger* then called for the Court to admit error and reverse the decision. The editorial demanded that "the states of the South [to] redouble their efforts to give 'separate but equal' facilities to Negroes as quickly as possible—the real and lasting solution after all,"[57] something that Southern states had begun to do in a desperate attempt to defend the failed "separate but equal" mantra.

CHAPTER 20

The Center Does Not Hold

The Evolution of an Editor

The desegregation decisions of the mid-1950s brought great changes to the *Messenger*'s outlook on the race problem. Editorials became more critical of federal government policies designed to break down the barriers of segregation, and increasingly defensive about Southern strategies to deal with the problem. Southern centrist editors still hoped that the gradualist approach would be successful, but clearly it was failing. These once-moderate editors did not appreciate the strong incentives for the racial status quo and, absent federal pressure, the virtually nonexistent incentives for moving forward to address the problem.

These editors and publishers had two choices: go against the tide of public opinion and their local business communities to support the efforts of the civil rights activists, or take the path of joining the segregationist white majority. The *Tuscaloosa News* took the former path. The *Messenger* and the *Advertiser* took the latter path. Nowhere was this clearer than in the racial divide over the integration of the University of Alabama campus.

The Mob Wins in Tuscaloosa

In 1956, a mild mannered young Black woman, Autherine Lucy, was admitted under court order to the rigidly segregated University of Alabama. The week before she started classes on February 3, eight crosses were burned on campus and on the lawns of university admissions administrators.

As Lucy arrived for class, Buford Boone of the *Tuscaloosa News*, was penning an editorial directed at the white citizens of Tuscaloosa and University of Alabama students, calling for acceptance of the court order. "The court decisions have gone in favor of our friends and fellow citizens, the Negroes of the South. They are a fine and patient people."[1]

Lucy's first day in class was uneventful on campus, but over the weekend a mob gathered in Tuscaloosa—first at the university president's house and then downtown. Most of the mob consisted of students, demanding the removal of Lucy. In speeches downtown, segregationists pumped up the crowd, while student body president Walter Flowers urged calm. Flowers asked the administration to stand firm on integration; anything less would be a capitulation to mob rule and the Klan.[2]

On Monday a large mob of around two thousand whites, many who were not students, gathered on campus, threatening Lucy. Lucy was accompanied to class by Dean of Women Sarah Healy and president's assistant Jefferson Bennett. The crowd became so threatening that Healy and Bennett decided to remove Lucy from campus. The mob attacked the car, throwing eggs and bottles at the three as they got into Healy's car. The trio managed a harrowing escape through the mob as members rocked the car and broke windows.

The threat continued, and the university capitulated, suspending and then expelling the unassuming innocent Lucy, a victim of the race hate that coursed through the veins of the Deep South. Disorder had prevailed over law. The state legislature passed all sorts of hate-filled anti-integration resolutions. Governor Folsom asked the legislature to keep the "rough edges" off the racial issue, but did not intervene otherwise. He had been muted by the increasing hostility to the racial moderation that had defined his first term as governor.[3]

Buford Boone was not silenced. His editorial, "What Price Peace" won the *News* a Pulitzer Prize for editorial writing. "There was a mob, in the worst sense, at the University of Alabama yesterday. Every person who witnessed the events there with comparative detachment speaks of the tragic nearness with which our great University came to being associated with a murder—yes, we said murder," Boone wrote, continuing,

> The target was Autherine Lucy. Her "crimes"? She was born black, and she was moving against Southern custom and tradition—but with the law, right on up to the United States Supreme Court, on her side. . . . What has happened here is far more important than whether a Negro girl is admitted to the university. We have a breakdown of law and order, an abject surrender to what is expedient rather

than a courageous stand for what is right. Yes, there's peace on the university campus this morning. But what a price has been paid for it![4]

Boone continued his assault on mob rule for days afterward. He wrote an incredibly insightful piece, "The Danger Is Friction among Extremists."[5] Boone wrote of the threats of mob violence, and those egging on the mob:

> Its members, white-faced and out of touch with reality, tried to do what a white-haired woman, perhaps mother of a student, kept shouting for them to do: "Kill her, kill her, kill her" . . . The area of hope lies . . . with people who are willing to think—to think about when one American is denied unjustly something that is justly his, we are all poorer.

He continued, "Gradual change has been taking place. But sometimes change cannot be continued in slow steps. There has to be a jump. When Autherine Lucy made the jump, all hell broke loose. . . . Agitation for more will bring strong groups of Citizens Councils and Ku Klux Klan Klaverns. The South is going to lose this one, too. But it is going to take longer than it took before."

Observing the mob's vitriol, the university's capitulation, and Lucy's simple, honest reactions to the chaos around her led columnist Murray Kempton to write one of the most poignant sentences ever written in American journalism: "What is this extraordinary resource of this otherwise unhappy country that it breeds such dignity in its victims?"[6]

Lucy was readmitted to the university in 1988 after she gave a talk to the History Department about her ordeal, and earned a masters' degree in education in 1992. In 2022, Bibb Graves Hall, the home of the Education School, was renamed for her, and she attended the renaming ceremony shortly before she died at the age of 92.

Boone's piece on the role of friction when major social problems are addressed is amazing in its grasp of the dynamics of social change. Many years later, Frank Baumgartner and I depicted a general path of public policy, which we termed "punctuated equilibrium." It involved forces for change meeting the friction generated by institutional bottlenecks and organized groups opposing change, leading first to gridlock and then, if the pressure to change continued, to large policy changes. Had we known of Boone's work, our explanations of the process may have been clearer.[7]

Boone knew the path he was treading was a dangerous one for an editor. He turned to a strategic praising of the Tuscaloosa Police, which was plagued with Klan members and sympathizers but nevertheless performed reasonably well, and of the university fraternity leadership, who urged their members to stay away from the mob action.[8]

Boone's role in the integration of the University of Alabama was not done; he played a major role in its final integration in 1963, a process I saw close-up as a freshman at the university.

The Degenerating Moderate Path

While the *Messenger* covered the mob invasion of the university with wire service articles, it made no comments on the incident. Even though the Klan was involved in the mob, the old crusading anti-Klan, pro-law-and-order *Messenger* of 1949 did not join Boone in his moral and strategic assault on the university's capitulation to the mob.

The *Messenger* instead went a step further and added fuel to the flame of segregation. One day after the *News* published Boone's "What Price Peace" editorial, the *Messenger* published an editorial entitled "States Rights Breakdown Foreseen Unless People Resist Encroachments." "In the wake of the Supreme Court's racial edict, an avalanche of bureaucratic rulings have been promulgated . . . seeking to break down the sovereign rights of the individual states. . . . Unless the trend is resisted with every power short of rebellion, the United States will become a Gestapo-fascist government."[9] The immediate purpose of the editorial was to praise George Wallace, then a county judge in nearby Barbour County, for threatening to jail FBI agents investigating grand jury activities in his county. It represented the "leave us alone" refrain many Southerners termed "freedom."

The *Messenger* used the old Southern claim of state sovereignty and elevated it to a governing principle. My father considered himself a moderate, calling frequently for progress in race relations and an end to extremist language. This most certainly was not a moderate editorial. It marked a serious turn from the gradualist path advocated by the *Messenger* through the early sparring over *Brown v. Board*.

The *Messenger* followed up a week later with a second defense of state sovereignty citing the 10th Amendment. The editorial that day claimed that the amendment "says all powers not specifically granted to the Federal government are reserved to the states."[10] The amendment says nothing of the kind, as my father surely knew. Inserting the word "expressly" or even worse "specifically" is an old states' rights technique to enflame defenders of segregation. My father's earlier editorials recognized that states' rights claims carried with them the responsibility to solve problems, including between the races. His later editorials elevated states' rights over racial justice.

With the increasing racial tension, Governor Jim Folsom called a conference of Black and white Alabama editors and publishers to address race problems. By his failure to send the National Guard to Tuscaloosa, he bore a large part of the responsibility for the success of the mob there, and belatedly hoped to address the damage. He proposed a biracial commission of white and Black newspapermen to work out a plan for addressing race problems without bloodshed. The group endorsed the plan, but the *Messenger* was critical of both Folsom and his commission, arguing that the Governor had ignored the race problem.[11] And indeed the moderate Folsom was finding the fire of segregationist sentiment too hot to handle.

Buford Boone said his paper had always sought a moderate course, explicitly not endorsing "such extremes as recommended by the Negro press." The more common claim of white editors was from the Birmingham *Post-Herald*'s James Mill, who said the editors would "do everything possible to find an honorable solution to the racial problem. Of course we know that it must be done within the framework of traditions deep-rooted in the South."[12] The Black press became more militant in its demands, while the white press had become more recalcitrant.

The commission seemed to have been stillborn, but at least Folsom tried to chart a moderate course with ideas about how to achieve some progress. The next three governors of Alabama—John Patterson, George Wallace, and Lurleen Wallace, George's wife and stand-in, spent their time on race issues defending segregation loudly and uncompromisingly.

Instead of participating in the conference, the *Messenger* published an editorial saying, "The Northern politicians, with more problems of their own than the smartest of them can ever solve, are ranting and raving, smugly smiling at their own press notices." It attacked the NAACP for "aiding and abetting the professional stirrer-uppers" and "think[ing] desegregation should be accomplished yesterday."[13] The Deep South had not moved on the segregation issue at all since "yesterday," spending its time fighting even the gradual progress Dad had so eloquently argued for "yesterday."

A month after the committee met, Buford Boone gave a talk to a group of journalists in Atlanta in which he called on moderate Southerners to "Bring some degree of sanity out of chaotic frenzy." Boone said that moderates had a patriotic duty to step forward and speak up on the racial problem, but "thus far there has been no leadership for such an element." He even suggested an integration program that should have appealed to moderates.[14] His program involved integrating the upper grades of high schools first, then moving down the ladder until the lower grades were integrated over the course of several years. The *Messenger* did not endorse Boone's plan, nor mention it beyond the front-page wire-feed article.

The environment for Southern moderate editors continued to deteriorate into the late 1950s. "In the feverish climate of 1958," wrote George Wallace biographer Dan Carter, "many respectable white southerners no longer regarded the Klan with horror."[15] Those upright white citizens, those upholders of civic virtue, were coming to accept—maybe even welcome—the Klan as a part of the resistance.

Grover Hall Faces the Intensity of White Racism

Grover B. Hall Jr. took over as editor of the *Montgomery Advertiser* in 1941, after the previous editor, his father, died unexpectedly of a heart attack. Grover Sr. had won a Pulitzer Prize in 1928 for his steadfast stance against the Klan and its infiltration into Alabama government. The younger Hall hoped to follow in his father's footsteps and leaned moderate in most of his editorials during his early career. Later, his editorials on the Montgomery Bus Boycott highlighted the moderation of the boycotters.[16]

The successes of the NAACP in school integration cases and the Autherine Lucy matter in Tuscaloosa led many civic leaders in Alabama toward resistance even to moderate paths toward integration. During the Montgomery Bus Boycott, Hall wrote to his friend, Supreme Court Justice Hugo Black, "Never in my nine years as editor have I seen Montgomery so enflamed as now. Trying to be a moderate, I've taken quite a mauling. Facts and reason are nothing to [white segregationist leaders]; you are either for white folks or you are against 'em."[17]

During the Autherine Lucy affair, the *Advertiser* highlighted not the violence but that the mob was composed of Alabamians, and "What should be grasped is the fact that the mob abhors race mixing in schools." Hall treated the action of the university in removing Lucy as reasonable and the integration effort as misguided for "the unwanted student."[18]

In the winter of 1956, Mississippi Senator James Eastland traveled to Montgomery for a White Citizens' Council Rally, and Hall had questions for him. They were basically softballs.[19] The White Citizens' Councils had originated in Mississippi and quickly spread throughout the Deep South. As Hall put it, they were "manicured Klanism" supporting "economic thuggery" against Blacks.[20] By appealing to manicured racists who owned businesses, White Citizens' Council members could threaten Blacks with loss of jobs and credit should they join the desegregation movement.

Hall was astounded at the support the White Citizens' Council received in Montgomery as Mississippi Senator James Eastland attacked the NAACP as backed by Communists. Hall toned down his criticism of the vicious segregationists, and his newspaper moved into a more rigid prosegregationist stance. Some of his segregationist editorials were about as contorted as one could imagine. He distinguished between a North Alabama Citizens Council headed by Asa Carter, a violent hatemonger and Klansman, and the Montgomery Chapter headed by State Senator Sam Englehardt, firebrand from Tuskegee. The Englehardt group "has but one aim—the preservation of segregation between the races, a desire that is shared by *The Advertiser*."[21]

Hall's editorials became more supportive of politicians pushing segregation and Black vote suppression, and were critical particularly of the Northern press for not becoming "enlightened" on the race problems in their back yards.[22] Hall's sensitivity to criticism of Southern resistance to desegregation by the Northern press led him to mount a major investigation into Northern racism. Not surprisingly, his research team found plenty of it. The failure of the series to bring national acclaim to Hall led to his increasingly vitriolic harangues against the *New York Times* as a symbol of Northern press hostility toward the South.

Hall was a major player in the landmark Supreme Court decision *New York Times v. Sullivan* (1964) on the extent to which the press could be held liable for stories it published. To establish liability, the Court ruled, it was necessary for the plaintiff in a suit to show knowledge of or "reckless disregard for" the truth. The case involved an advertisement placed in the *New York Times* in March of 1960 designed to raise money for the civil rights movement that had minor inaccuracies in it. L.B. Sullivan, the Montgomery Police Commissioner, sued the *Times* even though his name was not mentioned in the advertisement.

Clearly, Sullivan and his supporters, including Hall, brought the case to help stifle support for the civil rights movement in newspapers. Hall testified on behalf of Sullivan in the trial brought under Alabama's libel law, which Sullivan won. The Supreme Court overturned the verdict and established the Sullivan doctrine in 1964.[23]

The Path toward Resistance

Brown v. Board enflamed the South—but not immediately.[24] Initially a stunned silence gripped segregationists, politicians, and editorialists after Chief Justice Earl Warren read the decision. Segregationist James Kilpatrick called it "post-operative shock."[25] Moderates saw the initial calm and positive searches for solutions as good signs for that path.

Moderates ignored the astounding success of "the most potent segregationist organization to emerge during the modern civil rights movement, the Citizens' Council."[26] Councils were organizing all over the Deep South. There was no parallel mobilization to speak of among moderate whites that could have countered the building backlash.

Southern states needed to accomplish two goals to satisfy the court order. The first was to end legal segregation, and the second was to find a system of integrating school systems at the local level. The first would seem relatively easy: change state law and figure out implementation over time. Officials of seven border South states (Texas, Oklahoma, Missouri, Kentucky, West Virginia, Maryland, and Delaware) accepted the ruling and acted to dismantle de jure segregation of schools. The border South at least was passing the de jure test a few years after *Brown*, perhaps more because of persistent court attention than by choice. In the "rim South," Arkansas, Tennessee, and North Carolina, local integration of school districts was much more difficult. Local and state politicians poured gas on the smoldering embers, as Governor Faubus did in Little Rock. But de jure segregation in the three states had been eliminated.

That was not true of what the *Washington Post* called "the Citadel of Segregation."[27] Alabama, Mississippi, Louisiana, Georgia, Florida, South Carolina, and Virginia refused to repeal their segregation laws, and only a spare handful of school districts had made even the feeblest attempts at desegregation. The leader of the Citadel was Virginia, where the notion of "massive resistance" to desegregation was born. In November 1955 James Kirkpatrick of the Richmond *News-Leader* reincarnated John Calhoun's long discredited notion of interposition to describe the action.

In the "Citadel of Segregation," editors tended to be respected men in their communities, and had some influence on opinions there. But as tensions rose after *Brown*, "(e)ach of them felt a crushing pressure to conform, to fall into line with prevailing opinion, even to lead it. Some did, some didn't."[28]

The *Messenger* under Pressure

Southern editors, particularly in small towns, bore the brunt of increasingly strident pressure from white citizens, and they were susceptible to economic pressure from both subscribers and advertisers. White Citizens' Councils advocated such pressure, and members and sympathizers were present in every nook and cranny of the Deep South.

Politically my father called himself an "Independent Democrat." He was a staunch Loyalist, which was becoming increasingly difficult as South Alabama turned toward the Dixiecrat or States' Rights wing of the Democratic Party. I suspect the "Independent" meant that he did not agree with the civil rights push by national Democrats. He and other Southern moderates argued that the push was too fast and too strong.

During this period my father, as both editor and publisher, must have felt enormous pressure to conform to segregationist sentiment. His position was critical of existing Southern approaches to the race issue yet strongly rejected federal "interference." The *Messenger* lacked the more politically diverse white public that Tuscaloosa and even Montgomery had. Both advertisers and subscribers were tolerant of editorial stances up to a point, and that point was not very far from an increasingly harsh prosegregation sentiment. There were even threats of violence toward nonconforming editors. The home of a Florida editor of a weekly newspaper supporting integration was bombed twice in one week.[29]

The times had changed, and the attitudes of many moderate editors of the early 1950s were no longer relevant in the post-*Brown* era. Many editors calling themselves moderates in 1950 had not thought ahead to how legal segregation would be dismantled, and when the time came, as evidenced by Buford Boone's clarion call to begin incremental desegregation and Big Jim's biracial commission, Southern moderate editors mostly faded away.

In 1955, the state Senate Education Committee produced a bill that prohibited local boards from issuing school assignments to pupils based on race. The bill gave superintendents authority to assign students based on a set of criteria, including adequacy of preparation and scholastic aptitude, and relative intelligence. Such administrative discretion could easily keep schools segregated. The *Messenger* endorsed the proposal enthusiastically, saying that the bill "is the most sane and sensible approach to the problem of mixed schools that has been devised in the South."[30]

Governor Folsom was skeptical, putting his objections in class terms: "I wouldn't want to sign a bill that would let the rich folks send their kids all to one school and the poor folks to another school."[31] Of course his objection to class sorting would apply to race as well. Folsom remained a race moderate, even as he tried to rotate the conflict away from race and toward class.

Over time the *Messenger* edged toward a more segregationist stance, although never abandoning the gradualist possibility of peaceful disappearance of racial boundaries. In a 1956 editorial the *Messenger* managed both to excoriate the Court for its "ill advised, ill-timed, politically-dictated ruling" while gratuitously pointing out that Northerners were actually supporting Southern-style approaches to race relations. Still the *Messenger* did not rule out eventual integration. "Most of the Yankees are 'moderates' and want to see good sensible race relations. They, like the South, want race-mixing, if it occurs, to come about in a natural normal way without disturbing the confidence and peace of mind of anybody."[32]

In 1955 there also emerged Black resistance to inequality in public transportation with the Montgomery Bus Boycott. The *Messenger* was slow at covering the unfolding event, occurring just 50 miles from Troy, and treated it as a side issue unlikely to stir much interest. During the entire period not a single editorial was published on the situation. As Hall of the *Montgomery Advertiser* struggled to keep a moderate perspective in his editorials on the situation, the *Messenger* was silent.

Peanuts, Cotton, and International Affairs

Race relations may have been the most important issue facing Southern editors, Black and white, during the 1950s and 1960s, but it was by no means the only issue. Pike County was in a region of small farmers with more rural than town residents in the 1950s. In the early part of the decade, race was still not the burning issue it was soon to become. In Jim Folsom's run for the governorship in 1954, more rural whites of Pike County supported the race moderate and economic liberal Jim Folsom for reelection than did town dwellers. Class issues dominated the election. Folsom supported universal old age pensions and better roads, and promised to "Promote the General Welfare of All the People in the Fields of Education, Welfare, and Hospitals," as one of his ads highlighted. Race was on the backburner for whites, and farming conditions, especially the state of cotton and peanuts, were front and center.

Peanuts were deeply embedded in the local 1950s culture, even more than cotton. The Wiregrass was uniquely suited to peanut farming, and most of the nation's peanut crop then came from Southeast Alabama and Southwest Georgia. George Washington Carver of Tuskegee Institute had developed many new products from the lowly legume in the face of the cotton-destroying boll weevil epidemic. The move away from cotton caused the diversification of Southern agriculture in the early part of the 20th century. In the town of Enterprise, 35 miles to the south of Troy, town fathers had put up a statue of a woman in a flowing gown holding a tray with a boll weevil on it to laud the crop diversification caused by the insect's damage to cotton. Would not a statue of George Washington Carver have been more appropriate?

On the streets of Troy in the spring wounded war veterans sold bags of peanuts, picked from the vines when they were green and boiled in salted water. In the fall they sold parched peanuts, roasted when the legume was fully ripe. Our "hay rides" were on peanut hay, bails of peanut vines, which was prickly and uncomfortable. You simply could not escape the power of the peanut in the Wiregrass.

No wonder the *Messenger* was consumed with concerns of local farmers (as news and as subscribers), national farm policies, and the fates of peanuts and cotton. The paper advocated replanting quick-growing slash pine to replace the worn-out cotton farms and overproducing peanut farms. Slash pine was a poor but cheap substitute for the magnificent longleaf pines that once graced the region, but lumber was in demand while the prices of overproduced cotton and peanuts were propped up by Depression-era price supports.

Eisenhower's agriculture secretary, Ezra Taft Benson, probably garnered more *Messenger* coverage than the rest of the cabinet except Secretary of State John Foster Dulles. Benson wanted to move farm policies away from subsidies, established during the Depression years. Even worse, Benson was contemptuous of farmers using government subsidies, calling them "pampered." The *Messenger* called for his removal.[33]

International, national, and state news coverage followed the Associated Press wire, but there was considerable selectivity by the news editor. The *Messenger* gave heavy coverage to international affairs, including, for example, extensive lead story coverage to the French involvement in Indochina. Russia and the Cold War were news in small-town Alabama as well as the rest of the nation. Much of this coverage carried with it a strong anticommunist bent, and headlines and front-page stories called Communist leaders "commies."

The 1950s nationally were the highpoint of anticommunist fervor, bordering on hysteria. Senator Joseph McCarthy rode to fame with his list of alleged communists in the State Department. FBI Director J. Edgar Hoover, who authored the anticommunist screed *Masters of Deceit* in 1958, saw communism seemingly under every bed. The House Un-American Activities Committee (HUAC) conducted investigations into alleged communist infiltration into government, the media, and other aspects of American life. The *Messenger* joined in this fervor in news coverage and editorials.

Unfortunately, but probably predictably, the anticommunist fear increasingly focused on civil rights groups. In 1958 the *Messenger* published an article from the AP feed under the title "Group Trying to Uncover Commie Work in the South."[34] The "group" in the headline was HUAC; its investigators tried to pry admissions of Communist Party membership out of witnesses. Other headlines the same year included "Ike's Brother Faces Commie Agitation"; "Mexicans Thwart Commie Plot to Stone Dulles"; and "Commie Paper Strikes Back."[35]

I read *Masters of Deceit*, probably at my father's suggestion, and other books with an anticommunist theme. Being older by then, I did not swallow the theme of communist infiltration into civil rights groups to the extent that I swallowed the romanticism of the Lost Cause that I read when I was younger.

Progressivism Lives in South Alabama

Dad's editorials often took what would be called back then a progressive stance, not in sense that liberal Democrats use the word today but in the sense of the middle-class movement of the first half of the 20th century. Efficient and honest government, money for highways and education, establishing favorable conditions for economic growth, support for science, better public health and a belief in the inevitability of progress characterized the policies recommended by the paper. My father was acutely aware that poor government and backward policies, including on race, could deter business from moving South. Like his father, he supported an increased role in civic and economic life for women. Yet after 1954, if there was an editorial on race, it was almost always segregationist.

A whole series of editorials praised the development of the polio vaccine and urged citizens to get vaccinated. There was not resistance to vaccination then, even though a major mistake in vaccine manufacture during the first mass vaccination program in 1955 infected 40,000 children resulting in 200 cases of paralysis and 10 deaths.[36] My father's editorials suggested that vaccine resistance was more a result of inattention, indolence, and free-riding on the success of the vaccine than antiscience hostility.

In the summer of 1956 an outbreak of polio in Chicago infected 500 children and killed 11. Parents mobbed an inoculation center. "Wild-eyed in panic, they rushed, pushed, and shoved to get their dear children shot. . . . Why should the public, like animals, require a morbid circumstance to stir them into action?" He continued in a vein that resonates today: "If these same parents had heeded public appeals in the first place . . . the Chicago outbreak might have been averted." Local parents did not escape criticism. "The [Pike County] Health Office has vaccine cooling in refrigerators and nurses ready to give it to children who might be stricken at any time. But mothers aren't interested. They are keeping their children away."[37]

About the same time I recall standing in line with the other children in my 4th grade class as we were transported over to the Pike County Public Health Department for our first Salk vaccine shots. Blacks used a different door to enter, and nurses giving the shots were Black—Alabama prohibited white nurses from tending to Black patients.

For the period, Dad was open-minded on the gender issue. In 1956, the *Messenger* published an editorial urging parents in a small Southern town to break gender stereotypes and prepare their daughters for careers in science. The editorial quoted extensively comments made by an official for National Carbon Company, who cited the need for more scientists and urged U.S. parents to "start influencing the potential scientists at the grammar school age."[38]

Unusual for the 1950s, at the *Messenger* women held primary positions in the front office, even serving as editors. The high turnover of male editors in the early period of my father's publishership may have turned him toward a different strategy; if so it worked. After rotating through five male editors between 1949 and 1953, two women served in that position between 1953 and 1961.

No Room for Moderation: 1958–1961

Regardless of the diversity of issues that newspaper editors had to comb through, in the Deep South the main one was invariably race. One of the turning points for Alabama was the election of 1958, when it became clear that there was no room in politics for moderates on race.

In the determinative Democratic primary in May, three candidates looked viable at the outset: John Patterson, George Wallace, and Jimmy Falkner. Patterson, then attorney general of the state, had made his mark as a corruption fighter. Patterson was rewarded by serving as the hero of a Hollywood film noir movie, *The Phenix City Story*, and by getting elected as attorney general to replace his father, whom the criminal gangs in Phenix City had murdered.

As attorney general, Patterson continued his anticorruption work, but branched out into the segregation business. He gained recognition for his long-ranging legal vendetta against the NAACP, driving the civil rights organization out of the state for years.

The second notable candidate was George Wallace, the circuit judge in Baldwin County. The pugnacious Wallace gained fame for his threats to jail FBI agents investigating voting suppression in the county. He ran as a strong segregationist, but did not demagogue the issue to the extent that Patterson did.

The *Messenger* gave favorable front-page coverage to the third viable candidate, Jimmy Faulkner, a former state senator and a journalist from Bay Minette, near Mobile.[39] Faulkner, a friend of my father, was the most racially moderate candidate in the contest, and none of his advertisements in the *Messenger* (and presumably elsewhere) stressed segregation. "Jimmy Faulkner believes there is room in Alabama for everybody to prosper and work together in harmony and goodwill for the common good," stated a newspaper advertisement.[40]

Faulkner put great faith in economic development based on Northern capital as a mechanism to lift the South, as did my father. To both, that meant a sensible but gradualist strategy to deal with segregation. The *Messenger*'s endorsement in 1954, "Vote for the Kind of Man You Want to Hold Your Child's Hand" stressed Faulkner's human decency. The time for decency had passed, though, and Faulkner finished a weak third, behind the staunch segregationists Patterson and Wallace.

Grover Hall at the *Advertiser* endorsed Wallace, even working with his campaign. The paper exposed Patterson's explicit connections with the Alabama Klan Grand Wizard, Robert Shelton. The connection did not harm Patterson, who won easily.[41]

After 1958, *the Messenger*'s editorials generally avoided the race issue, focusing on local issues, particularly economic development in the region. When the paper focused on national affairs, it increasingly centered on limited government. In 1960, my father wrote an editorial titled "Government's Function," in which he alleged that "vast numbers of people regard the government as the proper source of almost every kind of handout, grant, and so-called benefits." The limited government framework was a platform to critique federal government policies on civil rights. Clearly the *Messenger* did not mean the farm subsidies and acreage allotments received by county farmers.

During much of the 1960s, the Alabama Democratic Party was consumed by a factional fight between Loyalist and States' Rights factions. After the Dixiecrat revolt of 1948, the Loyalist faction regained control of the party in 1950, restoring the Democratic Party label to the ballot in 1952 and 1956. The state went overwhelmingly for the Democrat Adlai Stevenson over the Republican Dwight Eisenhower in both elections. But in 1960 the States' Rights faction was able to implement a system that chose each elector separately. Democratic primary voters chose between uncommitted electors and those pledged for John F. Kennedy.

The unpledged slate, mostly from South Alabama, won six of the delegate seats to the 1960 Democratic National Convention; North Alabama loyalists held the remaining five seats. The old north-south split over politics in the state continued into the 1960s, with South Alabama more incensed over the race issue. States' Righters refused to pledge support to the national ticket if the nominee were to be "hostile to the South."[42] The *Messenger* did not comment on nor endorse candidates for delegates, likely because my father remained a Loyalist but was hesitant to raise the issue in a town that was increasingly turning to the States' Rights faction.

Preoccupation with "Communist Infiltration"

In May of 1961, student activists from the Congress of Racial Equality (CORE) initiated a campaign to challenge segregation on interstate buses and in bus terminals.[43] A major participant in the Freedom Rides was John Lewis of Pike County. The plan was a bus trip throughout the South, from Washington to New Orleans, integrating bus terminals to ensure the enforcement of two Supreme Court cases ruling segregation in interstate transportation unconstitutional.

In South Carolina a white mob beat John Lewis, but the major attacks came in Alabama. On May 14, a mob violently attacked one of Freedom Riders' buses, firebombing it and beating the riders. When a group of Freedom Riders were arrested in Birmingham, the U.S. Justice Department intervened, and the Freedom Riders traveled on to Montgomery. There, at the Greyhound Bus Terminal, the Montgomery Police stood by while a white mob viscously attacked the riders when they disembarked their buses.

The battered riders and members of the Montgomery Black community gathered in the First Baptist Church, where they were surrounded by a large white mob. Attorney General Robert Kennedy sent marshalls, but the scene was only cleared when Alabama Governor Patterson reluctantly mobilized the National Guard (Figure 20.1). The Freedom Riders traveled on to Jackson, Mississippi, where they were immediately jailed.

The *Messenger* dutifully reported on the rides in the news section, being careful to include "Freedom Riders" in quotation marks. However, the editorials during the Freedom Rides ignored the events, and focused instead on the anniversary of the start of the Civil War in 1861.

On May 15, the *Messenger* carried an editorial "Lee and Grant," recounting Grant's remembrances of Lee's surrender. The editorial closed with a dreamy metaphor: "Their behavior emphasizes the oft-used expression 'Gentleman's War' in referring to the Civil War."[44] The paper published several articles and editorials noting the 100th anniversary of the start of the Civil War, but what a day to carry the story. The next day the paper carried an editorial puff piece on Confederate nicknames.

After the worst of the violence against the Freedom Riders in Montgomery, the *Messenger* headline blared "Cradle of Confederacy Gripped by Martial Law." Rather than comment on the breakdown of law enforcement in Montgomery, the *Messenger* began a series of four editorials "explaining" racial tensions in the South as a product of communist infiltration of civil rights groups. The racial disturbances were not caused by local folks, because the white and colored in Alabama have enjoyed "a harmonious existence stretching over more than 100 years, and have an affection for each other that cannot be described. . . . The events that have transpired, as repulsive as they are, are strictly the making of a group of commies more concerned with disturbance than principles."[45]

The second editorial, the next day, asserted, "the commies come to Alabama through CORE." The *Messenger* claimed that these commies "fired [burned]

Figure 20.1 Soon after the Freedom Riders Were Battered in Montgomery, Governor John Patterson Donned Confederate Garb to Celebrate the Centennial of the Civil War.

Source: Alabama Department of Archives and History, Digital Collection [https://digital. archives.alabama.gov/digital/collection/photo/id/30483/rec/11].

a bus in a fashion so that their cohorts would not be hurt."[46] This was obviously not true. The third was downright weird, claiming that the commies chose Alabama as a target because they "want to encircle Florida, isolating it for military and subversive purposes." Cuba would serve as a springboard.[47]

The fourth editorial cites FBI Director J. Edgar Hoover as providing proof. The *Messenger* quotes Hoover as claiming communists manipulated minority groups, especially Blacks. The four-part commie infiltration commentary closes with this: "Anyone who thinks that the racial troubles of the South are not a part of the great communist conspiracy is being blind to realities."[48] Clearly the editorials were deeply influenced by FBI press releases and general news coverage influenced by Hoover.

The *Messenger*'s four-part screed during the Freedom Rides had strong roots in earlier coverage of infiltration. In 1958, the *Messenger* published an editorial about church and school bombings during the desegregation rulings in the 1950s titled "Bombings Not Southern Inspired." The editorial claimed that there was no proof that Southerners carried out the bombings, but that "What proof there is seems to indicate that the bombings are the work of 'hate group' agents, probably communists and or 'agents of the NAACP'" to divide the nation.[49] These kinds of false flag assertions became common, reaching a fever pitch in the explosion of bombings in Birmingham in 1963.

In the late 1950s my father created a partnership with two of his friends to purchase weekly newspapers, improve their economic viability, and sell them to members of the community. He spent more and more time on this venture, escaping the issues that were plaguing the *Messenger*. I am not sure he wrote the infiltration editorials, but they were his responsibility. And they were irresponsible.

Grover Hall at the *Montgomery Advertiser* also mostly ignored the Freedom Riders editorially. When he took notice his comments were critical of Black civil action. In his major editorial on the race riots in Montgomery, Hall called the Freedom Riders "incendiaries" and said the *Advertiser* "has no tears to shed for the stunning agitators [who] came to an inflamed area to incite riot."[50] He justified the beatings at the Montgomery bus station using the usual tactics of misdirection and false equivalence: "In all the five years of tumult that have made Montgomery an international symbol of violence, fewer, and fewer by far, people have been assaulted in Montgomery than in Central Park or Morningside Heights." He went on to call the Freedom Riders and Doctor King "inciters."[51]

Hall endorsed Wallace in 1962, explicitly attacking Jim Folsom, who was running for a third stint as governor, because of his moderate stand on segregation. He raised the specter of "Folsom registering every unqualified Negro in Alabama" and reminded readers of "Reconstruction days."[52] Hall continued to slip into the cesspool of demagogic racism, signing on as an advisor to Wallace in his gubernatorial campaign in 1962 and working with Klansman Asa Carter to draft Wallace's inaugural "segregation forever" speech.[53] In the wake of the 1963 bombing of the 16th Street Baptist Church that killed four young girls and horribly maimed another, Hall wrote in his column that Martin X (Hall's slur for Martin Luther King to associate him with Malcolm X) "thrives on violence," that Wallace had been slandered, and that President Kennedy "must bear some of the guilt" for the disorder in Birmingham by inflaming the man "who finally planted the dynamite at the church." Supposedly Kennedy had "inflamed the Negroes during the trouble by rehearsing their historic grievances."[54]

Hall went on to the editorship of the *Richmond News-Leader*, mouthpiece of "massive resistance," and finished out his career as an advisor to George Wallace. His career as a journalist ended with a truly abhorrent justification of evil in his commentary on the murders of little girls attending Sunday school.

Three Editors at the Brink

With the landmark Supreme Court decision to outlaw legal segregation in public schools, the third critical period of rapid change had begun. Entering the period, the three editors had much in common. All were segregationists, yet all were realists and supported some sort of gradual change in the status quo. All abhorred the Klan and wrote about its atrocities. All were critical of the Dixiecrats, promoting unification with the national Democrats.

All three of the editors changed in their stances on race and desegregation through the 1950s. They did not all change in the same direction, even though they started their editorships at similar moderate positions. None reached the sordid depths of the white supremacist editorships of papers such as *The Selma Times-Journal*, which lauded the White Citizens' Council and dreamed of a cross-class racist front unifying the increasingly tony Citizens' Councils and the "rednecks" of North Alabama.[55] Plenty of Southern newspapers consistently defended Jim Crow, as did *the Selma Times*. A sparse few adapted to the reality that separate but equal was impossible. Many more, but still a minority, dreamed of building a fairer system within a more limited "separate but equal" system. When that failed, most became defenders of segregation rather than adapting to the new reality.

The expressed opinions of editors depend on three factors: their general attitudes; the attitudes of their subscribers and advertisers; and the general climate of opinion in the regions where they lived and worked. All faced a similar climate of opinion, which was increasing Southern opposition to federal initiatives on desegregation and Black enfranchisement.

There were substantial differences in the local political environment. Tuscaloosa County teetered on the dividing line between the hills north of the Black Warrior River, which passed through the city of Tuscaloosa, and the flatlands of the Black Belt to the south of town. It is the home of the University of Alabama, and its business community was pragmatic, leading to more diverse opinion base than in Montgomery or Troy. George Van Tassel, a liberal Democrat, was mayor during the period. The setting was a more tolerant environment for Boone's editorials, but his stance on issues of race were nevertheless far ahead of the city's general racial tone.

Montgomery is the biggest city in the Black Belt, and Hall's editorials were crafted to appeal to white readers in the region. The county did not support Folsom, and whites harbored strongly conservative views on race.

Pike County is south of the Black Belt, a county of small yeoman and tenant farmers, both white and Black. The county, which included Troy, went solidly for Folsom in 1946, and again in Folsom's reelection campaign in 1954. Pike County white voters liked his focus on the less fortunate, and in the early years they tolerated his support for Blacks. That changed after *Brown v. Board* as race became a more prominent issue.

One of these three editors, Buford Boone of the *Tuscaloosa News*, dropped his early segregationist positions over time and searched for solutions to school integration that would work in the Deep South. He was one of the few white Southern editors willing to support integration. In Alabama, that included the progressive *Anniston Star* under the ownership of Harry Ayers and his son Brandt Ayers, where my father worked before going to the *Tuscaloosa News*.[56] I wonder if his experiences at these two North Alabama newspapers gave him a model for a South Alabama version of racial tolerance. If so it did not work.

The second of these editors, Grover Hall Jr., of the *Montgomery Advertiser*, was an inconsistent racial moderate even before Brown. Over time,

Hall's editorials became increasingly racially conservative. Hall was a fine writer, but his editorials had an elitist, condescending tone to them. His style did not save him. Among the three editors, he fell the furthest into the sinkhole of racism. He could not shake his Black Belt elitist sense of Black inferiority. I suspect the decline had much to do with his desire to be accepted by the Montgomery elites, many of whom joined or were sympathetic to the White Citizens' Council.

The third newspaperman, my father, set a path similar to Hall's, but was initially more progressive on race, and he did not sink so deep into Wallace-style racism. Like Hall, my father became increasingly conservative as the civil rights issue became more salient, and he failed to comment as critical events engulfed Alabama.

Hall and my father, and Southerners like them, really believed that a peaceful, gradualist approach would have worked, bettering the Black community but not threatening the white supremacist system that had governed the South their whole lives. Such men were angered by the "impatience" of civil rights activists, who seemingly could not see that the gradualist approach was working. The gradualist views were never realistic. These editors themselves realized that. Yet they built a not implausible world in which "separate but equal" was made a reality while integration grew across time.

My father had the toughest environment to navigate. As publisher and owner of the *Messenger*, he participated in civic affairs in a small town. He was an important member of the business community. Dad was president of the local Chamber of Commerce and member and president of the Rotary Club. He was on the Board of Stewards for the First Methodist Church, although to be honest I didn't see him there much. He would take my sister and me to Sunday School, and then go over to the *Messenger* office, and to work at the paper.

Having a local editor who owned a major interest in the local paper committed Dad to promoting economic betterment. He promoted Troy in the *Messenger* and in out-of-town papers as a small town with abundant amenities. He recognized early the value of a college in town, and highlighted educational improvement as an investment in the economic future of the town. The *Messenger* promoted every factory and many stores that opened in the region, touting them as adding to civic vitality while not spoiling the tranquility of the small town.

Local ownership meant focus on civic affairs and economic betterment for the white community, but it also implied a lack of editorial candor on segregation and failure to urge civic leaders to plan for the inevitable. Instead the *Messenger* offered a steadfast defense of "separate but equal" throughout the period after *Brown v. Board*.

I suspect the pressure from the community and its increasing clash with his support of moderation was a major reason that he got immersed in his business partnership of acquiring and improving weekly newspapers and selling them back to local owners. He was in the process of doing that in Oxford, Mississippi, when he died of a massive heart attack in 1961.

Moderate Newspapermen in an Unforgiving Climate

The final death throes of Jim Crow in the Deep South were ugly, violent, and destructive of the moderation that briefly flourished after the Second World War. My father and others like him were balancing their own views on race with the increasingly strident demands of their white supremacist subscribers and advertisers. Their own views were built on failures to update their segregationist attitudes with the deep-down knowledge that the Deep South held an unjustifiable and losing hand. To achieve balance, these editors gave up their early hopes that gradually a more just racial order could be achieved. These hopes fell because of their own frustrations at the pace of change and because of the increasing hostility to that change by their subscribers and advertisers. When that dream world collapsed, they resisted the intrusions of the federal government through continued appeals to gradualism, attacks on civil rights leaders as possible communists, and fake constitutional constructions to support states' rights. Of the three editors, Buford Boone alone was able to transcend the constraints of the Southern stance.

The sale of the *Messenger* after my father's death did not improve matters. The editorals under its new ownership took an even more strident segregationist stand. They were not only more vitriolic, but they also went into more sordid detail. The paper offered its readers rabid support of George Wallace, something that would have been unlikely had my father lived.

It has been hard for me to write these paragraphs, made even harder by the discovery of the early years of my Dad's editorship when right won out. My father, out of shifting beliefs and economic pressure, was desperately wrong in most of his editorial stances on racial justice after *Brown*. Because the editorials were unsigned, it is possible that others in the front office wrote these pieces, especially the four-part "commie" series when he was out of town. That matters little; he in the end was responsible. While I can understand his reasoning, I cannot condone it, even from the viewpoint of the standards of the day. By my late high school years, I was certain the system was broken, more from a sense or a feeling of unfairness than analysis. If he had been alive when I was in college, I suspect my visits back home from college would have been frank and sometimes unpleasant.

PART 6

The Collapse of Jim Crow

The long period of Jim Crow ended decisively during my junior year in college with "Bloody Sunday" and the Voting Rights Act. For the most part, the structure was ending generally peacefully in the border South and violently with massive resistance in the Deep South.

I serve as the observer in my family line of the last of the critical junctures I have followed in this book. Consequently, the observations recorded in the chapters in this part will take a more personal perspective.

In small-town South Alabama, the walls of segregation remained intact during much of the period. There were no civil rights marches or demands for desegregation, so the old rules stayed in place. There were only minimal Klan displays, and the one major cross-burning received a scathing review from the *Messenger*. I'm sure there were Klan members in the county, and probably a Citizens' Council unit, but I can find no reference to one in the files of the *Troy Messenger*. My friends and I, consumed with the trivialities of high school life, grew up with barely an inkling of the building pressure on Southern institutions. Even the violence against the Freedom Riders in Montgomery penetrated our limited attention spans only briefly.

Yet one could not be blind to the changes, and by the time I was a senior in high school I was becoming a thoroughgoing antisegregationist. I can't fully reconstruct how that happened, and I don't remember discussing it with my classmates, but I was pretty sure some of them felt as I did.

Then there was George Wallace. He turned my attempts to think through the system of segregation into horror for what he had wrought. I guess Wallace created one young desegregationist during his primary campaign in 1962.

I was fortunate enough to watch the system collapse while I was in college. Wallace's flaming racism in his inaugural speech in January 1962 and his "stand in the schoolhouse door" stunt at Foster Auditorium at the University

of Alabama in June 1963 turned me from a desegregationist to an integra-
tionist. I thank him for that, but the damage he did to Alabama and America
is incalculable.

By 1966, Wallace and the forces that he marshaled had mobilized many
white Americans nationally, and effectively began the tectonic shifts of party
realignment in Appalachia. I worked for a moderate candidate in the election of 1966. That election marked a clear reorientation of political parties in
Alabama. Black voters emerged from voter suppression to vote in large numbers for anti-Wallace candidates. Their electoral strength was offset by the shift
of North Alabama's support for Wallace. A new political alignment was emerging, undermining the dual South and reinforcing the birth of the single white
Southern mind.

CHAPTER 21

A Bad Hotdog and a Big Orange

After coming to Troy in 1949, we moved into a neighborhood where the woods met the town. The town of Troy straddled the Wiregrass–Black Belt divide. To the north and particularly the northeast, the soil was fertile and plantation agriculture thrived before the Civil War. A line of clay hills ran through the city, dividing the more productive soil in the north from the sandy grasslands stretching south. Most of the peanuts grew in the sandy soils to the south of town; cotton and abandoned fields and forests characterized the north. The town of about 8,500 was 40% Black, reflecting the divided geography. Our new home was just south of the clay hills, on the loose sandy soils of the Wiregrass.

At one time, I suppose, the street that our house faced was a country lane. In front of the large vacant field next to us were three old black walnut trees. The last one grew on the border between the vacant lot and ours, offering welcome shade in the summer. I imagine there once were several more trees along the lane that had been cut down to construct the houses slowly being built along Normal Avenue, so called not because the people along the street were normal, but because to the east toward town the street went by Troy Normal School (Troy State College by the time we got there).

The abundant vacant land in the neighborhood was covered with broomsedge (Figure 21.1), sour-weed, gourds, blackberry vines, rabbit tobacco, and pie melons. For a youngster, this was a cornucopia of useful stuff. Broomsedge is a beautiful grass that resembles little bluestem on the prairies of Texas but grows in acid soil and is not palatable to livestock. It grew tall enough that we could hide in it, and we regularly set up semipermanent campsites in the weeds. We used it as roofing for the huts we built. Pie melons taste terrible, but were useful for melon fights among neighborhood kids. Rabbit tobacco was useful in a different way. We'd ride our bikes to Elmore's five and dime downtown and buy corncob pipes. Then we'd dry

Figure 21.1 My Sister Carol, Me, and the Broomsedge Field
Source: Author's collection.

the rabbit tobacco (or just pull it up in the fall) and smoke it, pretending to be Huck Finn. Gourds grew vigorously in the vacant fields; I was fascinated by how this plant could generate such hard-skinned hollow vessels in the fall.

By far the best plants in the fields were the rapidly growing blackberry vines and their fruit, which always served as a welcome snack. Even better, when I could collect enough, Mother would make delicious blackberry pies.

On many hot and humid Alabama summer nights I'd take my bedroll into the fields all around our house and sleep out under the stars. The air was clear and clean and the stars not obscured by the lights of town back then, and I learned the constellations and the placement of the planets by reading *Sky and Telescope*, one of the many magazines I subscribed to. My family thought I was a little strange but tolerated my idiosyncrasies.

The neighborhood was served by a dirt road capped by red clay, and our postal address was a rural route. The postman had to know every house on the route, because letters were addressed to a person and the route number. Over time the street was transformed to tar covered over by slag, a gray stone byproduct of iron smelters in Birmingham. Cars traversing the road would work the slag into the tar, making it more durable and less subject to problems in the summer when the hot summer sun made the tar soft. But the tar stuck to the sides of the fenders of the cars going up and down the road.

The neighborhood was all-white, by custom not law. One could not imagine a Black family moving in to any white neighborhood, even one as wide open as ours was. I'm sure that no Blacks ever thought of it either. These customs reinforced the foundations of Jim Crow. We never thought of the possibility; segregation was the backdrop of our lives.

We moved into a modest house by today's standards. Probably around 1,200 square feet, it had three small bedrooms, a combined living room and dining room, and a compact kitchen. As was common in that day, the single bathroom was very small. In a more socially conservative time, bathrooms were anything but ostentatious.

It was a concrete block slab house with linoleum tiles glued to the concrete floors. The house had no central heat, only a big blower in the central hallway across from the bathroom, which was served by a propane tank next to the one-car attached garage. My sister Carol and I would rush to the blower in the winter after crawling out from the covers. While it was South Alabama, lows in January were in the mid-30s. Naturally there was no air conditioning, but we did have a large attic fan that circulated the cooler night air through the house in the summer.

We had a telephone, a party line shared with a family up the street, and it was still operator assisted. As a boy, I was mesmerized by the dial phones in Montgomery and Tuscaloosa. Troy seemed so backward! Entertainment centered on a big radio with large built-in speakers in the living room. There I listened to such programs as *Sky King*, *Sargent Preston of the Yukon*, and *Wild Bill*

Hickok before supper. After supper we read books and magazines in front of the fireplace; the *Saturday Evening Post* was our weekly.

We lived well if modestly by today's standards. I suspect it was the house my parents could afford, in large part because what savings they had were doubtless put into the *Messenger*. Rather than move, as the house began to feel too small for them they added on. First was to transform the garage into a kitchen—you had to go several steps downstairs to the kitchen. Quite strange. They added a cinder block garage in the back yard, then later, when I was in high school, an extra bedroom and bath for the adults. Complete with a window air conditioner! We kids were left with the attic fan.

Our home was located where the city melted into the countryside. From an early age, I wandered the woods and fields near our house. I remember a booklet, part of a series, in which you pasted stamps into the pages as you studied a topic. With these pamphlets, I studied turtles, frogs, tadpoles, and salamanders as I lay by a pool in a brook in the forest near my home. Unfortunately I lay in a huge patch of poison ivy, causing weeks of true misery. I guess I should have paid attention to plants as well as salamanders.

Reading consumed us during the hot summertime. At some point my parents bought a set of World Books. In the required summertime break after lunch—somehow that was supposed to prevent polio—I read the whole set over one summer.

I imagine my father spent a similar boyhood, and my grandfather's notes describe a bucolic childhood. That Penrod-style America, still alive and well in 1950s white Alabama, all but disappeared with the advent of television, air conditioning, and a more urban America.

To the west, across a large broomsedge field, Kleob Loflin and his widowed mother lived. That was really his name; I suppose it was a corruption of the biblical Caleb. Kleob was four years older than me, but was a truly decent guy, tolerating us younger kids in a way that I sensed even back then.

In the summer, I often ate lunch at his home, with his mother's fine Southern cooking. One day Mrs. Loflin called for Kleob to come home and do some chores, and he answered, "I'll be there directly." She shouted, "No you will not, Kleob Jr. I want you here right now." In the Southern dialect, "directly" did not mean "immediately."

Increasingly my father was absent from supper, consumed by work. Often he did not get home until 8:30 or 9:00 at night, having cold leftovers or cooking up something like hoecakes—basically corn meal, water, and a little grease.

He explained to me that the slaves working late in the field would build a fire and cook hoecakes on their hoes. I loved the things.

The Bicycle Incident

Segregation was a strange thing to me, both very familiar and somehow not logical. It was just there. I don't remember finding it irredeemably wrong until college. I recall the oiled floors and fascinating toy counters of the Elmore's next door to the *Messenger* where Blacks shopped freely, yet they allowed whites to bypass them in the purchase line. Nor could Blacks yet sit at the cafes on the square. The major street through the Black section of town was paved, but the side streets were not. Academy High, the Black high school in town, had much poorer facilities than Henderson High, the white high school. I recall seeing the Black football players practicing barefoot on the field next to Academy High.

Even as a boy I remember the averted eyes of the Black men as they moved away from whites on the sidewalks of the town. It was a sign of deference. My cousin, Jonnie, who lived in the smaller town of Brundidge to the southeast of Troy, recalls an even more severe segregation: "One of the things that I couldn't entirely understand as a child in Brundidge was why Black men had to step off the sidewalk to let whites by, including 6-year-olds."

The lack of logic in segregation really came home when I returned from a disastrous bike ride south to a small farm that my father briefly owned. The farm was around 35 acres and had two small houses on it. One was occupied by an elderly couple, tenant farmers; the other was abandoned and not in good shape. The land was divided between fields of peanuts and subsistence crops, and the rest was less productive forest land of pines and oaks.

My father had hoped to fix up the second house as a family retreat, but never got around to it. My friends and I occasionally would ride our bikes the 12 or so miles down to the place, check in with the tenant, and spend the day tramping around the woods in the back of the acreage. We'd spend the night sleeping on the creaky and drafty floors of the pier-and-beam abandoned house, and ride back to town the next morning.

On one trip when we got ready to go back to Troy I discovered my rear tire was flat. My buddies had things to do back in town, so I told them to go ahead. I pushed the bike to a filling station several miles away, pumped up the tire, and rode as fast as I could until the tire went back to its new, flat equilibrium.

Pushing a crippled bike with a flat tire on a hot and humid South Alabama summer morning was hard work, and it was well past noon when I got back to town.

On the town's outskirts was a hotdog stand, the Dairy Queen, with the obligatory two windows—white and colored. As my cousin noted, "[Many] things were just a 'given'—like that they had to sit upstairs in the movie theatre, use different restrooms/water fountains, come to our back door, and never use our water glasses. None of that I questioned." And neither did I. I went up to the "white" window to place an order.

A rail thin, somewhat scruffy white order clerk took food orders from both windows, and passed them back to the Black female cook, who prepared the hotdogs and hamburgers for both white and black customers. She passed the food to the order clerk, who handed it to the white customer through the White window and the Black customer through the Colored window. I ordered a chilidog and a Big Orange (all soft drinks seemed to be classified as either a "Coke" or a "Big Orange"—although a Dr. Pepper would do in a pinch).

The day was hot, there was no breeze, and the sticky summer South Alabama humidity caused my sweat glands to react aggressively. I was dehydrated and tired. After consuming the chilidog and Big Orange on my empty stomach, I got violently sick. I have had an aversion to chilidogs ever since, and to this day I cannot grasp why anyone would want to eat one with a Big Orange.

My time waiting at the Dairy Queen was a moment of enlightenment about segregation. When enlightenment came, it hit hard—and it stuck. A key justification by whites for segregation was that Blacks supposedly had more germs than whites. If this were so, why would Dairy Queen have two windows but one cook? It made no sense.

The experience further compounded my emerging sense of the ridiculousness of the apartheid system. The Pavlovian connection between pondering the stupidity of separate windows in the simple food stand and subsequently vomiting surely colored my later revulsion with segregation as well as with chilidogs and orange sodas. I called home and got a ride to the tire shop, and the incident faded in my mind, but it returned again and again when I saw the hypocrisy of segregation (Figure 21.2).

The revulsion I experienced at the Dairy Queen was an association reinforced by the Big Orange. I was not thinking things through. There was so much I did not understand. I failed to appreciate that the separate windows

Figure 21.2 Separate Segregated Windows at the Whoppaburger in Troy Alabama
Source: Reunion Troy [https://www.facebook.com/ReunionTroy/photos/pb.
100064529419079.-2207520000/2297472370538850/?type=3].

at the Dairy Queen was one part of a network of "public symbols and con-
stant reminders of [the Negro's] inferior position," as C. Vann Woodward put
it.[1] I am pretty sure by then that I had real problems accepting the idea that
Blacks were so thoroughly inferior as was ingrained in young people in the
late 1950s in the Deep South. I suspect that this reluctance to accept this system of rigidly enforced white superiority was part of a general rebellion against
the inflexible structure of small-town Alabama that my good friend Ed Walters
and I indulged. It was years later before I fully understood that the system was
designed to degrade, not to serve food efficiently.

Memes, Myths, Narratives, and Change

The justification for a social order includes memes, narratives, and myths generally supported by a set of recognized symbols. What happens when people
start to question these received "wisdoms"? The meme I absorbed that Blacks
carried more germs seemed suddenly at the Dairy Queen to be nonsense.

The evolutionary biologist Richard Dawkins employed the term "meme" to
denote a small unit of information that spreads across a population.[2] A meme

can evoke a more comprehensive narrative that need not be explained to grasp the underlying idea.

When memes and narratives, the building blocks of myths, are questioned, the full system justifying a social order may be questioned. Such questioning is unlikely to happen if the event itself is isolated, but if the context of the event is changing then it is likely it will be pushed to the background because it fits the social order. I cannot say just why the "Big Orange" event had such an effect on me, but without context of the broader civil rights movement I suspect I would have ignored it.

Times were changing. The civil rights movement was winning victories. In 1944 the Supreme Court in *Smith v. Allwright* declared the white primary, which was the major barrier to Black voting in most Southern states, to be unconstitutional.[3] In 1948, President Truman issued an executive order mandating desegregation of the military. The events that kept civil rights on the Southern mind kept coming: *Brown v. Board* in 1954; the Emmitt Till lynching and the Montgomery Bus Boycott in 1955; the Autherine Lucy denial of admission to the University of Alabama in 1956. The context surely made the "Big Orange" incident more salient.

Patsy

The Klan resurged throughout the South after *Brown v. Board* in 1954, and it was ugly. As we returned at night from a family visit in Tuscaloosa, on the dark and lonely road winding through the wooded hills toward Montgomery, we encountered a large traffic jam as cars and pickups full of locals from miles away came to participate in the burning of a huge cross by robed and hooded clan members.

We huddled in the car's back seat as Daddy inched it along, the flickering fire of the burning cross illuminating the white-robed and hooded participants. This Klan was not the "order restoring" Klan of Thomas Dixon's novels; it was deeply dark and threatening. I did not know that my father had published a series of virulently anti-Klan editorials a few years before. I could sense that he and my mother were fearful as we slowly moved through the disturbing scene.

The race-based dual labor market that relegated Blacks to the more menial and physically difficult jobs also gave whites of relatively modest incomes the ability to hire Black maids in their homes. As my father threw himself into his new business and my mother acted as the bookkeeper for the enterprise, they hired Patsy, a young woman who nevertheless had already lived a turbulent life. She kept house, cooked lunch, and cared for my preschool sister Carol, who adored her. Patsy had a large and very visible scar on her throat; we understood that her husband had grabbed a knife in a fit of rage and tried to slit her throat.

Patsy had no car, and Troy had no bus system, so my mother would drive her back and forth each day. If one could view traffic patterns during the early morning and late afternoon in many Southern towns, I suspect one could watch the cars going to and from the Black neighborhoods twice a day as middle-class white women ferried their maids to and from work. That pattern was not exclusively southern. In the mid-1970s I worked with the Detroit League of Women Voters on voter registration campaigns. I noted that the bus lines went from the Black center city neighborhoods to the white upper income suburbs of Grosse Pointe with connections peaking in the early morning and late afternoon.

As the civil rights movement heated up, Patsy left our employment, hoping to contribute to the civil rights cause. In any case, it no longer seemed appropriate to her to be employed as a maid in a white household. I do not know how her quest turned out.

Love Street and Officer Youngblood

My friends and I played pool in Vernon Quarles's pool hall on Three Notch Street. Quarles was a formidable character, a wounded Second World War veteran with a lame leg and a distinctive limp that contorted his still-powerful frame. Unlike most pool halls in "wet" counties in South Alabama, Quarles did not condone alcohol nor any misbehavior, which was a blessing to bored Troy youth whose parents would allow them to play pool there even as junior high students. Furthermore, Quarles would tolerate NO gambling!

Quarles backed up his pool hall order with a double-barreled 12-gauge shotgun behind his counter. In the front of the building were two "challenge" tables where winners held the table, and challengers signed up to play—again in orderly fashion. One weekday afternoon the third of my high school trio of friends, John Selman, and I held the second challenge table—we knew the norms and stayed off the front table, where the real pool players held sway.

Two fellows from further south who were around 20 years old or so challenged us to a match. We won, but they were not happy, and demanded a rematch. We pointed to the list of challengers and suggested that they sign up. They began to insist, we resisted, and the argument got heated. One of the out-of-towners slammed his cue on the table and both turned toward us with cues wielded like clubs. Suddenly Quarles was coming toward the table with his distinctive limp with his shotgun leveled, pointed at the out-of-towners. He marched them toward the front door at gunpoint and instructed them never to enter his place again. He mumbled something about out-of-towners not knowing the rules and limped back to his counter.

Love Street, named after Wallace Love, the most distinguished Black businessman in town, was only a block south of the town square with its north-facing Confederate soldier. Near where Love Street meets North Three Notch, a handful of Black cafes and bars served food during the day and drinks at night. For reasons that frankly I don't understand, given the strong norms of segregated living, the Love Street area was separated by several blocks from the main Black community along Academy Street.

The father of my close friend Ed Walters was a leading lawyer in town, and he owned several buildings on Love Street. John Walters hired Troy Police Officer Jean Hayden Youngblood to collect the Love Street rents for his buildings. He went by Hayden, but we only knew him as "Youngblood," and he was to us a friendly and open man generally respected by the white citizenry of Troy. The Troy Police Department was small, alleged to be the smallest of any town of its size in Alabama.

The café owners on Love Street did not share our benign view of Youngblood. I went occasionally with Ed to accompany Youngblood on his rent collecting rounds, and Youngblood was courteous to those Black businessmen. Nevertheless the discomfort of the Black owners was obvious to me. The symbolism (and implied threat) of rents being collected by Officer Youngblood represented the white legal power structure to the Black community. Even the banality of rent collection reinforced the role of public authority in maintaining the system of white supremacy.

One May afternoon in 1962, listening to the local radio station I heard a report that a man who shot and killed a teller in an Ozark bank, 30 miles south, was heading toward Troy, armed and dangerous. Youngblood drove south of town to a small rural store, where he waited inside with the owner. The bank robber circled the store, and when Youngblood crouched in the doorway the robber drove his car to the front, killing Youngblood with his .45 caliber hand-gun. He was the first Troy police officer to lose his life performing his duty since 1905.[4]

I went quickly over to Quarles's Pool Hall, where I suspected Ed would be shooting some afterschool pool; indeed, he was walking out as I approached. I told him of Youngblood's death and the events as the radio had reported them. Stunned at the news, without a word he walked straight to the police department, just around the block, and I followed. Because of Ed's connection to Youngblood, we occasionally dropped by the local police station to listen to the (mostly really dull) scanner and talk to the local officers. By that time, other Troy officers had picked up the chase and cornered the murderer in a ceme-tery north of town. Listening to the police radio we heard shots, then silence. The radio operator tried several times to reach the officers when finally one reported, "We got him." Two of my more daring classmates followed the action and arrived on the scene in time to hear the fatal shots—perhaps the local police figured if they did not tolerate us at the station, we might be crazy enough to chase the action. But of course such easy access to the police even in the midst of a crisis could not be envisioned for Troy's Black citizens.

The "Boy from Troy"

Martin Luther King always referred to John Lewis as "the Boy from Troy" from the time he first invited Lewis to Montgomery. Lewis, the famed civil rights leader who led the march across the Edmund Pettus Bridge in Selma to press for voting rights and later served as a congressman from Atlanta, was born and raised in rural Pike County, a few scant miles from my home. He was the son of sharecroppers who acquired land near the small commu-nity of Banks. Lewis was born four and a half years before me. He attended high school at the segregated Pike County Training School in Brundidge. If he had lived in Troy, he would have attended the segregated Academy High.

Even if we had been the same ages, and even if he been in the Troy attendance zone, I could not have known this remarkable person, because the system of segregation would have kept us apart. The Troy where I lived and the one John Lewis experienced were not the same place. It was neither the years separating us nor the differences between rural and town. It was the code of segregation that divided our worlds and instilled in me a different perception of Troy than the one John had.

Lewis came to Troy regularly, with his parents and alone, to shop and take advantage of such entertainment as was available to Blacks at the time. Three places in Troy illustrate how the world looked differently from the perspectives of a white and a Black boy.

During my high school years, after Sunday school at First Methodist, my friends and I would drop over to one of the three drugstores in town—Byrd's, Byrd-Watters, or McCloud's—and drink "combinations," a fountain drink which I later learned was called a "cherry coke" in the rest of the United States. In his award-winning memoir, *Walking with the Wind*, John Lewis recalled Byrd Drug as well, and he enjoyed an occasional combination there. However, he could not sit with his friends drinking and talking, as we did. He had to pay at the counter, and take his combination outside to drink. There an open bench directly faced the Confederate soldier on a high pedestal facing north, as was general custom. I'm sorry to say for most of my boyhood I never thought about the absence of Blacks inside Byrd's—or McCloud's, or at the two downtown restaurants.

The Troy five-and-dime is where I bought marbles, spinning tops, and corn-cob pipes. In that same store, Lewis noted the separate water fountains with one "modern chrome spouted water cooler, the other nothing more than a rusty spigot."[5] I don't recall that water fountain arrangement, but I clearly remember the oiled floors and counters with all sorts of interesting gadgets displayed. My memory could reflect the oblivion of what is now called white privilege.

On many Saturday afternoons, my friends and I would ride our bikes the two miles from our neighborhood into town. Our destination was the Enzor Theater on North Three Notch. The décor inside the theater was reminiscent of a Spanish garden, and the dark blue ceiling had lights resembling stars. For a dime, we could watch a double feature, a cartoon, and serials that carried the action from one week to the next to keep you coming. The features were often black-and-white cowboy movies featuring Hopalong Cassidy, the Lone Ranger, Lash Larue, and Whip Wilson, and sometimes Gene Autry and Randolph Scott. Sometimes the westerns featured a Union veteran paired with a former Confederate soldier, and the theme was reconciliation in a Lost Cause kind of format.

John Lewis remembered the Enzor too. A dime got him and his friends into the segregated balcony. The Enzor always seemed to be crowded on Saturdays with kids, on the main floor and the balcony, but we regulars learned to sit away from the end of the balcony overhang, as sometimes the patrons in the balcony "accidentally" would spill candy, popcorn, or an occasional partially consumed cup of coke onto the patrons on the main floor. We thought it funny that newcomers would sit under the balcony overhang, but we never thought about the source of the resentment that underlay such activities.

Lewis stopped attending the Enzor's Saturday matinees because of the indignity of sitting segregated in what Blacks called the "Buzzard's Roost."

The Enzor closed in 1957, leaving one remaining movie house in town, the Pike. Occasionally the Pike would reserve a late show slot for movies designed for Black audiences. *St. Louis Blues*, the story of W.C. Handy, featuring Eartha Kitt, Nat "King" Cole, Cab Calloway, Ella Fitzgerald, and Mahalia Jackson, played two nights at 9:30 in June 1958. Then the full theater was open to Blacks. Sometimes the balcony was open to whites but not Blacks—I sat in the balcony when the occasional traveling magician staged a show there—no Blacks allowed then.

John Lewis highlights the gross inequalities in life that reinforced white views of Blacks as inferior, built onto a system designed to keep them that way—from the poor schools to the single segregated public library in town, "but through whose doors I was not allowed to set foot."[6]

It was not just the inequality-causing system of inferior schools and services to which I was mostly oblivious. John Lewis noted as a boy it was the small indignities that added up to large assaults. In *The Southern Mystique*, Howard Zinn wrote, "It is incredible how many whites do not know, specifically, what Negroes experience in a segregated society." He asked his students in the fall of 1962 to write of their first encounters with racial discrimination. A girl from Georgia wrote of standing at a service window at a Dairy Queen until she was told always to go around to a side window, which "was the window for colored people."[7]

Lewis often used the term "good trouble" for the direct action he and other civil rights proponents took to try to change the corrupt and unfair system. The trouble was good because it was directed at a system that was not. The term makes perfect sense standing alone, but it also carries a historical connotation as well. White supremacists regularly distinguished between "good Negroes" and "troublemaking," "worthless," or "shiftless" Negroes. One of Lewis's legacies is that "Good Negroes" can and should cause "good trouble."

The Greyhound Bus to Tuscaloosa

My parents planned summer trips for me to Tuscaloosa and Birmingham to stay with relatives, perhaps to get to know them better, perhaps to get me out of town. My mother gave me bus fare and put me on the Greyhound Bus headed to Montgomery and then Birmingham. Blacks to the back and whites to the front. She instructed me carefully not to get off the bus in the busy station in Montgomery, later to become infamous for the mob attack on the Freedom Riders in 1961.

The link between the Trailways Bus to Tuscaloosa and the Greyhound headed to Birmingham was in Prattville. I recall it being out on the highway in a small filling-station sized building. Passengers stood outside until the Trailways bus pulled up and we got on. Blacks went to the back and whites to the front.

Aunt Joan, Mac's wife, met me at the bus station, and took me over to my grandmother's house. The house was a large and very drafty bungalow with a distinct musty smell near to the Alabama campus. Tuscaloosa's nickname is the Druid City for the water oaks that lined the streets. To this day, I associate the musty smell with the oaks and the nickname. Except, that is, when the Gulf States paper mill was not spewing its foul smell into the air. The house usually had a boarder, generally from South America, in the front bedroom to help my grandmother with expenses.

Aunt Joan made sure there was plenty to do during my visit. My cousins, McCoy and John, were playmates. We did a lot, but the Hurricane Creek swimming hole was my favorite. Tuscaloosa sits on the fall line with Appalachia to the north and the Black Belt prairies to the south. Hurricane Creek flows through the forests and over the rocky terrain of Appalachia before it connects to the Black Warrior River near Tuscaloosa. I recall jumping off the banks into the swimming hole next to a waterfall, so refreshing in the hot, humid, and non-airconditioned summer. The son of Joan's Black maid joined us there, as I recall.

After a week or so, Mother and Carol joined me in Tuscaloosa, and it was time for ice cream. We went over to the Tuscaloosa icehouse to buy bags of ice, and I was struck by how many of the customers were Black. The reason was clear. Many Black homes lacked electricity or electric refrigerators, making regular trips to the icehouse necessary. We packed the bucket with crushed ice, put rock salt on it, added the ice cream mix in the center container, and then I cranked away. There was a reward, though. I was the first to lick the dasher (mixer in the center of the ice cream container) when the ice cream had hardened.

Birmingham Visits

For a couple of years my cousin Marion, my mother's niece, invited me up to Birmingham to spend a week or two with her and her family. I was in grade school, maybe fifth grade, at the time. My mother took me down to the bus station in Troy, gave me bus fare, and told me to be sure not to get off the Greyhound until it stopped in Birmingham.

It was amazingly gracious of Marion to invite me to visit. She was nine years older than me, home from college, and having a tag-along was probably not high on her list of summer fun. I suspect now that she was filling a special request from my parents to get me out of town, surely a subsidized request. She had frequently joined us on our vacation trips to Florida as a child-minder. Nevertheless she was a marvelous host.

My relatives lived in Homewood, on Shades Mountain, to the South of Red Mountain and Birmingham, safe from the pollution from the still-thriving steel production plants in Birmingham and the industrial suburb of Bessemer. The location also created distance from the increasing number of Blacks in the city.

The lush mountain suburbs of Homewood and Mountain Brook were home to the Birmingham elites—the steel and coal company management, utilities executives, and the local business elites. Marion and her family lived on a beautiful large, tree-covered lot part way up the mountainside in a spacious ranch style home. My uncle by marriage was a vice president at Alabama Power Company, in our minds the most successful family member.

During Christmas visits to Tuscaloosa and other family gatherings there, the Homewood relatives would drive down to join us. Aunt Ruth was quiet and taciturn, and in Homewood spent much of her time in her bedroom. Mother told me she was ill. Her husband, Penn, as we called him, was outgoing and jovial, always with a few magic tricks for us.

Penn was jovial and open in Homewood as well when I visited. He came home promptly at around 6:00, unlike my father, who almost never joined us for dinner. He mixed himself a drink, offered me a ginger ale, and told stories.

Cousin Marion joined in, and I was mesmerized. When dinner was ready, we all came into the dining room, joining Aunt Ruth, as her husband continued his generally upbeat banter.

One day Penn came home in a truly dark mood. He mixed himself a drink but sat mostly quiet and sullen; it was clear that Marion and I should find something else to do before dinner. At dinner, we sat silently as Penn brooded. Then he let go of the most foul, hateful, and racist language that one could imagine. The "n" word flowed out of his mouth as easily as his jaunty jokes, but in a dark and threatening manner. Aunt Ruth and Marion looked down, almost afraid to catch his eye. Whatever happened at work, or elsewhere had nothing to do with Blacks. I do not recall at this time whether something in the news set him off. It was scary to a youngster to observe such a display while visiting relatives. I was shaken for days and never trusted his jovial moods again.

I was most shocked that a respected businessman would use such offensive language. I did not hear anything like this at home, or my friends' homes, or from other relatives. Certainly racist language was common on the streets, and racist jokes were far too common, but such language was mostly absent in general conversation. Many Southerners in the 1950s were paternalistic, thinking of Blacks as simpler folk, but they were not to be demonized. Racist language was the province of the less educated who supposedly were the carriers of the explicit racism and violence against Blacks.

Penn's language suggested a different explanation—that racism lies under the surface, and not that deep when the whole social structure is based on white supremacist norms. In a racist society, most are racists. The most successful rely on law and custom to maintain the trappings of status, while some turn to intimidation, degradation, and occasionally violence. Even for the most successful of whites, Blacks could become scapegoats for anything that might have gone wrong. Or so it seemed to me that evening in Homewood.

Reality was even more complex. The elites of Birmingham had a reputation for tolerating racism, fostered by the Planter–Big Mule alliance that so dominated state politics. By the late 1950s, the Birmingham industrial and utility businessmen had begun to separate themselves from the overt and vicious racism promulgated in the Black Belt, but the break went only so far. The elite element of Birmingham had long ago moved over Red Mountain, leaving the struggles over integration to the working class of the city.

When integration efforts came to a head in 1963, the business elite focused not on solving the festering sore of racism but rather zeroed in on the image of Birmingham nationally, an image that would not harm business.

When President Kennedy and his advisors met with executives from Birmingham, they pressed him to "get (Martin Luther) King and (the Birmingham pastor Fred) Shuttlesworth out of Birmingham."[8] Unlike the Tuscaloosa business and political community facing the integration of the University of Alabama, the Birmingham elites were unwilling to work with the Kennedy administration to restore calm and begin the long process of racial justice. I don't know what Penn's positions were on these issues, but the recalcitrance of Birmingham elites surely influenced him.

In 1985, Marion and her children came to Tuscaloosa for my mother's funeral. We had not seen each other in many years, and Marion was her old warm self. We spoke of my trips to Birmingham, and Marion's recollections of my mother, the aunt whom she adored, and the feeling was mutual. We recalled those trips to Florida she took with us; she was there to mind Carol and me so our parents could have some nights out alone.

Then, suddenly out of the blue, Marion went on what I perceived as racist rant about something I no longer recall. My mind immediately rushed back to the unpleasant incident in Homewood and Penn. Perhaps too quickly back. Now, however, I was not a schoolboy, and I confronted Marion on her comment, stating bluntly that was not language I could tolerate. She stood her ground, and so did I. The incident was diffused when someone came over and calmed us down.

The Collapse of Nostalgia

For John Lewis, growing up in Pike County carried little nostalgia, but nevertheless he writes of pleasant memories within a toxic system. For me, growing up in the 1950s and early 1960s had a nostalgic feel to it, but as I entered my teen years it began to feel superficial and not right. Segregation was often justified because Blacks could have harmful diseases, yet they prepared our food and made our beds. I failed to grasp the dual labor market—some jobs for whites, some for Blacks—that allowed middle-class Southern families to employ maids that otherwise would have been unaffordable. Over time, I was becoming increasingly aware of what I had ignored because it was so familiar and ever-present (Figure 21.3).

My high school friend Ed Walters was already developing into the class eccentric by our senior year in 1962. He felt stifled and incomplete, longing

Figure 21.3 Off to the National Boy Scout Jamboree as Part of a Segregated Alabama Contingent—A Few Years after the Bicycle Incident
Source: Author's collection.

to leave Troy for a different, less limited life. He would fume about the constraints of small-town life where uptight businessmen, as he put it, "scraped their faces raw, until they bled" and "tightened their ties to the choking point" as if to impose order on an increasingly chaotic world.

In my teenaged brain the stupid segregation system mixed with the "uptight" middle-class culture dominated by consumerism and upward mobility captured so well in *The Man in the Gray Flannel Suit*. The "beatnik" critique of that culture seeped into small towns all over the nation. Ed and I particularly became critical of the staid middle-class businessmen seemingly holding tight to a Southern order that could slip away at any minute. Whatever we did in life, we swore, would not involve returning to the stultifying culture of any small town anywhere.

In my high school years, I took down the Confederate flag over my bedroom desk, along with the bayonet acquired at a Virginia battlefield. The Lost Cause was lost for me. The Confederacy and its support of slavery meant that I had been on the wrong side of the divide. How I came to the recognition that romanticizing the Confederacy and justifying Jim Crow was wrong I cannot reconstruct. I am sure that the process was partly cognitive. Segregation increasingly made no sense. I could dimly see that the tenets of Southern segregation and the magnificent portrait of a free and sovereign America depicted by the founders and taught in American History clashed in a way that was not reconcilable. Racism was wrong, and reading *Huckleberry Finn* helped me to understand that. I just did not feel the animosity of racism nor the superiority of white supremacy.

Honestly, it was partly youthful rebellion: in my teenage brain, the stultification of a small town and Southern segregation could not be unwound. Both were unacceptable. I suspect that Iowa or New York small towns were as stultifying, but I did not know these towns. For me, stultification and segregation were as tightly bound as the double helix. Empathy for the plight of Blacks, I'm sorry to say, came later.

American Graffiti, Small-Town Style

Like the California kids in the movie *American Graffiti*, I graduated from high school in 1962. It is unbelievable how much our high school years resembled those of the make-believe Californians in the movie. We cruised to rock 'n' roll music just like the kids from Modesto. Kids without cars would hop from one ride to another. The kids in the movie tuned in to the legendary disk jockey Wolfman Jack. We could pick up disk jockey Dick Biondi, beamed south on the 50,000-watt Chicago station WLS.

Our cruising was sad compared to Modesto's. Driving back and forth between two drive-ins on a bypass, sometimes heading to the pool hall downtown, was just not the same as cruising Modesto's main drag. Cruising lost its charm much faster in Troy than in Modesto. I later learned that kids in Detroit cruised up and down Woodward Avenue from the Detroit River to Pontiac. Take that, Modesto.

If boredom set in, we'd find other stuff to do. Some nights we'd head over to the airport, with no operating license after dark, to watch a drag race, invariably the result of a challenge. Or head over to a country store out on Needmore Road where the compliant owner would fail to check IDs. Usually one of us would go in and pick up a six-pack. One evening it was Mike Manning's turn. He came back shaking and holding a pack of cigarettes, informing us that the local policeman was there, so he bought the cigarettes and left. Cigarettes were illegal for minors as well, so we had a good laugh and went on our way to try another store.

Sometimes it got interesting, as when the local bootleggers drove up to the Dari Delight Drive-In burger and ice cream joint on the bypass in their supercharged Ford Fairlane. The brothers, from the Brundidge area, showed us their car's powerful engine, and the false bottom in the trunk designed to carry the whiskey from Pike, a wet county, to the dry counties south. The false bottom did not deter the Pike County sheriff's deputies patrolling the roads. It was the car that deterred, the fastest road machine in the county.

Some weekend nights, I drove down Three Notch Street heading home, listening to the rock 'n' roll pumped out by DJ Dick Biondi. For a brief moment I encountered Black Troy without the submission required in the stultifying Jim Crow system. At the intersection of Three Notch and Love Street I'd watch the groups of Black men emptying the Love Street bars and cafes. The street was crowded, and occasionally fights would break out. As I came to realize later, the men were working off the built-up resentment endured from a week of submissively working for the Man.

The *Selma Times* Recognizes an "Opportunity"

After the Second World War there was to be a moment when liberal populists such as "Big Jim" Folsom and progressive editors, publishers, and businessmen thought that they could bring the South into alignment with national politics and slowly, slowly end the worst elements of Jim Crow. That faint hope flickered out in the explosion of white supremacist sentiment as national sentiment against segregation increased.

Resentment by whites toward Blacks pressing for an end to segregation sparked a statewide backlash. The backlash was far stronger in southern Alabama, and the voting patterns continued to display sectional patterns. This traditional class-based north-south division weakened in the late '50s and early '60s

The *Selma Times-Journal* recognized this as an opportunity to bolster white supremacy and the segregated social order. In 1956 the paper published an unabashedly pro–Citizens' Council editorial, "The 'Rednecks' Are Our Hope." The editor recognized changes in the composition of the Councils, from upper-class businessmen to a mix of businessmen, workers, and the poor. "There was a time that the [newspaper] composing room stood staunchly for Gov. James E. Folsom, but that time has passed." A wave of racism had smashed class politics. "With the aid of their skill and talent for organization, the so-called 'rednecks' can rule Alabama politics for generations to come."[9]

Jim Folsom on Television

Gubernatorial races immediately after the Second World War included both segregation and economic issues, but being conservative on both the race and economic issues was not popular. From 1946 through the Wallace years, Alabamians preferred economic liberalism. Race issues were prominent but did not deter economically disadvantaged voters from supporting racial moderate Jim Folsom.

By 1958 race was the prominent issue. The moderate candidate, Jimmy Faulkner in his second gubernatorial campaign, was eliminated in the first round, leaving Attorney General John Patterson, the eventual winner, and George Wallace in the runoff. I remember the campaign only sketchily, but I do recall attending a Jimmy Faulkner rally in the center of town, complete with the Statesmen Quartet, a gospel music group, and plenty of speech-making.

As the Democratic primary of 1962 approached, three major contenders emerged: George Wallace, former governor Jim Folsom, and Ryan DeGraffenreid, a young businessman from Tuscaloosa. All ran as segregationists, but Wallace ran a harshly racist campaign while Folsom and DeGraffenreid hewed to more moderate courses.

In March, Folsom came to Troy with his "Meat Grinders" band to give a speech. He attracted a large crowd, "including a large contingent of the Negro population."[10] Folsom remained highly popular among Blacks, but they generally could not vote. He pitched economics, especially education and pensions, but stayed away from the race issue until asked, and then defended segregation.

I had by then become fully emotionally invested in the politics of Alabama, disgusted with the race-baiting that reached a crescendo that year. I despised Wallace, who was busily overcompensating for what he saw as his failure to emphasize segregation and white supremacy strongly enough in 1958. Folsom endorsed segregation and ran a campaign with far more segregationist elements in it than in the past, reflecting a changed political climate. He was nevertheless the most moderate candidate in the race.[11] I thought DeGraffenreid had no chance, so I settled on Folsom as my candidate (of course, I had no vote).

Political candidates had learned to use radio to communicate their messages over the years. Folsom had used radio effectively in 1946 and 1954, and even ran limited television programs in 1954. In his runs for governor in 1954 and 1958, Faulkner bought large blocks of time on local stations for his "Talkathons" and even did a three-hour statewide version including questions from voters in 1958. By the early 1960s, radio was fading as a communication mechanism for politicians, and many had not mastered the techniques needed for the still-new medium of television. The night before the 1962 Democratic primary Folsom planned a half-hour television program, broadcast statewide, which would consist mostly of a film which Folsom and his family would introduce. I recall the other candidates presenting something similar.

I asked Mother if we could watch the program, and she said I could, but she was uninterested. Mostly I suspect it was distaste for both Wallace and Folsom. In any case as a Republican, she would not vote until the general election.

The film failed to get to the studio, and Folsom ad libbed. He was an infamous drinker, but he was just as famous for being able to hold it. I watched in horror as Folsom seemed confused and disoriented as the naturally gifted orator lost his ability to carry his theme. The next day, Folsom lost by less than 2,000 votes. Most analysts attributed his razor-thin loss to his abysmal television performance. I felt an acute sense of disappointment. In the runoff primary against DeGraffenreid, Wallace intensified his racist themes, attacking the federal government for its intervention, and won solidly. The Wallace era had begun. The one product that Wallace was best at selling—hate and race division—I was not buying, but I sensed that we were headed down the wrong path.

CHAPTER 22

The Pallbearer Who Couldn't Go into the Church

Frank Worthy was a quiet, muscular man of slightly more than average height. He worked in the back of the *Troy Messenger*, a steadfastly reliable jack of all trades, master of many.

All of the other office staff and print shop workers were white. At the time I knew all their names and I addressed them as "Mr." or "Mrs." (all of the women were married). But Frank was just Frank. I never knew Frank's last name until I started working on this project and looked it up. Not knowing Frank's last name reflected the Southern racial hierarchy, and referring to Black men by first names was reflexive in the ingrained racism, part of the background of systematic racism.[1]

Frank had worked at the *Messenger* longer than anybody and was an essential cog in the print shop. He knew all the jobs in the backroom and could substitute for most. The backroom crew knew him well and respected both his knowledge and his abilities, but he was invariably assigned the most unpleasant tasks.

The print shop was all hot metal, black ink, clanking linotype machines and the thunk-thunk of the noisy flatbed printing press. The modest front office, more or less air conditioned, faced North Three Notch Street, half a block from the town square and its north-facing Confederate soldier. Local legend claimed that Andy Jackson cut three notches on trees as he moved through the area toward New Orleans during the War of 1812, hence the street name. The Alabama Historical Society finds no evidence of that.

In the "modern" 1950s, the town fathers tore down the courthouse on the square and built a new one a short distance away, at the end of a dead-end street.

The Confederate monument remained the centerpiece of the small grassy park and larger parking lot that replaced the courthouse.

The small news and advertising staff worked in the front office of the *Messenger*. The staff wrote local stories and pulled material from the Associated Press teletype feeds for state and national items. The Associated Press sent engravings for pictures by express mail; any local pictures had to be engraved in Montgomery. My father's small office was adjacent to the un-airconditioned printing floor, which was unbelievably dirty with black ink covering floors, walls, machinery, almost everything. It was both hot in the humid South Alabama summer and noisy enough to require earplugs when the flatbed press was running.

Against the north wall were two linotype machines and a composing table, where the lead slugs produced by the magical linotypes were set and locked into plates. There was only one linotype operator in Troy, Martin Mershon. He was a member of the printers' craft union, the International Typographers' Union (ITU), served as the chairman of the school board, and was a major participant of the Methodist Church, supervising the Sunday school.

There is a funny thing about small Southern towns. On the one hand, church and civic participation encompassed pretty much all of the white community—from the guys that got their hands dirty, like the print staff at the *Messenger* and the mechanics at Troy Motors, to the operators of the pool halls and bars in town to the doctors, lawyers, and owners of the car dealerships. On the other hand, there was an unmistakable social ranking within the white community, and it mattered how long the family had been around.

The big divide, of course, was race.

The Print Shop

The linotype was a truly remarkable machine. It replaced hand typesetting in which typesetters set type letter by letter, first into lines and then the lines assembled into a page.[2] With the linotype, whole lines could be set at once. Mershon, machine operator, typed the copy generated by the front office on a keyboard that pulled molds from the storage magazine, lining them up backward (so they would print forward) and justifying (aligning) them.

Frank put lead alloy bars into an electric pot attached to the machine. The electric pot heated the lead bars to liquid, and the molten lead alloy was fed into the machine. Then the operator forced the hot metal into the molds, which produced the slugs with a "line of type" on the top of the slender rectangular slugs. The type came out as a single unit—hence the term "hot metal type-setting." The letter molds, called matrices, were returned automatically to the magazine.

The next step in the process was the composing table, where the typesetters locked down lines for the day's paper in a bed, or plate, one bed per page, and a small hand printing press lathered ink over the metal form and printed the proof sheet. The plates were flat, befitting a flatbed press—they are curved on a rotary press. Any mistakes were corrected, and the proof page was run again.

The linotypes were seemingly never silenced, but the aging flat-bed press was forever breaking down. The pressman and my father were pretty good at diagnosing and repairing minor problems, but more severe ones required a call to a press repairman in Montgomery, 50 miles away. That meant a very late night for the production staff, and the paperboys.

The jovial pressman locked the full day's paper onto the flatbed press, and the press run began. The pressman fed ink continuously into the press, rollers inked the plates, and the big rolls of paper mounted onto the press were fed onto the inked plates and pressed on them by a big cylinder. The press automatically pulled off the pages, folded them in proper order, and pushed the day's paper into an attached bin. The pressman and Frank continually emptied the bin and stacked the papers. A helper organized them into bundles tied with rough twine, each with the proper number for each paper route. After school the paperboys, many my friends, waited with their bicycles out at the loading dock behind the building.

Frank picked up the slugs from the linotype pots, disassembled the plates, separated the type and took them to the very back of the shop. He worked right next to the bathroom, a small single room (no colored and white signs here) with an ample supply of Lava soap. In big electric pots he melted the used lead and with a big ladle he poured the hot metal into molds for ingots. Frank took the ingots back up to the linotype machine to start the process over again.

During this process the heat, particularly in summer, was unbearable, and the work was dangerous. But I was fascinated with Frank's job, and watched him work until the heat became too much. Sometimes during a break he would talk, if only briefly, then go back to work. Some of the fascination came from my childhood imagination. In my mind, the ingots were just right for using as gold bars in pirate games, and sometimes I could convince Dad to bring one home. Unfortunately the ingots were highly toxic, and press workers were subject to lead poisoning.

Years later, in the 1970s, when we lived in Detroit, I was reminded of Frank when we toured Ford's River Rouge Plant, then the largest integrated industrial plant in the world. Iron ore went into the plant and automobiles emerged. The foundry floor was occupied almost exclusively by Blacks, while the assembly lines were almost totally white. The racial division of labor in a vast industrial plant and the tiny south Alabama printing plant were mirror images.

Jail and Release for Frank

Every so often on payday Frank would have too much to drink in one of the bars on Love Street, and get into an after-hours fight. The late-night call would come to our house, and my father would answer, knowing with a great deal of certainty what the call was about. I imagine the on-duty police officer that night would have said something like "Glenn, Frank was arrested fighting again, and we have him here in the station jail."

Invariably my father would get dressed and go down to the station, bail Frank out and drive him home. I suspect the drive home was stone silence, with Frank realizing how he had failed and my father suppressing his famous temper. Frank was a reliable worker, very good at his job. He deserved slack, but I suspect some nights my father thought seriously about other arrangements. Finding and training another reliable worker who would perform the dirty and exhausting tasks required, however, would not have been easy. And Frank knew that because he had a loyal patron, he would likely not be charged with a crime.

Such action was not uncommon in the 1950s South. James Madison Beck reports that his grandfather took similar action for Black workers at his sawmill in Glenwood, about 15 miles to the southwest of Troy. He bailed out the errant worker on Monday, after the worker had spent a couple of nights in jail.[3] For my father, getting up in the middle of the night was beyond the call of duty, and I am sure that the chastened Frank deeply appreciated the action. He was intensely loyal to my father. The system was paternalistic, but the connection between my father and Frank was more than that. It was a relationship between two decent men which would have been friends in a just world, but was structured by the rigid segregation and racial hierarchy imposed by the laws and folkways of mid-20th century Alabama.

The Call

The call came in the early morning of Saturday August 5, 1961, the day before my 17th birthday. My mother, always an early riser, answered the hall telephone. "You mean he's dead? OH NO," she shrieked, in words I can hear to this day. My father had suffered a massive heart attack while in Oxford, Mississippi, on business. He was part owner of the *Oxford Eagle* newspaper, and was in the process of arranging a sale. He had suffered a minor heart attack earlier in the summer while we were on vacation but like good parents of the early 1960s, they kept it from the kids. Later Mother told me that she was planning to go to Oxford to help with what she had assumed to be another nonfatal heart attack as she walked to the phone.

I went to my sobbing younger sister's bedroom to comfort her; she was only 13 years old. On completing the call, Mother told me to phone Mike Boisclair, the reliable business manager of the *Messenger*, which I did. Mike's stunned response was "What . . . that's something. . . . I can't believe it." My father and Mike had a close and productive working relationship. Mike was more than capable of bringing out the paper and solving the multitude of problems associated with it. Mother phoned her mother and my father's parents, and I phoned many of the rest of the relatives. The rest of the day was an emotional blur as we contacted pallbearers and chose the casket.

Pallbearers included Mike Boisclair, prominent businessman and leader of the town's small Jewish community Sigmund Rosenberg, and all the employees of the *Troy Messenger* as honorary pallbearers. Whether Mother recognized it or not, that meant she had invited Frank to attend the funeral.

On the Steps of the First Methodist Church of Troy

Methodism had discarded its radical roots based in class meetings decades before. Now its churches had too often become beacons of small-town respectability throughout the South and small-town America generally. For Ed Walters and me, they had become symbols of hypocrisy.

One Sunday at the start of services a heavyset man whom I did not recognize strode into the sanctuary, sitting down in the middle of a pew. He wore not the suits and ties required of even high school boys; rather he wore a pair of work pants and tee shirt that had gone through many a washing in its years of existence. This caused much consternation among the churchgoing Methodists. The church-folk, whispering among themselves, actively shunned the man.

I wondered why everyone regardless of class or background was not welcomed, and began to develop a sense of the hypocrisy of Southern religion. The churches reeking of respectability supported unjustifiable segregation and rigid norms of status among whites.

These beacons of Southern respectability were unbendingly segregated—the Methodist Church "had a constitutional framework in which Black churches and Black ministers were legally segregated from whites."[4] As massive resistance to integration built after the Supreme Court school desegregation decision *Brown v. Board* in 1954, some members of the Alabama Methodist Conference organized to support continued segregation in churches just two weeks after citizens of Selma organized the first White Citizens' Council in Alabama. One of the leaders of the movement was H. Paul Mathison, district superintendent of the Troy District.[5] Martin Luther King's famous observation that "the most segregated hour of Christian America is eleven o'clock on Sunday morning" was certainly true in Troy.

As Mother, Carol, and I began to walk up the steps of the church for my father's funeral, Governor John Patterson arrived in a black limousine. Patterson stepped out with an aide, gave Mother his sympathies, shook my hand and nodded to Carol, and went into the church.

I'm sure I knew of the chaos in the Freedom Rider protests in Montgomery just a few months earlier. I probably knew of Patterson's role as a rabid segregationist, and maybe of his reformist proclivities. But I cannot recall what I knew. I certainly knew of his failure to provide proper school funding, leading to "proration," that had led to cutting teachers' salaries that year—the teachers made sure we knew. As a high school junior, I knew of these happenings, but they seemed remote. Troy remained quiet, and most whites were oblivious (I am sure that Blacks were not). Still I was moved to tears that the governor of Alabama had attended my father's funeral.

As we continued up the steps, we noticed Frank sitting about halfway up, away from the door. Clearly he felt it necessary to be inconspicuous on the steps of our white church. That sort of deference was part of the network of social norms and countless indignities that buttressed legal segregation, reinforcing the inferior status of more than 40% of the population of Troy.

Frank was dressed in his Sunday clothes—dark suit, crisp white shirt, and conservative tie. He stood up as we approached, and nodded to us. "Frank, why don't you come on in?," my mother spontaneously blurted out, obviously touched that he would come. Frank responded, "Oh, no ma'm, that wouldn't be respectful."

Frank's heartbreaking response was surely in keeping with what was expected of him in Troy. There is little doubt in my mind that Frank could have suffered repercussions had he joined us. Nor is there doubt in my mind that the incident would have been the gist for serious town gossip, and Mother could have lost friends.

We continued up the stairs, into our white world, and Frank sat on the steps throughout the service. When we left, he stood up respectfully. He had stayed through the service, the honorary pallbearer who could not enter the church.

CHAPTER 23

Roll Tide at High Tide

I was an undergraduate at the University of Alabama from 1962 to 1966, the high tide of the civil rights movement. My undergraduate years were typical for the era, but those years were punctuated with all the major events that characterized a critical turning point in American history—the legal end of Jim Crow. As historian C. Vann Woodward wrote,

> The year 1965 would nevertheless remain one of historical importance in the record of American race relations. It did not mark the solution of a problem, but it did mark the end of a period—the period of legally sanctioned segregation of races. . . . If Jim Crow was dead, however, his ghost still haunted a troubled people and the heritage he left behind would remain with them for a long time to come.[1]

Discarding legalized racial segregation did not occur all at once in 1965. As with all critical junctures, events before and after 1965 included both pushes toward justice and backlashes against the change. These major events were concentrated in Alabama in my undergraduate years. They pushed the issue of de jure segregation onto the national policymaking agenda, resulting in the 1964 Civil Rights Act and the 1965 Voting Rights Act.

I entered college with a growing cognitive appreciation of the injustice imposed by the Jim Crow system, and an increasing moral sense that it was wrong. The more I observed the actions of Blacks and the vicious hateful and violent action of many whites and the silence of many more, the more I became emotionally incensed by the injustice of segregation. If there was a single event that brought about this revulsion, it was George Wallace's schoolhouse door stunt at the end of my freshman year. I became increasingly outspoken on the issue, sometimes to the irritation of those around me, who doubtless tired of the dialogue.

As the events unfolded, I became optimistic that the country had crossed an important threshold that would bring about a more equitable America. Like many Americans, I had the sense that the country was struggling to cross the worst barriers to decency and equality, and that it would succeed. I was not a dreamy-eyed optimist. The Vietnam War was unfolding at the same time, with its network of lies propagated by three administrations. I was so hopeful on segregation, perhaps because I thought it was obvious that it was unjustified.

I vastly underestimated the power of white backlash. I mistakenly believed that the backlash would be contained to a handful of extremists. I could not have been more wrong.

The Stand in the Schoolhouse Door

George Wallace had promised in his gubernatorial campaign to block the integration of Alabama schools even if he had to "stand in the schoolhouse door." Soon after his inauguration in June 1963, he got the opportunity to do just that.[2]

The stand has become one of the iconic images in American history, representing the end of both Jim Crow and the vicious white reaction to its end. The nonviolent but highly symbolic event was a result of a set of negotiations among five distinct groups: the two Black students themselves, Vivian Malone and James Hood, who were represented by the NAACP; George Wallace and his State of Alabama entourage; the University of Alabama community, led by President Frank Rose; the Justice Department of the Federal Government, charged with enforcing a federal judge's integration order; and the civic leaders of the City of Tuscaloosa.

In September of the previous year, James Meredith won an extended court battle over the right to be admitted to the University of Mississippi. When he arrived at the campus, he was met with a large white mob. In the white riot that followed, two bystanders were killed, 206 U.S. marshals were wounded, and 200 were arrested before order was restored by U.S. troops.[3] All were determined to avoid the violent fiasco at the University of Mississippi. Mississippi governor Ross Barnett had fought integration up until Meredith's admission, so Wallace was forewarned of the potential for violence. He nevertheless wanted to push the envelope as far as he thought he could, spewing his message of racial resentment to a national audience.

The mostly moderate Tuscaloosa white business community prepared for the upcoming Wallace challenge. Publisher Buford Boone used the *Tuscaloosa News* to promote racial moderation and urge calm, taking a few swipes at Wallace along the way. Banker George Lemaitre was closely bound to the national Democratic Party. He was a strong supporter of moderate Senators Lister Hill and John Sparkman, as well as John Kennedy in 1960 and Lyndon Johnson in 1964. In 1968, Robert Kennedy asked Lemaitre to serve as his Alabama coordinator, which he gladly accepted. Mayor George Van Tassel, former State Senator E.W. Skidmore, and my Uncle Mac Davidson, head of the Tuscaloosa Bar, were all part of the Labor-Liberal North Alabama coalition.

The day Wallace made his promise to defy the federal government over integration, Lemaitre spoke to the local Civitan Club, warning of the economic consequences of racial violence. He contended that no state official had the right to put himself above the law, and that includes a governor or a governor-elect. He received a standing ovation.[4] Lemaitre traveled the state explaining to businessmen that continued racial hostility would cost the state business, and the loss would be long-term.

The Kennedy administration negotiated with Wallace and separately with University President Frank Rose, banker Lemaitre, publisher Boone, Mayor Van Tassel, and the police chief of Tuscaloosa on a plan to unify the city and make sure the Klan-excited mobs did not reappear as they did in 1956. Wallace contacted Klan leader Bobby Shelton to urge him to keep the demonstrations in check, because Wallace thought it would undermine his national appeal.

Uncle Mac's son JD vaguely recalls his father telling him that Governor George Wallace would not bar the entry of the two Black students, Vivian Malone and James Hood, who were admitted and seeking to register for courses. Mac said, probably to reassure JD, that all would go well and that Wallace would step aside after a speech, and that indeed is what happened. It was likely that Mac was knowledgeable about (or perhaps involved in) the pre-event planning.

I decided to go down to campus and observe the event but found that the roads and sidewalks were blocked to all but summer school students. The university admitted Malone and Hood in the summer term when fewer people were on campus. There was little of the intense hatred generated by the Klan and the university student body in 1956, and none of the extensive riots of the year before at Ole Miss.

Both James Hood and Vivian Malone were under a great deal of stress in the summer. Under pressure from the university, Hood withdrew. In the fall, tension between the university administration and Governor George Wallace reached a fever pitch, with the governor pushing the university to remove Malone.

Several bombs exploded around the campus that fall. University administrator Jefferson Bennett drove to Montgomery to meet with Wallace, whom he suspected of encouraging the bombing. Wallace sneered at him, asking Bennett, "what he would do if 4 or 5 carloads of Alabama Highway Patrolmen attempted to remove Malone from [her dorm]." Shortly after, five National Guardsmen were arrested for setting the bombs.[5] Vivian Malone demonstrated great courage and persisted in her studies in the midst of an unfortunate display of the typical Southern bigotry of the day.

The Book Depository

Wallace's schoolhouse door stunt is what we would call today "performance politics." The symbolism of Wallace's act was part of a Southern governing system that included appeal to the worst instincts of the white mass public. In the typical performance, a "courageous politician" would stand up to the power of an evil and overbearing federal government. The federal monster stood accused of interfering with the right of white Southerners to operate a legally segregated system based on race.

Wallace laid the groundwork for his racist, grievance-riddled performance politics in his January 1963 inaugural speech. He called Alabama, with its 30% Black population, the "Very Heart of the Great Anglo-Saxon Southland," complained of "the tyranny that clanks its chains upon the South" and uttered the famous line, "segregation now . . . segregation tomorrow . . . segregation forever."

Performance politics are not only for show. Many times the performance led to anger and violence on the part of the audience. They can mobilize hate in the manner that Governors Ross Barnett and George Wallace did.

Behind the curtain of the performances Wallace was so adept at presenting was a thoroughly corrupt system in which businesses were allocated state contracts and grants of monopoly power to perform actions on behalf of the State. The State granted contracts and licenses based on political connections, campaign contributions, and outright bribes. In return, the system delivered low taxes and cheap labor to the Big Mules. The masses got symbolic morality plays about the Southern status system; the oligarchs got state contracts and conservative economic policies.

After my freshman year, I needed a summer job. After looking over the possibilities in the *Tuscaloosa News* help wanted ads, I applied for a position as a traveling salesman, selling pots and pans. The company sent me to Birmingham for training.

All sales were through commission; the pots were expensive and sold on an installment plan. The trick was to demonstrate the fantastic quality of the pans (taught to us in the training session). Clearly the stuff was overpriced, but we were supposed to overcome the resistance by adding a free set of dinnerware.

What a racket. They handed us a page of out-of-date "leads" from our region of the state, and a sample kit, and off we went. We built other leads from the friends and acquaintances of those young women we contacted. Mostly I contacted working women who lived in the country, often with their mothers looking on with disapproval. After a couple of sales, I felt worse, not better. Something about saddling working women with overpriced merchandise with an installment arrangement. I turned in my sample case and went back to the help wanted ads.

One of my friends worked in the Alabama Book Depository in Northport, just on the other side of the Black Warrior River from Tuscaloosa. A resignation there opened up a slot, and he recommended me for it. A Tuscaloosa businessman named Paul Malone owned Malone's Bookstore, which sold university textbooks. Malone obtained a state contract to supply books on a state-approved list to school districts throughout the state. The process for getting and holding the contract for supplying all the textbooks in the state was political and corrupt, as I would find out soon enough.

The work involved pulling books from the shelves in the unairconditioned warehouse, loading them on large pallets, and bringing them down near the loading dock. Packers packed and labeled the books, and loaded them on trucks for shipping. The pay was good, and I got to know the crew well. Often we'd go out for beers after work. Soon I was "promoted" from the heavy work of book puller to the much easier job of "head packer." Even better, I was set with a summer job for the rest of my college career, because the first offers each summer went to the previous workers.

Corruption in Alabama had been endemic long before George Wallace took office. As Wallace biographer Dan Carter noted, "Alabama state government had a long tradition of financial kickbacks and outright corruption between contractors and political leaders."[6] Malone admitted that he had "played politics" to get his original contract in 1956; he was aided by Senator E.W. Skidmore, my uncle Mac's law partner. There was no evidence that Skidmore benefited from the connections.

Malone got very favorable terms on his contract and no-bid extensions of it, leading to enormous profits. When the arrangement was disclosed a fight over the contract ensued.[7] When the Wallace administration assumed control of state government, the Board canceled Malone's contract and awarded a close Wallace ally a no-bid five-year contract, but a Tuscaloosa judge enjoined the action.[8] In the end Malone lost his contract, transferring ownership to Wallace's friend, and was prosecuted. The outcome for me amid the corruption and political gaming was that I lost my "plum" summer job.

Wallace ran on a "clean government" platform in 1962, but soon discovered the virtues of contractor kickbacks. He used the system masterfully to build a powerful statewide machine. The huge building program necessitated by his imaginative state trade school system was a great source of income for the machine, as all contractors were required to hire political operatives who did little work but were loyal to the governor. In the 1966 election, when Governor Wallace prevailed on his wife, Lurleen, to run because the state constitution prohibited consecutive terms, businessmen doing contract work with the State received "pledge cards" from the state's purchasing agent.[9]

The two Montgomery newspapers, *The Alabama Journal* and *The Montgomery Advertiser*, made public evidence of considerable corruption in the first Wallace administration, including the abuse of no-bid contracts. The state signed road asphalt contracts with Gerald Wallace, the governor's brother, whose shakedown program was well known to Montgomery insiders. Reporter Bob Ingram commented, "There's a double standard in Alabama politics. George Wallace can do things and things can happen in his administration which would destroy any other public official. . . . For some reason the people just say, 'Well, George didn't know anything about it.'"[10.]

Wallace was a charismatic orator who attracted adoring supporters through his message of racial resentment. His strong defense of segregation drove home the possibility of state action against the supposedly unconstitutional interference by the Federal Government in the "out Southern way of life," which of course included racial segregation. The "fighting little judge" could be excused by his enthusiastic followers for building a corrupt machine, especially a machine that was built, in the minds of his supporters, to forward racial division.

Speaking Out

It can be difficult to speak out on sensitive issues such as racial change; but things left unsaid can fester. On the other hand, tone can matter—sometimes honey does work better than vinegar.

At home watching the news from Birmingham in spring 1963, my mother, my Aunt Mary Elizabeth, and I were all appalled at Bull Connor's fire hoses and police dogs breaking up the children's march. Still like so many racial moderates, Mother asked rhetorically, "Why does he (Martin Luther King) have to have it all now? Why can't he go slower?" My aunt, more liberal than Mother, nevertheless agreed. I blurted out, "I think he's doing great things for America." Neither one of them spoke to me the rest of the evening. I probably could have handled that in a more sophisticated manner.

A few of my fraternity brothers were in the same accounting class as Vivian Malone in the fall 1963. They came back complaining about having to attend class with her—I guess I was unsure why, since they were not known as avid class attenders. Their tone changed when they realized she was the most conscientious student in the class, and as the midterm approached, the refrain from the late sleepers was, "She always goes to class. Let's see if we can get her notes." I did enjoy needling them about their inconsistencies.

When I was a freshman, it became apparent that one of the upperclassmen, Bob Hughes, was, to put it mildly, a vocal racist. He continually ridiculed the Black staff, with particular derision for the kitchen manager, Perry. Hughes not infrequently mocked Blacks more generally. Sometimes his younger brother, Marion, joined in. Although I would attempt to reassure the Black staff, and I let my close friends know how disturbing I found Bob, as a freshman I did not confront him, which I regret.

The next year his brother decided to run for chapter president. This time I hit the roof, letting all who would listen that I would not support his candidacy. I went to his room completely steaming and told him in no uncertain terms that I would not support him and would leave the fraternity if he were elected. Marion's response was neither defensive nor evasive. He condemned his brother, admitted his role, and promised that would not happen again. He had not engaged in racist behavior since his brother had graduated, so I gave him the benefit of the doubt. I never heard him engage in racist dialogue, and he went out of his way to treat the staff with respect.

I was not driven to confront Marion because of any thoughtful strategy; I was simply angry. Nevertheless such a strategy exists. In a system in which white supremacy ruled the day, simple acts of calling out incidences of racist behavior may help to contain the infection; many acts of confrontation in the face of obvious injustice, even small ones, can aid in healing even the most severe wound.

As I look back, I feel no remorse for condemning the perceived injustices that I observed, even where I was wrong or overemphasized the injustice. But I do regret those moments when I remained silent (Figure 23.1).

Although I left Alabama with the conviction that racism was on the decline, that was nothing more than a pipe dream. Many years later, I attended a conference at Virginia Tech, in the hills of southwestern Virginia. After a session a few of us, including Larry Terry, who was Black, went over to the Blacksburg town center to a tavern. I went up to the bar to get a round of beers, but the bartender nodded toward Larry, saying "You can't have *him* in here."

At first I had no idea what he was talking about. When I realized what had just happened, I, well, exploded. "It's been twenty years since the Civil Rights Act was passed, and what you are doing is illegal," I almost shouted. The bartender leaned over the counter in a threatening manner and demanded that we get out. I responded, "Absolutely not; call the cops if you want," but Larry came over and pulled me away. Turned out to be easy to find a nondiscriminatory tavern in a university town.

The Schism in the Machine

University of Alabama student politics are even today alleged to be controlled by a secret society termed "the Machine." It has apparently existed since 1914 and consists primarily of fraternity and sorority representatives, and has served as a system for preparing students for higher political office.[11] In the 1960s, the Machine had become more inclusive, including large and small fraternities and sororities, but as one might expect the participation was left to the guys. Smaller fraternities and independents were becoming more successful at getting elected to student government and chosen to lead other organizations, especially those generally based on merit. More women were choosing to become involved as well, which was causing some headaches among the prestigious fraternity leaders.

Figure 23.1 College at the University of Alabama. At the time this photograph was taken, under ten Black students attended the University of Alabama.
Source: Author's collection.

I served as a representative to the meetings of the Machine. Basically it con-sisted of a meeting in some fraternity's basement once a year. I recall these as mostly being "who are we going to endorse for SGA president" discussions. Usually there was one candidate who was clearly qualified and got the nomina-tion; for example he or she had served as SGA vice president, or associate editor of the yearbook or student newspaper. So the trick was to get your candidate on the "ladder" to success early and let them work themselves up.

In 1964 the Machine experienced a major schism. The organization could not come to a consensus on whom to nominate for SGA president. Jewish fraternities and sororities and most of the smaller fraternities supported Don Siegal, who would be the first Jewish student body president at the university. I do not recall the second candidate, but he was supported by the prestigious fraternities and their allies.

Hence the schism. Supporters of Siegal, including me, developed an "expand the electorate" strategy. I worked with debate star Boots Gale, Jack Drake, and others from the dorms and small fraternities to organize networks of independents who did not normally vote in campus elections, tied up as they were with more important matters. We organized similarly among the less prestigious fraternities. Antisemitism played an unspoken part in the schism, but I remember more clearly wanting to defeat the pompous, classically Southern frats like the Kappa Alphas, with their "Old South" party in which members dressed up in Confederate garb and their dates wore hoop skirts.

At the time, the most discussed theory of political parties in the Political Science Department was that of V.O. Key, who argued that a two-party system would increase participation as the party organizations strove to integrate new voters into the system. We were mimicking Key's ideal two-party system, and we underdogs won. Siegal served as 55th SGA president.

I hoped that the two-faction system would become the new model rather than the oligarchical Machine. Unfortunately the system failed as a major fraternity defaulted from our side, and the campus oligarchy based on disinterest restored itself.

Tuscaloosa 1964

Ed Walters, my high school friend, entered the University of Alabama after a reasonably successful year at another college, and our paths crossed again. We continued our quirky rebellion against the "uptight" establishment. We cheered as the cocky Cassius Clay beat Sonny Liston to win the Heavyweight Boxing Championship in February. Many white Americans had a deep distaste for the boasting, taunting Clay, thinking of Liston as a more acceptable Black man, but of course that is exactly why we cheered Clay (later Muhammad Ali) on.

We watched the Republican Convention in the summer of that year, rooting for the insurgent Goldwater as he overthrew the moderate Eastern wing of the Republican Party. We weren't Republicans or Democrats, but we were antiestablishment.

On July 2, 1964, President Lyndon Johnson signed into law the Civil Rights Act, a key priority of President Kennedy before he was assassinated the previous fall. The law prohibited racial discrimination by private businesses. Because of its dramatic and virtually instantaneous ending of the system of segregation, and because it interfered with the "right" of business owners to discriminate in their own businesses, it was a very difficult vote for Southern congressmen. Only six of the 105 congressmen from the old Confederacy voted for the act.

One was Jake Pickle from Texas, who held the Austin area district that Lyndon Johnson held before he was elected to the Senate in 1948.[12]

The resistance to the legislation in the Deep South was strong and immediate—especially among the owners of lunch counters and cafes catering to working-class and rural whites. Lester Maddox, owner of the Pickrick Café in Atlanta passed out axe handles to his customers to stop Blacks from entering. He rode his subsequent fame to victory in his 1966 run for governor of Georgia.

Tuscaloosa was already on edge in June of 1964 after the police had beaten, gassed, and arrested a group of Black marchers as they started out from the First African Baptist Church to protest the white-only drinking fountains at the new Tuscaloosa Court House. Reverend T.Y. Rogers had been leading a series of marches to protest segregation at the courthouse. The Tuscaloosa police chief William Marable, determined to stop the permit-less marches, confronted Rogers and a group of marchers that day. Marable had deputized a large group of white men, mostly from the Klan. Both the police and the Klan attacked the marchers. Thugs and cops injured 33 marchers badly enough that they were hospitalized, and the police arrested another 94 individuals. In many ways, this violence was worse than Selma. The event deservedly became known as "Bloody Tuesday."[13]

In the period before "Bloody Sunday," I went downtown to observe one of Reverend Rogers's marches. I stood with downtown shoppers, mostly Black, on the sidewalk watching the marchers as they walked down Greensboro Avenue. The local police walked alongside the marchers, hurrying them along and keeping a watchful eye for any trouble. A young boy, no older than 11 or 12 and tired and thirsty from the hot Alabama sun had fallen a few yards behind the main group of marchers. Using his baton, one of Tuscaloosa's finest pushed the child to the ground. The boy scrambled to his feet and hurried to join the other marchers. Such a gratuitous degrading of the innocent was the action of an armed bully. I should have spoken out.

The week following the signing of the Civil Rights Act on July 2nd of 1964, all hell broke loose. The Klan resurged, and in Tuscaloosa set up picket lines in front of theaters and lunch counters that were at risk of integration. Black citizens entered cafeterias and the movie theaters without major difficulties, but the situation quickly deteriorated as the Klan reacted. Robert Shelton, imperial wizard of the United Klans of America, lived in Tuscaloosa, so for him integration there was "ground zero."

City elites urged citizens to follow the law and Buford Boone warned of mob violence in the *Tuscaloosa News*. Boone taunted the Klan as a group of weaklings. A university professor, James Jaquith, his wife, and several University of Alabama students crossed the Klan picket line at the Capri Theater, finding their car tires slashed on leaving. Klan members rode around in cars intimidating Blacks and any whites that defied the picket lines. On July 8, a group of Black students integrated the Druid Theater on University Avenue, only to be attacked by a Klan-led group of hostile whites when they left. They escaped safely, apparently due to the intervention of an armed Black defense group.[14] On July 9, a Klan-led mob trapped actor Jack Palance and his family, in town to visit relatives, in the Druid Theater. The actor and his family were led out the back door and down an alleyway to safety. Tuscaloosa police dispersed the mob with fire hoses and tear gas.[15] I walked over to the site of the incident later that night, out of curiosity, and left with eyes burning from the canisters of teargas.

The university administration advised students to avoid provoking the Klan, which in effect meant they should stay away from the targeted Tuscaloosa businesses.[16] Things settled down, but generally whites stayed away from the movie theaters. Only a few brave Black Tuscaloosans, previously relegated to the balconies of movie theaters there and all over the South, went to sit in on the main floor—for the first time.

In mid-July, after a couple of beers Ed and I decided to attend a movie at the Bama Theater on Greensboro Avenue, because "no damn Klan guys are going to keep us from going to see a movie." At the theater a small number of sign-carrying men from the local Klan chapter stood in front—signs warning potential patrons that Blacks were in the theater. One leaned over to us and informed us "there's niggers in there." I replied that we didn't care, we wanted to see the movie, which was a particularly poor excuse for a film.

Inside there were only a few patrons, all Black and all seated on the main floor, watching the movie. As the only white patrons that night, we felt self-satisfied at our defiance of the Klan, and left the theater, again crossing the Klan's picket line, and receiving dirty looks and threatening mutters from the pickets. We were less pleased when a car parked in front of the theater followed us home and remained out front of our house for a while. For weeks after, we got phone calls with only breathing in response to our 'Hello'—clearly the Klan.

I wish I could say that we integrated the Bama for moral reasons, or because we empathized with the abused Black citizens, and I wish I could say that we did the same at other businesses throughout the summer, but I cannot. While both of us were pro-integration and sympathetic to the plight of Blacks, we entered the Bama because of the opportunity to defy the Klan and assert our right to attend a movie. It felt like part of our defiance of Southern norms that we had pursued since high school.

Ed and I drifted apart during the next couple of years, with our paths crossing only sporadically. The last time I saw Ed was at the University Student Union café known as the "Supe" Store, where we sat down for a cup of coffee. As we drank our coffee, he told me that he was planning to apply to study theater at Yale on what he called a "Take a Chance" program. I commented that I thought such programs were for disadvantaged minorities. He was undeterred and said whatever happened he planned to pursue his dream of becoming a playwright.

Although we lost touch after college, he apparently followed his dream, landing in New York City to pursue his craft. Sadly, he judged himself a failure at it, and, deeply depressed, he ended his life by leaping into Grand Canyon, leaving a suicide note.[17]

The Democratic Convention

In mid-August 1964, three friends and I decided to take a road trip to New York before classes began. The itinerary included New York City and Atlantic City, designed around the Democratic National Convention to satisfy the political scientist in me. Somehow, we managed to secure scruffy, inconveniently located hotel rooms in both places. In New York we did all the touristy stuff: Central Park, Statue of Liberty, Empire State Building, Museum of Natural History, Carnegie Delicatessen, a Yankee baseball game, the Bowery (I had seen too many Bowery Boys movies at the Enzor Theater), and getting tossed out of an Irish bar.

We left New York City and headed down to Atlantic City for the Democratic National Convention. Although Lyndon Johnson's nomination was assured, the Mississippi Freedom Democratic Party challenged the Mississippi delegation on the grounds of the state Democratic Party's denial of due process to Black citizens. Fanny Hammer gave riveting televised testimony to the Credentials Committee about the hostility of Mississippi political leaders to the Freedom Summer activities directed at getting Blacks registered to vote. Four civil rights workers were murdered, Fannie Hammer was beaten in jail, and numerous Black businesses and churches were bombed.

We arrived at our run-down hotel, wandered the Boardwalk, and headed down to the Convention Center to see if we could join the action on the floor after Lyndon Johnson was nominated. The staff informed us that we could get in the Center only after the nomination and then only if we had passes from our delegation.

In 1964 the Alabama States' Rights faction had swept the delegate slate for the National Convention. For the first time no Loyalists, those pledged to support the national ticket, could participate. The Alabama Delegation members were meeting at their hotel to discuss whether to walk out of the convention because of the compromise devised by the Credentials Committee. The compromise would recognize one nonvoting delegate from the Mississippi Freedom Democrats, a plan that satisfied neither the regulars nor the Freedom Democrats. The all-white Mississippi delegation had already walked out. The Alabama delegation split, with most voting to leave the convention.

Fortuitously we arrived at the hotel as the meeting adjourned. As the delegates poured out of the room, we asked what had happened, and a couple of them said, "We're leaving!" I asked about tickets for entering the Convention Center as guests, and one said, "We can do better than that. Take our credentials; we don't need them."

We showed up at an open door to the Convention Hall—things were so much more casual back then—and presented our credentials to the guards. It took them only a glance, and one of them responded, "This is not you" and they confiscated our passes. Oh, how much I wish I had kept those treasures! What a prop to use in teaching political science!

We were not ready to leave. We hung around the doorway, watching the voting proceed until Johnson had the nomination and the celebration broke out. Crowds of delegates marched around the convention floor, joined by spectators from the galleries. We were able to slip past the distracted guards into the celebrating crowd, minus, of course, most of the Alabama delegation.

The Corolla Incident

In 1963–1964, as a sophomore, I served as an associate editor of the Alabama yearbook, the *Corolla*. The university had just integrated, and part of my duties was to ensure that the photographic department at the university got the photographs done on time and that the pictures of students were in the right order for the engraving and printing of the volume. We sent the pictures to Alabama Engraving in Birmingham, run by a man named Robert Faerber, who forwarded the engraved plates to Paragon Press in Montgomery for printing and binding.

The job was a large one for Faerber, and he worked to keep the goodwill of the *Corolla*'s staff. He had a tradition of inviting the editor and the associate editors to dinner at one of Tuscaloosa's best restaurants. He knew that it was highly likely that next year's editor would be one of this year's associates. Faerber wanted to stay on good terms with the editorial staff; good reviews would help him maintain a lucrative contract. As associate editor, I attended with editor Kathie Simon and the other two associate editors, Janice Rogers and Virginia McCahan.

Things went along smoothly at first, but after a couple of martinis Faerrber came forth with an appalling stream of racist comments. Janice, Virginia, and I tried hard to turn the conversation toward the *Corolla*, his engraving business, how the connection between engraving and printing worked, anything, but the more Faerber drank, the more he drifted back into racist language.

As we put together the yearbook, we gladly accepted volunteer workers from sororities, fraternities, and the dormitories to do the exacting layout work of matching names and biographies with the photographs. I was disappointed that Vivian Malone had not had her picture taken for the yearbook. But as I supervised the layouts, I saw a Black student who I presumed had entered in the second term.

I remembered his name when the proofs came back from the printer in Montgomery. I proudly showed our interns the student . . . but a white face looked back at us from the yearbook proofs. I was furious, knowing full well that the picture had to have been pulled at the engravers, as the block of pictures were locked down at the engravers before being sent to the printer. The picture had to have been pulled by Faerber. Or so I thought.

I was appointed editor for the coming year. All summer I fumed over Faerber's sin. I tried to direct my anger toward productive problem-solving, with little success. As the fall term began, I finally developed a strategy. When Faerber contacted me about the customary dinner, I met with the associate editors and told them I'd be meeting Faerber alone.

At dinner, Faerber asked me why the associates had not joined us, and I responded that they had other obligations. After we sat down for dinner and had engaged in some small talk, I informed Faerber about the missing Black student picture. I didn't blame him but told him in a no-nonsense tone for a college kid talking to a middle-aged businessman that "one of his shop workers" had likely pulled the picture.

Faerber looked increasingly anxious. Then I overplayed my hand, saying that if it happened again, I would bring the issue up with the University's Publication Board and try to get his contract revoked. I was a member of the Publication Board, but it was highly doubtful I could have got his contract canceled. There was no doubt that I could have caused trouble, and I was enough of a hothead to follow through. Faerber quickly responded that he would make sure that would not happen again.

Years later as I reconstructed the event, I cannot confirm that there was a Black student at the university other than Vivian at the time. It is possible that my misinterpretation led to my anger and caused me to put together a plan to make sure that Black students would participate in the process. On the other hand, Faerber was a vocal racist, and I never regretted speaking out even if I was wrong on the facts.

During the threatening environment on campus in the fall of 1963, University President Frank Rose had confronted the campus police because he did not trust them to carry out their security duties when these duties involved race.[18] That problem characterized much of the white university staff. In working with photographic services, I had heard comments from the photographers expressing distress at the integration of the university. I feared that hostility on the part of the university's photographic staff could deter the handful of Black students on campus from having their photographs taken. I convened a meeting of the head of photographic services and our associate editors, picture editors, and Mac Cowden, our copy editor. I put the onus on the photographic services director to keep his staff honest, which he promised to do. I told him that should I hear that any photographers had engaged in discrimination or hostility, I would contact him again and recommend action at the Board of Publications. I had little trust in the photographic services, so I sent along Mac to accompany the photographers to the dorm sessions. Similarly, one of our female staff members took on the duty to make sure that Black women were encouraged to participate in the yearbook's photographic efforts.

Six Black students, most of those who had started school in the autumn of 1964, appeared in the book, one of whom was Vivian Malone.[19] It is a sad footnote that the 1965 *Corolla* was the first Alabama Yearbook to include photographs of Black students. I believe these were all who attended at the time. Two of these students, Patricia Marcus and Josephine

Powell, had integrated West End High School in Birmingham, where they had endured racial epithets and threats of violence. Patricia was particularly active on campus. She graduated in 1968, the first Black student from the College of Arts and Sciences. Vivian graduated from the Business School.

Goldwater and the Changing Deep South

In September 1964, Republican Presidential Nominee Barry Goldwater headed south for a tour of the former Confederate states. Political reporter Richard Rovere followed the action, seeing it clearly for what it was.

> By coming South, Barry Goldwater had made it possible for great numbers of unapologetic white supremacists to hold great carnivals of white supremacy . . . the Goldwater movement, whether or not it can command a majority, remains an enormous one in the South and appears to be a racist movement and almost nothing else. On his tour, Goldwater seemed fully aware of this and not visibly distressed by it.[20]

Goldwater was a master of the code word. It quickly became clear that he was a reckless foreign policy hawk and was not above making a thinly veiled appeal to white supremacy. I ran into my friend Ed on the Quad, and we had come to the same conclusion: we could not support him. As if that mattered. We were not old enough to vote as the voting age was 21 at the time.

Every four years, the university held a mock presidential election, which the students took very seriously. That was especially true in fall 1964. The Young Democrats and Young Republicans organized rallies, put signs all over the Quadrangle, while fraternities, sororities, and dorm groups urged participation. A sizable portion of the student body voted. Goldwater won, with two-thirds of the student vote. Given the tenor of the state and university, this outcome was not surprising, but it was clearly a harbinger of what was to come.

Earlier in May, voters in the Alabama Democratic Primary had selected a slate of unpledged electors promoted by Wallace over a Loyalist slate supported by both Alabama senators, Lister Hill and John Sparkman. The Wallace slate easily carried the state, including most of the North Alabama counties, previously a stronghold of Loyalist Democrats. It was clear that Wallace was building a single Alabama political mind centering on race and resentment.[21]

In the 1964 general election Alabama voters were forced to choose between Goldwater and the unpledged slate. The Democratic Party "nominee" was a set of electors who refused to commit to the sitting president, Lyndon Johnson, or any other individual. Even though the unpledged elector scheme had been devised by Wallace, he announced his support for Goldwater, who won the state easily.

State sectionalism emerged nevertheless, but in a bizarre manner. The Tennessee Valley counties voted against Goldwater, likely because of his threat to privatize the Tennessee Valley Authority. The traditionally Republican-leaning mountain counties voted for Goldwater, but at lower rates than the Black Belt counties, where Blacks generally could not vote. Goldwater had appeal throughout the state, but his appeal was greatest where white racism was strongest.

Judgment at Selma

As our deadlines to get the yearbook to the engraver and printer approached, our work schedule intensified. During the period, I spent many late evenings assembling, checking, and double-checking as we prepared the material headed off to Paragon Press. On Sunday night, March 7, I had gone to the *Corolla* offices to continue the task, but didn't stay late. I walked back to the fraternity house, and saw several guys watching a movie on television. I asked them what it was, "Judgment at Nuremberg," answered one. I sat down to watch.

We were blissfully unaware of the happenings in Selma, just 75 miles to the South, earlier that day, "Bloody Sunday." Instead of a gripping trial centering on the failure of the Allies to hold the "minor" Nazis accountable, the television program switched to show an Alabama Highway Patrol calvary unit, sent by the Alabama Director of Public Safety, attacking defenseless civil rights protestors. I was deeply shaken, as were the other movie watchers.

The national uproar that ensued led to the Selma to Montgomery march and King's famous "How Long? Not Long" speech. It gave President Johnson the opportunity to introduce the Voting Rights Act in a speech to both houses of Congress.

Johnson understood that Southern states achieved Black disenfranchisement by requiring potential voters to perform some act that would be more difficult for Black voters—such as pass a literacy test or fulfill a "good character" clause as defined by the registrar. Johnson made sure that the Act prohibited such measures, stating, "For the fact is that the only way to pass these barriers is to show a white skin." The answer was to remove the discretion of local officials to discriminate through legal procedures. The brilliance of the 1965 system was to empower the Federal Government to block the implementation of state and local laws and administrative actions in states where discrimination had been widespread—primarily the former Confederate states. Congress passed and Johnson signed the Act on my 21st birthday—on the date I could first vote.

The Voting Rights Act of 1965 was an easier vote for Southern congressmen than the Civil Rights Act of 1964—23 congressmen from the old Confederacy voted for it. Even the Deep South broke on the issue—two congressmen from Georgia and two from Louisiana voted for the act, while Florida, Tennessee, and Texas generated 18 of the 23 pro votes. All Alabama congressmen and both senators voted no, unsurprisingly.

In March 1966, I walked over to Foster Auditorium, where Wallace had staged his "stand in the schoolhouse door" less than three years before. Robert Kennedy was in town for a symposium titled "The Student Role in a Democratic Society." George Wallace had been the keynote speaker the day before, which I skipped.

The auditorium was filled with RFK enthusiasts, including me. When Kennedy said that "Negroes must be as free as other Americans . . . not because it is economically advantageous, not because the law says so, but because it is right," we cheered lustily.[22] As he left the auditorium, students reached out to grasp his hand; I did so as well. It really felt like a chapter was closing in Alabama, with the state joining the nation in unity.

Boy, was I wrong.

Thinking through Segregation

I spent many hours pondering the issues raised by Southern segregation and voting suppression. Making trade-offs between values is one of those things that comes late in the development of the prefrontal cortex.[23] I kept thinking about the trade-offs presented by the Civil Rights Act of 1964 and the Voting Rights Act of 1965. The segregationists kept up the states' rights argument and the private property claim—why could not a property owner keep Blacks out of his restaurant or lunch counter or hardware store if he wanted to? Was not that the American way?

It's not that I had any sympathy with segregation. I had in my high school years rejected the idea that segregation made any sense—it obviously did not. It was nothing more—but nothing less—than a system to ensure the superior status of whites.

I found it easy to grasp that state government had no business excluding Blacks from universities, nor setting up separate water fountains or bathrooms, nor segregating schools. In these cases, public property is the main issue. The strategies used by segregationists to prevent Blacks from voting were obviously unjustifiable. I was less sure about prohibiting segregation in the case of private property.

Segregationists made it easy for me to grapple with this issue by the truly terrible arguments they made. I don't think that today there is much appreciation of the arguments made by whites about why Blacks should not be allowed to vote. Atticus Finch in Harper Lee's *Go Set a Watchman* tells Scout, "Negroes down here are still in their childhood, as a people. They've made terrific progress in adapting themselves to white ways, but they are far from it yet . . . can you blame the South for resenting being told what to do about its own people by people who have no idea of its daily problems?"[24] These were the ridiculous and unsubstantiated claims of the segregationists, but they were common. When these arguments failed, the segregationists retreated to "protecting our Southern way of life," which meant "I really don't have a reason for denying Blacks the rights and responsibilities of citizenship."

The power of the segregationist culture was evident when students returned to the university after a summer at home. Patricia Marcus, one of the Black students enrolled in 1964, commented to a reporter that racial hostility was worse in the fall, "after white students have come back to school from segregationist homes."[25]

In the end, for me, it was voting. Denying the right to vote was a central injustice of segregation and white supremacy. Even if the private property claim was valid, why deny Blacks the right to vote? How could Blacks influence political outcomes without the power of the vote? Could not they use the vote to improve their schools the way whites had? In the end for me the whole system of white supremacy broke upon the shoals of vote denial.

Jerry Franks, one of the handful of fraternity brothers who shared my political values, and I sometimes sat on the steps of the fraternity house talking politics. One evening after a lengthy discussion, he finally said, "And I thought I was liberal!" I don't think I was a liberal except on voting rights and Jim Crow because I saw these as moral issues. I began to see that the whole set of issues were interconnected, and that interconnectedness caused the whole states' rights, Southern way of life, and private property arguments to fall apart because the whole system was set up on the foundation of undemocratic vote denial.

I had stopped going to church because, well, it was boring and irrelevant to the critical issues of the day, but Mother asked me to go again. I did, but the "sermon" involved building an annex to the Sunday school building. The civil rights activity led by Reverend T.Y. Rogers was going on at the time. Here we were enmeshed in the most important human rights issue facing Tuscaloosa, Alabama, and the nation, and the congregation was debating expansion.

It was true that white churches had isolated themselves from the most important moral issues of the region and indeed the nation. In his *Letter from a Birmingham Jail*, Martin Luther King indicted churches for staying on the sidelines mouthing "pious irrelevances and sanctimonious trivialities." Actually, I never heard such "sanctimonious trivialities," but only silence. Maybe a Methodist Church taking a stand on civil rights would have kept me there. As I well knew, the deep segregation in Southern churches made that impossible, so I took the easy route out. Plus it allowed me to sleep in on Sunday mornings.

Carl Elliott and Lurleen Wallace

In spring 1966, things in Alabama seemed to me to be improving, and rapidly. The university had integrated and students appeared to be accepting their Black colleagues, if sometimes resentfully. Goldwater had carried Alabama and four other states of the deepest South, but his racist Southern strategy coupled with a hawkish foreign policy caused him to lose overwhelmingly. Tuscaloosa had weathered the worst of the collapse of Jim Crow after the passage of the Civil Rights Act in 1964, and the Voting Rights Act in 1965, and had emerged shaken and changed, but only after Blacks had suffered state-sanctioned violence on "Bloody Tuesday." Many Alabama counties complied quickly with the requirements of the Voting Rights Act, and more did so with

some serious pressure from federal attorneys. Deputized federal voting registrars were deployed rapidly to the recalcitrant counties, mostly in the Black
Belt.

George Wallace had a popular first two years in the governor's office, spewing racial resentment and preaching white supremacy, and building a machine
through corrupt state contracting. The legislature generally passed whatever
he requested. He promoted some liberal policies, but proved to be more pro-
business than his earlier years as a Folsom supporter would have suggested.
His stand in the schoolhouse door at Foster Auditorium was highly popular,
even outside the South. The images of his state troopers attacking unarmed
and nonthreatening voting rights marchers at Selma undercut his claims of
pursuing constitutional government.

Alabama's constitution prohibited the governor from serving two successive
terms. Wallace was determined to get that provision out of the constitution.
He planned a 1968 presidential run, and wanted to use the office to promote
himself. The succession amendment failed in the Senate, leading to vitriolic
attacks by Wallace and constituents on the senators who voted "no." The
attacks were so severe that one senator committed suicide. Wallace pushed his
wife, Lurleen, even though diagnosed with cancer, into the race as his surrogate. The "Fighting Judge" seemed weaker than he had since the start of his
term.

In addition to Lurleen Wallace, Alabama Democrats would have an array of
choices in the upcoming gubernatorial primary, from ex-governor John Patterson's strong segregationist but governmental reformist stance to Attorney
Richmond Flowers's direct appeal to Black voters. Folsom ran again, but clearly
was not going anywhere—his time had passed.

Two candidates occupied the space between Wallace and Flowers. Ryan
deGraffenried offered a pro-business stance and moderation on race. Finally
there was former congressman Carl Elliott, described by Wallace biographer
Dan Carter as "a man of unshakable rectitude, a 'moderate' on racial matters
and a colorblind pro-labor liberal on economic issues."[26]

I wanted to get involved. Perhaps Alabama had reached a turning point.
Maybe the entry of around 100,000 Black voters in Alabama would make possible new coalitions—perhaps a moderate politician could mobilize Blacks and
moderate whites from North Alabama in a cross-race coalition, reestablishing
the famed Populist coalition.

I had followed deGraffenried's trajectory since he lost to Wallace in 1962, and
he was an impressive man whose racial positions I found acceptable, but his

overly pro-business positions were problematic for me. Labor was weak in the state, but was a key lynchpin in a reconstructed Folsom Populist-style coalition. Although I was an economic moderate but racial liberal, in all honesty I wanted to support the candidate that had the best chance of beating Wallace. If that were deGraffenried, so be it.

Unfortunately in February of 1966 deGraffenried was killed in a crash of his small airplane on one of his campaign trips, eliminating the strongest contender. While I had sympathy for the uncompromising Richmond Flowers, who had personally prosecuted the Klan killers of Viola Liuzzo in Lowndes County, I did not think he could win.

I turned to Carl Elliott and his direct appeal to a coalition of newly enfranchised Black voters and moderate white voters. Elliott's appeal was explicitly to moderates on the race issue, and labor liberals on economics. I thought that pairing had a chance of winning. At first, things looked pretty good as deGraffenried's formal support went over to Elliott. Elliott also got unified support from organized labor, unusual for that famously fragmented movement.[27]

In his autobiography, Elliott told a story about the 1966 campaign that graphically illustrates the state's traditional sectional divide. He was campaigning in the south Alabama town of Greenville. "When my talk was done," he wrote, "I shook hands with the crowd, black and white alike." Then he went into the courthouse to thank the probate judge, who responded, "You have violated Southern tradition, shaking hands with those niggers." Elliott retorted, "Don't you tell me about Southern tradition, by God. I'm a mountain man and you're a Black Belt fellow, but I'm as much of a Southerner as you are." As Elliott left, the probate judge continued to scream at him about violating Southern tradition.[28]

I went down to Elliott's Tuscaloosa campaign headquarters and volunteered. I suggested some work on campus, but that was not where the votes were. Voting age was 21 back then, so most students could not vote. They asked me to serve as a speaker at the various community gatherings that organized "meet the candidate" (or the candidate's representative if he were not available) gatherings.

The Tuscaloosa campaign organization was seriously disorganized, and that was obvious at the time. Soon with no instructions I was off representing Elliott at a town hall at Duncanville in the southeastern part of Tuscaloosa County. There several representatives of the candidates made short presentations to a small but interested group of white men in overalls who were respectful and asked good questions.

I felt pretty good about it and found it was great fun. Then I heard nothing from campaign headquarters. After a while I called, but there seemed nothing but disarray. Finally the campaign manager called and asked me to speak at a Northport rally to take place in the Tuscaloosa County High Stadium. That was going from the minor league to the majors!

I showed up to what I expected would be a handful of hearty politics junkies. To my surprise, one side of the stadium was filled. I offered the Elliott line, starting with "My friends, Carl Elliott is a moderate." Wallace had poisoned the air with attacks on "liberals," so talking about Elliott's labor liberalism seemed unwise. I went on to promote higher teachers' salaries, improved roads, and a fair shake for Blacks. I got a smattering of unenthusiastic applause.

Then Lurleen Wallace's stand-in stepped up to the microphone, and presto! Pandemonium, hats waved in the air, cheers, hoots, rebel yells. After every line. I knew we were doomed. There were no moderates on race anymore. "Too late Elliott realized that Alabama had no 'moderate' white constituency for any but the most cosmetic adjustments to the collapsing system of white racial domination," as Wallace biographer Carter put it.[29] Combined with the Black vote going solidly for Flowers, Elliott came in third, with most of his votes coming from the mountain counties.

The election was notable in its high turnout. Lurleen won without a runoff, carrying all counties except the seven Black Belt counties won by Flowers. The 100,000 new Black voters were matched by even more new white voters.[30] Political scientists have noticed for some time that high turnout does not consistently advantage one party over the other.[31] Certainly the 1966 election followed that pattern, with a strong white reaction endorsing racial divisions in response to the addition of the new Black voters.

I was downcast after Wallace's complete victory in 1966. I fretted at the time that Alabama and the Deep South could not be salvaged from the tragedy of white supremacist politics. Whites always seemed subject to the siren song of race politics.

The End of State Sectionalism

In the 1950s, it seemed possible for Southern Progressives like Alabama Senators Lister Hill and John Sparkman and congressmen like Carl Elliott of the North Alabama hills and Bob Jones from the Tennessee Valley to weather the white resentment generated by *Brown v. Board*. It might have taken some accommodation to segregation, but over time, these men thought that they were on the right side of history. After all, Jim Folsom served as governor from 1947 to 1951, and had been reelected overwhelmingly in 1955–1959, without the need for the typical Southern Democratic primary run-off.

The dream of Alabama moderates was a reconstruction of the old interracial coalition of the Progressive era. It was Elliott's explicit dream, and I fell for it. It was no longer possible. Political developments in the 1950s and 1960s and the demagoguery of George Wallace and his masterful use of resentment politics made the old farmer-labor-liberal coalition impossible.

In his infamous uncompromisingly white supremacist inaugural speech of 1963, Wallace started by thanking those folks of his home county, the south Alabama county of Barbour, and ticking off a list of towns and villages there. Then he said,

> And I shall forever remember that election day morning as I waited. Suddenly at ten o'clock that morning the first return was flashed around the state and carried the message: Wallace 15; Opposition, zero. The result came from the Hamrick Beat at Putnam's Mountain where lived the great hill people of the state. May God bless the mountain man . . . his loyalty is unshakable; he'll do to walk down the road with.

Mountain men walking with Wallace would have been unthinkable a generation before. They walked with Folsom. Wallace had successfully unified the white voter in Alabama around white supremacy and Southern resentment, undermining Folsom's politics of economics. The South was changing. White supremacy was increasingly popular in the places where it had been least important: the mountains of Appalachia. And Wallace, more than any single person, had forged that Solid [white] South.

Wallace in 1962 and Goldwater in 1964 were part of the same conservatism sweeping the South—a conservatism more rooted in racial identities than economic issues. Old-style sectionalism in the South was dying, to be replaced by a modern style. As Blacks gained the vote, Black Belt counties increasingly voted Democratic whereas Appalachia became the bedrock of Republican support.

In my first paper in graduate school, I traced county voting patterns from the election returns in 1966 and found only a faint trace of the old sectionalism embedded in Alabama since before the Civil War. The two minds of the Deep South were merging into one.

Demagogues

Some politicians, religious figures, and leaders of broad social movements form bonds with large swaths of the public in a manner unfathomable to most of us. Sometimes the bonds form around positive sentiments, but many times they are based in resentment.

Two Alabama leaders, Jim Folsom and George Wallace, forged those bonds with the Alabama's mass public in the 1950s and 1960s. Folsom unified public sentiment around class-based appeals, attacking the industrialists and bankers, but painting a positive future for the common folk. Folsom's policies centered on making the common man and woman better off. The working man and small yeoman farmer were being exploited by the rich industrialists and planters, but Folsom promised to make life better for each person, whether white or Black. Bringing down rich people was less a part of the Folsom message than elevating poor folks. Folsom's message was class politics at its best.

Wallace's power "sprang from the governor's passionate support, support rooted in the elemental hatreds and longtime grievances of white voters."[32] Wallace's message always included strong doses of resentment, emphasizing the erroneous but common racist claim that Blacks were often shiftless and no-good, but treated better than whites. Included in Wallace's message was a claim that he was not a racist, but he was a segregationist, because Blacks were just not ready for the responsibilities of citizenship and economic management. Status politics required using resentments to reinforce the sense of entitlement held by whites, and resentment toward Blacks had always been the major lever used by Southern conservative politicians.

In spring 1966, I went over to a Klan "rally" at the Tuscaloosa County Fair Grounds, complete with amusement rides, booths selling home-made pies, and small children running around in white robes and the conic hats characteristic of the Klan uniform. I mused that the cleaned-up Klan on display there signified the end of its power. Organizationally that was true; the Klan of Bobby Shelton was headed for the ash heap of American history. I overlooked the success that George Wallace was having in his program to gain power by incorporating the political ideas of what we would call today "white nationalism" into the mainstream of American politics.

Economist Albert O. Hirschman published a book in 1970 that summarizes a classic dilemma we all face. In the face of deteriorating quality of an organization, or a service, or a location, a person faces the three options captured by the book title: exit, voice, or loyalty.[33] The harsh backlash against what I saw as progress made me certain that exit from Alabama was my only choice. I joined the many Deep Southern expatriates for whom the stultifying white supremacist social structure seemingly would not change, and where the limited intellectual climate could not thrive.

CHAPTER 24

Looking Back to See Forward

You cannot see something that never changes. The background becomes everything. Even minor blips in the background are ignored as artificial and it seems that nothing important has changed. Seldom do we notice injustices when they have become incorporated into the social structure reinforced by supporting narratives and myths.

We notice injustices during periods when there are major shifts in the landscape on which lives are played out. These critical junctures jumble the social system, changing the basic structure of government, the economy, and peoples' daily lives.

I've followed the traces of my ancestors through four critical junctures in Southern history—Indian removal; the Civil War and Reconstruction; the Populist Rebellion; and the Civil Rights movement. Between each of these critical junctures were periods of relative stability in the sociopolitical structures—the background. These periods of stability, however, often incorporated mechanisms that empowered resistance even to gradual change—as Southern white moderates discovered when they tried to nudge the South forward on desegregation in the 1950s. Such resistance made the coming critical juncture much more destabilizing than otherwise would have been the case, simply because the proponents of change had to push much harder to achieve that change.

I was fortunate enough to have a front row seat to the end of segregation de jure and I learned from it. I intuitively grasped what *Tuscaloosa News* editor Buford Boone meant when he wrote, "Gradual change has been taking place. But sometimes change cannot be continued in slow steps. Sometimes there has to be a jump." I naively thought that we had made that jump with the Civil Rights Act and Voting Rights Act, and a new era was upon us.

I was wrong. Friction, resistance, and backlash were far more important than I ever imagined.

Moving West

As Boone had predicted, the large steps forward made by civil rights activists in the 1960s brought about a huge backlash. The backlash to overcoming racial injustices was almost as powerful as the great event itself.

Immediately after the landmark destruction of the legal superstructure of de jure segregation in 1964–1965, Lurleen Wallace, running for Alabama governor as a surrogate for her husband George, won a smashing victory in 1966. The massive mobilization of white voters for Wallace overwhelmed the new Black voters empowered by the Voting Rights Act. And the landslide swept away the traditional north-south divide in Alabama politics.

And it did more. It energized George Wallace, fueling his second run for the presidency. I watched in dismay as he stoked the fires of white resentment and racial hate throughout the state and beyond. Wallace biographer Dan Carter argues that Wallace was the vessel for the spreading of racial hate across the nation, and I think he is right. Wallace didn't create it, but he was its earthly messenger.

As these forces gained ascendency in Alabama, I turned my back on my home state and left for graduate school. I had been rejected at two of the four schools where I applied, and chose the University of Texas above the University of Virginia because of V.O. Key's description of both states in *Southern Politics*. Choosing graduate school based on a book written almost two decades before is probably a first and last. Key depicts Virginia as a "political museum piece," run by a racist political machine supporting massive resistance. On the other hand, changes since the Civil War, wrote Key in the middle of the 20th century, "weakened the heritage of southern traditionalism, revolutionized the economy, and made Texas more western than southern."[1] He saw a dynamic system in which factions within the Democratic Party divided along class lines, and the politics of race and other "irrelevances" are pushed aside. The modern view of both states today is considerably different.

Reaching Austin just before Labor Day in 1966, I found most of Key's observations to be true. Compared with Alabama, Texas was a dynamic place. No wonder that John Albert Dean, the disaffected Blount County Populist and my great-grandfather, came to seek his fortune there when he saw that he had no political future in Alabama. All politics did not collapse to the race issue, as was the case in Alabama. There was an active Liberal faction thriving but mostly losing within the Democratic Party. I learned there were three racial groups instead of two: Anglos, Blacks, and Mexican-Americans (sometimes Tejanos).

As Labor Day approached, considerable excitement gripped Austin. Cesar Chavez of the United Farm Workers, Eugene Nelson of the National Farm Workers Association, and two local organizers, Margil Sanchez and Lucio Galvan, led 800 marchers up Congress Avenue to the state Capitol. The march originated from a farm workers' strike in the Rio Grande Valley against the low wages paid by growers there. Getting no satisfactory response, the farm workers marched the 380 miles from Rio Grande City to Austin in the Texas August heat to urge state officials to establish a state minimum wage. I was one of the 10,000 onlookers cheering for the marchers as they climbed the gentle hill from the Colorado River to the Capitol grounds.[2]

However, the politics of status and class still played out in Texas; the struggle was just more complex. When the La Raza march finished in Austin, and the farmworkers went back to Starr County, the strike continued out of the limelight of the media. Landowners called the Texas Rangers back, and they continually harassed and attacked the workers. The law enforcement powers of the state were put to work on behalf of the ranch owners. Captain A.Y. Allee, brutal head of the Rangers, finally broke the strike. Did not the ranch owners resemble Alabama's plantation owners? Was A.Y. Allee the Texas version of Al Lingo, George Wallace's head of State Troopers at Selma?

In Texas, class politics could not as easily be snuffed out as in Alabama, but if the Texas business and agricultural elites—oilmen, industrialists, bankers, and Rio Grande landowners—always won, how much difference did that make?

Will the Concern for Status Always Dominate?

The writer Tom Wolfe asserted, "I think every living moment of a human being's life, unless the person is starving or in immediate danger of death in some other way, is controlled by a concern for status."[3]

Class politics involves redistribution, but at its best it can aim at providing collective goods that make most people better off regardless of race or other indicators of status. Class politics involves debates about such issues as universal healthcare or child tax credits or food aid. The better off get taxed more to provide such collective goods, but if done properly the tax system is designed so as not to undermine capitalist incentives. Nothing destroys the capacity of a nation to provide collective goods as fast as undermining capitalism—except the resentment and vitriol of status politics.

The politics of race is a politics of status. Often it is THE politics of status, as it has been historically and, in many ways, still is. Making one race better off ensures that another race will be worse off. Status politics—the politics of white supremacy and anti-immigration—always divides the coalitions that must be built to provide collective goods. Heather McGee's *The Sum of Us* makes this point brilliantly.

The potential disruption of Southern white supremacy wrought by the Populist uprising in the 1890s required cross-race coalitions, and a challenge to the status politics of the day. Ruling Bourbon Democrats rolled out the standard canards of the threat of Black Rule and the romanticism of the Lost Cause, but that was not enough. Massive election cheating and economic and physical intimidation of Blacks joined with the mythology of the Lost Cause to staunch the class-based wave threatening to overwhelm the oligarchical planter-banker class. At the same time, as economic times improved, high levels of voting for Populists by whites declined, making it easier for the Bourbons to restore white supremacy and seal the fate of class politics in the South. The threat was over in an instant, locked in by the Jim Crow constitutions.

The disenfranchisement of both Southern Blacks and a large proportion of the common white farmers and laborers relegated the South to backwater oligarch-dominated politics. Southern class politics in the Jim Crow era was a within-party matter, with the conservative faction nearly always dominating.

The whole American political system adjusted to Jim Crow. Once the bastion of democratic values, the Republican Party drifted back to its Whiggish roots, failing to develop a serious Southern presence centering on democratic participation and equality.

In the 1950s a new breed of Republican emerged in the South—V.O. Key called them "Eisenhower Republicans" because they were made up of business and professional men and women, mostly in the big cities, and were generally thought to be moderate on the race issue. Actually paternalists would be a better characterization. An emerging politics of economics based in the new commercial business class aligned against a coalition of urban labor, middle-class progressives, and yeoman farmers seemed entirely possible. On the one hand a "growth coalition" would advocate economic growth through the building of local capital rather than relying on investment from out of the region. On the other hand, a "populist coalition" would advocate a fairer distribution of the social product to citizens regardless of race. The result would be a two-party system based in arguments about economic matters.

Alas the ideal of Key and other political scientists studying Southern political development did not emerge. Losing the opportunity to integrate Blacks more firmly into the national political scene, the Republican Party instead became hostile to desegregation and resistant to civil rights. Writer William F. Buckley and journalist James J. Kilpatrick were in the vanguard of the new right that pursued massive resistance to racial equality. Arizona senator and 1964 Republican presidential candidate Barry Goldwater brought the ideas into mass politics. Goldwater and his supporters proposed a new Republicanism—which was the old Republicanism with white supremacy structured in. The new Republicanism appealed first to Dixiecrats and Wallace worshipers. Republican presidents Richard Nixon and Ronald Reagan made the package attractive to a broader coalition of voters.

During the period, most of my relatives were Republicans of the Eisenhower brand. Indeed the South was so firmly Republican that claiming a Democratic allegiance was as strange as my mother's Republican allegiance in South Alabama in the 1950s. At a Jones family reunion in 1996, when my cousin James Sentell discovered I claimed the Democratic label he called his two children over and told them to "go talk to the Democrat" to give them a sense of diversity.

As the Republicans became the party of whites and the Democrats continued to struggle with factionalism, the matters of civil rights and social justice were left to an indigenous and vigorous civil rights movement. Such visionaries as M.L. King, Fred Shuttlesworth, and John Lewis pushed another visionary, President Lyndon Johnson, to make the Democratic Party the carrier of social justice.

Today's Republican Party has shifted rapidly toward a Bourbon stance—a combination of white supremacy rhetoric and voter suppression that resembles the conservative Democratic Bourbons of the 1890s. The Bourbons destroyed the incipient Populist democracy of "free vote, fair count" then, and we face such a danger today.

The slow and uneven movement of the Republican Party toward incorporating white supremacy accelerated with the election of Barack Obama, our first Black president. Some sanitized the divide between the parties as one over "cultural issues." But race led the agenda. It is no accident that the screeching of hate in our school boards was first about the inclusion of honest discussions about race in the curriculum. Republicans decry critical race theory—CRT—as a code phrase for promoting white supremacy. As Alabama journalist Kyle Whitmire put it, "CRT is the mechanism Republican candidates can use to accuse Black people of being the *real* racists."[4] Then there is almost a systematic searching for the next subject to heap scorn and hate onto—to continue the scourge of status politics.

Many issues that we thought were solved returned in force. In 1963, Governor George Wallace was the star attraction in a gathering of proponents of private segregated white academies, promising state aid.[5] Today Governor Greg Abbott of Texas demands that the legislature pass "vouchers" for private schools including "Christian academies" seemingly modeled on the 1960s segregationist system. In both cases, the governors called the system "school choice," with Wallace highlighting that the schools would remain segregated and Abbott leaving the obvious unsaid.

The dual mind of the white South was swallowed in the ascendency of race politics. The rural regions of Populism and New Dealism collapsed into the one mind of the (white) South with the rise of George Wallace. It was a mindset resentful of Yankee intruders and Black protesters, and obedient to the oligarch-based conservatives and their political allies. As in the case of the original Bourbon rule, today's version has a hierarchical bent—economic and political elites stoke the demagoguery, resentment, and racism that motivate many white voters.

Katherine Kramer and Jonathan Metzel have independently shown how resentment can feed on itself, becoming a strong force in politics. In the process, resentment relegates economic interests to the sidelines.[6]

To conclude that the one white mind thesis holds today would nevertheless be hasty. It is true that Southern Republicanism rests on the single Southern mind of white supremacy. The scramble by Republican politicians to cobble together regimes based on voter suppression and racial resentment are signs of an underlying fear of emerging minority power.

New coalitions in America's cities unifying Blacks and other minorities with urban professionals and other liberal-minded whites are filling the void left by the demise of the old mountain Populist and Black coalition of earlier years. Rob Mickey sees this as a process of democratizing "enclaves" in Southern states. Focusing on the Deep South states of Georgia, Mississippi, and South Carolina, Mickey shows the dynamics of a South transforming from "Dixie" to the new democratized enclaves.[7] In part, the new dynamics of enclaves were a product of socioeconomic changes—urbanization and diversification. In part it was due to federal intervention to restore democracy—the Civil Rights Act and Voting Rights Act in particular. What failed in 1865 and 1900 succeeded in 1965.

Unfortunately, the backlash to democratization has not run its course. If today we re-ran the Reconstruction or Populist campaigns, the democratic forces in many Southern states would likely lose to the oligarchs, as they did in those periods. The oligarchic coalition represented by those such as James Powell Carr, my slaveholding ancestor from Sumter County who engaged in election fraud, again bests John Albert Dean, the vibrant Populist tax assessor from Blount County and my great grandfather, who helped jump-start the Populist revolt. In Alabama, Mississippi, and South Carolina, an updated form of Bourbon rule continues to suppress the emerging shoots of democracy. Arkansas, Tennessee, and Florida are becoming less democratic. Urban and diverse Texas is governed by right-wing Republicans funded by economic oligarchs. Throughout the former Confederacy voter suppression is rampant, stimulated by the Supreme Court decision in *Shelby v. Holder*. Although there is no doubt that the urban coalition is transforming America, neither is there doubt that the massive voter suppression program led by conservative economic elites and hate-spewing politicians can deter or even overwhelm the South's emerging democratic enclaves.

The Bellwether of an American Tragedy?

For the distinguished political scientist Walter Dean Burnham, political change could happen quickly. Following his mentor V.O. Key Jr., Burnham developed a theory of *critical elections*—those in which voter allegiances shifted rapidly from one political party to another. I too am fascinated by sudden political shifts. Dean and I had quite a few lunches discussing punctuated changes while both of us were in Austin.

Yet critical junctures in history are not completely defined by a single moment. There is usually an extended period during which the pressure for change intensifies. That happened in the 1890s. This churning happened again during the Civil Rights movement of the 1960s. As in the 1890s there was no one single point in time or election that can be pinpointed as THE critical instant. The key is to look for challenges to the existing social and economic order, and watch for the inevitable backlash from threatened interests. The backlash can be stronger than the challenge to the status quo, as was the case in the 1890s.

Over the 1950s and 1960s the sectional class-based divide vanished in Alabama politics. Something more was also going on, a trend that political scientists first saw as positive: the replacement of the sectional structure in the South more generally with a two-party system.

In a prescient article, Dean Burnham studied the 1962 Alabama Senate general election between New Deal Democrat and racial moderate Senator Lister Hill and James Martin, a Republican businessman from industrial Gadsden.[8] Martin ran a strong campaign, earning 49% of the vote by appealing to the Eisenhower business-oriented Republicans with conservative economic policies. But he also made crystal clear that he was a strong segregationist, and that the Southern version of the Republican Party would support Dixiecrat policies on race. Hill ran a strictly liberal economic campaign, arguing that national Democratic economic policies had pulled many Alabamians out of poverty.

Burnham produced a county-by-county map of the vote division, presented below (Figure 24.1). The reader's first reaction would probably be: "Nothing to see here. Same old north-south division the author has been harping on the whole book."

But look again. The map is *upside down*—with regard to party preferences. South Alabama, then virtually devoid of Republican identifiers, voted for the Republican by large majorities. North Alabama voted for the economic liberal and racial moderate Loyalist Democrat. There were two exceptions: Republican Jefferson County (Birmingham), where urban Republicanism was blooming, and the Free State of Winston, sticking to its post–Civil War roots.

Burnham and other political scientists studying Southern political development saw that this was a big deal. Was this the long-predicted realignment between the parties, an abrupt shift in party preferences that matched the class-based preferences of voters? Burnham saw "a political re-emergence of Alabama's ancient regional and socio-economic antagonisms" in which the poorer northern counties and Blacks supported the Democratic Party, more aligned to the class interest of these groups. He went on to show that Blacks were mostly allowed to vote in the northern, more open, part of the state.

V.O. Key's claim that the Solid South led to a politics dominated by planter and Big Mule elites and that the cure was vigorous two-party competition seemed on the verge of reality. Certainly it was the talk of the University of

RESULTS OF ALABAMA SENATORIAL ELECTION, 1962

☐ Counties for Hill (D)

■ Counties for Martin (R)

Figure 24.1 Counties Carried by the Republican Candidate James Martin in the Senatorial Election of 1962

Source: Redrawn from Walter Dean Burnham, "The Alabama Senatorial Election of 1962," *Journal of Politics* 16 (1964), 799, Map I.

Alabama's Political Science Department, still steeped in the glory of V.O. Key's research team from back in the late 1940s. It seemed that the urban better-off were moving toward Republicanism, and there were hints of an emergence of a Black-labor-farmer Democratic coalition in the North. This slow development seemed to many political scientists to be the bromide the region needed to overcome its backwardness.[9]

Unfortunately, the white backlash was just starting. A cross-race partisan alignment based on class interests was not what was going on. Burnham was right—1962 was a bellwether of realignment, but it was a status-centered realignment anchored in race politics rather than a class-based one. Segregation was the motivator, and the politics of resentment was the vehicle. It was not an alignment of economic interests, but one of racial resentments.

South Alabama whites showed how correct Burnham was in predicting "abrupt jump-shifts in party percentages rather than by secular trends."[10] They rushed to the new Republicanism, quickly dropping their former Democratic allegiances. But many were already not loyal Democrats. Many Black Belt Democrats had supported the Dixiecrat faction of the Democratic Party since the late 1940s. Now the Wiregrass farmers were joining in. The States' Rights wing of the Democratic Party paved the way for this transition—from New Deal Loyalist Democrats to Dixicrats to Republicans.

The pattern was not evident in North Alabama, where many voters were accustomed to voting for Democratic Party Loyalists even although many of their neighbors still voted for the Republicans. Democrats actually gained votes in North Alabama compared to the 1960 presidential election. There the strong vote for Loyalist Lister Hill seemed to be a bellwether for a class-based two-party system.

Political scientists of the day missed the indicator of the real realignment. Republicans did not bother to run a candidate against the Democratic nominee for governor, George Wallace, who won with 96% of the vote against an independent. South Alabama voted for the Democrat Wallace and for the Republican Martin. It was likely they were voting for the most racially aggressive candidate and against Lister Hill's association with the Kennedy administration and its antisegregation policies.

In 1962, North Alabama's traditional preferences for liberal economic policies and moderate racial policies had remained in place. But not for long. Instead, these regions moved toward the New Republicanism advocated by Martin. The 1964 Republican candidate for president, Barry Goldwater, perceived, as had Jim Martin, that many whites in the South were resentful of the national Democrats' increasing embrace of civil rights for Blacks. Goldwater recommended that Republicans "go hunting where the ducks are"—that is, compete for Southern white votes and stop trying to be competitive for Black votes.

A Return to Bourbon Rule?

A vibrant Southern two-party system had plenty of opportunities to flour-ish after 1965. Indeed, there were positive signs for establishing Southern democratic rule based on two-party competition not centered on racial fears. The Voting Rights Act and its speedy implementation gave many great hope for the future. The cross-party consensus in Congress that passed and reau-thorized the Act was built by men and women of good will, even as the Republican Party became more Southern and more conservative on racial poli-cies. Congress and the president renewed and extended the Voting Rights Act in 1970, 1975, 1982, and 2006. The 2006 extension included a unanimous Senate vote on the Act. Surely the nation had reached a consensus on the democratic principle that all adult citizens should vote.

White racism and status politics is strong, and it is hard for one party to pass up the opportunity to mobilize it.[11] That is the route that the Republican Party took in its Southern strategy following the victories of the civil rights move-ment. Is this strategy getting "locked in" the way the Bourbons locked in legal segregation through Supreme Court decisions and the white supremacist state constitutions at the end of the 19th century?

There are alarming signs. In 2013 the Supreme Court, in its *Shelby County v. Holder* decision, authored by voting rights opponent Chief Justice John Roberts, swept away that consensus on voting rights and opened the door for politicians to suppress votes of minority citizens. The subsequent attempts to suppress minority votes came quickly and mostly from the very Southern states that had been the targets of the original Voting Rights Act. The Court fol-lowed up with a series of decisions unfavorable to the Act and to the democratic nation its authors sought to build.

The Court and Congress have made it easier for the rich to influence and even dominate politics. In the *Citizens United* case in 2010 the Supreme Court allowed outside groups to spend unlimited money on campaigns, leading to massive spending by interest groups and political action committees.[12] With the urging of Republican presidents, Congress has passed large tax cuts for the rich and for corporations, making money available for capital investment—unfortunately including investment in skewing government policies toward the rich.

A great deal has been written about the move of the Republican Party toward supporting white supremacy since 1968. In essence, the party fused conservative economic policy generally harmful to the working class—witness the stagnation of incomes for low- and middle-income Americans in the face of an increasing GDP—with conservative social policies. Those conservative social policies were generally anchored in white supremacist policies of the past, and that connection is becoming increasingly clear today.

Scholars and political practitioners have traced this connection back to the 1950s, highlighting the increasing influence of white supremacist notions on the party's strategies.[13] That was evident in ideas as well as policies. William Buckley, one of the conservative intellectuals who helped to forge the connection between economic and social conservatism, was an avowed white supremacist. He wrote in the *National Review* as late as 1957 that the key issue for racial relations in the South "is whether the White community in the South is entitled to take such measures as are necessary to prevail, politically and culturally, in areas in which it does not pre-dominate numerically? The sobering answer is Yes—the White community is so entitled because, for the time being, it is the advanced race." Buckley's writings in the period oozed Bourbonism; the new conservatism he advocated promoted government from an oligarchic hierarchy of superior white rulers.

Bourbon rule is more than crass racism—it is racism to further elite rule. Recall that antiplanter Populists used the term Bourbon to connote the desire of the planters to restore an antebellum hierarchical South that relegated Blacks to the bottom and the white poor higher but by no means on an equal with the "civilized" planter and industrialist class.

The 1962 Alabama senatorial campaign was not a bellwether for a realignment based on economics. Such a realignment would have led to a politics focused on the need for the accumulation of capital to invest in new enterprises versus the need to redistribute wealth among all classes. Rather it was precursor to a realignment based on status competition, which invariably leads to a politics based on out-group resentment and hate—and the ability of oligarchs to prosper. Such was the antebellum South. Such was the South after the Populist uprising and the imposition of Jim Crow. And, sadly, such is the current state of our politics today.

The 2024 presidential election could be a critical moment for American (not just Southern) politics. It could represent the lock-in point for Bourbon rule. The strong victory for Republicans and the racist demagogue Donald Trump was generated by an alliance between elements of the industrial and commercial elite and large segments of the white working and middle classes. Highly unequal and highly diverse societies foster Bourbon alliances, and that is what the United States has become since the 1980s. Today's alliance supports economic policies that benefit the wealthy few, and, through its political leaders, generates racism, misogyny, religious bigotry and seething resentment for consumption by working and middle-class citizens. Most importantly, it offers white supremacy to the status deprived. Policies developed by Democrats that aid the less well-off or foster the common good are often ignored by the pumped-up Bourbon supporters.

The strategy is not new, as we have seen in this book. The only question left is whether the system can be locked in, in a way reminiscent of the early 1900s in the South. The tactics will be different today, but the outcome could be similar.

Notes

FOREWORD

1. Frank Baumgartner and Bryan Jones, *Agendas and Instability in American Politics* (Chicago: University of Chicago Press, 1993).
2. Angie Maxwell and Todd Shields, *The Long Southern Strategy* (New York: Oxford University Press, 2019); Stuart Stevens, *It Was All a Lie* (New York: Alfred A. Knopf, 2020).
3. Donald E. Collins, *When the Church Bells Rang Racist* (Macon, GA: Mercer University Press, 1988), 19.
4. Carl Elliott Sr. and Michael D'Orso, *The Cost of Courage* (Tuscaloosa: University of Alabama Press, 1992), 21.

CHAPTER 1

1. Testimony in *Lynch v. Alabama* (2011), quoted in Ira W. Harvey, *The Property Tax in Alabama* (Center for Leadership and Public Policy, Alabama State University, Montgomery, AL, 2012), 6.
2. Thomas Frank, *The People, NO* (New York: Metropolitan Books, 2020).
3. V.O. Key Jr., *Southern Politics in State and Nation* (New York: Vintage, 1949), 284–285.
4. Paul Pierson, *Politics in Time* (Princeton, NJ: Princeton University Press, 2004), 2.
5. Kyle Whitmire, "Ambushed in Eufaula: Alabama's Forgotten Race Massacre," AL.com, January 16, 2022 [https://www.al.com/news/2022/01/ambushed-in-eufaula-alabamas-forgotten-race-massacre.html], accessed 01/17/2022.
6. William Faulkner, *Intruder in the Dust* (New York: Random House, 1948), 193.
7. The concept of a critical juncture is what social scientists call a heuristic. It is based on the notion that history unfolds in fits and starts, but the particulars of what is and is not a specific critical juncture is debated. Social scientists use two additional concepts in describing disjoint historical change—a buildup of pressures for change before the critical juncture, and a backlash that often happens after the change.
8. Robert Merton, "The Matthew Effect in Science," *Science, New Series* 159, no. 3810 (January 5, 1968), 56–63.
9. Elizabeth Shanahan, Michael D. Jones, Mark K. McBeth, and Claudio M. Radaelli, "The Narrative Policy Framework," in Christopher M. Weible and Paul Sabatier, eds., *Theories of the Policy Process, Fourth Edition* (New York: Westview Press 2018), 173–214; Robert H. Bates, Avner Greif, Margaret Levi, Jean-Laurent Rosenthal, and Barry R. Weingast, "The Analytic Narrative Project," *American Political Science Review* 94 (2000), 696–702; Robert J. Shiller, *Narrative Economics* (Princeton, NJ: Princeton University Press, 2019).
10. Daina Ramey Berry, *Swing the Sickle for the Harvest Is Ripe* (Champaign-Urbana: University of Illinois, 2007); Daina Ramey Berry, *The Price for Their Pound of Flesh* (Boston: Beacon Press, 2017); Chandra Manning, *What This Cruel War Was Over* (New York: Vintage, 2007).
11. Kendra T. Field, "The Privilege of Family History," *American Historical Review* 127 (2022) 600–623; Field, *Growing Up with the Country: Family, Race, and Nation after the Civil War* (New Haven, CT: Yale University Press).

12. Edward Ball, *Slaves in the Family* (New York: Farrar, Straus and Giroux, 1998); *Life of a Klansman* (New York: Farrar, Straus and Giroux, 2020).

13. William Horne, "White Americans Fail to Address Their Family Histories," *The Activist History Review*, February 8, 2018 [https://activisthistory.com/2018/02/09/white-americans-fail-to-address-their-family-histories/], accessed 05/26/2022.

Chapter 2

1. "North and South Alabama," *Sumter County Sun*, April 11, 1889.

2. David Hackett Fischer, *Albion's Seed: Four British Folkways in America* (New York: Oxford University Press, 1991); Colin Woodard, *American Nations* (New York, Penguin, 2011).

3. E. Han, P. Carbonetto, R. Curtis, et al., "Clustering of 770,000 Genomes Reveals Post-Colonial Population Structure of North America," *Nature Communications* 8, 14238 (2017) [https://doi.org/10.1038/ncomms14238], accessed 01/24/2022

4. V.O. Key Jr., *American State Politics: An Introduction* (New York: Alfred A. Knopf, 1956), 209.

5. Walter Dean Burnham, "The Alabama Senatorial Election of 1962: Return of Inter-Party Competition," *Journal of Politics* 26 (1964), 798–829, 801.

6. Joseph H. Taylor, "Populism and Disfranchisement in Alabama," *The Journal of Negro History* 34 (1949), 411. Editorial appeared on November 1, 1874.

7. W.J. Cash, *The Mind of the South* (New York: Alfred A. Knopf, 1941).

8. Ralph J. Bunche, "The Negro in the Political Life of the United States," *The Journal of Negro Education* 10 (1941), 567–584, quote at 568–569.

9. Cash, *Mind*, 305, 336.

10. W.E.B. Du Bois, *Black Reconstruction in America* (New York: The Free Press 1935), 319–320.

11. Kyle Whitmire, "Ambushed in Eufaula: Alabama's Forgotten Race Massacre," AL.com, January 19, 2020 [https://www.al.com/news/2022/01/ambushed-in-eufaula-alabamas-forgotten-race-massacre.html], accessed 01/24/2020.

12. J.D. Vance, *Hillbilly Elegy* (New York: Harper, 2016).

13. Key, *Southern Politics*, 6.

14. Avidit Acharya, Matthew Blackwell, and Maya Sen, *Deep Roots* (Princeton, NJ: Princeton University Press, 2018); see also David A. Bateman and Eric Schickler, "Deeper Roots," *Journal of Historical Political Economy* 3 (2023), 1–30.

15. John O'Brien, "North Alabama Was Never Entirely Confederate," *Left in Alabama*, June 10, 2017 [http://leftinalabama.com/north-alabama-was-never-entirely-confederate/], accessed 07/26/2019.

16. C. Vann Woodward, *The Strange Career of Jim Crow, Second Edition* (New York: Oxford University Press, 2002).

17. Key, *Southern Politics*, 668.

18. The notion of enclaves of democracy is from Robert Mickey, *Paths Out of Dixie* (Princeton, NJ: Princeton University Press, 2015).

19. Bunche, "Negro in Political Life," 569.

20. Cash, *Mind*, 171.

21. Keri Leigh Merritt, *Masterless Men* (New York: Cambridge University Press, 2017); see also Wayne Flynt, *Poor but Proud* (Tuscaloosa: University of Alabama Press, 1989).

22. Isabel Wilkerson, *Caste* (New York: Random House, 2020).

23. Nikole Hannah-Jones, Caitlin Roper, Ilena Silverman and Jake Silverstein, eds., *The 1619 Project: A New Origin Story* (New York: New York Times, 2021).

24. Jefferson Cowie, *Freedom's Dominion* (New York: Basic Books, 2022).

25. Ted Robert Gurr, *Why Men Rebel* (Princeton, NJ: Princeton University Press, 1970).

26. Harvey H. Jackson III, *Inside Alabama: A Personal History of My State* (Tuscaloosa: University of Alabama Press, 2004), 14.

Chapter 3

1. The Ulster-Scots Society of America, "The Great Migration from Ulster to America'" [https://www.electricscotland.com/history/ulster_scots/ulster4.htm], accessed 04/25/2022.

2. John Cannon, "Henry McCulloch and Henry McCulloh," *The William and Mary Quarterly* 15 (1958), 71–73.

3. There are differences of opinion on the specifics of this tale. James Osborn Carr, in "The Carr Family of Duplin County," written around 1920, states that Barbara grew up in Holland and was traveling with Beverett, who was her husband, and that Joseph Carr was on the boat as well. Immigration records point to the storyline above.

4. Ball, *Slaves in the Family*, chapter 11.

5. J.O. Carr, "The Battle of Rockfish Creek in Duplin County," *The North Carolina Booklet* 6 (1907), 177–184 [http://penelope.uchicago.edu/Thayer/E/Gazetteer/Places/America/United_States/North_Carolina/_Texts/journals/The_North_Carolina_Booklet/6/3/The_Battle_of_Rockfish_Creek*.html], accessed 01/22/2020.

6. Steadman Hall Carr, "Application for Membership, Florida Chapter of the Sons of the American Revolution," June 2, 1960.

7. "Dale County and Its People during the Civil War: Reminiscences of Mary Love (Edwards) Fleming," *Alabama Historical Quarterly* 19 (1957), 6.

8. Matthew Yglesias, "America's Slaves Were More Valuable Than All Its Industrial Capital Combined," *Slate* [https://slate.com/business/2013/07/america-s-slave-wealth.html], accessed 07/28/2013; Thomas Piketty and Gabriel Zuckman, "Capital Is Back: Wealth-Income Ratios in Rich Countries, 1700–2010," *Quarterly Journal of Economics* 129 (2014).

9. Samuel H. Williamson and Louis P. Cain, "Measuring Slavery in 2016 Dollars," *Measuring Worth* [https://www.measuringworth.com/slavery.php], accessed 12/13/2020.

10. Albert W. Neimi Jr., "Inequality in the Distribution of Slave Wealth," *Journal of Economic History* 37 (1977), 747–754.

11. John P. Bowles, "American Indian Removal beyond the Removal Act," *Native American and Indigenous Studies* 1 (2014), 65–87; Ethan Davis, "An Administrative Trail of Tears," *The American Journal of Legal History* 50 (2008–2010), 49–100. The latter article explains how the federal government constructed an entire administrative state to accomplish removal, an indication of the rules changes that occur after a critical juncture.

12. Will of James Pearsall, Duplin County, North Carolina, 1837.

13. Trail of Tears, History.com, July 7, 2020 [https://www.history.com/topics/native-american-history/trail-of-tears#:~:text=It%20was%2C%20one%20Choctaw%20leader%20told%20an%20Alabama,out%20for%20Oklahoma%20did%20not%20survive%20the%20trip.], accessed 1/5/2021.

14. Frederick Douglass, *Narrative of the Life of an American Slave Written by Himself*, Electronic Version, Documenting the American South [https://docsouth.unc.edu/neh/douglass/douglass.html], accessed 10/13/2023.

15. James Marone, *Hellfire Nation: The Politics of Sin in America* (New Haven, CT: Yale University Press, 2004).

16. "Autobiography of R. G. Christopher," from a typed copy made by Nell Marshall Reid, Tuscaloosa, Alabama, 1975.

17. "Livingston Methodist Church," *Bulletin of the Livingston Methodist Church*, Alabama, United States, Marriages, Deaths, Wills, Court, and Other Records, 1784–1920.

18. William B. Lawrence, "Slavery and the Founders of Methodism," UM News, August 12, 2020 [https://www.umnews.org/en/news/slavery-and-the-founders-of-methodism], accessed 12/03/2021.

19. Becky Little, "Why Bibles Given to Slaves Omitted Most of the New Testament," *History*, August 2019 [https://www.history.com/news/slave-bible-redacted-old-testament], accessed 02/12/2022.

20. Tom Blake, "Sumter County: Largest Slaveholders from 1860 Census Schedules," transcribed October 2001 [https://sites.rootsweb.com/~ajac/biggest16.htm], accessed 08/06/2023.

21. Wilkerson, *Caste*.

22. Merritt, *Masterless Men*, 58.

23. Nellie Jenkins, *Pioneer Families of Sumter County Alabama* (Greenville, SC: Southern Historical Press, 1961), 15.

24. Merritt, *Masterless Men*; Ball, *Slaves in the Family*.

25. Alan Brown and David Taylor, eds., *Gabr'l Blow Sof'* (Livingston: Livingston Press, University of West Alabama, 1997), i.

26. Brown and Taylor, *Gabr'l Blow Sof'*, 40.

27. Brown and Taylor, *Gabr'l Blow Sof'*, 13–15.

28. Writers tried to capture the Negro dialect as faithfully as they could, incorporating them into the narratives.

29. Brown and Taylor, *Gabr'l Blow Sof'*, 17.

30. Brown and Taylor, *Gabr'l Blow Sof'*, 34.

31. Brown and Taylor, *Gabr'l Blow Sof'*, 33–34.

32. Brown and Taylor, *Gabr'l Blow Sof'*, 13.

33. Brown and Taylor, *Gabr'l Blow Sof'*, 48.

CHAPTER 4

1. "The 56th Alabama Cavalry Regiment, Partisan Rangers, The American Civil War" [http://www.americancivilwar101.com/units/csa-al/al-cav-56-reg-rangers.html], accessed 03/05/2021.

2. "Confederate Guerrilla Warfare, 1861–1865: Partisan Rangers and Guerrilla Commands," MyGen [http://www.mygen.com/users/outlaw/csa.html], accessed 03/05/2021.

3. Kara E. Kozikowski, "Guerilla Warfare," *American Battlefield Trust* [https://www.battlefields.org/learn/articles/guerrilla-warfare], accessed 08/06/2023.

4. Phillip Ager, L. Platt Boustan, and K. Eriksson, "The Intergenerational Effects of a Large Wealth Shock: White Southerners after the Civil War," Centre for Economic Policy Research (CEPR) Discussion Paper 13,660 (2019) [https://cepr.org/publications/dp13660], accessed 10/13/2023.

5. Merritt, *Masterless Men*, 44. Carr's estimates from the U.S. Censuses of 1860 and 1870.

6. William E. Laird and James R. Reinhart, "Deflation, Agriculture, and Southern Development," *Agricultural History* 42, no. 2 (1968), 115–124.

7. Ball, *Slaves in the Family.*

8. "Beat" is an archaic term for an election district.

9. William Warren Rogers Jr., *Reconstruction Politics in a Deep South State* (Tuscaloosa: University of Alabama Press, 2021), 53.

10. Walter Lynwood Fleming, *Civil War and Reconstruction in Alabama* (New York: Columbia University Press, 1905), 358–360.

11. "The New Election Law," *Livingston Journal*, October 23, 1868; Rogers, *Reconstruction*, 97.

12. *Livingston Journal*, November 6, 1868.

13. *Livingston Journal*, various dates.

14. *Livingston Journal*, August 6, 1868.

15. "North and South Alabama," *Sumter County Sun*, April 11, 1889. These words were written in a different time, but certainly represented the sentiments of the planter elites of the county.

16. Woodward, *Strange Career*, 88.

17. "How It Was Done," *Livingston Journal*, November 8, 1872.

18. "To Election Officials," *Livingston Journal*, July 14, 1876.

19. "Historic Sumter," *Livingston Journal*, August 4, 1876.

20. Allen Johnston Going, *Bourbon Democracy in Alabama 1874–1890* (Tuscaloosa: University of Alabama Press, 1952), 320.

21. U.S. Selected Federal Census, Agriculture Schedules, 1880, Alabama, Sumter, Gaston.

22. Donna Barton, "Memories of a Father: The Life and Times of Judge Carr," *Anniston Star*, June 18, 2017.

CHAPTER 5

1. Joel Chandler Harris, "Introduction," *Uncle Remus: His Songs and Sayings* (New York: Appleton, 1880).

2. Harris, *Uncle Remus*, xvii.

3. Harris, *Uncle Remus*, 236.

4. Fleming, *Civil War*, 209–210.

5. Morgan York, "The Dunning School of Thought," *Making History* [https://unm-historiography.github.io/intro-guide/essays/20th-Century/The-Dunning-School-of-Thought.html], accessed 6/2/2021.

6. Ty Seidule, *Robert E. Lee and Me* (New York: St. Martin's Press, 2020).

7. Nicole Maurantonio, *Confederate Exceptionalism* (Lawrence: University Press of Kansas, 2019); David W. Blight, *Race and Reunion* (Cambridge, MA: The Belknap Press of Harvard University Press, 2001); Patrick Gerster and Nicholas Cords, eds., *Myth and Southern History, Volume 1: The Old South, Second Edition* (Urbana and Chicago: University of Illinois Press, 1989).

8. Sarah Fowler, "'It's What I Think': Mississippi Official Makes Racist Comments after Confederate Statue Vote," *Jackson Clarion-Ledger*, June 16, 2020.

9. Steven McDonald and Leslie Mayer, "Long-Run Trends and Fluctuations in Cotton Prices," World Agricultural Outlook Board, USDA, Economic Research Service, USDA, January 22, 2018. [https://mpra.ub.uni-muenchen.de/84484/], accessed 02/23/2020.

PART 2

1. "Sundown Towns in the United States," website created and maintained by James W. Loewen [http://sundown.tougaloo.edu/content.php?file=sundowntowns-whitemap.html], accessed 02/23/2020.

2. James W. Loewen, *Sunset Towns: A Hidden Dimension of American Racism* (New York: Touchstone Books, 2006).

3. Dan Carter, "Forgotten Story of America's Whites-Only Towns," UU World Bookshelf [http://www.uuworld.org/articles/forgotten-story-americas-whites-only-towns], accessed 09/12/2024.

CHAPTER 6

1. Leonard Bloom, "The Acculturation of the Eastern Cherokee," *North Carolina Historical Review* 19 (1942), 323–358, 325.

2. Bartholomew H. Sparrow, "The Other Point of Departure: Tocqueville, the South, Equality, and the Lessons of Democracy," *Studies in American Political Development* 33 (2019), 178–208, 208.

3. Register of Deeds, Buncombe County, NC, "As Long as the Grass Shall Grow," September 17, 2021 [https://storymaps.arcgis.com/stories/e9913eb717dc4e68aebe7a7c7d3f42c3], accessed 2/2/2022.

4. A considerable amount of genealogical information is available on the Davidsons, part of a general interest in Americans of Scottish descent. I've relied on Mildred Davis Davidson, *Frederick Davidson, Revolutionary Soldier, and His Descendants* (Carmichael, CA, 1987), and John A. Burrison, *Brothers in Clay* (Athens: University of Georgia Press, 2008), 244–246.

5. For a map of Alabama and Georgia in 1823, including the borderlands, see Figure 12.1.

6. See the map for Georgia Indian land cessions reproduced at the website *Indian Land Cessions in the American Southeast* [http://www.tngenweb.org/cessions/], accessed 9/12/2024.

7. The last record of his activities in South Carolina is a land sale in October of 1820, and his third son, John, was born in South Carolina in 1819. Davidson, *Frederick Davidson*, 247.

8. I define the area as the two census pages around Frederick's name.

9. Adam Jeffrey Pratt, *Regulating the Republic: Violence and Order in the Cherokee-Georgia Borderlands* (Dissertation submitted to the Department of History, Louisiana State University, Baton Rouge, 2012).

10. The record, reproduced by Mildred Davidson, *Frederick Davidson*, 34, states that the seizure affected "Lot # 24, drawn by Mrs. Sky of Chatham Co. GA."

11. Burrison, *Brothers in Clay*, 240.

12. Burrison, *Brothers in Clay*, 7.

13. "Grand Jury Summation, October Term 1832," reprinted in Davidson, *Frederick Davidson*, 13.

14. Clay Jenkinson, Hedgehogs and Foxes, "Alexis de Tocqueville: An Alphabetical List of Authors Writing on Tocqueville" [https://hedgehogsandfoxes.org/index.php/alexis-de-tocqueville-an-alphabetical-list-of-authors-writing-on-tocqueville/], accessed 10/04/2024.

15. Pratt, *Regulating the Republic*, 3.

16. Pratt, *Regulating the Republic*, 22.

17. Pratt, *Regulating the Republic*, 22.

18. Pratt, *Regulating the Republic*, 5.

19. David Williams, "Gold Rush," *New Georgia Encyclopedia*, 2003 (updated 2016). [https://www.georgiaencyclopedia.org/articles/history-archaeology/gold-rush/], accessed 10/13/2023.

20. James Smith, *Cherokee Land Lottery* (New York: Harper Brothers, 1838, 242), [https://openlibrary.org/books/OL23693654M/The_Cherokee_land_lottery], accessed 10/04/2024.

21. Davidson, *Frederick Davidson*, 172.

22. Pratt, *Regulating the Republic*, chapter 3.

23. Pratt, *Regulating the Republic*, 187.

24. Davidson, *Frederick Davidson*, 31–39; Burrison, *Brothers in Clay*, 240.

25. Alexis de Tocqueville, *Democracy in America*, volume 2, section 2, chapter 13.

26. Sparrow, "The Other Point."

27. Steve Inskeep, *Jacksonland* (New York: Penguin, 2015).

28. Pratt, *Regulating the Republic*, 254.

29. Pratt, *Regulating the Republic*, 3.

CHAPTER 7

1. He is listed in the 1840 Census in Chattooga County and 1850 Census in Walker County, both formally parts of the Cherokee Nation. 1840 *United States Federal Census*, Georgia, Chattooga, District 925; 1850 *United States Federal Census*, Georgia, Walker County, Chattanooga Valley; Davidson, *Frederick Davidson*, 31.

2. 1860 *United States Federal Census*, Alabama, DeKalb County, Division 2.

3. Joey Brackner, *Alabama Folk Pottery* (Tuscaloosa: University of Alabama Press, 2006); Countryman-Forbes Stoneware Collection: Davidson [https://sites.google.com/site/jjudkinsfor/davidson?authuser=0], accessed 10/14/2023.

4. Davidson, *Frederick Davidson*, 33.

5. A.S. Davidson, "Davidson," *Alabama Christian Advocate*, January 7, 1909, 14. Reprinted in Davidson, *Frederick Davidson*, 58–59.

6. Bessie Martin, *A Rich Man's War, a Poor Man's Fight* (Tuscaloosa: University of Alabama Press, 2003), 53–57. Originally published by Columbia University Press in 1932.

7. Martin, *Rich Man's War*, 53–57; Fleming, *Civil War*, 199.

8. "Letters from Alabama," in Davidson, *Frederick Davidson*, 170–171.

9. Ken Roberts, *The Cedar Choppers* (College Station, Texas: Texas A&M Press, 2018).

10. Merritt, *Masterless Men*.

11. Davidson, *Frederick Davidson*, 33.

CHAPTER 8

1. J. William Harris, "Portrait of a Small Slaveholder: The Journal of Benton Miller," *The Georgia Historical Society* 74 (1990), 1–19.

2. 1850 Slave Schedule, District 11, Walker County Alabama, transcribed by Veneta McKinney [http://genealogytrails.com/ala/walker/census_1850slave.html], accessed 10/04/2024.

3. James Oakes, "Intermittent Slave Ownership: Texas as a Test Case: A Response," *The Journal of Southern History* 51 (1985), 23–28.

4. The Alabama 1855 Census shows that Joseph held no slaves.

5. Samuel H. Williamson and Louis P. Cain, "Measuring Slavery in 2016 Dollars," *Measuring Worth 2021* [https://www.measuringworth.com/index.php], accessed 9/16/2024.
6. Brian Lyman, "A Permanent Wound: How the Slave Tax Warped Alabama Finances," *Montgomery Advertiser*, February 4, 2017, updated December 26, 2017 [https://www.montgomeryadvertiser.com/story/news/politics/southunionstreet/2017/02/05/permanent-wound-how-slave-tax-warped-alabama-finances/97447706/#], accessed 9/16/2024.
7. Martin, *A Rich Man's War*, 54–55.
8. The above was reconstructed from records archived in Fold3, a division of Ancestry.com; and "The Civil War Battle Unit Details," National Park Service [https://www.nps.gov/civilwar/search-battle-units-detail.htm?battleUnitCode=CAL0019RI], accessed 11/13/2024.
9. U.S. Census for 1880.
10. *Birmingham Iron Age*, February 5, 1878.

CHAPTER 9

1. Key, *Southern Politics*, 6.
2. Fleming, *Civil War*, 28–38.
3. Martin, *A Rich Man's War*, chapter 2.
4. Martin, *A Rich Man's War*, chapter 2
5. Robin Sterling, *Blount County, Alabama, Confederate Soldiers* (Compiled and Annotated by Robin Sterling, 2012).
6. Key, *Southern Politics*, 286–287.
7. Fleming, *Civil War*, 163.
8. Du Bois, *Black Reconstruction*, 319–320.
9. Du Bois, *Black Reconstruction*, 320.
10. Wayne Flynt, "Alabama's Shame: The Historical Origins of the 1901 Constitution," *Alabama Law Review* 53 (2001), 67–76, 69.
11. The specifics of A.S. Davidson's neighbors are drawn from the U.S. Census of 1970.
12. Robin Sterling, "The Rise of the Klan in Blount County," *Tales of Old Blount County* (Compiled and Edited by Robin Sterling 2013), 144–148.
13. Joey Brackner, *Alabama Folk Pottery* (Tuscaloosa: University of Alabama Press, 2006), 127–128, 142.
14. Sterling, *Tales of Old Blount County*, 193.
15. *Journal of the House of Representatives, State of Alabama, 1878–79*, 4; Albert Burton Moore, *The History of Alabama and Her People* (Chicago: The American Historical Society, 1927). I have found that Moore's biographies are not always factually correct; he seems to have had a habit of embellishing them.
16. "Warrior Dots," *Blount County News-Advocate*, April 5, 1888.
17. Robin Sterling, *Tales of Old Blount County*, 2013, 254–255; Sterling says that T.M. Davidson, a son of A.S. Davidson and half-brother to T.H. Davidson, was the representative, but the Alabama House of Representatives lists T.H. Davidson.

CHAPTER 10

1. "Interstate Commerce Act (1887)," *Milestone Documents*, National Archives [https://www.archives.gov/milestone-documents/interstate-commerce-

act#:~:text=The%20railroad%20monopolies%20had%20the,none%20for%20short%2
Dhaul%20oruns.], accessed 8/10/2023

2. "John A. Dean, Tax Assessor of Blount County Refused to Accept. . .," *Montgomery Advertiser*, August 25, 1885.

3. Charles Bernard and John Jones, *Farm Real Estate Values in the United States by Counties, 1850–1982*, Department of Agriculture, Economic Research Service, Washington, DC, 1987. Table 2.

4. Alabama Department of Revenue, "Assessed Value Fixed by Alabama Constitution," Alabama Department of Revenue [https://www.revenue.alabama.gov/], accessed 07/25/2024. The "Redemption Constitution" of 1875 put stringent limits on both assessed values and tax rates. Susan Pace Hamill, "Constitutional Reform in Alabama," *Cumberland Law Review*, October 15,2002, 15 n.39.

5. "Synopsis of the Commissioners' Court," *Blount County News-Dispatch*, August 13, 1885.

6. William Warren Rogers Sr., *The One-Gallused Rebellion* (Tuscaloosa: University of Alabama Press, 2001).

7. Samuel L. Webb, *Two Party Politics in the One-Party South* (Tuscaloosa: University of Alabama Press) 1997, chapter 4.

8. Elizabeth Sanders, *Roots of Reform* (Chicago: University of Chicago Press 1999), 128–129.

9. Rogers, *One-Gallused Rebellion*, 187.

10. Samuel Proctor, "The National Farmers' Alliance Convention and Its 'Ocala Demands,'" *Florida Historical Quarterly* 28 (1950), 161–181.

11. "Blount for Jones," *Birmingham News*, May 14, 1892.

12. "Solid for Tom Jones and Good Government," *Birmingham News*, May 13, 1892.

13. Rogers, *One-Gallused Rebellion*, 208.

14. Rogers, *One-Gallused Rebellion*, 212.

15. Rogers, *One-Gallused Rebellion*, 212.

16. Rogers, *One Gallused Rebellion*, 214.

17. Paul Horton, "Testing the Limits of Class Politics in Alabama," *The Journal of Southern History* 57 (1991), 63–84.

18. "Safe," *Birmingham Daily News*, August 2, 1892.

19. Rogers, *One Gallused Rebellion*, 226.

20. "Both Sides Theirs," *Eufaula News-Dispatch*, August 24, 1893.

21. One clever business placed a front-page ad in his hometown newspaper, "Jones and Kolb have engaged the attention of the masses, but if you want to be happy, just call on Porter, Martin and Company and see what great bargains they have for both Jones and Kolb men. *Jacksonville Republican*, August 6, 1892.

22. Rogers, *One Gallused Rebellion*, chapter 9.

23. "Jeffersonian Democratic Convention," *Blount County News-Dispatch*, January 11, 1894.

24. Rogers, *One Gallused Rebellion*, chapter 8; "The Jeffersonians," *Birmingham News*, February 15, 1894.

25. Woodward, *Strange Career*, 78–79.

26. I examined reports from several papers, all of which reported the same county returns. Sources: "The Official Vote," *Livingston Journal*, August 24, 1894. The tabulation here gives the official totals for 1892 and 1894; the following sources used to validate the figures: "The Count of the Votes Cast in Last Monday's Election," *Montgomery Advertiser*, August 13, 1892; "Majorities for Governor," *Livingston Journal*, August 17, 1894. See as well the analysis of Taylor, "Populism and Disfranchisement."

27. The equation for the line is: $y = -0.08 + 1.04x$, with an r-square of 0.64.

28. Taylor, "Populism and Disfranchisement," 417.

29. Daron R. Shaw and John R. Petrocik, *The Turnout Myth* (New York, Oxford University Press, 2020).

30. "The Vote Cast," *Blount News-Dispatch*, August 30, 1894.

31. Daniel C. Reed, "Reevaluating the Vote Market Hypothesis: Effects of Australian Ballot Reform on Voter Turnout," *Social Science History* 38 (2014), 277–290.

CHAPTER 11

1. "The Barbeque," *Blount County News-Dispatch*, July 9, 1896.

2. "Blount County Reform Convention Alive, Not Dead or Sleeping," *Peoples Weekly Tribune* [Birmingham], June 4, 1896.

3. Sterling, *Tales of Old Blount County*, 239.

4. "Blount County, Reform Convention Alive."

5. V.O. Key Jr., "A Theory of Critical Elections," *Journal of Politics* 17 (1955), 16.

6. David R. Mayhew, *Electoral Realignments* (New Haven, CT: Yale University Press, 2004).

7. "The Middle of the Road Was Taken by the Pops," *Birmingham News*, September 4, 1896; "Kolb and Bowman," *Chattanooga Times*, October 26, 1896; "Kolb and Bowman Removed," *Choctaw Alliance*, October 27, 1896.

8. "County Democrat," *Our Mountain Home* [Talladega, AL], July 1, 1896.

9. "North Carolina Redeemed," *Progressive Age* [Scottsboro], November 24, 1898.

10. *Oneonta Southern Democrat*, November 17, 1898.

11. Ronnie W. Faulkner, "Fusion Politics," *North Carolina History Project* [https://northcarolinahistory.org/encyclopedia/fusion-politics/], accessed 06/12/ 2021.

12. Gregg Cantrell and Scott Barton, "Texas Populists and the Failure of Biracial Politics," *The Journal of Southern History*, 55 (1989), 660; Key, *Southern Politics*, 534.

13. "John Burdyne Davidson," *History of Alabama and Her People, Volume II: Alabama Biography* (Chicago and New York: The American Historical Society, 1907). Silas's son, John Burdyne Davidson, was also a Democrat.

14. Sheldon Hackney, *Populism to Progressivism in Alabama* (Princeton, NJ: Princeton University Press, 1969).

15. Taylor, "Populism and Disfranchisement," 418.

16. Sanders, *Roots of Reform*.

17. Webb, *Two Party Politics*, chapter 8.

18. Hackney, *Populism to Progressivism*, 111.

19. Blount County News-*Dispatch*, July 22, 1897.

20. *Oneonta Southern Democrat*, January 19, 1899.

21. "Trustee Sale," *Oneonta Southern Democrat*, November 9, 1899.

22. Boyce House, "Spindletop," *Southwestern History Quarterly* 50 (1946), 36–43.

23. Aldon Moore, "Sabinal, Texas," *Southern Democrat*, May 30, 1907.

24. Hackney, *Populism to Progressivism*, 113.

25. "The District Convention," *Birmingham News*, September 15, 1896.

26. "The Populite Committee," *Birmingham News*, December 31, 1897.

27. "Wimbs Won Out," *Birmingham News*, September 7, 1898.

28. "Row among Republicans," *Montgomery Advertiser*, November 17, 1899, 5.

29. Bunche, "Negro in Political Life," 579–580.

30. *Southern Democrat*, September 6, 1906, and September 13, 1906.

31. "Confederate Reunion," *Oneonta Southern Democrat*, September 24, 1903.

32. "Inequality of Representation," *Birmingham Times*, October 17, 1902.
33. Luke Keele, William Cubbison, and Ismail White, "Suppressing Black Votes: A Historical Case Study of Voting Restrictions in Louisiana," *American Political Science Review* 115 (2021), 694–700.
34. "Julius Davidson May Be in the Race for Chairman of Republican Committee," *Morning Mercury Sun* [Huntsville], March 11, 1906.
35. C. Vann Woodward, *Tom Watson, Agrarian Rebel* (New York: Oxford University Press, 1963); Carol Pierannunzi. "Thomas E. Watson," in *New Georgia Encyclopedia*, last modified 2020 [https://www.georgiaencyclopedia.org/articles/history-archaeology/thomas-e-watson-1856–1922/], accessed 04/17/2024.
36. Boris Heersink and Jeffery Jenkins, *Republican Party Politics and the American South, 1865–1968* (New York: Cambridge University Press, 2020).
37. "Jefferson County Republicans," *The Birmingham Times*, September 19, 1902.
38. "Republicans in Convention," *The Birmingham Times*, September 19, 11902.
39. "Lily Whites Will Rule the Convention," *Birmingham Age-Herald*, September 16, 1902.
40. "Judge Roulhac Gets the Plum," *The Birmingham News*, October 8, 1902.
41. *Bessemer Herald-Journal*, October 11, 1902.
42. Webb, *Two-Party Politics*, 198.
43. "Thompson Wins Factional Fight" and "Leaders of the Opposing State Republican Factions," *Birmingham News*, June 6, 1908.
44. Woodward, *Strange Career*, 54.
45. Du Bois, *Black Reconstruction*, 322.
46. Glenn Feldman, *The Disfranchisement Myth* (Athens: University of Georgia Press, 2004).
47. Feldman, *Disfranchisement Myth*, 170.

INTERLUDE

1. Key, *Southern Politics*, 254.
2. Margaret Sizemore Douglass, "Alabama Horse and Buggy Minister-Doctor," *Annals of Northwest Alabama* 2 (1959), 91.
3. W.M. Harris, "Rev. Marvin McCoy Davidson, D.D.," Obituaries, Committee on Memoirs, North Alabama [Methodist] Conference. Reprinted in Davidson, *Frederick Davidson*, 52–53.
4. "M.M. Davidson Married," *Southern Democrat*, January 6, 1908.
5. Frank, *The People NO*.

PART 3

1. Cowie, *Freedom's Dominion*, chapter 12.
2. Cash, *Mind*, 352.
3. Cash, *Mind*, 351.
4. Richard J. Neuhaus, "Ortega e Gasset Revisited," *Commentary* July, 1986 [https://www.commentary.org/articles/richard-neuhaus/ortega-y-gasset-revisited/], accessed 09/28/2023.

CHAPTER 12

1. "Edmund Jones," Will Book B 1786–1793, Abstract of Charleston District, 205.

2. Julia Floyd Smith, *Slavery and Plantation Growth in Antebellum Florida, 1821–1860* (Gainesville, FL: LibraryPress@UF, 2017), 3 [https://ufdcimages.uflib.ufl.edu/AA/00/06/19/96/00001/9781947372627_Smith.pdf], accessed 10/04/2024.

3. Donald Scott, "Evangelicalism as a Social Movement," TeacherServe, National Humanities Center, 2000 [http://nationalhumanitiescenter.org/tserve/nineteen/nkeyinfo/nevansoc.htm]. Accessed 10/04/2024.

4. Joseph A. Thacker, "Methodism and the Second Great Awakening," Lecture at the Oxford Reading and Research Seminar, Regents College, Oxford England in the summer of 1975 [https://place.asburyseminary.edu/cgi/viewcontent.cgi?article=1560&context=asburyjournal], accessed 10/04/2024.

5. One of Charley's descendants has possession of a book, *Methodism, Preachers' Excellence*, in which Charley had written "Chas. S. V. Jones, his book April 1813" in the inside front cover. See Sam Carnley and Bruce Cosson, "Alaqua Pioneer C.S.V. Jones Honored and Remembered," *Walton Relations and History* 8.(Walton County Heritage Association, May, 2017) 3-10. [https://www.waltoncountyheritage.org/GenSoc/NL2017May.pdf], accessed 9/20/2024.

6. Carnley and Cosson, "Alaqua Pioneer." The U.S. Census locates Charley and his family in Talfair County in 1820.

7. Carnley and Cosson, "Alaqua Pioneer," 7. Charley wrote on the back inside cover of his book "State of Georgia from Pulaski County, August 5th 1821. 1817, Taught school here awhile."

8. In 1821 he wrote in *Preachers' Excellence*, "I moved on to Henry County, Alabama," with several of his children.

9. The following relies on several sources. Carolyn Mays Brevard, "The Scotch Pioneers of Euchee Region: Scottish History, Part Two, Chapter Four," in *A History of Florida*, 1904 [https://www.google.com/books/edition/A_History_of_Florida/qXEAAAAAYAAJ?hl=en&gbpv=1] accessed 9/20/2024; John L. McKinnon, "History of Walton County, 1911," reproduced at *Floridapedia* [https://fcit.usf.edu/florida/docs/e/euchee.htm], accessed 9/20/2024; "The MacKinnons Move to Walton County," Rootsweb.com [http://homepages.rootsweb.com/~cmddlton/mckmig1.html#anchor749587], accessed 9/20/2024.

10. "1818 James Monroe—Andrew Jackson Invades Florida. First Seminole War, Part 2," *State of the Union History* [http://www.stateoftheunionhistory.com/2017/03/1818-james-monroe-andrew-jackson.html]; "1818 James Monroe-An Unauthorized Act of War—First Seminole War, Part 3" [http://www.stateoftheunionhistory.com/2017/03/1818-james-monroe-unauthorized-act-of.html], both accessed 12/22/2020.

11. "Charles Shepherd Vincent Jones," WikiTree [https://www.wikitree.com/wiki/Jones-56725], accessed 8/12/2023.

12. Michael Portier, "From Pensacola to St. Augustine in 1827: A Journey of the Rt. Rev. Michael Portier," *The Florida Historical Society* 26 (1947), 135–166, 138.

13. Samuel R. Overton and Joseph M. White, "A Report of Claims to Land in West Florida," *Congressional Quarterly*, May 25, 1824, 62–63, reprinted in "Very Early Northwest Florida Genealogy Records," *Northwest Florida History and Genealogy Records* [https://nwfloridahistory.files.wordpress.com/2016/08/1824-congressional-record.pdf], accessed 12/23/2020.

14. "Reverend Charles Shepard Vincent Jones, Alaqua's First Preacher," *The Circuit Writer, A Quarterly Publication of the South Alabama-West Florida Circuit of the United Methodist Church*, Summer 2018.

15. Jim Martin, "Jones Descendants Honor Ancestors with Markers," *Walton Relations and History* 9 (Walton County Heritage Association June 2018), 4–7. [https://www.waltoncountyheritage.org/GenSoc/NL2018Jun.pdf], accessed 9/20/2024.

16. Ed M. Johnson, "Navigation of the Choctawhatchee River," September 17, 1903. Ms. in the author's possession.

17. Frederick J. Turner, "The Significance of the Frontier in American History (1893)," American Historical Association [https://www.historians.org/about-aha-and-membership/aha-history-and-archives/historical-archives/the-significance-of-the-frontier-in-american-history], accessed 01/08/2021.

18. Richard Hofstadter, "Turner and the Frontier Myth," *The American Scholar* 8:4 (1949), 433–443, 439.

19. Hofstadter, "Turner and the Frontier Myth," 439.

CHAPTER 13

1. In 1827, Georgia conducted a land lottery for the last Creek lands in the state. William Chalker is listed as an illegitimate and under 18. *1827 Land Lottery Reprint*, courtesy of Donna Eldredge [http://www.usgennet.org/usa/ga/county/fulton/decatur/1827LANDLOTTERYdecatur.pdf], accessed 4/9/2022.

2. Tommy Craig Brown, *Deep in the Piney Woods* (Tuscaloosa: University of Alabama Press, 2018).

3. Mary Love Edwards Fleming, "Dale County and Its People during the Civil War," *Alabama Historical Quarterly* 19 (1957) 61-109.

4. The above discussion is based on the U.S. 1860 Censuses, including Agricultural and Slave Schedules. For John Edmond Jones: Alabama, Coffee County, Precinct 1; For William Chalker: Alabama, Dale County, precinct not stated.

5. James P. Faust, *The Fighting Fifteenth Alabama Infantry* (Jefferson, NC: McFarland and Company, 2014).

6. William C. Oates, *The War between the Union and the Confederacy and Its Lost Opportunities* (New York: Neal Publishing, 1905), 497–498 [https://www.google.com/books/edition/The_War_Between_the_Union_and_the_Confed/IMgvAQAAMAAJ?hl=en&gbpv=1].

7. Edward H. Bonekemper III, *The Myth of the Lost Cause* (Washington, DC: Regnery History, 2015).

8. Key, *Southern Politics*, 7.

9. W.A. Edwards, "A Most Interesting Letter," *Southern Star*, November 15, 1915.

10. *A.N. Edwards Memoir, Dictated to Emma Irene Edwards Garland in 1930.* (Enterprise, AL: Fleming Multimedia).

11. *A History of Company E, 15th Alabama Infantry Regiment* (Enterprise, AL: Fleming Multimedia).

12. Civil War battles often have two names because the Union usually named battles according to nearby geographic features, while the Confederacy used nearby towns.

13. W.A. Edwards, "A Most Interesting Letter."

14. W.A. Edwards, "A Most Interesting Letter."

15. *A History of Company E, 15th Alabama Infantry Regiment.*

16. Edwards, "A Most Interesting Letter."

17. Oates, *The War*, 77.

18. Oates, *The War*, 79.

19. Faust, *The Fighting Fifteenth.*

20. Civil War Soldiers, 3-Fold [https://www.fold3.com/image/10082629].

21. 3-Fold [https://www.fold3.com/image/10082719].

22. Edwards, "A Most Interesting Letter."

23. Faust, *The Fighting Fifteenth.*

24. The Battle of Fair Oaks and Darbytown Road: October 27–28 1864, *The Siege of Petersburg Online* [http://www.beyondthecrater.com/resources/bat-sum/petersburg-siege-sum/sixth-offensive-summaries/the-battle-of-fair-oaks-and-darbytown-road-october-27-28-1864/], accessed 9/20/2024.

25. National Park Service, Appomattox Court House, "Alphabetical Listing for Parole Passes" [https://www.nps.gov/apco/learn/historyculture/parole-passes-a.htm], accessed 8/20/2024.

26. "Paroles of E. Co, Ala 15th Appomattox", *Civil War Talk* [https://civilwartalk.com/threads/15th-alabama-unit-history.135579/], accessed 9/20/2024. This list by company is a copy of one provided by Col. A.A. Lowther, the 15th's commanding officer at the surrender, and includes C.C. Jones of Company E. The list was drawn from J. William Jones, editor, *Southern Historical Society Papers* 15, 1887. List is in possession of author.

27. Laura Carr Jones, "Tribute to Charles Cade Jones," typescript March 1960. Copy in possession of author. She began her remarks by noting, "I am assured that I have a sympathetic and understanding audience," surely indicating the UDC.

28. Thomas G. Jones, "Sketch of the Life of Charles Cade Jones," typescript, n.d. Copy in possession of author.

29. "Lessons from the Personal Memoirs of U.S. Grant," National Park Service [https://www.nps.gov/articles/lessons-from-the-personal-memoirs-of-u-s-grant.htm#:~:text=I%20felt%20like%20anything%20rather,there%20was%20the%20least%20excuse], accessed 9/20/2024.

CHAPTER 14

1. Oates, *The War.*

2. Key, *Southern Politics*, 37–41.

3. Paul McWhorter Pruitt Jr., "William Calvin Oates.,' *Encyclopedia of Alabama* 2007, updated 2014 [http://www.encyclopediaofalabama.org/article/h-1410], accessed 9/20/2024.

4. "Ozark's Oldest Business Moved Here from Newton in 1870," *Ozark Southern Star*, October 15, 1970. USGenWeb Archives [http://files.usgwarchives.net/al/dale/newspapers/nw96ozarksol.txt], accessed 9/20/2024.

5. Adams's biography in Thomas McAdory Owen's *History of Alabama and Dictionary of Alabama Biography* (Chicago: S.J. Clarke Publishing Company 1921); author's survey of issues of the *Ozark Star* during the 1890s.

6. William N. Byrd Jr., *Wiregrass: The Transformation of Southeast Alabama, 1880–1930* (Dissertation submitted to Auburn University, Auburn, Alabama, May 9, 2009).

CHAPTER 15

1. Cash, *Mind*, 288.

2. C. Vann Woodward, *Origins of the New South* (Baton Rouge: Louisiana State University Press, 1951), 58–64.

3. Thomas Collins, "Alabama Man Sets Example for Retiring," *Birmingham News*, November 28, 1952.
4. "Pastor: Rev. Thomas G. Jones," *Greenville Advocate*, March 11, 1931.
5. Collins, *When the Church Bell Rang Racist*.
6. "Minister Okehs Amendment No. 2," *Troy Messenger*, August 27, 1956.
7. Heather McGhee, *The Sum of Us* (New York, One World, 2021), 25–26.

PART 4

1. Although I do not deal with these issues in this book, my coauthors and I explore this and other facets of Jim Crow in Bryan Jones, Wilbur Rich, and Clarence Stone, *Remembrances of Jim Crow* (in preparation).
2. Joseph Madison Beck, *My Father and Atticus Finch* (New York: W.W. Norton, 2016).

CHAPTER 16

1. Gene Roberts and Klibanoff, *The Race Beat* (New York: Vintage Books, 2006), 9.
2. "Taken to Blount County to Stand Trial on Charge of Murder—Talk of Lynching," *Birmingham Age-Herald*, December 15, 1899; "Tunstall Quiet and in Safety," Birmingham Age-Herald, July 28, 1899; "Brought to Birmingham," Birmingham News, July 27, 1899.
3. "Mistrial Entered," *Birmingham News*, December 22, 1899.
4. "A Lynching Threatened in Alabama," *The Wilmington Messenger*, July 28, 1899; *Norfolk Landmark*, July 27, 1899.
5. *Cullman Tribune-Gazette*, August 10, 1899.
6. *Lynching in America, Third Edition* (Montgomery, AL: Equal Justice Institute, 2017); *Lynchings by State and Race*, 1882–1968, Tuskegee University Archives Repository [http://archive.tuskegee.edu/repository/wp-content/uploads/2020/11/Lynchings-Stats-Year-Dates-Causes.pdf], accessed 9/20/2024.
7. *Atlanta Constitution*, July 21, 1897.
8. "The Thrilling Story of the Hanging," *Atlanta Constitution*, July 21, 1897. The race of the victim was not mentioned in the story, indicating that he was white. Southern lawlessness transcended the racial divide until after the turn of the century, as did yellow journalism.
9. *Blount County News Dispatch*, December 1, 1887.
10. "A Black Fiend Burned at Stake," *Fort Payne Journal*, April 6, 1899.
11. "Burned at Stake," *Russell Register*, April 6, 1899.
12. "A Protest against the Burning and Lynching of Negroes," *Birmingham Age-Herald*, February 29, 1904.
13. "Lynching in America: County Data Supplement, Updated 2020" (Montgomery, AL: Equal Justice Institute, 2021) [https://eji.org/wp-content/uploads/2020/02/02-07-20-lynching-in-america-county-supplement.pdf], accessed 9/20/2024.
14. "Lynching in Cullman County," *Blount County News-Dispatch*, August 20, 1891; "A Legal Hanging," *Blount County News-Dispatch*, October 12, 1893.
15. "Troops Ordered Out," *Norfolk Landmark*, July 27, 1899.
16. "Troops Ordered Out."
17. "Some Danger," *Birmingham News*, October 14, 1899.
18. "Mistrial Entered."
19. "Davidson Has No Audience," *Gadsden Times-News*, October 22, 1910.
20. "Hard Luck for a Tiger," *Gadsden Times-News*, April 27, 1909.

21. "Mountainboro's Clan Freed of Conspiracy," *Gadsden Times-News*, May 5, 1910.

22. "Seaborn Wright to Prosecute Jay Smith!," *Gadsden Times-News*, February 26, 1912.

23. "Elkins Life Hangs by Thread," *Gadsden Times-News*, May 24, 1910; "John Elkins Given Life Sentence," *Gadsden Times-News*, May 25, 1910.

24. "Something's Up at White Top," *Gadsden Times-News*, July 20, 1909.

25. "The North Alabama Collecting Agency," *Southern Democrat*, April 2, 1914.

26. "George Lige Must Hang for Crime," *Gadsden Times-News*, May 27, 1910.

27. "Black Murderer Is Brought to Gadsden," *Gadsden Time-News*, December 12, 1909.

28. "This Negro May Hang," *Gadsden Times-News*, May 6, 1910.

29. "George Lige Must Hang for Crime."

30. "George Lige's Lawyer Failed to Carry Up an Appeal," *Gadsden Times-News*, September 26, 1910.

31. "George Lige to Hang on the 29th of July," *Montgomery Times*, June 6, 1911.

32. Executions in Alabama, DeathPenaltyUSA [http://deathpenaltyusa.org/usa1/state/alabama2.htm], accessed 5/15/2021.

33. "Lige Is Reprieved," *Birmingham News*, August 23, 1911.

34. "Gadsden Murderer Is Respited by the Governor," *Montgomery Advertiser*, June 24, 1911.

35. "Emmet O'Neal (1911–15)," *Encyclopedia of Alabama*, 2017 [http://www.encyclopediaofalabama.org/article/h-1585], accessed 5/17/2021.

36. "Another Big Meeting Held in Aurora Beat," *Gadsden Times-News*, November 2, 1909; "Something Is Up with White Top"

37. *Marion Times*, October 6, 1911; *Executions in Alabama*, 1901–1925.

38. Beck, *My Father and Atticus Finch*.

39. Feldman, *Disfranchisement Myth*, 15.

CHAPTER 17

1. Bob Ingram, "Loyalist Faction Wins; 'White Supremacy' Goes," *Birmingham News*, January 21, 1966.

2. Flynt, "Alabama's Shame.

3. Flynt, "Alabama's Shame, 76.

4. Woodward, *Origins of the New South*.

5. Woodward, *Origins of the New South*, 373.

6. "How Racism Split the Suffrage Movement," *Bust Magazine*, Winter 2021 [https://bust.com/feminism/19147-equal-means-equal.html], accessed 02/07/2021.

7. "Vote against Woman Suffrage," The Georgia Association Opposed to Woman's Suffrage, c. 1915 (HR64A-F20.4), Records of the U.S. House of Representatives, Record Group 233; National Archives Building, Washington, DC [https://www.docsteach.org/documents/document/ga-opposed-woman-suffrage-card], accessed 02/07/2021.

8. Nick Chiles, "Nine Ways Franklin D. Roosevelt's New Deal Purposely Excluded Black People," *Atlanta Black Star*, February 4, 2015, 3 [https://atlantablackstar.com/2015/02/04/9-ways-franklin-d-roosevelts-new-deal-purposely-excluded-blacks-people/3/], accessed 02/07/2021.

9. Curtis Thomasson, "Sentell Descendants Excelled in Education, Legal Fields," *Andalusia Star News*, August 12, 2011.

10. Patricia Hoskins Morton, "Crenshaw County," *Encyclopedia of Alabama*, September 2007; updated May 2019 [http://www.encyclopediaofalabama.org/article/h-1342], accessed 09/29/2019.

11. Joe R. Sport, "Early History of Crenshaw County," 1957 [http://genealogytrails.com/ala/crenshaw/history1.html], accessed 10/2/2019.

12. Sport, "Early History of Crenshaw County.

13. Thomasson, "Sentell Descendants."

14. Thomasson, "Sentell Descendants."

15. Flynt, "Alabama's Shame."

16. Feldman, *Disfranchisement Myth*, 15.

17. Hackney, *Populism to Progressivism*, 180.

18. Hackney, *Populism to Progressivism*, 181.

19. "Alabama's 1901 Constitution: Instrument of Power," University of Alabama School of Law, December 9, 2016 [https://www.law.ua.edu/specialcollections/2016/12/09/alabamas-1901-constitution-instrument-of-power/], accessed 4/29/2022.

20. "Alabama's 1901 Constitution: Instrument of Power," 175.

21. Feldman, *Disfranchisement Myth*, 55.

22. Hackney, *Populism to Progressivism*, Appendix III.

23. Feldman, *Disfranchisement Myth*, 75.

24. Feldman, *Disfranchisement Myth*, 138.

25. Feldman, *Disfranchisement Myth*, 99.

26. Feldman, *Disfranchisement Myth*, 98.

27. Feldman, *Disfranchisement Myth*, 90.

28. Feldman, *Disfranchisement Myth*, 243.

29. Feldman, *Disfranchisement Myth*, 90.

30. Feldman, Disfranchisement Myth, 95.

31. Feldman, *Disfranchisement Myth*, 243, n.72.

32. Feldman, *Disfranchisement Myth*, 95.

33. Feldman, *Disfranchisement Myth*, 15.

34. Hackney, *Populism to Progressivism*, Appendix III.

35. Flynt, "*Alabama's Shame*," 74–75.

36. Feldman, *Disfranchisement Myth*, 82.

37. *Giles v. Harris* (1903) 189 U.S. 475.

38. Flynt, "Alabama's Shame," 75.

39. Bryan Stevenson, *Just Mercy* (New York, One World, 2014), 17.

40. "Opening Comments by Gerald Stern," in "Symposium: Voices of the Civil Rights Division: Then and Now (October 28, 2011)," *McGeorge Law Review* 44 (2013), 13.

41. Dan T. Carter, *The Politics of Rage, Second Edition* (Baton Rouge: Louisiana State University Press, 2000), 99.

42. Jack Bass, "Frank M. Johnson Jr.," *Encyclopedia of Alabama* [http://www.encyclopediaofalabama.org/article/h-125], accessed 10/23/2019; International Civil Rights Walk of Fame, "Judge Frank Johnson, 1918–1999," Martin Luther King National Historic Site, National Park Service [https://www.nps.gov/features/malu/feat0002/wof/Frank_Johnson.htm], accessed 10/24/2019.

43. John Lewis, *Walking with the Wind: A Memoir of the Movement* (New York: Simon and Schuster, 1998), 340, 344.

44. "Viola Liuzzo," *Encyclopedia of World Biography*, updated October 11, 2019 [https://www.encyclopedia.com/people/history/historians-miscellaneous-biographies/viola-liuzzo], accessed 10/19/2019.

45. *Williams v. Wallace*, 240 F Supp. 100 (Middle District of Alabama 1965).

46. *Brief for Appellee Collie Leroy Wilkins, Jr., and Eugene Thomas, Appellants, v. United States of America, Appellee*, The United States Court of Appeals for the Fifth Circuit.

47. Arnold Foster and Benjamin R. Epstein, *Report on the Ku Klux Klan* (New York: Anti-Defamation League of B'nai B'rith, 1965).

48. Foster and Epstein, *Report on the Ku Klux Klan*, 11.

49. "Viola Liuzzo."

50. "Comments by James P. Turner, Symposium: Voices of the Civil Rights Division: Then and Now (October 28, 2011)," *McGeorge Law Review* 44 (2013), 11 [https://law.yale.edu/sites/default/files/documents/faculty/papers/FissDoar_McGeorge.pdf], posted 7/19/2013, accessed 9/21/2024.

51. "Comments by James P. Taylor," 12.

52. "Pictorial Summary of a Tragicomic Mistrial," *Life Magazine*, May 21, 1965, 33–39.

53. "Collie Leroy Wilkins Trial: 1965," *Law Library—American Law and Legal Information Notable Trials and Court Cases—1963 to 1972*, 3 [https://law.jrank.org/pages/3141/Collie-Leroy-Wilkins-Trial-1965.html], accessed 10/29/2019.

54. "Pictorial Summary," 38.

55. "Collie Leroy Wilkins Trial: 1965."

56. "Comments by Turner," 12.

57. "Comments by Turner," 12.

58. "Comments by Turner," 13.

59. "Collie Leroy Wilkins Trial: 1965," 4.

60. *Collie Leroy Wilkins, Jr., and Eugene Thomas, Appellants, v. United States of America*, Appellee, 376 F.2d 552 (5th Cir. 1967).

61. "'Mr. J.O.' Retires," *Court News: Newsletter of the Alabama Judicial System*.6, no.7 (July 1982), 4.

CHAPTER 18

1. Tom Brokaw, *The Greatest Generation* (New York, Random House, 1998), xxxviii

2. Division History, 4th Infantry Division, National 4th Infantry (IVY) Division Association [https://www.4thinfantry.org/content/division-history], accessed 3/7/2021.

3. The 4th Infantry Division during World War II, *Holocaust Encyclopedia*, United States Holocaust Memorial Museum [https://encyclopedia.ushmm.org/content/en/article/the-4th-infantry-division], accessed 3/07/2021

4. "E.W. Skidmore, Candidate for Re-Election for State Senate," *The Alabama Citizen*, April 10, 1954.

5. *NAACP v. Alabama ex rel. Flowers*, 377 U.S. 288 (1964).

6. "E.W. Skidmore," *Montgomery Advertiser*, May 31, 1958.

7. "Truckers Oppose Repeal," *Birmingham News*, April 7, 1957.

8. "Skidmore Bids for Votes in North Alabama," *Birmingham News*, March 30, 1958.

9. "Alabama CIO Elects James Battles of Birmingham Secretary-Treasurer," *Birmingham News*, April 26, 1955.

10. "A Message to the Men and Women Who Do Not Have a Million Dollars," *Troy Messenger*, May 28, 1958.

11. Carter, *Politics of Rage*, 95.

12. "Big Business Opposes Him, Says Skidmore," *Birmingham News*, May 28, 1958.

13. "Stronger Resistance to Civil Rights, Labor Setback for Next 4 Yrs. Here," *Alabama Citizen*, June 21, 1958.

14. *Birmingham News-Age Herald*, June 16, 1935; *Anniston Star*, June 23, 1935, and August 4, 1939.

CHAPTER 19

1. *Troy Messenger*, January 4, 1949.
2. "Tuscaloosa Graphic," *Troy Messenger*, August 11, 1961.
3. "And This 'Invisible Empire' Fell before a People's Wrath," *Birmingham News*, June 26, 1949.
4. Roberts and Klibanoff, *Race Beat*.
5. Glenn Feldman, *Politics, Society, and the Klan in Alabama, 1915–1949* (Tuscaloosa: University of Alabama Press, 1999), 290.
6. "Ku Klux Klan Attempts Revival," *Troy Messenger*, May 10, 1946.
7. "Klan Criticizes Folsom, Warren," *Troy Messenger*, December 13, 1949.
8. Glen Jeansonne, "Huey Long and Racism," *Louisiana History* 33 (1992), 265–282.
9. Carl Grafton and Anne Permaloff, "James E. 'Big Jim' Folsom Sr. (1947–51; 1955–59)," *Encyclopedia of Alabama* [http://www.encyclopediaofalabama.org/article/h-1423], accessed 10/04/2024.
10. Feldman, *Politics, Society, and the Klan*, 288.
11. Carl Grafton and Anne Permaloff, *Big Mules and Branchheads* (Athens: University of Georgia Press, 1985), 68.
12. "1948 Presidential Election in Alabama," *Wikipedia* [https://en.wikipedia.org/wiki/1948_United_States_presidential_election_in_Alabama], accessed 4/30/2024.
13. Grafton and Permaloff, *Big Mules*, 132.
14. Bem Price, "Klan's Power Is Lessening in a Changing South," *Anniston Star*, April 17, 1949.
15. Counts calculated from Newspapers.com using the keyword "Klan."
16. "Six Flogged by Hooded Fiends," *Troy Messenger*, June 20, 1949.
17. Price, "Klan's Power."
18. "Three Floggings Reported in Clay," *Troy Messenger*, June 30, 1949.
19. "We Progress," *Montgomery Advertiser*, July 29, 1949.
20. Roberts and Klibanoff, *Race Beat*, 23.
21. Editorials are almost always unsigned, but they represent the position of the paper. The *Messenger* editorials during this period were certainly my father's, given the turnover of editors and their limited newspaper experience.
22. "Bad Business in Montgomery," *Troy Messenger*, May 23, 1949.
23. 'Infamy for Georgia," *Troy Messenger*, May 31, 1949.
24. "Hooded Hoodlums," *Troy Messenger*, June 14, 1949
25. "Anti-Mask Legislation," *Troy Messenger*, June 16, 1949.
26. Then and Now," *Montgomery Advertiser*, June 22, 1949.
27. "The Dixiecrats: Past, Present, and Future," *Montgomery Advertiser*, November 7, 1948.
28. "A Worm, Maybe," *Troy Messenger*, November 2, 1949.
29. "Lycurgus and Dixiecrats," *Troy Messenger*, August 8, 1949.
30. "Cross Burners," *Troy Messenger*, June 23, 1949.
31. "Clark Orders Investigation in Alabama," *Troy Messenger*, June 24, 1949.
32. "Crime Never Pays," *Troy Messenger*, June 27, 1949.
33. "Klan in the Pulpit," *Troy Messenger*, July 14, 1949.
34. "More Floggings Seen in Alabama," *Troy Messenger*, July 1, 1949.
35. "Legion to Discuss Hooded Mob Action," *Troy Messenger*, July 1, 1949.

36. "The Maxwell Field Business," *Montgomery Advertiser*, June 24, 1949.

37. "Alabama Refuses to Aid in War Effort If It Means Any Form of Racial Integration," *Equal Justice Institute*, July 23, 2022 [https://calendar.eji.org/racial-injustice/jul/23], accessed 7/23/2022.

38. "The Truman Order," *Troy Messenger*, July 1, 1949.

39. *Troy Messenger*, July 8, 1949.

40. Elliott, and D'Orso, *The Costs of Courage*, 80.

41. Roberts and Klibanoff, *Race Beat*, 122–123.

42. "Goats on the Hill," *Troy Messenger*, June 10, 1949.

43. "He Who Laughs Last. . .," *Troy Messenger*, August 2, 1949.

44. "Overdoing It," *Montgomery Advertiser*, May 3, 1949.

45. Grafton and Permaloff, *Big Mules and Branchheads*, 126.

46. Roberts and Klibanoff, *Race Beat*, 10.

47. "Ku Klux Klan No Longer Has Dixie Bluffed," *Selma Times-Journal*, April 17, 1949.

48. "Regional Education," *Troy Messenger*, July 13, 1949.

49. "Folsom Blasts Legislature in Courthouse Address Here," *Troy Messenger*, March 29, 1949.

50. Sparkman advertisement, *Troy Messenger*, April 30, 1954.

51. "Vote for the Kind of Man You Want To Hold Your Child's Hand," *Troy Messenger*, May 3, 1954.

52. "Segregation Won't Expire Suddenly," *Montgomery Advertiser*, May 18, 1954.

53. "Educators Adopt 'Waiting' Attitude on Segregation," *Troy Messenger*, May 18, 1954.

54. "Freedom of Choice May Mitigate Segregation Decision," *Troy Messenger*, May 19, 1954.

55. "B'ham Leader Gives School Plan to Gov. Persons," *Alabama Citizen*, January 23, 1954.

56. "North Practices Segregation in Schools and Elsewhere," *Troy Messenger*, June 2, 1954.

57. "Not Too Late for Supreme to Reverse Its Segregation Decision," *Troy Messenger*, September 8, 1954.

CHAPTER 20

1. B.J. Hollars, *Opening the Doors* (Tuscaloosa: University of Alabama Press, 2013), 19.

2. Flowers become a close ally of George Wallace, serving as his campaign manager in Wallace's 1972 presidential race. He voted for the impeachment of President Nixon in 1974.

3. Wayne Phillips, "University Ousts Miss Lucy because of Her Charges," *New York Times*, March 2, 1956.

4. "What Price Peace," *The Tuscaloosa News*, February 7, 1956.

5. Reprinted in the *Montgomery Advertiser*, February 14, 1956.

6. Roberts and Klibanoff, *Race Beat*, 132.

7. Baumgartner and Jones, *Agendas and Instability in American Politics*; Bryan D. Jones and Frank R. Baumgartner, *The Politics of Attention* (Chicago: University of Chicago Press, 2004).

8. Hollars, *Opening the Doors*; E. Culpepper Clark, *The Schoolhouse Door* (Tuscaloosa: University of Alabama Press, 1995).

9. "States' Rights Breakdown Foreseen Unless People Resist Encroachments," *Troy Messenger*, February 8, 1956. The paper listed only a news editor during this period.

10. "Does the Tenth Amendment Mean What It Says or Not?," *Troy Messenger*, February 15, 1956.

11. "The Newspapers Will Probably Lie about Folsom's Conference," *Troy Messenger*, February 23, 1956.

12. "Folsom Seeks Creation of Bi-Racial Commission," *Troy Messenger*, February 24, 1956.

13. "In Tempestuous Segregation Issue Vital Leadership Is Basic Need," *Troy Messenger*, February 22, 1956.

14. "Publisher Calls for 'Moderates' in Race Frenzy," *Troy Messenger*, March 23, 1956.

15. Carter, *Politics of Rage*, 95.

16. Roberts and Klibanoff, *Race Beat*, 125.

17. Roberts and Klibanoff, *Race Beat*, 124.

18. "The Only Course," *Montgomery Advertiser*, February 9, 1956.

19. "Senator Eastland May See Fit to Tell Us," *Montgomery Advertiser*, February 10, 1956.

20. Roberts and Kilbanoff, *Race Beat*, 124.

21. "A Difference in Two Councils," *Montgomery Advertiser*, June 25, 1956.

22. Roberts and Klibanoff, *Race Beat*, 214.

23. Kermit L. Hall, "Dignity, Honor, and Civility: *New York Times v. Sullivan*," *OAH Magazine of History*, Winter 1995. The author's interpretation of Hall's motivation is incorrect, in my view. He sees Hall as a Southern moderate editor, which he was in the early 1950s, but not by the time he was involved in supporting Sullivan's suit.

24. Roberts and Klibanoff, *Race Beat*, chapter 3.

25. Roberts and Klibanoff, *Race Beat*, 65.

26. Roberts and Klibanoff, *Race Beat*.

27. "Segregation's Citadel Unbreached in Four Years," *Washington Post*, May 11, 1958; David Fernsler, "South Is Still the South but Segregation Will End," *Guam Daily News*, May 21, 1958.

28. Roberts and Klibanoff, *Race Beat*, 112.

29. "Florida Editor's Home Bombed Twice," *Troy Messenger*, February 24, 1956.

30. "State's School Bill Product of Alert, Keen Legal Minds," *Troy Messenger*, June 21, 1955.

31. "Folsom Balks at Comment on School Bill," *Troy Messenger*, June 21, 1955.

32. "Opposition Mounting in the North Against Integration Moves," *Troy Messenger*, April 4, 1956.

33. "Benson's Latest Mistake Cannot Be Forgotten by U.S. Citizens," *Troy Messenger*, February 9, 1956.

34. *Troy Messenger*, July 20, 1958.

35. July 8, 1958; December 3, 1958; June 18, 1958.

36. Michael Fitzpatrick, "The Cutter Incident: How America's First Polio Vaccine Led to a Growing Vaccine Crisis," *Journal of the Royal Society of Medicine* 99 (2006), 156.

37. "Polio Epidemic Aroused Mothers to Panic in Seeking Salk Vaccine Shots," *Troy Messenger*, August 24, 1956.

38. "Big Future for Women, Girls Opened in Scientific World," *Troy Messenger*, September 13, 1956.

39. "Faulkner Brings Vote Drive to Troy, Brundidge," *Troy Messenger*, March 25, 1958.

40. *Troy Messenger*, May 3, 1954.

41. Carter, *Politics of Rage*, 95–96.

42. "An American Plague" and "Canvas Gives States Righters Majority," *Troy Messenger*, July 7, 1960.

43. "Freedom Rides," The Martin Luther King, Jr. Research and Education Institute, Stanford University [https://kinginstitute.stanford.edu/encyclopedia/freedom-rides], accessed 10/1/2021.

44. "Lee and Grant," *Troy Messenger*, May 15, 1961.

45. "The Commie Technique in Alabama," *Troy Messenger* May 22, 1961.

46. "How the Commies Won Their Point," *Troy Messenger* May 23, 1961.

47. "Why Commies Chose Alabama," *Troy Messenger* May 24, 1961.

48. "J. Edgar Hoover Gives Evidence," *Troy Messenger* May 25, 1961.

49. *Troy Messenger* October 27, 1958.

50. "The Road Back," *Montgomery Advertiser*, May 23, 1961.

51. "Inside Out," *Montgomery Advertiser*, June 2, 1961.

52. "Wallace For Governor," *Montgomery Advertiser*, April 15, 1962.

53. Carter, *Politics of Rage*, 10.

54. "Academic Serfdom at Yale," *Montgomery Advertiser*, September 22, 1963. See also Carter, *Politics of Rage*, 182.

55. "The 'Rednecks' Are Our Hope," *Selma Times-Journal*, reprinted in the *Montgomery Advertiser*, May 24, 1956.

56. H. Brandt Ayers and Carlo Nunnelly, *Cussing Dixie, Loving Dixie* (Tuscaloosa: University of Alabama Press, 2015).

CHAPTER 21

1. Woodward, *Strange Career*, 7.

2. Richard Dawkins, *The Selfish Gene* (Oxford, UK: Oxford University Press, 1989).

3. Robert Mickey, *Paths Out of Dixie* (Princeton, NJ: Princeton University Press, 2015).

4. Bill Rice Jr., "Chiropractor Gault Left 'Trail of Blood' through South Alabama," *Troy Life*, publication of the *Troy Messenger*. (2021).

5. Lewis, *Walking with the Wind*, 36.

6. Lewis, *Walking with the Wind*, 36.

7. Howard Zinn, *The Southern Mystique* (New York: Alfred A. Knopf, 1964), 139.

8. Carter, *Politics of Rage*, 183.

9. Reprinted in *The Montgomery Advertiser*, May 24, 1956.

10. "Big Crowd Greets Big Jim in Troy," *Troy Messenger*, March 22, 1962.

11. Grafton and Permaloff, *Big Mules and Branchheads*, 226–236.

CHAPTER 22

1. Thanks to Carter Wilson for pointing this out.

2. "The Linotype Typesetter that Changed the Printing World," *The Printing Times* [https://www.printersdevil.ca/linotype-machine/], accessed 10/7/2023.

3. Beck, *My Father and Atticus Finch*, chapter 2.

4. Collins, *When the Church Bell Rang Racist*, 19.

5. Collins, *When the Church Bell Rang Racist*, 20.

CHAPTER 23

1. Woodward, *Strange Career*, 191.

2. Earl H. Tilford, *Turning the Tide* (Tuscaloosa: University of Alabama Press, 2014); Clark, *Schoolhouse Door*; Hollars, *Opening the Doors*.

3. "UM History of Integration," The University of Mississippi [https://50years.olemiss.edu/james-meredith/], accessed 5/5/2024.

4. "George A. Lemaitre, Lawyer, Banker, Educator, Civic Leader," *The Alabama Business Hall of Fame* [https://abhof.culverhouse.ua.edu/members/], accessed 3/31/2022.

5. Clark, *Schoolhouse Door*, 248–249.

6. Carter, *Politics of Rage*.

7. "Politics Won Book Pact, Operator Says," *Birmingham News*, January 3, 1963; Hugh Sparrow, "Sweeping Changes May Follow School Book Disclosures," *Birmingham News*, January 6, 1963.

8. "Malone Moves to Halt Delivery of Textbooks," *Alabama Journal*, June 29, 1964.

9. Carter, *Politics of Rage*, 403.

10. Mary Palmer, *An Enigma: The Complex Life of Alabama's Most Controversial and Divisive Governor* (Point Clear, AL: Intellect Publishers 2016), e-book location 1292 of 4206.

11. Lynsey Eidell, "What Is the Machine in 'Bama Rush'? Everything to Know about the Controversial Secret Society," *People*, May 23, 2023.

12. Jake Pickle and Peggy Pickle, *Jake* (Austin: University of Texas Press, 1997), 91, 95.

13. Liz Ryan, "Tuscaloosa v. United Klans of America," November 17, 2021 [https://www.alreporter.com/2021/11/17/tuscaloosa-v-united-klans-of-america/], accessed 4/22/2022; "'Bloody Tuesday': Tuscaloosa Remembers Civil Rights Marchers Brutalized 50 Years Ago," Associated Press, June 10, 2014; John M. Giggie, *Bloody Tuesday* (New York: Oxford University Press, 2024).

14. "Repression and Resistance in Tuscaloosa (Jun–Aug)," Civil Rights History, Veterans of the Civil Rights Movement Archives [http://www.crmvet.org/"tim/timhis63.htm], accessed 9/23/2024.

15. "At Large: When Actor Jack Palance Met Southern Mob Hospitality," *Tuscaloosa News*, May 1, 2011 [http://www.tuscaloosanews.com/opinion/20110501/at-large-when-actor-jack-palance-met-southern-mob-hospitality], accessed 9/23/2024.

16. Tilford, *Turning the Tide*, 42–47.

17. Steven Stack and Barbara Bowman, "Suicide in the Grand Canyon National Park," in David Lester and Steven Stack, eds., *Suicide as a Dramatic Performance* (Brunswick, NJ: Transaction Publishers, 2015), 124–146.

18. Clark, *Schoolhouse Door*, 247.

19. "125 Years of Women in the College of Arts and Sciences," *Collegian* (2018), 30. Clark, *Schoolhouse Door*, 249, reports ten Black students in the spring of 1965.

20. Richard Rovere, "The Campaign: Goldwater," *The New Yorker*, October 3, 1964.

21. "Unpledged Slate Wins in Alabama," *New York Times*, May 6, 1964.

22. Hollars, *Opening the Doors*, 212–213.

23. H. Richard Winn, "Prefrontal Cortex," *Science Direct* [https://www.sciencedirect.com/topics/medicine-and-dentistry/prefrontal-cortex], accessed 01/17/22.

24. Harper Lee, *Go Set a Watchman* (New York: Harper Luxe, 2015), 297–302.

25. "125 Years," 30.

26. Carter, *Politics of Rage*, 286.

27. "Elliott Wins Labor Support," *Anniston Star*, April 12, 1966.

28. Elliott and D'Orso, *Cost of Courage*, 282.

29. Carter, *Politics of Rage*, 285.

30. Carter, *Politics of Rage*, 285.

31. Shaw and Petrocik, *Turnout Myth*.

32. Carter, *Politics of Rage*, 226.

33. Albert O. Hirschman, *Exit, Voice, and Loyalty* (Cambridge, MA: Harvard University Press, 1970).

CHAPTER 24

1. Key, *Southern Politics*, 254.

2. James Harrington, "The Longest and Largest March in Texas State History," *Mexican American News*, September 5, 2016 [https://mexican-american.org/history/20th-century/1960s/ufw-labor-day-march-of-1966.html], accessed 9/23/2024.

3. "Tom Wolfe: Jefferson Lecture 2006," National Endowment for the Humanities [https://www.neh.gov/about/awards/jefferson-lecture/tom-wolfe-biography?msclkid=d3a4d118bc3411eca3c5034271b3840e], accessed 4/14/2022.

4. Kyle Whitmire, "Legislating While Black in Alabama: CRT and the Struggle for Respect," AL.com, April 5, 2022 [https://www.al.com/news/2022/04/legislating-while-black-in-alabama-crt-and-the-struggle-for-respect.html], accessed 4/5/2022.

5. Dave Langford, "Governor Pledges Private School Aid," *Birmingham News*, October 30, 1963.

6. Katherine J. Kramer, *The Politics of Resentment* (Chicago: University of Chicago Press, 2016); Jonathan Metzel, *Dying of Whiteness* (New York: Basic Books, 2019).

7. Mickey, *Paths Out of Dixie*.

8. Walter Dean Burnham, "The Alabama Senatorial Election of 1962," *Journal of Politics* 16 (1964), 798–829.

9. Earl Black and Merle Black have documented the Southern realignment in three books that trace that realignment: Earl Black and Merle Black, *The Rise of Southern Republicans* (Cambridge, MA: Harvard University Press, 2003); *The Vital South* (Cambridge MA: Harvard University Press, 1992); *Divided America* (New York: Simon and Schuster, 2007).

10. Burnham, "Alabama Senatorial Election, 821.

11. There is evidence that Key recognized this as he examined state parties more generally in the United States. David Mayhew, "Why Did V.O. Key Draw Back from His 'Have Nots' Claim?," in Milton C. Cummings Jr., ed., *V.O. Key and the Study of American Politics* (Washington, DC: American Political Science Association, 2008), 24–38.

12. Tim Lau, "*Citizens United* Explained," Brennan Center for Justice, December 2019 [https://www.brennancenter.org/our-work/research-reports/citizens-united-explained?ref=foreverwars.ghost.io], accessed 5/6/2024.

13. Maxwell and Shields, *Long Southern Strategy*; Stevens, *All a Lie*; Eric Schickler, *Racial Realignment: The Transformation of American Liberalism, 1932–1965* (Princeton, NJ: Princeton University Press, 2016); Bryan D. Jones, Sean Theriault, and Michelle Whyman, *The Great Broadening* (Chicago: University of Chicago Press, 2019). Recent research indicates that almost all of the Southern realignment was due to shifts by racially conservative whites. Ilyana Kuziemko and Ebonya Washington, "Why Did the Democrats Lose the South? Bringing New Data to an Old Debate," *American Economic Review*, 2018, 108: 2830-2867.

Index

Figures are indicated by an italicized *f* following the paragraph number.

For the benefit of digital users, indexed terms that span two pages (e.g., 52–53) may, on occasion, appear on only one of those pages.